Marcia Jorgenson
March 2015

FORWARD

America's Presidents From Washington to Obama

Q. David Bowers

Dave Lifton

Whitman Publishing, LLC
Publishing Since 1934

Atlanta, Georgia

Whitman Publishing, LLC
PUBLISHING SINCE 1934
www.whitman.com

3101 Clairmont Road • Suite G • Atlanta, GA 30329

Correspondence concerning this book may be directed to the publisher, Attn: Forward, at the address above.

ISBN: 0794837247
Printed in the United States of America

Contents

I.

THE PRESIDENCY OF BARACK OBAMA

44th President (2009–2016)

BARACK OBAMA

Born August 4, 1961

Political party: Democratic

Vice president: Joe Biden (2009–2016)

First Lady and family: Married Michelle Robinson on October 3, 1992. The couple had two daughters: Malia Ann (1998–) and Natasha ("Sasha") (2001–).

Especially remembered for: First African-American to be elected president. Dealing with difficult economic conditions and worldwide unrest.

"Four More Years"

After nearly two years of campaigning, it all came down to one night—November 6, 2012—as nearly 120 million people cast their ballots. Most of the focus was on the swing states, where the race was the closest. As the results came in, it became clear that most of them were leaning toward Obama.

At approximately 11:12 p.m. Eastern, the networks called Ohio for Obama, which gave him the necessary 270 electoral votes needed to win a second term. Although he won the popular vote by a fairly slim margin, 50.5% to 47.9%, Obama's victories in eight of the nine most hotly contested states gave him a massive 332-206 decision in the electoral college.

Romney conceded nearly two hours later, when the remaining incoming results proved too conclusive to work out in his favor. In his gracious concession speech, he called for the nation to put partisanship aside and work together to solve the nation's problems.

Shortly thereafter, the now two-term president took to the stage at McCormick Place in Chicago. He congratulated the Romney-Ryan campaign and praised his family, Vice President Biden, and his staff. Then he turned his focus to the American people, reminding them that, for all its messiness, the democratic process is vital to our growth as a nation because it shines a spotlight on our shared values.

He closed by echoing words with which he had struck such a chord during the 2004 Democratic National Convention. "I believe we can seize this future together because we are not as divided as our politics suggests," he said. "We're not as cynical as the pundits believe. We are greater than the sum of our individual ambitions, and we remain more than a collection of red states and blue states. We are and forever will be the United States of America."

The Making of a President

The Early Years

The rise of Barack Obama is truly an "only in America" story. He was born on August 4, 1961, in Honolulu, Hawaii. His father, for whom he is named, was a Kenyan student at the University of Hawaii at Manoa. While there, Barack Sr. fell in love with Stanley Ann Dunham, a native of Kansas whose family had moved to Hawaii in 1959 as impending statehood offered the dream of prosperity. It appeared to be a truly American story: a child of the heartland meets a promising immigrant as manifest destiny extends beyond the oceans—but the dream wouldn't last long. When Barack was two years old, his father received a scholarship to attend Harvard University, but could not afford to take the young family. He left them in Hawaii and went to Massachusetts in pursuit of his doctorate, and eventually returned to Kenya. Ann and Barack Sr. divorced in 1964.

Obama's mother would soon marry another student, Lolo Soetoro, who with other scholars from that country was recalled to Indonesia in 1967 when military leader Suharto came to power. The family moved with Lolo's to his native Indonesia, where, from age six to ten, Barack attended school in Jakarta. Ann, who was working as an English teacher at the American embassy, stressed to her son the importance of an education to rise above the poverty surrounding them. In 1970 a daughter, Maya,

Above: Barack Obama Jr. with his mother, Ann Dunham, during the 1960s. Left: Barack Obama Sr. Ann and Barack Sr. married in 1960; Obama Jr. was born on August 4, 1961.

arrived, but the new family did not stay together long. A year later Barack moved to Hawaii to live with his maternal grandparents, Madelyn and Stanley Dunham, and to receive an American education at the prestigious Punahou Academy. In December 1971, his father returned to America for a month-long visit, giving the 10-year-old Obama his lasting only memories of his father.

After graduating from Punahou in 1979, Barack attended Occidental College, a small liberal-arts school in Los Angeles. It was here that he became politically active. In his sophomore year, he helped organize, and spoke at, an anti-apartheid rally for corporate divestment in South Africa. That day he learned that he had the power to affect people simply by speaking from the heart.

After two years at Occidental, Obama transferred to Columbia University in New York in 1981 to complete his degree in political science. Scarcely a year later, he received a phone call from an aunt in Kenya, who bore the news that his father had been killed in a car accident.

Obama moved to Chicago in 1985 to take a job as the director of the Developing Communities Project, a faith-based organization based on the South Side. There he worked as a community organizer, helping create jobs, prepare students, for college and remove asbestos from a local housing project. The experience taught him how to bring people together, as well as the responsibilities of government toward the less fortunate.

In 1988, he was accepted to Harvard Law School. Before classes began, he traveled to Kenya to visit his extended family and to learn more about the father of whom he knew so little. This journey would form the emotional conclusion to his best-selling 1995 memoir, Dreams From My Father: A Story of Race and Inheritance.

After his first year at Harvard, he got an internship at Sidley & Austin, a prominent downtown Chicago law firm. One of the associates was a recent Harvard Law graduate named Michelle Robinson.

Young Barack in a t-shirt from the University of Hawaii, where his parents met.

A Remarkable Woman

Herself a graduate *cum laude* of Harvard Law School, Michelle Robinson gave much of her free time to the Harvard Legal Aid Bureau, working under the supervision of a practicing attorney. Upon graduation in 1988, she was offered a job with Sidley & Austin, a noted Chicago law firm that encourages its associates to do pro bono work.

A year later, Michelle was assigned to mentor a 28-year-old first-year Harvard Law student who was working at the firm for the summer. As Michelle told it on the campaign trail, upon hearing his name, she wondered, "What's a Barack Obama?"

The future president was instantly smitten with Michelle, and he turned on the charm. But the career-minded lawyer felt it was inappropriate to date a co-worker, much less someone she was mentoring. She even tried to set him up with some of her friends.

Barack finally convinced her to join him at a community meeting in a church basement. He rolled up his sleeves and began to talk, not about how the world is, but about how it should be. The community organizers were persuaded, and so was Michelle—but in her case, of more than just the issues on the table that day. Michelle saw that, despite coming from different backgrounds, they shared the same values. Her resistance began to break down, and they began dating.

"What I saw in him on that day was authenticity and truth and principle," she would tell the *Washington Post* in 2007.

On their first proper date, they started at the Art Institute of Chicago, in the Loop. Afterwards, they walked up Michigan Avenue for a drink at the Signature Room on the 95th floor of the Hancock Building, which features stunning panoramic views of the city. They finished the day by seeing the Spike Lee movie *Do The Right Thing*, followed by ice cream at Baskin-Robbins. Her only major complaint about him was that he smoked.

Michelle still felt like she needed a second opinion, so she asked her brother, Craig, to take her new boyfriend out to play basketball, to get a better sense of who he is. Craig was impressed—not necessarily with his game, but with his confidence, lack of selfishness, and natural leadership ability on the court. "He didn't just pass me the ball because he was dating my sister," the former draft pick of the Philadelphia 76ers said. "Whenever a player gets tired, he reverts back to the player he truly is . . . and we played for hours. That's how I could tell."

Starting a Family for the Future

Obama first gained national attention in his second year at Harvard, when he became the first black president of the Harvard Law Review. As with his work in Chicago, his ability to bring people of different backgrounds and agendas together would form the backbone of his political successes.

After graduating magna cum laude from Harvard in 1991, Obama returned to the Windy City, where he would soon split his time between practicing civil rights law and teaching at the University of Chicago, where he was a visiting law and government fellow. He became an active presence on various local boards, making the necessary connections for him to begin his career in public service.

Michelle, meanwhile, was reevaluating her relationship with Barack. The two were in love, but he was ambivalent about marriage. Given that his father had abandoned the family when Barack was only two years old, his doubts were understandable. But Michelle was adamant that she wanted a family like the one in which she grew up.

Shortly after his graduation, the couple was having dinner at a fancy restaurant. The long-running debate started up again. Michelle told him that he should get serious about their relationship because she wasn't going to hang around forever. Eventually, it was time for dessert. On Michelle's plate was a box with an engagement ring inside. "That kind of shuts you up, doesn't it?" her new fiancé said.

Michelle and Barack were married on October 3, 1992, at the Trinity United Church of Christ, by the Rev. Jeremiah Wright, who would later be the source of much controversy during the 2008 presidential campaign. Santita Jackson, Michelle's old friend from high school, sang during the wedding. The reception was held at the South Shore Cultural Center (previously a country club that did not accept blacks or Jews). Their two daughters, Malia and Sasha, would follow in 1998 and 2001.

Barack Obama and his bride, Michelle Robinson, on their wedding day, October 3, 1992, in Chicago. After his first year at Harvard, Obama was a summer associate at a corporate law firm in Chicago; Robinson, another Harvard law graduate, was his adviser. They later married, and had two daughters, Malia and Sasha.

A Star Rising

Obama's political and public-service career didn't slow down for his personal life. From April through October of 1992, Obama directed Project Vote!—an effort that was nothing short of amazing. With 10 staffers and several hundred volunteers, the project registered about 150,000 new voters, mostly African Americans, in Illinois. (Project Vote! was helped by a liberal organization called ACORN, which later ran into trouble for a variety of reasons, some of them real, some manufactured by political enemies. The temporary association of Project Vote! and ACORN would be a problem for Obama during the 2008 campaign.)

In 1993 Obama joined the law firm of Davis, Miner, Barnhill, and Galland as an associate. The firm's particular interests were civil-rights litigation and neighborhood economic development. As his reputation grew, he began to serve on the boards of directors of numerous charitable organizations. In 1995, his first book, *Dreams From My Father: A Story of Race and Inheritance,* was published.

In 1996 Obama was elected to the Illinois State Senate from the 13th District, which comprised neighborhoods on the South Side of Chicago. He where he worked on successful legislation for campaign finance and health-care reform, as well as becoming a reliable vote on traditional Democratic issues like gun control and against racial profiling. Reelected to the senate in 1998, Obama made a run in 2000 for the Democratic nomination for the U.S. House of Representatives, but lost to the four-term incumbent.

Despite this setback, his statewide star was rising; he was reelected to the state senate in 2002, but Obama began to aim even higher. In March 2004, he became the Democratic nominee for the U.S. Senate, receiving nearly 70% of the votes, more than twice as many votes as his nearest competitor. He was only the third African American ever elected to the U.S. Senate. He held a spot on the powerful Foreign Relations Committee, and he successfully introduced or sponsored legislation on arms reduction, government spending and lobbying reform, and reduction of greenhouse gasses. By that time he had also spoken out against the Bush administration's 2003 invasion of Iraq, which was said to be meant to eliminate reported weapons of mass destruction (which proved to be nonexistent).

But it was on July 24, 2004, that Barack Obama became a national sensation when he delivered the keynote address at the Democratic National Convention. His masterful speech connected his life story to the ideals upon which America was founded. He summed up his political philosophy with the now-legendary phrase, "Tonight, there is not a liberal America and a conservative America; there is the United States of America."

In October 2006 Obama released his second book, *The Audacity of Hope: Thoughts on Reclaiming the American Dream,* which quickly reached the top of the *New York Times* and Amazon.com's best-seller list. The calls for him to run for President grew louder.

Delivering the keynote address at the 2004 Democratic National Convention.

2004 Democratic National Convention Keynote Address

by Barack Obama

Delivered to the Democratic National Convention at the Fleet Center in Boston, Massachusetts, July 27, 2004

Thank you so much. Thank you. Thank you. Thank you so much. Thank you so much. Thank you. Thank you. Thank you, Dick Durbin. You make us all proud.

On behalf of the great state of Illinois, crossroads of a nation, Land of Lincoln, let me express my deepest gratitude for the privilege of addressing this convention.

Tonight is a particular honor for me because, let's face it, my presence on this stage is pretty unlikely. My father was a foreign student, born and raised in a small village in Kenya. He grew up herding goats, went to school in a tin-roof shack. His father—my grandfather—was a cook, a domestic servant to the British.

But my grandfather had larger dreams for his son. Through hard work and perseverance my father got a scholarship to study in a magical place, America, that shone as a beacon of freedom and opportunity to so many who had come before.

While studying here, my father met my mother. She was born in a town on the other side of the world, in Kansas. Her father worked on oil rigs and farms through most of the Depression. The day after Pearl Harbor my grandfather signed up for duty; joined Patton's army, marched across Europe. Back home, my grandmother raised a baby and went to work on a bomber assembly line. After the war, they studied on the G.I. Bill, bought a house through F.H.A., and later moved west all the way to Hawaii in search of opportunity.

And they, too, had big dreams for their daughter. A common dream, born of two continents.

My parents shared not only an improbable love, they shared an abiding faith in the possibilities of this nation. They would give me an African name, Barack, or "blessed," believing that in a tolerant America your name is no barrier to success. They imagined—They imagined me going to the best schools in the land, even though they weren't rich, because in a generous America you don't have to be rich to achieve your potential.

They're both passed away now. And yet, I know that on this night they look down on me with great pride.

They stand here—And I stand here today, grateful for the diversity of my heritage, aware that my parents' dreams live on in my two precious daughters. I stand here knowing that my story is part of the larger American story, that I owe a debt to all of those who came before me, and that, in no other country on earth, is my story even possible.

Tonight, we gather to affirm the greatness of our Nation—not because of the height of our skyscrapers, or the power of our military, or the size of our economy. Our pride is based on a very simple premise, summed up in a declaration made over two hundred years ago:

"We hold these truths to be self-evident, that all men are created equal, that they are endowed by their Creator with certain inalienable rights, that among these are Life, Liberty and the pursuit of Happiness."

That is the true genius of America, a faith—a faith in simple dreams, an insistence on small miracles; that we can tuck in our children at night and know that they are fed and clothed and safe from harm; that we can say what we think, write what we think, without hearing a sudden knock on the door; that we can have an idea and start our own business without paying a bribe; that we can participate in the political process without fear of retribution, and that our votes will be counted—at least most of the time.

This year, in this election we are called to reaffirm our values and our commitments, to hold them against a hard reality and see how we're measuring up to the legacy of our forbearers and the promise of future generations.

And fellow Americans, Democrats, Republicans, Independents, I say to you tonight: We have more work to do—more work to do for the workers I met in Galesburg, Illinois, who are losing their union jobs at the Maytag plant that's moving to Mexico, and now are having to compete with their own children for jobs that pay seven bucks an hour; more to do for the father that I met who was losing his job and choking back the tears, wondering how he would pay 4500 dollars a month for the drugs his son needs without the health benefits that he counted on; more to do for the young woman in East St. Louis, and thousands more like her, who has the grades, has the drive, has the will, but doesn't have the money to go to college.

Now, don't get me wrong. The people I meet—in small towns and big cities, in diners and office parks—they don't expect government to solve all their problems. They know they have to work hard to get ahead, and they want to. Go into the collar counties around Chicago, and people will tell you they don't want their tax money wasted, by a welfare agency or by the Pentagon. Go in—Go into any inner city neighborhood, and folks will tell you that government alone can't teach our kids to learn; they know that parents have to teach, that children can't achieve unless we raise their expectations and turn off the television sets and eradicate the slander that says a black youth with a book is acting white. They know those things.

People don't expect—People don't expect government to solve all their problems. But they sense, deep in their bones, that with just a slight change in priorities, we can make sure that every child in America has a decent shot at life, and that the doors of opportunity remain open to all.

They know we can do better. And they want that choice.

In this election, we offer that choice. Our Party has chosen a man to lead us who embodies the best this country has to offer. And that man is John Kerry.

John Kerry understands the ideals of community, faith, and service because they've defined his life. From his heroic service to Vietnam, to his years as a prosecutor and lieutenant governor, through two decades in the United States Senate, he's devoted himself to this country. Again and again, we've seen him make tough choices when easier ones were available.

Via Delia sells her homemade Obama buttons along 14th Street in downtown Denver during the convention.

His values and his record affirm what is best in us. John Kerry believes in an America where hard work is rewarded; so instead of offering tax breaks to companies shipping jobs overseas, he offers them to companies creating jobs here at home.

John Kerry believes in an America where all Americans can afford the same health coverage our politicians in Washington have for themselves.

John Kerry believes in energy independence, so we aren't held hostage to the profits of oil companies, or the sabotage of foreign oil fields.

John Kerry believes in the Constitutional freedoms that have made our country the envy of the world, and he will never sacrifice our basic liberties, nor use faith as a wedge to divide us.

And John Kerry believes that in a dangerous world war must be an option sometimes, but it should never be the first option.

You know, a while back—awhile back I met a young man named Shamus in a V.F.W. Hall in East Moline, Illinois. He was a good-looking kid—six two, six three, clear eyed, with an easy smile. He told me he'd joined the Marines and was heading to Iraq the following week. And as I listened to him explain why he'd enlisted, the absolute faith he had in our country and its leaders, his devotion to duty and service, I thought this young man was all that any of us might ever hope for in a child.

But then I asked myself, "Are we serving Shamus as well as he is serving us?"

I thought of the 900 men and women—sons and daughters, husbands and wives, friends and neighbors, who won't be returning to their own hometowns. I thought of the families I've met who were struggling to get by without a loved one's full income, or whose loved ones had returned with a limb missing or nerves shattered, but still lacked long-term health benefits because they were Reservists.

When we send our young men and women into harm's way, we have a solemn obligation not to fudge the numbers or shade the truth about why they're going, to care for their families while they're gone, to tend to the soldiers upon their return, and to never ever go to war without enough troops to win the war, secure the peace, and earn the respect of the world.

Now—Now let me be clear. Let me be clear. We have real enemies in the world. These enemies must be found. They must be pursued. And they must be defeated. John Kerry knows this. And just as Lieutenant Kerry did not hesitate to risk his life to protect the men who served with him in Vietnam, President Kerry will not hesitate one moment to use our military might to keep America safe and secure.

John Kerry believes in America. And he knows that it's not enough for just some of us to prosper—for alongside our famous individualism, there's another ingredient in the American saga, a belief that we're all connected as one people. If there is a child on the south side of Chicago who can't read, that matters to me, even if it's not my child. If there is a senior citizen somewhere who can't pay for their prescription drugs, and having to choose between medicine and the rent, that makes my life poorer, even if it's not my grandparent. If there's an Arab American family being rounded up without benefit of an attorney or due process, that threatens my civil liberties.

It is that fundamental belief—It is that fundamental belief: I am my brother's keeper. I am my sister's keeper that makes this country work. It's what allows us to pursue our individual dreams and yet still come together as one American family.

E pluribus unum: "Out of many, one."

Now even as we speak, there are those who are preparing to divide us—the spin masters, the negative ad peddlers who embrace the politics of "anything goes." Well, I say to them tonight, there is not a liberal America and a conservative America—there is the United States of America. There is not a Black America and a White America and Latino America and Asian America—there's the United States of America.

The pundits, the pundits like to slice-and-dice our country into Red States and Blue States; Red States for Republicans, Blue States for Democrats. But I've got news for them, too. We worship an "awesome God" in the blue states, and we don't like federal agents poking around in our libraries in the red states. We coach Little League in the blue states, and yes, we've got some gay friends in the red states. There are patriots who opposed the war in Iraq, and there are patriots who supported the war in Iraq. We are one people, all of us pledging allegiance to the Stars and Stripes, all of us defending the United States of America.

In the end—In the end—In the end, that's what this election is about. Do we participate in a politics of cynicism or do we participate in a politics of hope?

John Kerry calls on us to hope. John Edwards calls on us to hope.

I'm not talking about blind optimism here—the almost willful ignorance that thinks unemployment will go away if we just don't think about it, or the health care crisis will solve itself if we just ignore it. That's not what I'm talking about. I'm talking about something more substantial. It's the hope of slaves sitting around a fire singing freedom songs; the hope of immigrants setting out for distant shores; the hope of a young naval lieutenant bravely patrolling the Mekong Delta; the hope of a millworker's son who dares to defy the odds; the hope of a skinny kid with a funny name who believes that America has a place for him, too.

Hope—Hope in the face of difficulty. Hope in the face of uncertainty. The audacity of hope!

In the end, that is God's greatest gift to us, the bedrock of this nation. A belief in things not seen. A belief that there are better days ahead.

I believe that we can give our middle class relief and provide working families with a road to opportunity.

I believe we can provide jobs to the jobless, homes to the homeless, and reclaim young people in cities across America from violence and despair.

I believe that we have a righteous wind at our backs and that as we stand on the crossroads of history, we can make the right choices, and meet the challenges that face us.

America! Tonight, if you feel the same energy that I do, if you feel the same urgency that I do, if you feel the same passion that I do, if you feel the same hopefulness that I do—if we do what we must do, then I have no doubt that all across the country, from Florida to Oregon, from Washington to Maine, the people will rise up in November, and John Kerry will be sworn in as President, and John Edwards will be sworn in as Vice President, and this country will reclaim its promise, and out of this long political darkness a brighter day will come.

Thank you very much everybody. God bless you. Thank you.

Barack and Michelle wave to delegates after he delivered his keynote address. It had the feel of an old Broadway plot: Barack Obama walked on stage an unknown, and walked off a star.

Barack Obama, Presidential Candidate

An Auspicious Beginning

On February 10, 2007, on the steps of the Illinois State Capitol in Springfield, Obama announced his candidacy for President of the United States. His campaign platform included ending the occupation of Iraq, increasing domestic energy production, and expanding health care to cover all citizens. New York senator and former first lady Hillary Clinton was considered the front-runner, while John Edwards, the vice-presidential candidate in 2004, was seen as her only real challenger.

But Obama shocked the political world by winning the Iowa caucuses, the traditional start of the campaign season, in January 2008. Clinton came back to win a close victory in the New Hampshire primary a week later. Edwards soon lost steam and dropped out, essentially making it a two-person race between Clinton and Obama.

The next four months became a knock-down, drag-out battle. By the end of February, Obama had a solid lead. Clinton fought strong, with victories in early March that put her back in the race. But she was unable to catch up to Obama, and on early June 7 she ended her campaign and endorsed Obama.

Democratic presidential candidate Senator Barack Obama, and his vice-presidential running mate, Senator Joe Biden, in an appearance in Springfield, Illinois.

Rosario Dawson and Jessica Alba on the final night of the convention, August 28.

A stuffed Obama doll in Denver. His face is seemingly everywhere in shop windows and on the streets near the convention.

Seven-year-old Sasha Obama leans on her mom's lap as her dad gives his acceptance speech.

Barack Obama was officially the Democratic nominee. He would face Republican senator John McCain of Arizona in the race to become the 44th president of the United States.

Preparing for Battle

With the nomination sewn up, Barack Obama began his search for a running mate. Many saw Hillary Clinton as the obvious choice: her presence on the ticket would unify a fractured party, and she could help deliver states where he had trouble. But on the eve of the Democratic National Convention, Obama chose Senator Joe Biden of Delaware. The pick was another inspired move. Biden was widely seen by both parties as a leading Senate expert on foreign policy, and his blue-collar background would help deliver votes in the predominantly white, blue-collar Eastern states where Obama had faltered in the primaries.

The convention, held in Denver in late August, was designed to educate the public about Barack Obama. On the first night appeared Senator Ted Kennedy, who had rarely been seen in public since being diagnosed with a brain tumor in May. Kennedy, who had endorsed Obama in February, gave a rousing speech that named Obama as the inheritor of the ideals his brothers had championed. The evening concluded with Michelle speaking to the public of her history with Barack, portraying him as a loving husband and father working for a better world.

In Hillary Clinton's address on Tuesday, she unequivocally confirmed her support of Obama with six words: "No way. No how. No McCain." She went one step further on Wednesday afternoon when she interrupted the official roll call to move the vote be suspended and that Obama be nominated by acclamation. It was a remarkable piece of political theater. Following Biden's acceptance speech at the Pepsi Center, Obama made a surprise appearance, sending the crowd into ecstasy. But it would be nothing compared to the next night.

On Thursday, August 28, the convention moved to INVESCO Field at Mile High, home of the Denver Broncos. In front of 84,000 people and 38 million more watching at home, Barack Obama delivered another of his classic speeches, "We Cannot Stand Alone." He forcefully stated that the American government had failed its citizens over the last eight years by not remaining true to the founders' ideals of equal opportunity. He laid out his belief that he was the right man, with the intelligence and vision, to lead the country through the next four years.

Obama, Michelle, and their two daughters, Malia (second from left) and Sasha, take the stage after Obama addresses supporters at Lawrence North High School in Indianapolis.

The Fight Turns Bloody

The next morning, before the world could digest the magnitude of Obama's speech, John McCain announced his running mate, Governor Sarah Palin of Alaska. The Republican National Convention began three days later, and then the general election was officially underway.

The candidates were running neck-and-neck through much of September. Although nationally unknown, Sarah Palin energized Republican conservatives who had not completely warmed up to McCain, and Obama fell behind in the polls. But then, several major U.S.-based financial institutions collapsed, plunging the global economy into crisis. As the month ended, McCain announced that he was suspending his campaign and returning to Washington to work on the solution.

To the undecided voter, the contrast was striking—Obama came across as calm and presidential while McCain seemed out of touch. Obama took the lead again as the campaign and debates continued.

The McCain-Palin campaign turned negative, with Palin in particular questioning Obama's patriotism. While her words were popular with conservatives, she was alienating the moderate Republicans and swing voters who had long honored McCain's lifetime of public service and history of "straight talk."

Greeting supporters before introducing Senator Biden in Springfield, Illinois.

We Cannot Walk Alone

by Barack Obama

Delivered to the Democratic National Convention at INVESCO Field in Denver, Colorado, August 28, 2008

To Chairman Dean and my great friend Dick Durbin; and to all my fellow citizens of this great nation.

With profound gratitude and great humility, I accept your nomination for presidency of the United States.

Let me express my thanks to the historic slate of candidates who accompanied me on this journey, and especially the one who traveled the farthest—a champion for working Americans and an inspiration to my daughters and yours—Hillary Rodham Clinton. To President Bill Clinton, who made last night the case for change as only he can make it; to Ted Kennedy, who embodies the spirit of service; and to the next vice president of the United States, Joe Biden, I thank you. I am grateful to finish this journey with one of the finest statesmen of our time, a man at ease with everyone from world leaders to the conductors on the Amtrak train he still takes home every night.

To the love of my life, our next first lady, Michelle Obama, and to Malia and Sasha—I love you so much, and I'm so proud of you.

Four years ago, I stood before you and told you my story—of the brief union between a young man from Kenya and a young woman from Kansas who weren't well off or well-known, but shared a belief that in America, their son could achieve whatever he put his mind to.

It is that promise that has always set this country apart—that through hard work and sacrifice, each of us can pursue our individual dreams but still come together as one American family, to ensure that the next generation can pursue their dreams as well. That's why I stand here tonight. Because for 232 years, at each moment when that promise was in jeopardy, ordinary men and women—students and soldiers, farmers and teachers, nurses and janitors—found the courage to keep it alive.

We meet at one of those defining moments—a moment when our nation is at war, our economy is in turmoil, and the American promise has been threatened once more.

Tonight, more Americans are out of work and more are working harder for less. More of you have lost your homes and even more are watching your home values plummet. More of you have cars you can't afford to drive, credit card bills you can't afford to pay, and tuition that's beyond your reach.

These challenges are not all of government's making. But the failure to respond is a direct result of a broken politics in Washington and the failed policies of George W. Bush.

America, we are better than these last eight years. We are a better country than this.

This country is more decent than one where a woman in Ohio, on the brink of retirement, finds herself one illness away from disaster after a lifetime of hard work.

We're a better country than one where a man in Indiana has to pack up the equipment he's worked on for 20 years and watch it shipped off to China, and then chokes up as he explains how he felt like a failure when he went home to tell his family the news.

We are more compassionate than a government that lets veterans sleep on our streets and families slide into poverty; that sits on its hands while a major American city drowns before our eyes.

Tonight, I say to the people of America, to Democrats and Republicans and independents across this great land—enough! This moment—this election—is our chance to keep, in the 21st century, the American promise alive. Because next week, in Minnesota, the same party that brought you two terms of George Bush and Dick Cheney will ask this country for a third. And we are here because we love this country too much to let the next four years look just like the last eight. On November 4, we must stand up and say: "Eight is enough."

Now let there be no doubt. The Republican nominee, John McCain, has worn the uniform of our country with bravery and distinction, and for that we owe him our gratitude and our respect. And next week, we'll also hear about those occasions when he's broken with his party as evidence that he can deliver the change that we need.

But the record's clear: John McCain has voted with George Bush 90 percent of the time. Sen. McCain likes to talk about judgment, but really, what does it say about your judgment when you think George Bush has been right more than 90 percent of the time? I don't know about you, but I'm not ready to take a 10 percent chance on change.

The truth is, on issue after issue that would make a difference in your lives—on health care and education and the economy—Sen. McCain has been anything but independent. He said that our economy has made "great progress" under this president. He said that the fundamentals of the economy are strong. And when one of his chief advisers—the man who wrote his economic plan—was talking about the anxieties that Americans are feeling, he said that we were just suffering from a "mental recession," and that we've become, and I quote, "a nation of whiners."

A nation of whiners? Tell that to the proud autoworkers at a Michigan plant who, after they found out it was closing, kept showing up every day and working as hard as ever, because they knew there were people who counted on the brakes that they made. Tell that to the military families who shoulder their burdens silently as they watch their loved ones leave for their third or fourth or fifth tour of duty.

Striding onto the stage to deliver his acceptance speech.

These are not whiners. They work hard and they give back and they keep going without complaint. These are the Americans I know.

Now, I don't believe that Sen. McCain doesn't care what's going on in the lives of Americans. I just think he doesn't know. Why else would he define middle-class as someone making under $5 million a year? How else could he propose hundreds of billions in tax breaks for big corporations and oil companies but not one penny of tax relief to more than 100 million Americans? How else could he offer a health care plan that would actually tax people's benefits, or an education plan that would do nothing to help families pay for college, or a plan that would privatize Social Security and gamble your retirement?

It's not because John McCain doesn't care. It's because John McCain doesn't get it.

For over two decades, he's subscribed to that old, discredited Republican philosophy—give more and more to those with the most and hope that prosperity trickles down to everyone else. In Washington, they call this the Ownership Society, but what it really means is that you're on your own. Out of work? Tough luck. You're on your own. No health care? The market will fix it. You're on your own. Born into poverty? Pull yourself up by your own bootstraps—even if you don't have boots. You are on your own.

Well it's time for them to own their failure. It's time for us to change America. And that's why I'm running for president of the United States.

You see, we Democrats have a very different measure of what constitutes progress in this country.

We measure progress by how many people can find a job that pays the mortgage; whether you can put a little extra money away at the end of each month so you can someday watch your child receive her college diploma. We measure progress in the 23 million new jobs that were created when Bill Clinton was president—when the average American family saw its income go up $7,500 instead of go down $2,000 like it has under George Bush.

We measure the strength of our economy not by the number of billionaires we have or the profits of the Fortune 500, but by whether someone with a good idea can take a risk and start a new business, or

whether the waitress who lives on tips can take a day off and look after a sick kid without losing her job—an economy that honors the dignity of work.

The fundamentals we use to measure economic strength are whether we are living up to that fundamental promise that has made this country great—a promise that is the only reason I am standing here tonight.

Because in the faces of those young veterans who come back from Iraq and Afghanistan, I see my grandfather, who signed up after Pearl Harbor, marched in Patton's Army, and was rewarded by a grateful nation with the chance to go to college on the GI Bill.

In the face of that young student who sleeps just three hours before working the night shift, I think about my mom, who raised my sister and me on her own while she worked and earned her degree; who once turned to food stamps but was still able to send us to the best schools in the country with the help of student loans and scholarships.

When I listen to another worker tell me that his factory has shut down, I remember all those men and women on the South Side of Chicago I stood by and fought for two decades ago after the local steel plant closed.

And when I hear a woman talk about the difficulties of starting her own business or making her way in the world, I think about my grandmother, who worked her way up from the secretarial pool to middle-management, despite years of being passed over for promotions because she was a woman. She's the one who taught me about hard work. She's the one who put off buying a new car or a new dress for herself so that I could have a better life. She poured everything she had into me. And although she can no longer travel, I know that she's watching tonight, and that tonight is her night as well.

Now, I don't know what kind of lives John McCain thinks that celebrities lead, but this has been mine. These are my heroes. Theirs are the stories that shaped my life. And it is on behalf of them that I intend to win this election and keep our promise alive as president of the United States.

What is that American promise?

It's a promise that says each of us has the freedom to make of our own lives what we will, but that we

also have the obligation to treat each other with dignity and respect.

It's a promise that says the market should reward drive and innovation and generate growth, but that businesses should live up to their responsibilities to create American jobs, to look out for American workers, and play by the rules of the road.

Ours is a promise that says government cannot solve all our problems, but what it should do is that which we cannot do for ourselves—protect us from harm and provide every child a decent education; keep our water clean and our toys safe; invest in new schools and new roads and science and technology.

Our government should work for us, not against us. It should help us, not hurt us. It should ensure opportunity not just for those with the most money and influence, but for every American who's willing to work.

That's the promise of America—the idea that we are responsible for ourselves, but that we also rise or fall as one nation; the fundamental belief that I am my brother's keeper; I am my sister's keeper.

That's the promise we need to keep. That's the change we need right now. So let me spell out exactly what that change would mean if I am president.

Change means a tax code that doesn't reward the lobbyists who wrote it, but the American workers and small businesses who deserve it.

You know, unlike John McCain, I will stop giving tax breaks to corporations that ship jobs overseas, and I will start giving them to companies that create good jobs right here in America.

I'll eliminate capital gains taxes for the small businesses and the start-ups that will create the high-wage, high-tech jobs of tomorrow.

I will, listen now, cut taxes—cut taxes—for 95 percent of all working families. Because in an economy like this, the last thing we should do is raise taxes on the middle-class.

And for the sake of our economy, our security and the future of our planet, I will set a clear goal as president: In 10 years, we will finally end our dependence on oil from the Middle East. We will do this.

Washington's been talking about our oil addiction for the last 30 years, and by the way John McCain's been there for 26 of them. And in that time, he's said no to higher fuel-efficiency standards for cars, no to investments in renewable energy, no to renewable fuels. And today, we import triple the amount of oil that we had as the day that Sen. McCain took office.

Now is the time to end this addiction, and to understand that drilling is a stop-gap measure, not a long-term solution. Not even close.

As president, I will tap our natural gas reserves, invest in clean coal technology, and find ways to safely harness nuclear power. I'll help our auto companies re-tool, so that the fuel-efficient cars of the future are built right here in America. I'll make it easier for the American people to afford these new cars. And I'll invest $150 billion over the next decade in affordable, renewable sources of energy—wind power and solar power and the next

generation of biofuels; an investment that will lead to new industries and 5 million new jobs that pay well and can't be outsourced.

America, now is not the time for small plans.

Now is the time to finally meet our moral obligation to provide every child a world-class education, because it will take nothing less to compete in the global economy. You know, Michelle and I are only here tonight because we were given a chance at an education. And I will not settle for an America where some kids don't have that chance. I'll invest in early childhood education. I'll recruit an army of new teachers, and pay them higher salaries and give them more support. And in exchange, I'll ask for higher standards and more accountability. And we will keep our promise to every young American—if you commit to serving your community or our country, we will make sure you can afford a college education.

Now is the time to finally keep the promise of affordable, accessible health care for every single American. If you have health care, my plan will lower your premiums. If you don't, you'll be able to get the same kind of coverage that members of Congress give themselves. And as someone who watched my mother argue with insurance companies while she lay in bed dying of cancer, I will make certain those companies stop discriminating against those who are sick and need care the most.

Now is the time to help families with paid sick days and better family leave, because nobody in America should have to choose between keeping their job and caring for a sick child or ailing parent.

Now is the time to change our bankruptcy laws, so that your pensions are protected ahead of CEO bonuses; and the time to protect Social Security for future generations.

And now is the time to keep the promise of equal pay for an equal day's work, because I want my daughters to have the exact same opportunities as your sons.

Now, many of these plans will cost money, which is why I've laid out how I'll pay for every dime—by closing corporate loopholes and tax havens that don't help America grow. But I will also go through the federal budget, line by line, eliminating programs that no longer work and making the ones we do need work better and cost less—because we cannot meet 21st century challenges with a 20th century bureaucracy.

And Democrats, we must also admit that fulfilling America's promise will require more than just money. It will require a renewed sense of responsibility from each of us to recover what John F. Kennedy called our "intellectual and moral strength." Yes, government must lead on energy independence, but each of us must do our part to make our homes and businesses more efficient. Yes, we must provide more ladders to success for young men who fall into lives of crime and despair. But we must also admit that programs alone can't replace parents; that government can't turn off the television and make a child do her homework; that fathers must take more responsibility to provide love and guidance to their children.

Individual responsibility and mutual responsibility—that's the essence of America's promise.

And just as we keep our promise to the next generation here at home, so must we keep America's promise abroad. If John McCain wants to have a debate about who has the temperament, and judgment, to serve as the next commander in chief, that's a debate I'm ready to have.

For while Sen. McCain was turning his sights to Iraq just days after 9/11, I stood up and opposed this war, knowing that it would distract us from the real threats that we face. When John McCain said we could just "muddle through" in Afghanistan, I argued for more resources and more troops to finish the fight against the terrorists who actually attacked us on 9/11, and made clear that we must take out Osama bin Laden and his lieutenants if we have them in our sights. You know, John McCain likes to say that he'll follow bin Laden to the Gates of Hell—but he won't even go to the cave where he lives.

And today, as my call for a time frame to remove our troops from Iraq has been echoed by the Iraqi government and even the Bush administration, even after we learned that Iraq has $79 billion in surplus while we are wallowing in deficits, John McCain stands alone in his stubborn refusal to end a misguided war.

That's not the judgment we need. That won't keep America safe. We need a president who can face the threats of the future, not keep grasping at the ideas of the past.

You don't defeat a terrorist network that operates in 80 countries by occupying Iraq. You don't protect Israel and deter Iran just by talking tough in Washington. You can't truly stand up for Georgia when you've strained our oldest alliances. If John McCain wants to follow George Bush with more tough talk and bad strategy, that is his choice—but that is not the change that America needs.

We are the party of Roosevelt. We are the party of Kennedy. So don't tell me that Democrats won't defend this country. Don't tell me that Democrats won't keep us safe. The Bush-McCain foreign policy has squandered the legacy that generations of Americans—Democrats and Republicans—have built, and we are here to restore that legacy.

As commander in chief, I will never hesitate to defend this nation, but I will only send our troops into harm's way with a clear mission and a sacred commitment to give them the equipment they need in battle and the care and benefits they deserve when they come home.

I will end this war in Iraq responsibly, and finish the fight against al Qaeda and the Taliban in Afghanistan. I will rebuild our military to meet future conflicts. But I will also renew the tough, direct diplomacy that can prevent Iran from obtaining nuclear weapons and curb Russian aggression. I will build new partnerships to defeat the threats of the 21st century: terrorism and nuclear proliferation; poverty and genocide; climate change and disease. And I will restore our moral standing, so that America is once again that last, best hope for all who are called to the cause of freedom, who long for lives of peace, and who yearn for a better future.

These are the policies I will pursue. And in the weeks ahead, I look forward to debating them with John McCain.

But what I will not do is suggest that the senator takes his positions for political purposes. Because one of the things that we have to change in our politics is the idea that people cannot disagree without challenging each other's character and each other's patriotism.

The times are too serious, the stakes are too high for this same partisan playbook. So let us agree that patriotism has no party. I love this country, and so do you, and so does John McCain. The men and women who serve in our battlefields may be Democrats and Republicans and independents, but they have fought together and bled together and some died together under the same proud flag. They have not served a Red America or a Blue America—they have served the United States of America.

So I've got news for you, John McCain. We all put our country first.

America, our work will not be easy. The challenges we face require tough choices, and Democrats as well as Republicans will need to cast off the worn-out ideas and politics of the past. For part of what has been lost these past eight years can't just be measured by lost wages or bigger trade deficits. What has also been lost is our sense of common purpose. That's what we have to restore.

We may not agree on abortion, but surely we can agree on reducing the number of unwanted pregnancies in this country. The reality of gun ownership may be different for hunters in rural Ohio than they are for those plagued by gang-violence in Cleveland, but don't tell me we can't uphold the Second Amendment while keeping AK-47s out of the hands of criminals. I know there are differences on same-sex marriage, but surely we can agree that our gay and lesbian brothers and sisters deserve to visit the person they love in the hospital and to live lives free of discrimination. You know, passions may fly on immigration, but I don't know anyone who benefits when a mother is separated from her infant child or an employer undercuts American wages by hiring illegal workers. But this, too, is part of America's promise—the promise of a democracy where we can find the strength and grace to bridge divides and unite in common effort.

I know there are those who dismiss such beliefs as happy talk. They claim that our insistence on something larger, something firmer and more honest in our public life is just a Trojan Horse for higher taxes and the abandonment of traditional values. And that's to be expected. Because if you don't have any fresh ideas, then you use stale tactics to scare voters. If you don't have a record to run on, then you paint your opponent as someone people should run from.

You make a big election about small things.

And you know what—it's worked before. Because it feeds into the cynicism we all have about government. When Washington doesn't work, all its promises seem empty. If your hopes have been dashed

again and again, then it's best to stop hoping, and settle for what you already know.

I get it. I realize that I am not the likeliest candidate for this office. I don't fit the typical pedigree, and I haven't spent my career in the halls of Washington.

But I stand before you tonight because all across America something is stirring. What the naysayers don't understand is that this election has never been about me. It's about you. It's about you.

For 18 long months, you have stood up, one by one, and said enough to the politics of the past. You understand that in this election, the greatest risk we can take is to try the same old politics with the same old players and expect a different result. You have shown what history teaches us—that at defining moments like this one, the change we need doesn't come from Washington. Change comes to Washington. Change happens because the American people demand it—because they rise up and insist on new ideas and new leadership, a new politics for a new time.

America, this is one of those moments.

I believe that as hard as it will be, the change we need is coming. Because I've seen it. Because I've lived it. Because I've seen it in Illinois, when we provided health care to more children and moved more families from welfare to work. I've seen it in Washington, where we worked across party lines to open up government and hold lobbyists more accountable, to give better care for our veterans and keep nuclear weapons out of the hands of terrorist.

And I've seen it in this campaign. In the young people who voted for the first time, and the young at heart, those who got involved again after a very long time. In the Republicans who never thought they'd pick up a Democratic ballot, but did. I've seen it in the workers who would rather cut their hours back a day even though they can't afford it than see their friends lose their jobs, in the soldiers who re-enlist after losing a limb, in the good neighbors who take a stranger in when a hurricane strikes and the floodwaters rise.

You know, this country of ours has more wealth than any nation, but that's not what makes us rich. We have the most powerful military on Earth, but that's not what makes us strong. Our universities and our culture are the envy of the world, but that's not what keeps the world coming to our shores.

Instead, it is that American spirit—that American promise—that pushes us forward even when the path is uncertain; that binds us together in spite of our differences; that makes us fix our eye not on what is seen, but what is unseen, that better place around the bend.

That promise is our greatest inheritance. It's a promise I make to my daughters when I tuck them in at night, and a promise that you make to yours—a

promise that has led immigrants to cross oceans and pioneers to travel west; a promise that led workers to picket lines, and women to reach for the ballot.

And it is that promise that 45 years ago today, brought Americans from every corner of this land to stand together on a Mall in Washington, before Lincoln's Memorial, and hear a young preacher from Georgia speak of his dream.

The men and women who gathered there could've heard many things. They could've heard words of anger and discord. They could've been told to succumb to the fear and frustration of so many dreams deferred.

But what the people heard instead—people of every creed and color, from every walk of life—is that in America, our destiny is inextricably linked. That together, our dreams can be one.

"We cannot walk alone," the preacher cried. "And as we walk, we must make the pledge that we shall always march ahead. We cannot turn back."

America, we cannot turn back. Not with so much work to be done. Not with so many children to educate, and so many veterans to care for. Not with an economy to fix and cities to rebuild and farms to save. Not with so many families to protect and so many lives to mend. America, we cannot turn back. We cannot walk alone. At this moment, in this election, we must pledge once more to march into the future. Let us keep that promise—that American promise—and in the words of Scripture hold firmly, without wavering, to the hope that we confess.

Thank you, God Bless you, and God Bless the United States of America.

With Michelle, after delivering an eloquent and moving acceptance speech.

Obama's Best Lieutenant

America today has a love affair with Michelle Obama, and appreciates her style, grace, and overall demeanor; but that was not always the case. Early on in the presidential campaign she was criticized for her sarcasm and dry humor. Some comments, often those intended as jokes, did not translate well in print, and she eventually toned them down.

Near the beginning of the campaign Michelle made a sage attempt to present her husband as a mortal. In an interview with *Glamour* magazine, she revealed personal foibles, such as Barack often failing to pick up his dirty socks. Some readers criticized her for disclosing such things.

Michelle said that she was sharing with the world that her husband was just a man. "People understood that this is how we all live in our marriages," she said of the comments. "And Barack is very much human. So let's not deify him, because what we do is we deify, and then we're ready to chop it down."

In hindsight, Michelle's words would seem prophetic. After the inauguration an emphasis was placed on the fact that Barack Obama should not be expected to fix everything simply by having taken the oath. "He's just a man," people said. "He's only one person," they added. Three years later, during Obama's bid for reelection, this argument would be reiterated in the face of criticism that he hadn't solved all of America's problems in a single term.)

Most people appreciated the fact that Michelle came across as genuine. Many women across America also identified with her on the basis of her personal style—she was known for wearing her own clothing and for dressing comfortably and buying off the rack. "It makes her seem more like me," one woman said of Michelle's ready-to-wear purchases.

A strong woman, Michelle had to learn to tone down her delivery at first.

Even though voters eventually came to identify with Michelle, she first had to undergo her fair share of scrutiny. She hit a major bump when, during a stump speech for her husband, she said, "For the first time in my life I am really proud of my country." Conservative pundits were quick to react. Michelle Obama sustained more criticism than any other candidate's spouse. She was referred to as an angry black woman, as Barack's "baby-mama" (a slang term that implied she and Barack were unmarried), and even as a terrorist. The mockery, most notoriously an ad by the Tennessee Republican Party, grew so critical that Barack Obama interceded to demand that people "lay off [his] wife."

Michelle Obama, to her credit, seemed to take it all in stride, and while her approach changed a bit over the course of the campaign, she still maintained her own identity and style. "Barack and I have been in the public eye for many years now, and we've developed a thick skin along the way. When you're out campaigning, there will always be criticism. . . . At the end of the day, I know that it comes with the territory," she said.

Another striking factor on the campaign trail was that Michelle did not allow it to disrupt her children's lives. Early in the campaign she limited her involvement to only two days a week, and traveled overnight only if daughters Malia and Sasha could come along. This early reluctance to become too involved in the campaign worked to the Obamas' advantage: First, it made it clear to everyone that Michelle's number-one priority is the well-being of her children. Second, it made people more curious about who she was and what she was like.

The public became familiar with Barack Obama's story early on, but Michelle's story was almost a secret weapon for the Obama campaign. She had achieved what is considered to be the American Dream; this made people admire her even more. The woman once perceived as sarcastic and aloof was more and more seen as hardworking, driven, and accomplished—and that only bolstered America's confidence in her husband.

In her speech at the Democratic National Convention, Michelle was able to speak to Barack's experience and vision in a way that was personal yet relatively objective. Where in the past she had described him as a mere human, she now talked about the visionary who "talked about the world as it is and the world as it should be." She explained that "he said that all too often we accept the distance between the two, and we settle for the world as it is, even when it doesn't reflect our values and aspirations."

She also made tangible Barack Obama's work as a community organizer. His opponents had poked fun at his work, but Michelle described "what he did all those years ago in Chicago." She made it clear that Barack's work as a community organizer was nothing to laugh it, in spite of his opponents' attempts to deride the experience. She described

his "setting up job training to get people back to work and after-school programs to keep kids safe; working block by block to help people lift up their families. It's what he did in the Illinois Senate, moving people from welfare to jobs, passing tax cuts for hardworking families, and making sure women get equal pay for equal work."

She made clear what it was that he had done, and the impact that his work had on people. This helped the campaign tremendously. Many voters were already identifying with his dream and his push for change; now, for supporters and critics alike, hearing his story from Michelle—someone who knew the story because it was part of her own.

Delivering a speech at the 2008 Democratic National Convention.

Victory

Obama and McCain were running neck-and-neck through much of September. But during the campaign, the economy plunged into the worst crisis since the Great Depression, and undecided voters responded more to Obama's policies and calm temperament.

As the campaign headed into its final weeks, Obama had a clear lead in both the popular and electoral votes. On November 4, 2008, record numbers cast their ballots to elect a new leader. At 11:00 Eastern Time, seconds after every contiguous state had closed its polls, the television networks predicted Barack Obama as the next president of the United States.

After a gracious concession by McCain, Obama took the stage at Chicago's Grant Park in front of hundreds of thousands of jubilant citizens. In his final speech of the campaign, he thanked his family and supporters. He quoted Abraham Lincoln. He referenced singer Sam Cooke's stirring civil rights anthem, "A Change Is Gonna Come," and, most emotionally, the Rev. Dr. Martin Luther King Jr.'s "I've Been to the Mountaintop" speech.

Obama closed with a challenge to the American people. "This is our moment. This is our time—to put our people back to work and open doors of opportunity for our kids; to restore prosperity and promote the cause of peace; to reclaim the American dream and reaffirm that fundamental truth—that out of many, we are one; that while we breathe, we hope, and where we are met with cynicism, and doubt, and those who tell us that we can't, we will respond with that timeless creed that sums up the spirit of a people: Yes We Can."

With the Bidens at an election-night party at Grant Park in Chicago, November 4, 2008.

From Election to Inauguration

The New Administration

After the presidential election, Barack Obama set upon the task of assembling his cabinet and senior staff. On November 6, a key piece of the puzzle was put into place when he named Congressman Rahm Emanuel of Illinois to be his chief of staff. Emanuel, who had also worked in the Clinton White House, had a reputation as a hard-nosed Democratic politician, but one who could work across the aisle.

With the country in the midst of a recession, Obama had to promptly gather his economic advisers. He picked Timothy Geithner, president of the Federal Reserve Bank of New York, to be his secretary of the Treasury. Also named to the team were former Treasury secretary Lawrence Summers, and Paul A. Volcker, who was chairman of the Federal Reserve under presidents Carter and Reagan.

Ever since Hillary Clinton ended her presidential campaign, there were questions about what role she would play in the new administration. Shortly after the election, word got out that the president-elect had offered her the position of secretary of state. This became official on December 1, when Obama introduced his former political opponent as part of his foreign affairs and national security team. Former White House chief of staff Leon Panetta was nominated as the director of the Central Intelligence Agency.

To maintain continuity in the ongoing war efforts, Robert Gates would continue as secretary of defense. Two other cabinet nominees were named that day: Arizona governor Janet Napolitano as secretary of homeland security, and Eric Holder as attorney general, the first African American to be nominated for that position.

Through December and January, other cabinet and cabinet-level appointments would be revealed: Arne Duncan, secretary of education. Tom Vilsack, secretary of agriculture. Shaun Donovan, secretary of housing and urban development. Ray LaHood, secretary of transportation. Hilda Solis, secretary of labor. Eric Shinseki, secretary of veterans affairs. Ken Salazar, secretary of the interior. Steven Chu, secretary of energy. Lisa Jackson, administrator of the Environmental Protection Agency. Ronald Kirk, U.S. trade representative. Susan Rice, ambassador to the United Nations.

With one-time foe Hillary Clinton, now his pick for secretary of state.

There were a few complications with the president-elect's choices, but not many. Dianne Feinstein, chairwoman of the Senate Intelligence Committee, raised doubts about Panetta's intelligence experience. Eric Holder's confirmation was delayed due to a controversial pardon he arranged while working for President Bill Clinton. During Geithner's confirmation hearings, it was revealed that he had failed to pay taxes on time (he would be confirmed after the inauguration); Tom Daschle withdrew his own nomination as Health and Human Services secretary for similar reasons. There were questions also about whether Bill Clinton's work with his global foundation would create conflicts of interest with his wife as America's chief diplomat. In early January, Obama's first choice for secretary of commerce, New Mexico governor Bill Richardson, withdrew when it was learned that his administration was under investigation for corruption. (Obama's second choice for the post, New Hampshire senator Judd Gregg, a Republican, would later withdraw his own consideration, citing policy disagreements with the administration.) These situations were unusual; most of the incoming president's cabinet-level picks were confirmed without incident.

With a bulldog temperament, Congressman Rahm Emmanuel is a natural pick for chief of staff.

Getting the Residence in Order

On November 10, Barack Obama met with President George W. Bush to discuss the transition of power. Despite Obama's frequent criticisms of Bush during the campaign, the departing leader offered his full cooperation in providing the incoming administration with whatever it needed. During their conversation, First Lady Laura Bush gave Michelle Obama a tour of the White House, spending most of their time in the executive residence.

Speculation about where Malia and Sasha would continue their education was answered on November 21, when it was announced that they would attend the elite Sidwell Friends School in Northwest Washington, D.C. Chelsea Clinton, Julie and Tricia Nixon, and Al Gore III had all attended Sidwell Friends during their parents' service in Washington. The school's experience in handling the Obama daughters' unique security requirements played a major role in the decision.

Less than two weeks before the inauguration, the Obama family released the news that Marian Robinson, Michelle's mother, would move into the White House to help care for Sasha and Malia. In 2007 Mrs. Robinson had retired from her job as an executive secretary at a bank to look after her granddaughters while their parents were campaigning.

President Bush walks with President-elect Obama down the Colonnade of the White House on November 10, en route to the Oval Office.

A Distraction From Illinois

On December 9, Illinois governor Rod Blagojevich was arrested on corruption charges, including allegedly attempting to sell the Senate seat Obama vacated when he resigned on November 16. U.S. Attorney Patrick Fitzgerald said from the outset that neither Obama nor anybody on his staff was a suspect in the scandal. The day after Blagojevich's arrest, Obama called for the governor's resignation.

To assuage concerns, Obama began an internal investigation of his team's contacts with Blagojevich. Two days before Christmas, he released his report, which found no inappropriate contact by any member of his staff in their conversations with Blagojevich. The scandal momentarily distracted the famously disciplined Obama team from its transition work. (Before the end of January, "Blago" would be impeached and unanimously voted out of office by the state legislature. "Today ends a painful episode for Illinois," Obama would write on January 29 as he welcomed the incoming governor, Patrick Quinn.)

First lady Laura Bush and Michelle Obama have a quiet visit in the private residence of the White House.

Getting Sasha, 7, and Malia, 10, ready for their first day of school at Sidwell on January 5. Jan. 5, 2009. For the moment, the family lives at the Hay Adams Hotel in Washington.

Ben's Chili Bowl

Located near Howard University in the Shaw section of Washington, D.C., the U Street Corridor has long been the cultural heart of Washington's African American community. In the 1950s it became known as the "Black Broadway" for the number of theaters and jazz clubs that lined the street. Legendary jazz composer Edward Kennedy "Duke" Ellington grew up nearby, and a mural of him overlooks U Street on the wall of the True Reformer Building.

The neighborhood has undergone many changes over the past 50 years and is currently a thriving multicultural hotspot. But Ben's Chili Bowl at 1213 U Street NW has remained a constant. Opened in 1958 by Ben and Virginia Ali, Ben's Chili Bowl has served countless plates of its signature dish, the chili half-smoke. It rose to national prominence in 1985, when Bill Cosby, who discovered the restaurant in the 1960s, held a press conference there to celebrate his hit television show. In 2003, to commemorate Ben's Chili Bowl's 45th anniversary, the alley adjacent to the restaurant was named "Ben Ali Way."

Because its clientele is representative of Washington's diverse population, Ben's is frequently used by local politicians for photo opportunities, and news reporters when they want to take the pulse of the city. Photographs of famous African Americans who have eaten there, including Denzel Washington and Chris Rock, line its walls.

President-elect Obama had been in Washington since becoming a senator in 2005, but he had yet to experience a meal at Ben's Chili Bowl. On January 10, 2009, Washington mayor Adrian Fenty took him to the landmark restaurant for a lunch of a chili half-smoke, cheese fries, and sweet tea. As a crowd gathered outside, Obama joked and posed for pictures with the staff and patrons.

Although a sign lists the Obama family as eating for free—Cosby is the only other on the list—the future president insisted on paying for his meal, handing $20 to the cashier.

The Inaugural Express

The legacy of Abraham Lincoln was a constant presence in the period leading up to the inauguration. News commentators frequently searched for angles to connect Obama and Lincoln, from their Illinois roots to their oratorical skills. Obama's cabinet, which includes former political opponents and two Republicans, invites comparisons to Lincoln's famed "team of rivals."

But few moments were as designed to draw parallels between the 16th and 44th presidents as the

Waving to onlookers after a bite at the iconic Ben's Chili Bowl.

"Inaugural Express." Recreating the train ride that brought Lincoln to Washington, D.C., in 1861, the Obama family left Philadelphia's 30th Street Station around noon on January 17, 2009, which was also Michelle's 45th birthday.

In Wilmington, Delaware, they picked up Vice President–elect Joe Biden and his wife, Jill. Before boarding, Biden, who famously traveled by train daily from his home in Wilmington to Washington, addressed the crowd that had gathered to send off their hometown hero.

As the train, the *Georgia 300,* made its way south towards the nation's capital, many supporters, from large crowds at the stations to individuals living along the route, braved the bitter cold to cheer, chanting Obama's name and waving flags.

The *Georgia 300* is a privately owned car built by the famous Pullman Standard Company in 1930. Although retired in 1982, it has since been used by presidents Jimmy Carter, George H.W. Bush, and Bill Clinton. It features a master bedroom, two other bedrooms, two showers, a large dining room, an observation room, and an open rear platform. Attached to the *Georgia 300* were 10 Amtrak cars carrying the president-elect's staff, journalists, and 41 citizens whom Obama had met during the campaign.

The train made one other stop, in Baltimore, Maryland, where Obama spoke to a crowd of 40,000 people. At approximately 7:00 p.m., the Inaugural Express completed the 137-mile journey by pulling into Washington's historic Union Station, located steps from the U.S. Capitol. The Obamas were then taken by motorcade to Blair House, the official residence where they would live until after the inauguration.

Greeting Amtrak conductor Noel Powell at Philadelphia's 30th Street Station before embarking on Obama's inaugural whistle-stop train trip to Washington.

We Are One

On the chilly afternoon of Sunday, January 18, an estimated crowd of 400,000 people gathered at the Lincoln Memorial for a star-studded tribute to the inauguration of Barack Obama. The concert, called "We Are One," was telecast live, and HBO opened up its signal so the entire country could view it for free. The show was picked up by television networks around the world. The audio was broadcast across the country on National Public Radio.

Following an invocation by the Right Rev. Gene Robinson—the nation's only openly gay Episcopalian bishop—the Bidens and Obamas were presented to the crowd. They emerged from the memorial, walked down its marble steps, and took their place in a separate section off to the side. Academy Award–winning actor Denzel Washington delivered introductory remarks about the symbolism of the monuments to George Washington, Thomas Jefferson, and Abraham Lincoln. He also spoke of how Obama's message of unity and hope has inspired people around the country to help create the more perfect union the Founding Fathers dreamed about.

Then, Bruce Springsteen, who endorsed Obama during the primary season, kicked off the musical proceedings. Backed by a red-clad choir, Springsteen performed an inspiring version of "The Rising," the hymn-like song that was frequently used at Obama campaign rallies.

In between the musical performances were readings designed to put Barack Obama's inauguration into historical context. Laura Linney and Martin Luther King III, on the same steps where his father gave his famous "I Have A Dream" speech, spoke of the inaugural addresses by Franklin Delano Roosevelt and John F. Kennedy. Jamie Foxx quoted Thurgood Marshall, the first African American named to the U.S. Supreme Court, and delighted the crowd with his impression of Obama's election-night victory speech in Chicago's Grant Park.

President-elect Barack Obama and Michelle Obama arrive at the "We Are One: Opening Inaugural Celebration at the Lincoln Memorial" in Washington on January 18.

Beyoncé performs at the inaugural celebration at the Lincoln Memorial.

Tom Hanks recited a solemn but moving rendition of Aaron Copland's "A Lincoln Portrait," complete with Copland's orchestral accompaniment. Queen Latifah spoke of how gospel singer Marian Anderson was denied an opportunity to sing at Washington's Constitution Hall in 1939, only to have First Lady Eleanor Roosevelt arrange a performance for her at the Lincoln Memorial. Tiger Woods, the son a U.S. Army lieutenant colonel, paid tribute to the sacrifices made by our men and women in uniform and their families. And Samuel L. Jackson spoke of the legacy of Rosa Parks and the March on Washington.

The guests of honor also addressed the crowd. Joe Biden spoke passionately of how the promise of America can be achieved through hard work. Near the end, Obama spoke—as he had throughout the election—of the threads that bind Americans together, and of the challenges that currently face the country.

The emotional high point of the concert followed, as folk icon Pete Seeger walked onstage escorted by his grandson Tao Rodriguez-Seeger and Bruce Springsteen. Seeger was blacklisted in the 1950s for his views, but never lost his commitment to civil rights and social justice, or his optimism. Springsteen ceded the spotlight to the 89-year-old Seeger, who led everybody in a sing-along of his friend Woody Guthrie's "This Land Is Your Land." He included a rarely sung verse that seemed to sum up not only his entire career, but also the spirit of the forces of change that made the weekend possible.

Nobody living can ever stop me,
As I go walking that freedom highway;
Nobody living can ever make me turn back
This land was made for you and me.

The concert concluded with Beyoncé leading all of the day's performers in "America the Beautiful."

Voices Calling for Change

by Barack Obama

Speech delivered at the Lincoln Memorial in Washington, D.C., on January 18, 2009

I want to thank all the speakers and performers today for reminding us, through song and through words, just what it is that we love about America. And I want to thank all of you for braving the cold and the crowds and traveling in some cases thousands of miles to join us here today. Welcome to Washington, and welcome to this celebration of American renewal.

In the course of our history, only a handful of generations have been asked to confront challenges as serious as the ones we face right now. Our nation is at war. Our economy is in crisis. Millions of Americans are losing their jobs and their homes; they're worried about how they'll afford college for their kids or pay the stack of bills on their kitchen table. And most of all, they are anxious and uncertain about the future—about whether this generation of Americans will be able to pass on what's best about this country to our children and their children.

I won't pretend that meeting any one of these challenges will be easy. It will take more than a month or a year, and it will likely take many. Along the way there will be setbacks and false starts and days that test our fundamental resolve as a nation.

But despite all of this—despite the enormity of the task that lies ahead—I stand here today as hopeful as ever that the United States of America will endure—that the dream of our founders will live on in our time.

What gives me that hope is what I see when I look out across this mall. For in these monuments are chiseled those unlikely stories that affirm our unyielding faith—a faith that anything is possible in America. Rising before us stands a memorial to a man who led a small band of farmers and shopkeepers in revolution against the army of an Empire, all for the sake of an idea. On the ground below is a tribute to a generation that withstood war and depression—men and women like my grandparents who toiled on bomber assembly lines and marched across Europe to free the world from tyranny's grasp. Directly in front of us is a pool that still reflects the dream of a King, and the glory of a people who marched and bled so that their children might be judged by their character's content. And behind me, watching over the union he saved, sits the man who in so many ways made this day possible.

And yet, as I stand here tonight, what gives me the greatest hope of all is not the stone and marble that surrounds us today, but what fills the spaces in between. It is you—Americans of every race and region and station who came here because you believe in what this country can be and because you want to help us get there.

It is the same thing that gave me hope from the day we began this campaign for the presidency nearly two years ago; a belief that if we could just recognize ourselves in one another and bring everyone together—Democrats, Republicans, and Independents; Latino, Asian, and Native American; black and white, gay and straight, disabled and not—then not only would we restore hope and opportunity in places that yearned for both, but maybe, just maybe, we might perfect our union in the process.

This is what I believed, but you made this belief real. You proved once more that people who love this country can change it. And as I prepare to assume the presidency, yours are the voices I will take with me every day I walk into that Oval Office—the voices of men and women who have different stories but hold common hopes; who ask only for what was promised us as Americans—that we might make of our lives what we will and see our children climb higher than we did.

It is this thread that binds us together in common effort; that runs through every memorial on this mall; that connects us to all those who struggled and sacrificed and stood here before.

It is how this nation has overcome the greatest differences and the longest odds—because there is no obstacle that can stand in the way of millions of voices calling for change.

That is the belief with which we began this campaign, and that is how we will overcome what ails us now. There is no doubt that our road will be long. That our climb will be steep. But never forget that the true character of our nation is revealed not during times of comfort and ease, but by the right we do when the moment is hard. I ask you to help me reveal that character once more, and together, we can carry forward as one nation, and one people, the legacy of our forefathers that we celebrate today.

Thank you, America. God bless you.

A Letter to Malia and Sasha

On the eve of the inauguration, President-elect Barack Obama wrote a letter to his daughters, Malia, 10, and Sasha, 7. In it, he eloquently told them the reasons he ran for president—that they were rooted in his desire to do all he can to make the world better for them, and for every child in America.

Obama explained that this meant giving them the chance to go to schools "that challenge them, inspire them, and instill in them a sense of wonder about the world around them." He also wrote of his desire to make the planet cleaner and safer through improvements in science and technology.

He struck a solemn tone when he told them that he understood that there would be times when he would have to use force to protect the American way of life. "I want every child to understand that the blessings these brave Americans fight for are not free," he wrote. "That with the great privilege of being a citizen of this nation comes great responsibility."

He wrote that he learned this from his mother, who passed away before they were born. She would often read to him the Declaration of Independence and explain that those who marched for equality

Walking on Kailua Beach in Hawaii with Malia and Sasha, August 2008.

were trying to bring the words in that document to fruition.

He concluded with a challenge for them to continue his life's mission of working to give others the opportunities that they have had, and by saying that he loved them and was proud of them. The letter would be published later in PARADE magazine. The full text follows.

Dear Malia and Sasha,

I know that you've both had a lot of fun these last two years on the campaign trail, going to picnics and parades and state fairs, eating all sorts of junk food your mother and I probably shouldn't have let you have. But I also know that it hasn't always been easy for you and Mom, and that as excited as you both are about that new puppy, it doesn't make up for all the time we've been apart. I know how much I've missed these past two years, and today I want to tell you a little more about why I decided to take our family on this journey.

When I was a young man, I thought life was all about me—about how I'd make my way in the world, become successful, and get the things I want. But then the two of you came into my world with all your curiosity and mischief and those smiles that never fail to fill my heart and light up my day. And suddenly, all my big plans for myself didn't seem so important anymore. I soon found that the greatest joy in my life was the joy I saw in yours. And I realized that my own life wouldn't count for much unless I was able to ensure that you had every opportunity for happiness and fulfillment in yours. In the end, girls, that's why I ran for President: because of what I want for you and for every child in this nation.

I want all our children to go to schools worthy of their potential—schools that challenge them, inspire them, and instill in them a sense of wonder about the world around them. I want them to have the chance to go to college—even if their parents aren't rich. And I want them to get good jobs: jobs that pay well and give them benefits like

The young Obama family on election night in 2004, awating results of Barack's Senate run.

health care, jobs that let them spend time with their own kids and retire with dignity.

I want us to push the boundaries of discovery so that you'll live to see new technologies and inventions that improve our lives and make our planet cleaner and safer. And I want us to push our own human boundaries to reach beyond the divides of race and region, gender and religion that keep us from seeing the best in each other.

Sometimes we have to send our young men and women into war and other dangerous situations to protect our country—but when we do, I want to make sure that it is only for a very good reason, that we try our best to settle our differences with others peacefully, and that we do everything possible to keep our servicemen and women safe. And I want every child to understand that the blessings these brave Americans fight for are not free—that with the great privilege of being a citizen of this nation comes great responsibility.

That was the lesson your grandmother tried to teach me when I was your age, reading me the opening lines of the Declaration of Independence and telling me about the men and women who marched for equality because they believed those words put to paper two centuries ago should mean something.

She helped me understand that America is great not because it is perfect but because it can always be made

better—and that the unfinished work of perfecting our union falls to each of us. It's a charge we pass on to our children, coming closer with each new generation to what we know America should be.

I hope both of you will take up that work, righting the wrongs that you see and working to give others the chances you've had. Not just because you have an obligation to give something back to this country that has given our family so much—although you do have that obligation. But because you have an obligation to yourself. Because it is only when you hitch your wagon to something larger than yourself that you will realize your true potential.

These are the things I want for you—to grow up in a world with no limits on your dreams and no achievements beyond your reach, and to grow into compassionate, committed women who will help build that world. And I want every child to have the same chances to learn and dream and grow and thrive that you girls have. That's why I've taken our family on this great adventure.

I am so proud of both of you. I love you more than you can ever know. And I am grateful every day for your patience, poise, grace, and humor as we prepare to start our new life together in the White House.

—Love, Dad

President Barack Obama, First Lady Michelle Obama, and their daughters, Sasha and Malia, sit for a family portrait in the Green Room of the White House, September 1, 2009.

A National Day of Service

Coincidentally, the day before the inauguration was the national observation of the birthday of Dr. Martin Luther King Jr. Since 1994, the holiday has been set aside by Congress as a national day of service to continue Dr. King's work and legacy.

With President-elect Obama publicly committing to the day of service, thousands of Americans followed his example. The Corporation for National and Community Service, which coordinates the event, noted record numbers for volunteers, with more than double the previous year's number of projects taking place. Across the country, men and women donated their time to plant trees, prepare and deliver food to the hungry, clean up neighborhoods, and act as mentors to at-risk children.

It was a fitting lead-in to the next day's proceedings.

Painting during a renovation project at Sasha Bruce Youthwork, a shelter for homeless or runaway teens, in Washington.

Visiting Calvin Coolidge High School, where students, military families, and volunteer service groups are working on various projects supporting the troops.

Vice president–elect Joe Biden hangs drywall with volunteers at a Habitat For Humanity home renovation effort in Washington.

Mr. Obama Goes to Washington

Blair House

After arriving in Washington, D.C., on January 17 on the "Inaugural Express," President-elect Barack Obama and his family were escorted to Blair House, across from the White House, diagonally over Pennsylvania Avenue. Blair House is the official state guest house for visiting dignitaries and heads of state. It is the traditional residence for incoming presidents before they move into the White House.

Built in 1824, Blair House began as a private home for Joseph Lovell, the eighth surgeon general of the United States. Twelve years later, it was bought by newspaper publisher and presidential advisor Francis Preston Blair. The house remained in his family for the next century before the U.S. government purchased it in 1942.

President Harry S. Truman lived in Blair House for much of his time in office while the interior of the White House underwent major structural renovations. Truman had to cross Pennsylvania Avenue every day.

Throughout the years, Blair House has expanded beyond its origins as an urban home to incorporate the three adjacent townhouses, which are internally connected. Within the complex's 70,000 square feet are 119 rooms, including 14 guest bedrooms, eight staff bedrooms, 35 bathrooms, four dining rooms, an exercise room, a flower shop, and a fully equipped hair salon.

Blair House is operated under the supervision of the chief of protocol of the United States, an officer of the State Department.

A City for Ceremony

In 1791, President George Washington gave Major Pierre Charles L'Enfant the responsibility of designing the newly designated federal capital. L'Enfant's vision was to create a city built for ceremony. Inspired by the great capital cities of Europe, he proposed a grid system—but with wide diagonal avenues named after the original 13 states. At the intersection of these avenues he specified open spaces devoted to noted citizens so that

Inauguration day: President-elect Obama and Michelle Obama leave the Blair House on the way to a church service at St. John's Episcopal Church, across from the White House.

the public could reflect on their statesmanship in a contemplative, recreational environment.

By 1901, however, another aspect of L'Enfant's vision—the National Mall, an open green area directly west of the Capitol Building—was blighted by railways, barracks from the Civil War, and even cattle. A commission consisting of noted architects Daniel Burnham, Frederick Law Olmstead Jr., and Charles F. McKim, and famous sculptor Augustus Saint-Gaudens, was created to determine how to restore the Mall to its proper grandeur.

The committee was chaired by Senator James McMillan of Michigan. The commission set upon the task of redesigning the Mall. This was the beginning of the system of parks, museums, and monuments in Washington, D.C., that visitors from all over the world enjoy to this day.

The inauguration of President Barack Obama brought a record audience of some 1.8 million people to the National Mall. Thousands more lined Pennsylvania Avenue between the Capitol and the White House for the inaugural parade.

The sun rises on the already crowded National Mall on inauguration day as people continue to gather in anticipation of the swearing-in of the president elect.

Preparing for the Inauguration

Putting on an event of the magnitude of the inauguration requires an incredible amount of planning and coordination. With so many of the festivities taking place on or around the National Mall, the National Park Service was charged with the tasks of maintaining the facilities used, and ensuring the safety of the visitors.

With record crowds expected to pass through Washington, the NPS called in its Central Incident Management Team, normally located in Utah's Bryce Canyon National Park, to help coordinate with the park rangers on duty. The U.S. Park Police, a unit of the NPS, also called in officers from New York City and San Francisco to help manage the crowds. (The NPS reported no arrests, assault, robberies, or serious injuries during any of the inaugural events.)

The NPS was also responsible for the construction, maintenance, and removal of all temporary structures used during the weekend. This included all temporary stages, bleachers, and media trailers, and the parade reviewing stand. Boxes were built to protect the trees along Pennsylvania Avenue from parade viewers.

In mid-December, the NPS created an inaugural section of its Web site for those seeking information about the weekend. The site featured maps, frequently asked questions, inauguration history, news releases, and kids' activities. The NPS also provided locations and granted permits to groups wishing to exercise their constitutional right to assemble and protest the policies of the government.

Park rangers gave more than 250 interpretive talks designed to inform visitors of the nation's inaugural history. Special maps of the National Mall were printed to help visitors make their way around the area. Other national parks throughout the region created programs and events with presidential themes.

The entire city was getting ready for what would be the largest public gathering in its history.

The inaugural platform at the west front of the Capitol in Washington, under construction in early December for the January ceremony.

U.S. service members prepare for the 56th presidential inauguration rehearsal in Washington on Sunday, January 11, 2009. More than 5,000 men and women in uniform are providing military ceremonial support to the event, a tradition dating back to George Washington's 1789 inauguration.

Chris Bullock, of Landover, Maryland, works on inaugural seals at Hargrove Inc. in preparation for the big day.

Army Staff Sgt. Derrick Brooks stands in for President-elect Barrack Obama. Stand-ins for the president, vice president, and their families were selected due to height, weight, gender, and ethnic similarities.

"A New Birth of Freedom"

Inauguration Day

As dawn broke on January 20, 2009, Americans could sense the excitement in the air. The spirit of optimism that had swept the nation over the past year was about to reach its zenith in a town usually noted for being cynical and jaded.

Despite the bitter cold, people had been arriving at the National Mall since the night before. Those with tickets lined up at the designated security checkpoints, which opened at 8:00 a.m. Those without headed toward the western side of the Mall, up to the Washington Monument and beyond.

For the president-elect and his family, the hours leading up to the inauguration were steeped in tradition. In the morning, the Obamas, the Bidens, and several close friends attended a multi-denominational service at historic St. John's Episcopal Church, located one block from the White House. The precedent of an incoming president going to church on the day of his inauguration goes back to George Washington in 1789.

After church the Obamas went to the White House, where they were greeted at the north portico by President and Mrs. Bush. Michelle Obama presented Laura Bush with a gift—a leather-bound journal and a pen engraved with the date, for the former first lady to use in her memoirs. The Bushes

President Barack Obama waves before giving his inaugural address.

and Obamas then went inside the mansion to converse, a tradition which began with the inauguration of Rutherford B. Hayes in 1877. Also participating in the gathering, which took place in the Blue Room, were the Bidens, Vice President Dick Cheney, and members of the Congressional Escort Committee.

After coffee, the outgoing and incoming first families rode together from the White House to the east side of the U.S. Capitol, a trip that has been taken at every inauguration since 1837. The ride marked the official debut of the new presidential limousine. As the motorcade made its way down Pennsylvania Avenue, cheers rang out from the mass of people that lined the historic street.

The inauguration, whose theme was "A New Birth of Freedom," began at 10:00 a.m. with music provided by the U.S. Marine Band, America's oldest professional musical organization. The band, known as "The President's Own," has performed at every inauguration since Thomas Jefferson's in 1801.

The San Francisco Boys Chorus and the San Francisco Girls Chorus then performed a selection of patriotic songs including "America the Beautiful," the Oscar Peterson / Harriette Merolla civil-rights anthem "Hymn to Freedom," and "I Hear America Singing." They also gave the world premiere of a new work by composer David Conte, "An Exhortation," which featured words spoken by Barack Obama in his victory speech on November 4, 2008.

As the music played, distinguished guests emerged from inside the Capitol and took their seats on the platform on the West Front. The group included members of Congress, Supreme Court justices, and all living past presidents, vice presidents, and their wives. Barack Obama was the last person to be introduced, and a thunderous ovation rang out. As he walked down the steps, he hugged Georgia's Representative John Lewis, a veteran of the civil rights movement.

Enthusiastic crowds gather in the chilly morning just before dawn.

As the chairwoman of the United States Congress Joint Committee on Inaugural Ceremonies, Senator Dianne Feinstein was given the role of master of ceremonies. In her opening remarks, she described the day as "a turning point for our nation," and praised the process of democracy over violence as an agent of change.

The invocation was delivered by the Rev. Dr. Rick Warren of the Saddleback Church in Lake Forest, California. Warren, who had held a forum in August 2008 with Obama and Republican presidential nominee John McCain, asked God to grant the new president the wisdom, courage, and compassion to lead the country. Warren also referenced the historical significance of the day by saying that "Dr. King and a great cloud of witnesses are shouting in Heaven."

Aretha Franklin, the "Queen of Soul," stepped to the microphone, turning "My Country 'Tis of Thee" into a spiritual. Franklin's father, the

Rev. Dr. C.L. Franklin, was a Baptist preacher whose recorded sermons were influential in the rise of activism in African American churches in the 1960s.

Senator Robert Bennett of Utah then introduced Associate Justice of the Supreme Court John Paul Stevens to administer the oath of office to Joe Biden. At 88 years of age, Stevens is currently both the oldest justice of the Supreme Court and its longest-serving member. With his wife Jill at his side, Biden placed his hand on the Bible and repeated after Stevens.

Aretha Franklin wears a gray felt custom-designed hat as she performs at the inauguration ceremony. She says it would be hard to part with the hat since the day was "a crowning moment in history," but that she will consider donating it to the Smithsonian Institution for an exhibit.

I, Joseph Robert F. Biden Jr., do solemnly swear that I will support and defend the Constitution of the United States against all enemies, foreign and domestic; that I will bear true faith and allegiance to the same; that I take this obligation freely, without any mental reservation or purpose of evasion; and that I will well and faithfully discharge the duties of the office on which I am about to enter. So help me God.

Obama's swearing-in drew closer. But it would have to wait a little bit longer, as another musical interlude followed. To commemorate the event, John Williams, best known for his film scores, composed "Air and Simple Gifts." The piece evoked Aaron Copland's 1944 score for the Martha Graham ballet, "Appalachian Spring," in its adaptation of "Simple Gifts," a famous Shaker song. The piece was performed by three giants in the classical world: violinist Itzhak Perlman, cellist Yo-Yo Ma, and pianist Gabriela Montero, along with clarinetist Anthony McGill of the Metropolitan Opera.

Feinstein then introduced Supreme Court Chief Justice John Roberts to administer the presidential oath of office, and asked everybody in attendance to stand. The spirit on the Mall, which had been growing all day, intensified as Roberts and the Obama family took center stage for the official transition of power. A platform was provided for Malia and Sasha to stand on. "That's for you," Obama told his daughters. Michelle held the Bible used by Abraham Lincoln during his first inauguration as Obama placed his left hand on the sacred book and raised his right hand. Although this was the first time in

Chief Justice John Roberts delivers the oath of office to the president elect.

history a chief justice swore in a president who had voted against his confirmation, there were smiles all around as Roberts asked if Obama was ready to take the oath:

> *I, Barack Hussein Obama, do solemnly swear that I will faithfully execute the office of president of the United States, and will to the best of my ability preserve, protect, and defend the Constitution of the United States. So help me God.*

But the seemingly simple administering of the oath of office did not go as well as planned. First, Obama did not wait for Roberts to say "do solemnly swear" before repeating his part. Then, Roberts, perhaps flustered by Obama's interruption, accidentally put the word "faithfully" in an improper place, after "president of the United States." Obama noticed the mistake and waited for Roberts to correct himself. But in trying to correct himself, Roberts got tongue-tied, and Obama recited the words as Roberts originally misspoke them.

Although there was no argument that Obama's presidency was legitimate, the wording of the oath of office in the Constitution is clear. To remove any potential doubt among constitutional scholars and partisan pundits, Roberts re-administered the oath in the Map Room of the White House the next day.

But none of that mattered at the time. To the world, at 12:05 p.m., Barack Obama had become the 44th president of the United States of America.

Instantly, hundreds of thousands of people on the Mall who had come from all over the world to witness the inauguration became connected by their presence at history. Strangers cheered, hugged, and cried together with an intimacy usually reserved for family. The scene was mirrored throughout the world, in large cities and small villages, in schools and pubs, and in public squares and private homes.

Two minutes later, Senator Feinstein had the distinct honor of presenting the new leader of the free world.

The 44th president of the United States, Barack Obama.

"A New Era of Responsibility"

Any questions from political opponents about whether Barack Obama's extraordinary command of the English language was simply "empty words" were rebuked in his inaugural address. Displaying little of the soaring rhetoric he frequently used on the campaign trail, Obama took a sober, but no less inspiring, tone as he addressed the still-ecstatic crowd on the Mall.

In the 19-minute speech with the theme of "A New Era of Responsibility," Obama began by painting a grim picture of an America that was in economic crisis because of "our collective failure to make hard choices." In order to restore the country to prosperity for all its citizens, he declared an end to the days of carelessness. It was now time to "pick ourselves up, dust ourselves off, and begin again the work of remaking America." Obama said that the grand scope of his ambitions would be met because it is "the risk takers, the doers, the makers of things" who shape the nation's destiny.

The president then laid out his foreign-policy agenda, emphasizing diplomacy and coalitions over the unilateralism of recent years. American ideals, he said, outlasted the threats of "fascism and communism not just with missiles and tanks, but with sturdy alliances and enduring convictions."

Despite the change in tone, the speech was not without a few of Obama's trademark flourishes. He described how America has gained strength and purpose through hard times, including "the bitter swill of civil war and segregation." Citing the Founding Fathers' belief in the rights of all men, Obama rejected "as false the choice between our safety and our ideals." He also issued a diplomatic challenge to rogue nations by saying "we will extend a hand if you are willing to unclench your fist."

Obama concluded with a quote from Thomas Paine's *The American Crisis* article in December 1776, which, a year later in Valley Forge, George Washington ordered to be read to his troops. "Let it be told to the future world," wrote Paine, "that in the depth of winter, when nothing but hope and virtue could survive, that the city and the country, alarmed at one common danger, came forth to meet [it]."

After Obama's speech, Elizabeth Alexander recited a poem she wrote, called "Praise Song for the Day." Alexander, who teaches in the Department of African American Studies at Yale University, was only the fourth poet to read at an inauguration. Robert Frost was the first, reading at John F. Kennedy's inauguration in 1961, and both of Bill Clinton's inaugurations featured poets. Maya Angelou read in 1993 and Miller Williams in 1997.

The final speaker of the afternoon was the Rev. Dr. Joseph E. Lowery, who offered the benediction. Lowery, who helped lead the 1955 bus boycott in Montgomery, Alabama, following the arrest of Rosa Parks, asked God to bestow his blessings on the new president, as Rick Warren had in the invocation. But at the end, Lowery added a touch of levity in contrast to the majesty of the afternoon:

> *"[W]e ask you to help us work for that day when black will not be asked to get back; when brown can stick around; when yellow will be mellow; when the red man can get ahead, man; and when white will embrace what is right."*

Two musical performances concluded the ceremony. First, the U.S. Navy Band "Sea Chanters" sang "The Star Spangled Banner." Then the U.S. Marine Band played several of John Philip Sousa's classic marches, including "The Stars And Stripes Forever," as the president led the way up the Capitol steps.

Opposite: Delivering a powerful inaugural address, "A New Era of Responsibility."

A New Era of Responsibility (2009 Inaugural Address)

by Barack Obama

Speech delivered in front of the United States Capitol Building in Washington, D.C., on January 20, 2009, before a record audience

My fellow citizens:

I stand here today humbled by the task before us, grateful for the trust you have bestowed, mindful of the sacrifices borne by our ancestors. I thank President Bush for his service to our nation, as well as the generosity and cooperation he has shown throughout this transition.

Forty-four Americans have now taken the presidential oath. The words have been spoken during rising tides of prosperity and the still waters of peace. Yet, every so often the oath is taken amidst gathering clouds and raging storms. At these moments, America has carried on not simply because of the skill or vision of those in high office, but because We the People have remained faithful to the ideals of our forbearers, and true to our founding documents.

So it has been. So it must be with this generation of Americans.

That we are in the midst of crisis is now well understood. Our nation is at war, against a far-reaching network of violence and hatred. Our economy is badly weakened, a consequence of greed and irresponsibility on the part of some, but also our collective failure to make hard choices and prepare the nation for a new age. Homes have been lost; jobs shed; businesses shuttered. Our health care is too costly; our schools fail too many; and each day brings further evidence that the ways we use energy strengthen our adversaries and threaten our planet.

These are the indicators of crisis, subject to data and statistics. Less measurable but no less profound is a sapping of confidence across our land—a nagging fear that America's decline is inevitable, and that the next generation must lower its sights.

Today I say to you that the challenges we face are real. They are serious and they are many. They will

not be met easily or in a short span of time. But know this, America—they will be met. On this day, we gather because we have chosen hope over fear, unity of purpose over conflict and discord. On this day, we come to proclaim an end to the petty grievances and false promises, the recriminations and worn-out dogmas, that for far too long have strangled our politics.

We remain a young nation, but in the words of Scripture, the time has come to set aside childish things. The time has come to reaffirm our enduring spirit; to choose our better history; to carry forward that precious gift, that noble idea, passed on from generation to generation: the God-given promise that all are equal, all are free, and all deserve a chance to pursue their full measure of happiness.

In reaffirming the greatness of our nation, we understand that greatness is never a given. It must be earned. Our journey has never been one of shortcuts or settling-for-less. It has not been the path for the faint-hearted—for those who prefer leisure over work, or seek only the pleasures of riches and fame. Rather, it has been the risk-takers, the doers, the makers of things—some celebrated but more often men and women obscure in their labor, who have carried us up the long, rugged path towards prosperity and freedom.

For us, they packed up their few worldly possessions and traveled across oceans in search of a new life.

For us, they toiled in sweatshops and settled the West; endured the lash of the whip and plowed the hard earth.

For us, they fought and died, in places like Concord and Gettysburg; Normandy and Khe Sanh. Time and again these men and women struggled and sacrificed and worked till their hands were raw so that we might live a better life. They saw America as bigger than the sum of our individual ambitions; greater than all the differences of birth or wealth or faction.

At the National World War II Memorial, crowd members watch the inaugural speech on a monitor.

This is the journey we continue today. We remain the most prosperous, powerful nation on Earth. Our workers are no less productive than when this crisis began. Our minds are no less inventive, our goods and services no less needed than they were last week or last month or last year. Our capacity remains undiminished. But our time of standing pat, of protecting narrow interests and putting off unpleasant decisions—that time has surely passed. Starting today, we must pick ourselves up, dust ourselves off, and begin again the work of remaking America.

For everywhere we look, there is work to be done. The state of the economy calls for action, bold and swift, and we will act—not only to create new jobs, but to lay a new foundation for growth. We will build the roads and bridges, the electric grids and digital lines that feed our commerce and bind us together. We will restore science to its rightful place, and wield technology's wonders to raise health care's quality and lower its cost. We will harness the sun and the winds and the soil to fuel our cars and run our factories. And we will transform our schools and colleges and universities to meet the demands of a new age. All this we can do. All this we will do.

Now, there are some who question the scale of our ambitions—who suggest that our system cannot tolerate too many big plans. Their memories are short. For they have forgotten what this country has already done; what free men and women can achieve when imagination is joined to common purpose, and necessity to courage.

What the cynics fail to understand is that the ground has shifted beneath them—that the stale political arguments that have consumed us for so long no longer apply. The question we ask today is not whether our government is too big or too small, but whether it works—whether it helps families find jobs at a decent wage, care they can afford, a retirement that is dignified. Where the answer is yes, we intend to move forward. Where the answer is no, programs will end. And those of us who manage the public's dollars will be held to account—to spend wisely, reform bad habits, and do our business in the light of day—because only then can we restore the vital trust between a people and their government.

National Guard citizen-soldiers of Joint Task Force 29, led by the 29th Infantry Division, coordinate the activities of some of the 9,300 National Guard soldiers and airmen supporting the inauguration.

Nor is the question before us whether the market is a force for good or ill. Its power to generate wealth and expand freedom is unmatched, but this crisis has reminded us that without a watchful eye, the market can spin out of control—and that a nation cannot prosper long when it favors only the prosperous. The success of our economy has always depended not just on the size of our Gross Domestic Product, but on the reach of our prosperity; on our ability to extend opportunity to every willing heart—not out of charity, but because it is the surest route to our common good.

As for our common defense, we reject as false the choice between our safety and our ideals. Our Founding Fathers, faced with perils we can scarcely imagine, drafted a charter to assure the rule of law and the rights of man, a charter expanded by the blood of generations. Those ideals still light the world, and we will not give them up for expedience's sake. And so to all the other peoples and governments who are watching today, from the grandest capitals to the small village where my father was born: know that America is a friend of each nation and every man, woman, and child who seeks a future of peace and dignity, and that we are ready to lead once more.

Recall that earlier generations faced down fascism and communism not just with missiles and tanks, but with sturdy alliances and enduring convictions. They understood that our power alone cannot protect us, nor does it entitle us to do as we please. Instead, they knew that our power grows through its prudent use; our security emanates from the justness of our cause, the force of our example, the tempering qualities of humility and restraint.

The West Front of the Capitol takes on a festive appearance for the inauguration.

We are the keepers of this legacy. Guided by these principles once more, we can meet those new threats that demand even greater effort—even greater cooperation and understanding between nations. We will begin to responsibly leave Iraq to its people, and forge a hard-earned peace in Afghanistan. With old friends and former foes, we will work tirelessly to lessen the nuclear threat, and roll back the specter of a warming planet. We will not apologize for our way of life, nor will we waver in its defense, and for those who seek to advance their aims by inducing terror and slaughtering innocents, we say to you now that our spirit is stronger and cannot be broken; you cannot outlast us, and we will defeat you.

For we know that our patchwork heritage is a strength, not a weakness. We are a nation of Christians and Muslims, Jews and Hindus—and nonbelievers. We are shaped by every language and culture, drawn from every end of this Earth; and because we have tasted the bitter swill of civil war and segregation, and emerged from that dark chapter stronger and more united, we cannot help but believe that the old hatreds shall someday pass; that the lines of tribe shall soon dissolve; that as the world grows smaller, our common humanity shall reveal itself; and that America must play its role in ushering in a new era of peace.

To the Muslim world, we seek a new way forward, based on mutual interest and mutual respect. To those leaders around the globe who seek to sow conflict, or blame their society's ills on the West—know that your people will judge you on what you can build, not what you destroy. To those who cling to power through corruption and deceit and the silencing of dissent, know that you are on the wrong side of history; but that we will extend a hand if you are willing to unclench your fist.

To the people of poor nations, we pledge to work alongside you to make your farms flourish and let clean waters flow; to nourish starved bodies and feed hungry minds. And to those nations like ours that enjoy relative plenty, we say we can no longer afford indifference to the suffering outside our borders; nor can we consume the world's resources without regard to effect. For the world has changed, and we must change with it.

As we consider the road that unfolds before us, we remember with humble gratitude those brave Americans who, at this very hour, patrol far-off deserts and distant mountains. They have something to tell us, just as the fallen heroes who lie in Arlington whisper through the ages.

We honor them not only because they are guardians of our liberty, but because they embody the spirit of service; a willingness to find meaning in something greater than themselves. And yet, at this moment—a moment that will define a generation—it is precisely this spirit that must inhabit us all.

A U.S. Army trumpeter sounds a fanfare during the inauguration ceremonies.

For as much as government can do and must do, it is ultimately the faith and determination of the American people upon which this nation relies. It is the kindness to take in a stranger when the levees break, the selflessness of workers who would rather cut their hours than see a friend lose their job which sees us through our darkest hours. It is the firefighter's courage to storm a stairway filled with smoke, but also a parent's willingness to nurture a child, that finally decides our fate.

Our challenges may be new. The instruments with which we meet them may be new. But those values upon which our success depends—honesty and hard work, courage and fair play, tolerance and curiosity, loyalty and patriotism—these things are old. These things are true. They have been the quiet force of progress throughout our history. What is demanded then is a return to these truths. What is required of us now is a new era of responsibility—a recognition, on the part of every American, that we have duties to ourselves, our nation, and the world—duties that we do not grudgingly accept but rather seize gladly, firm in the knowledge that there is nothing so satisfying to the spirit, so defining of our character, than giving our all to a difficult task.

This is the price and the promise of citizenship.

This is the source of our confidence—the knowledge that God calls on us to shape an uncertain destiny.

This is the meaning of our liberty and our creed—why men and women and children of every race and every faith can join in celebration across this magnificent mall, and why a man whose father less than sixty years ago might not have been served at a local restaurant can now stand before you to take a most sacred oath.

So let us mark this day with remembrance, of who we are and how far we have traveled. In the year of America's birth, in the coldest of months, a small band of patriots huddled by dying campfires on the shores of an icy river. The capital was abandoned. The enemy was advancing. The snow was stained with blood. At a moment when the outcome of our revolution was most in doubt, the father of our nation ordered these words be read to the people:

"Let it be told to the future world . . . that in the depth of winter, when nothing but hope and virtue could survive . . . that the city and the country, alarmed at one common danger, came forth to meet [it]."

America, in the face of our common dangers, in this winter of our hardship, let us remember these timeless words. With hope and virtue, let us brave once more the icy currents, and endure what storms may come. Let it be said by our children's children that when we were tested we refused to let this journey end, that we did not turn back nor did we falter; and with eyes fixed on the horizon and God's grace upon us, we carried forth that great gift of freedom and delivered it safely to future generations.

Thank you. God bless you. And God bless the United States of America.

The new president concludes his remarks on a historic day.

Witnessing History

The inauguration of President Barack Obama was seen in person by an estimated crowd of 1.8 million people, a record for the National Mall. Some came from the Washington, D.C., area, others from all parts of the country. Here are stories told by people who were there on that historic day.

Albert Klyberg, Lincoln, Rhode Island: In 1960, I was actively engaged in the election as chairman of the College Young Democrats in Ohio. I received an invitation to attend the Kennedy inauguration only to be stranded by a snow storm. This time, I was determined to make up for the

earlier disappointment, and we obtained two tickets through our congressman, Patrick J. Kennedy. We boarded a train at Providence on Saturday. There were a few delays that set us back about two hours. We got into D.C. at just about the same time as a system-wide delay caused by the pre-inaugural train ride from Philadelphia to Washington. We even passed their train at the Baltimore station!

Frank Chang, Fairfax, Virginia: I wanted to be able to tell my nine-month- old daughter that I was there. This is the first inauguration since I became an American. I have been living in this country since I was two. I am now 41 and just became a U.S. citizen. I served in the U.S. Army for six years and have followed the politics of this country forever. Obama has improved my feeling about my adopted country. As someone that is not from this country and born half- Asian and half-white, there is finally someone of real power in this world who, I believe, understands things I have had to go through in my life.

James Heiberg, Alexandria, Virginia: When you live in Washington you do try to take advantage of being able to go to big political events. Even though I am a Republican and voted for McCain, I like Obama and I've always liked Biden. This was the first election where I wasn't going to be upset regardless of who won. So while Obama wasn't my guy, I have a positive opinion of him. That he is also the first black president, coupled with the level of enthusiasm for his election that I'm not sure I'll ever see repeated in my lifetime, made going to his inauguration something of a no-brainer.

Marie Lawrence, Atlanta, Georgia: I overheard a phone conversation in the crowd where the individual on the phone said, "There are no commercials where I am." That was exactly my point: live and in person. The opportunity to witness the 56th inauguration could not be put into words. This inauguration represented inclusion, that all men are created equal. The election process has always felt as if it were passive, but viable candidates in 2008 that were diverse and qualified created an interest and a feeling that one could be vested in the process.

Bundled-up onlookers gather around and even climb onto a bronze statue on the National Mall.

Howard Scott, Arlington, Virginia: I was born and raised overseas. My mother went to Fisk University in Tennessee, an all-black college, which exposed her to the full force of Jim Crow laws. While there, she met some black GIs who told her that she should go to Europe, because white people didn't discriminate in Europe like they did in the United States. Shortly after she graduated, she left the U.S. and moved to Paris, where she met and married my dad. While she has returned to the U.S. to visit many times, she has not lived here since the early 1950s. She considered coming here to attend the inauguration. But eventually she was put off by the warning of huge crowds and freezing-cold weather.

I am still amazed and proud that America has chosen a black man to lead them, but my reasons for attending were somewhat more political than racial. My main motivation for going to the inauguration was the same as my reason for dancing and cheering in front of the White House on Election Day: to rebuke the Bush administration and all who have ever supported him.

Louise Johnson, Norcross, Georgia: The only way I could have watched the inauguration of the 44th president of the United States was to personally be there. Yes, I could have watched the events on TV, however, that would not have been sufficient. This inaugural was *history*, because the president just happened to be an African American. *Wow.* It was a moment in time that I could not and would not be a mere spectator of. I knew I had to be a participant. Therefore I went with two of my friends to this most awesome and spectacular event.

Jon Cummings, Westlake Village, California: I was an early Obama supporter. As early as election night my wife and I had discussed attending the inauguration, but work deadlines made it impossible for her. Nearly two months later she surprised me with plane tickets and a hotel reservation for a solo trip. She felt strongly that our family needed to be represented. When I got to LAX I found that my first flight had been delayed two hours. Thankfully, my connecting flight at O'Hare had also been delayed, and I got into D.C. on Saturday night.

Marcel Hillie, Alexandria, Virginia: When I came to D.C. in 1993 to attend Howard University, part of the appeal was being in a city that contained so much culture and history. The ability to watch Barack Obama become president of the United States was something I could not possibly miss. I honestly never thought as a child that I would live to see a black man be elected president. And when I thought about all of the issues and where all of the candidates stood on them, Obama was simply the best candidate.

Daniel Baskes, Chicago, Illinois: We flew in from Chicago on Monday morning, arriving in D.C. just past noon. I am not a hugely political person, nor have I ever been extremely involved in an election. But Obama's charisma and desire for change were pushing me to get involved for the first time. On two separate occasions, including Election Day, my wife and I drove to Laporte, Indiana, to knock on doors and push the Obama vote. When given the opportunity to attend the inauguration, I could not turn it down, because it was this man who had been elected that had driven me to become involved.

Jossie Redmond, of Crawford, Mississippi, is moved to tears during the inaugural ceremonies on the National Mall leading up to the swearing-in ceremony.

Hannah Stuart, of Seattle, Washington, dances and waves a flag on the National Mall.

Dana Compton, Alexandria, Virginia: I was so happy to see and hear people being optimistic that I felt like I couldn't miss it. Everyone talked about it. Everyone was excited about it. I've never, ever seen an inauguration where so many people were so interested. It was a once-in-a-lifetime opportunity. And even if there are some things about Obama that I don't 100% agree with, you can't deny his unbelievable ability to motivate and inspire people.

Marie: I submitted my name to Georgia congressman Jim Marshall and Senator Saxby Chambliss's office for tickets to the inauguration. After two letters of acknowledgement and one rejection letter, the prospect of securing tickets was slim, but I could not be deterred. The day before the inauguration, I visited Senator Chambliss's office, and put my name on a waiting list. I returned around the cut-off time and was fortunate enough to receive silver tickets to the inauguration.

Louise: The feeling of hope and joy started with our drive up to Washington on the 17th. "Why?" you ask. Because we found it a joy to count the cars with Obama/Biden stickers with license plates from Texas, Louisiana, North and South Carolina, and Virginia. We would pass them and honk and get either a smile or a thumbs-up.

James: My wife wisely made arrangements for us and our group of friends to spend Monday night near U Street at the house of friends who would be out of town for the inauguration.

Spectators in Times Square cheer the inaugural address.

Jon: I had a chat on inauguration eve with a gregarious, 70-something African American man in a three-piece suit and fedora, who'd come up from Atlanta. We considered whether it was worthwhile to join the line at Ben's Chili Bowl on U Street, where Obama had been the week before. He said, "If I don't get my Barack dog now, when am I ever gonna get it?" and headed off toward the end of the line.

Marie: A friend of a friend has an office on Pennsylvania Avenue. Our plan was to sleep in the office and start out around 5:00 a.m. When we saw crowds walking towards the Capitol at 1:30 a.m., we decided to pack up the pillows and blankets and walk to the Mall, where a line had formed at the silver gate. We learned that people began the line the night before, around 11:00 p.m.

Jon: I was awakened at 5:15 a.m. by the alarm clock in the next room. The atmosphere on the Metro was surprisingly electric for a packed, predawn train. I was greeted by so many strangers' smiles as I got on board that I couldn't help but blurt out, "Mornin', everybody!" The response was heartwarming, and the mood remained high even though it took nearly an hour and a half to reach the District.

Daniel: We had pedicabs [bicycle rickshaws] pick us up in Adams-Morgan at 8:00 a.m. It was a great way to get down to the Mall quickly because we could cut through streets closed to automobiles. However, we were purple-ticket holders and were stuck in a massive throng of people at 1st and Constitution. We did not gain access to the Mall until 11:30.

Marcel: My friends and I woke up early and walked down to the Mall. It was surreal to see D.C. so deserted even on a Tuesday morning and then see more and more people the closer we got to the Mall.

Albert: We took a bus from the Adams-Morgan neighborhood, where we were staying, that got us very close to our goal of 3rd and C streets. But then we had to walk through a long tunnel under the plaza in front of the Capitol and then find the end of our ticket line, which stretched nearly to the Smithsonian Castle. At one point we thought we had lost our place, but one of the volunteers appeared to lead our section right to the gate.

Howard: Because of the huge crowds that were anticipated, inauguration officials closed all the bridges, from Virginia into downtown D.C., to car traffic. The only way for people coming from Virginia to get downtown was to take the Metro or to walk. I left around

8:30 a.m. and parked my car in a spot between the Pentagon and Arlington National Cemetery. I took a picture of the house of Robert E. Lee, because he fought hard to keep a day such as this from ever happening. I crossed the Memorial Bridge on foot, and by 9:30 I had arrived at the foot of the Lincoln Memorial.

Frank: I met a friend and her daughter at a friend's house. We took the Metro from there to Rosslyn, and walked across the bridge to the Lincoln Memorial. The hardest part was that my friend's daughter is three, so we had to do lots of carrying! We originally planned on biking downtown, but since we were running late we just took the Metro. It actually worked out great.

Sergeant James Bishop, at right, and other soldiers watch the inauguration at Camp Liberty in Baghdad, Iraq. "My mother always wanted to be here," said Bishop, 39, who wiped away tears as he watched.

Jon: I met up with a friend at the Gallery Place Station. At first glance, the scene was like a Hollywood disaster-movie set, until we witnessed the eagerness to cooperate with the crowd management and security measures. Everybody knew there would be video screens and a good sound system not too far away.

Albert: Our tickets got us along the rim of the Capitol reflecting pool. With binoculars, we had a good sightline to the podium and were right near a screen. The raised edge of the reflecting pool provided a place to sit, which we hadn't expected.

The National Mall is carpeted with spectators and well-wishers.

James: We ended up very close to the base of the Washington Monument. You couldn't see the screens too clearly but you could hear the PA pretty well. The Capitol, of course, was a mile off in the distance.

Marie: I stood about half a mile from the Capitol steps. I had an upfront view of the screen, but you had to squint to see the actual platform where the inauguration took place.

Daniel: We were in the West Purple section, which was straight back, and a little to the left of the podium. We were the first section of people standing behind those with seats. I would say we were roughly 200 yards from the president.

Frank: We found a spot near the Lincoln and Korean War memorials. The place we picked was close to a big screen, but on a rise of land where not many others were sitting.

Jon: We were about 50 feet to the north of the monument. Unfortunately, cell-phone coverage in Washington was dicey throughout the weekend, so my hopes for a grand gathering of my friends went unrealized. But afterward I learned that four groups of my friends were within 100 yards of us!

Marcel: The diversity of people stood out to me, from the good friends that I was there with to the lady from Connecticut who overheard our wisecracks to the college tour groups, to the large amounts of older couples who could not stop talking about how special the day was. It may be a cliché but I kept thinking to myself, "This is America."

Dana: We met a guy from Massachusetts who took a picture of our group since we were his "Mall neighbors" for the day. Everyone was friendly and excited about Obama. That seemed to be the only thing that really mattered to people.

Mattie J. Moore cheers as President Barack Obama finishes the oath of office on a restaurant television in the Hyde Park neighborhood of Chicago.

James: I saw one woman wearing a homemade t-shirt proclaiming that for the first time she was proud to be an American. I was a bit put off by that, but hopefully Obama's election will help those who have believed themselves to be alienated from being an American to feel they are part of this country.

Marie: I stood next to a young man from Albany, New York, who appeared to be very reflective. He traveled to the event alone and his mood was extremely somber. I could sense the importance of the inauguration to him, and it immediately took you to a place of reflection as well.

Albert: For a few minutes we were stuck in a crowd with the Rev. Jesse Jackson about 10 feet away. I had met him briefly in Providence years ago, at a statehouse function for the Rhode Island Black Heritage Society, but the crowd in D.C. that day was just too jammed for us to get close enough to greet him.

Frank: I got a picture of a guy who was wearing shorts during the entire thing, which was pretty nuts since it was so cold. I met two women with U.S. and Aussie flags and they said that they came all the way from Australia specifically for this event.

Curt Thompson, state senator, Georgia: These are the two most profound things I witnessed at the inauguration. First, seeing how truly happy and proud everyone was—not just African Americans proud of a 'first,' but all Americans happy with the end of the Bush presidency and proud of the nation for stepping into this new era. Second, seeing the young people climbing into trees and on top of things to get photos, and straining to see history. It hit me, watching these kids climbing up to catch just a glimpse, or to get a photo for themselves, that this truly was an event that changed America.

Jon: When Obama walked out behind Harry Reid and Nancy Pelosi, both more than 20 years his senior, I was struck by the sudden and stunning sense of Obama's youthfulness. The torch indeed seemed to be passed to a new generation, *my* generation. The sense of new responsibility being thrust upon my generation, so long in the shadow of the boomers, was palpable. I was thinking about that when he took the oath of office. I felt the crowd around me collectively holding its breath, as though the nation's renewal depended upon him getting to the words, "So help me God." All morning the mood had been jovial and even irreverent, but suddenly the import of the moment swept over us and left us silent, right up until he completed the oath, at which point we let loose the most joyous roar I've ever heard. I've never hugged and high-fived so many total strangers as I did once that moment had finally come. I imagined it was like V-J Day.

Marie: The moment that President Barack Obama completed the oath was emotional. People in the crowd cheered, cried, and applauded. The reality of it all was joyous.

Daniel: I was not driven to tears as I thought I might be, but I did find myself feeling elation, pride, and an almost instantaneous sense of relief. I felt as though we had accomplished something that no one thought possible two years earlier.

Howard: The crowd erupted when Obama was sworn in! In fact they erupted whenever he, or Michelle, or the Obama daughters, appeared on the screen. I felt ecstatic, vindicated after years of being told I was wrong.

James: I got a little choked up at the moment Obama was inaugurated. I'm not much for symbolic political acts but it seemed to me that America had taken another significant step to wipe away the stain of the "original sin" of slavery and racism from its past.

Over a million people gathered on the National Mall to watch the Inauguration of President Barack Obama and Vice President Joe Biden on January 20, 2009.

Marcel: There was still a bit of disbelief. Did that really just happen? Then the crowd roared, absolutely roared. That really brought home the fact that I just witnessed history.

Louise: You see, there was no TV screen large enough to capture the moment, the energy, the spirit, the excitement, the hope, the joy, the sense of renewal and the atmosphere of *change* that was moving through the throngs of people in Washington as well as through the country and the world.

Marie: I witnessed the events for myself and for those in my family who are no longer present. It rendered me speechless. My father, Sergeant First Class Thomas A. Lawrence, fought in the Korean and Vietnam wars and died on July 16, 2001. The changes that have occurred since measure up significantly to those that Dad experienced in his lifetime, and I consider myself fortunate to be alive during this generation.

Dana: Obama's speech was so, so, so much better than the actual swearing in. When he was talking, I actually forgot how cold I was. I was absolutely amazed that so many people could be so quiet for so long just mesmerized by what he was saying. Seeing him speak in person made the whole thing worth it.

Howard: As soon as Obama said ". . . and God bless America!" I turned tail and headed home. It was *a very* cold day, and although I was wearing five layers, I had been standing in the cold for about four hours and I wanted to get somewhere warm!

Frank: We got home pretty quickly. I wasn't feeling very well before I went out that day, so I went home to lie on the sofa and watch the parade.

James: The Mall had been fairly empty behind us when we got there, but now the mass of humanity was just unbelievable! My wife and I got separated from our group and made our way back to a friend's house for hot food and warmth. Because of all the road closures, it took us nearly two hours to get back to Alexandria.

Marie: Having stood for approximately 10 hours, we decided to travel back to Laurel, Maryland, to rest. We stopped for warm drinks and nothing else.

Dana: We finally made it back to Alexandria, cold and tired and hungry. My husband and I took the

hottest showers we could stand, and ordered sushi. I called my Dad, who said he wished he had flown in from Arizona to be there, and told him all about it. Then I ate and went to sleep. I don't know how the people who went to the balls did it. I would have fallen asleep on my feet.

Jon: On the Metro ride back, I saw an African American woman, elegantly turned out in a chinchilla coat and matching hat, berating a pair of teenagers who had skipped the swearing-in. "Why weren't you out there for Barack? He's our man!" she asked. "He's not just our man," said one of the

teens, turning toward me. "A bunch of white people voted for him. . . . You voted for him, right?" After I responded affirmatively, the other kid said, "We were going to go down there, but when we saw how many people were in the streets we decided to go do something else." The woman was incredulous: "But this was a once-in-a-lifetime thing! You'll never see anything like this again." The first kid laughed. "We see him every day. He's on the TV, like, 24 hours a day. If I need to see him, I'll just turn on CNN."

Marcel: After taking a little while to rest and warm up at a friend's, I went back out to a bar in town that I knew well to meet up with an old friend from high school who had come into town. We had a good time catching up and talked to people the next table over that also traveled in for the inauguration. It was a low-key end to the day, and exactly what I needed.

Albert: Following the benediction we left the grounds to return home to our daughter's apartment, where we were staying. We were emotionally and physically drained, not only from the day, but from the prior events, like the great concert Sunday afternoon at the Lincoln Memorial and the miles of walking. We needed the time to reflect on all the events and think about the resolution of all of the historical trends and threads.

Jon: A friend invited me to join his family in a corporate hospitality suite at the JW Marriott overlooking Pennsylvania Avenue. After hours of standing on the frozen Mall, it felt almost obscenely luxurious to be able to watch the parade pass by while sitting on a comfy sofa in front of a picture window.

Dana: I'm thrilled that I went, and I'll never, ever forget what it felt like to be there. That I could feel this way even though we walked about five miles in the cold, stood outside for hours, and fought through ridiculous crowds amazes me.

Jon: Through Craigslist, I got a ticket for the Western Ball. On Sunday evening I got an email from a friend who had moved out of the D.C. area, and I convinced her to be my (wife-approved) date for the event, which was held in a massive ballroom at the Washington Convention Center.

Marc Anthony took the stage at about 9:30 p.m., and Jennifer Lopez came out from the wings to duet with her husband on the last number. The couple left the stage just moments before the Bidens emerged for a quick speech and an even quicker spin around the stage, both of which were received rapturously. The Obamas arrived about an hour later. The first lady's casual elegance and the president's undeniable charm made an indelible impression and left tongues wagging all over the ballroom.

Daniel: We were able to go to the Homestate Ball, which was jointly hosted by Illinois and Hawaii, the two states Obama has called home. It was at the Washington Convention Center. Unfortunately, we were running late and missed the appearance by the new first family by 10 minutes.

Jon: I had decided to stay up all night, as I had to catch a 6:00 a.m. flight home anyway. My friend had graciously agreed to push through with me. We proceeded to an all-night establishment near Dupont Circle that quickly filled up with post-ball revelers. We said our farewells at 3:00 a.m., with our hearts full and our memories of the day cemented—and with her camera still in my pants pocket.

Albert: For most events in history there is more the sense of being on a great arc rather than experiencing an identifiable turning point. But on January 20th, 2009, that was achieved. To be an eyewitness to such an event was exhilarating. In our lifetime it would be like being at the tearing down of the Berlin Wall or the announcement of V-J Day in August of 1945, which I fondly remember. Of all the similar times, and there are not that many I recall over almost 70 years, the taking of the oath of office by Barack Obama has to rank as the most memorable for me.

James: Every day since the election I've seen people wearing Obama hats and t-shirts with the same sense of pride as if it were their favorite bands or sports teams. I cannot imagine any other politician being able to inspire in the same way. It seems to be a throwback to a time when people trusted their political leaders and held them in high esteem. I hope that they're not all just being naïve and that Obama's election may really end an era of extreme cynicism towards politics, and that he lives up to their trust in him.

Louise: It was the most memorable four days of my life, because I witnessed *change* coming to America.

Josh Shapiro, state representative, Pennsylvania: It took Americans from all walks of life to rally around this messenger, to make Barack Obama's ascendency to the office of president a reality. The story is about the country coming together behind an extraordinary man, who is also African American, and his message of hope. This was most apparent at the inauguration, where people from all walks of life gathered in the cold to bear witness to history. The diverse crowd was pleasant, despite the physical obstacles to being there. We all felt optimistic, despite the challenges that lie ahead for our country. I kept thinking, if we could somehow harness this positive feeling and spread it throughout our country, the world would be a dramatically better place.

The crowd disperses on the National Mall after the swearing-in ceremony.

Snapshots From Inaugural Week

The Lincoln Bible

To his millions of supporters, President Barack Obama is the man described by composer Paul Dresser in "Give Us Just Another Lincoln" (1900):

1.
With war on ev'ry side of us our nation great and grand,
To guide the Ship of State aright, will need a master hand,
The cry goes up in this great land of freedom dearly won,
Bring forth some one to bear the flag, a man to lead us on!

REFRAIN

Give us just another Lincoln, or a Thomas Jefferson,
Give to us a Grant or Jackson, whose fame lives on and on,
One who's loyal to his country, One whose work when done
Shall be beloved by all the nation, As they loved George Washington.

2.
The mother in her humble home thinks of her boy in blue,
Who fights in some far distant land, to his country ever true,
She loves the flag, also her boy, from whom she had to part,
But war broke up her little home, and also broke her heart!

When Barack Obama took the oath of office, he made yet another connection between himself and Abraham Lincoln. During the swearing-in, Obama placed his left hand on the Bible used by the 16th president in his first inauguration, in 1861.

Although in the press it was frequently referred to as the "Lincoln Bible," the book was not owned by Abraham Lincoln. Supreme Court Clerk William Thomas Carroll purchased the Bible because Lincoln's family book was still en route to Washington from Springfield, Illinois. The burgundy velvet-bound volume currently resides in the protective care of the Library of Congress.

The seal of the Supreme Court is stamped into the back of the Bible, which features the following inscription:

President-elect Barack Obama rests his hand on President Lincoln's inaugural Bible, which Michelle Obama holds as he takes the oath of office.

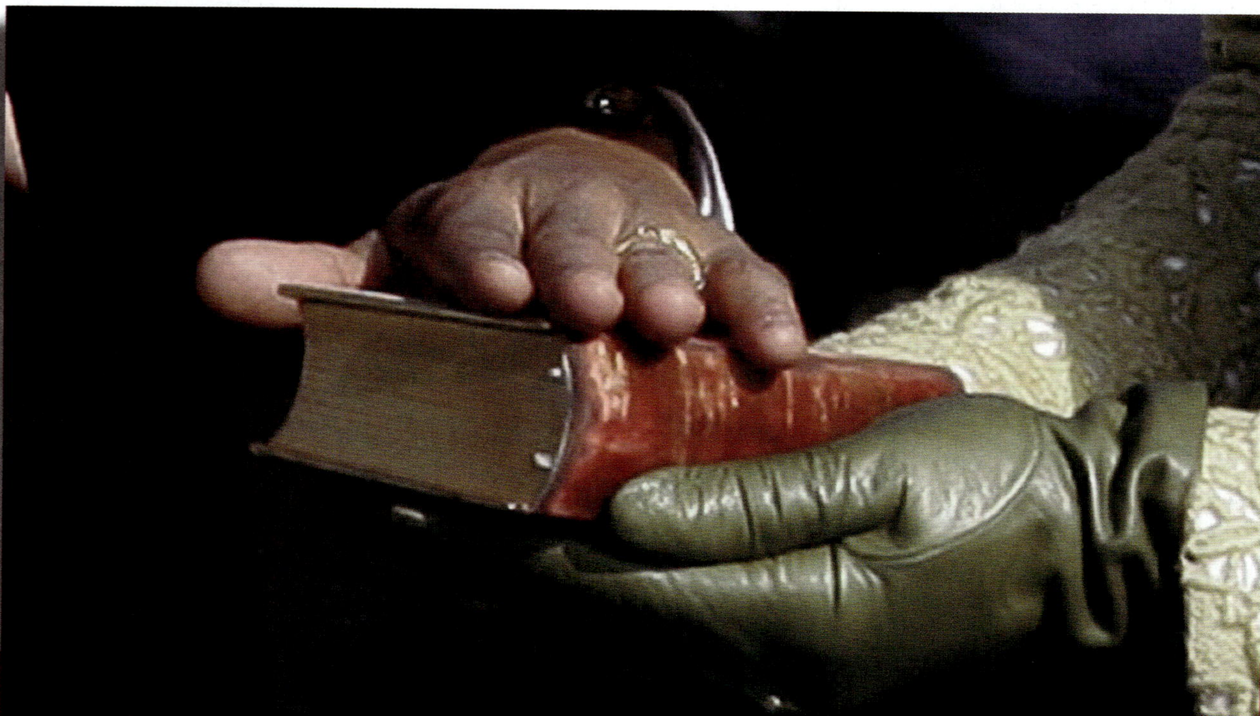

> *I, William Thomas Carroll, clerk of the said court do hereby certify that the preceding copy of the Holy Bible is that upon which the Honble. R. B. Taney, Chief Justice of the said Court, administered to His Excellency, Abraham Lincoln, the oath of office as President of the United States. . . .*

The use of that particular Bible in the Obama inauguration carries perhaps even greater symbolism from the other side of the presidential podium. The man who swore in Abraham Lincoln, Chief Justice Roger Brooke Taney, wrote the majority opinion in *Dred Scott v. Sandford* in 1857. The Dred Scott decision, as it became known, declared that slaves and their descendants were "beings of an inferior order, and altogether unfit to associate with the white race." The decision is widely considered one of the worst Supreme Court rulings in American history.

A curator displays the burgundy velvet, gilt-edged Lincoln inaugural Bible at the Library of Congress. Obama is the first president to use it since Abraham Lincoln at his swearing-in on March 4, 1861.

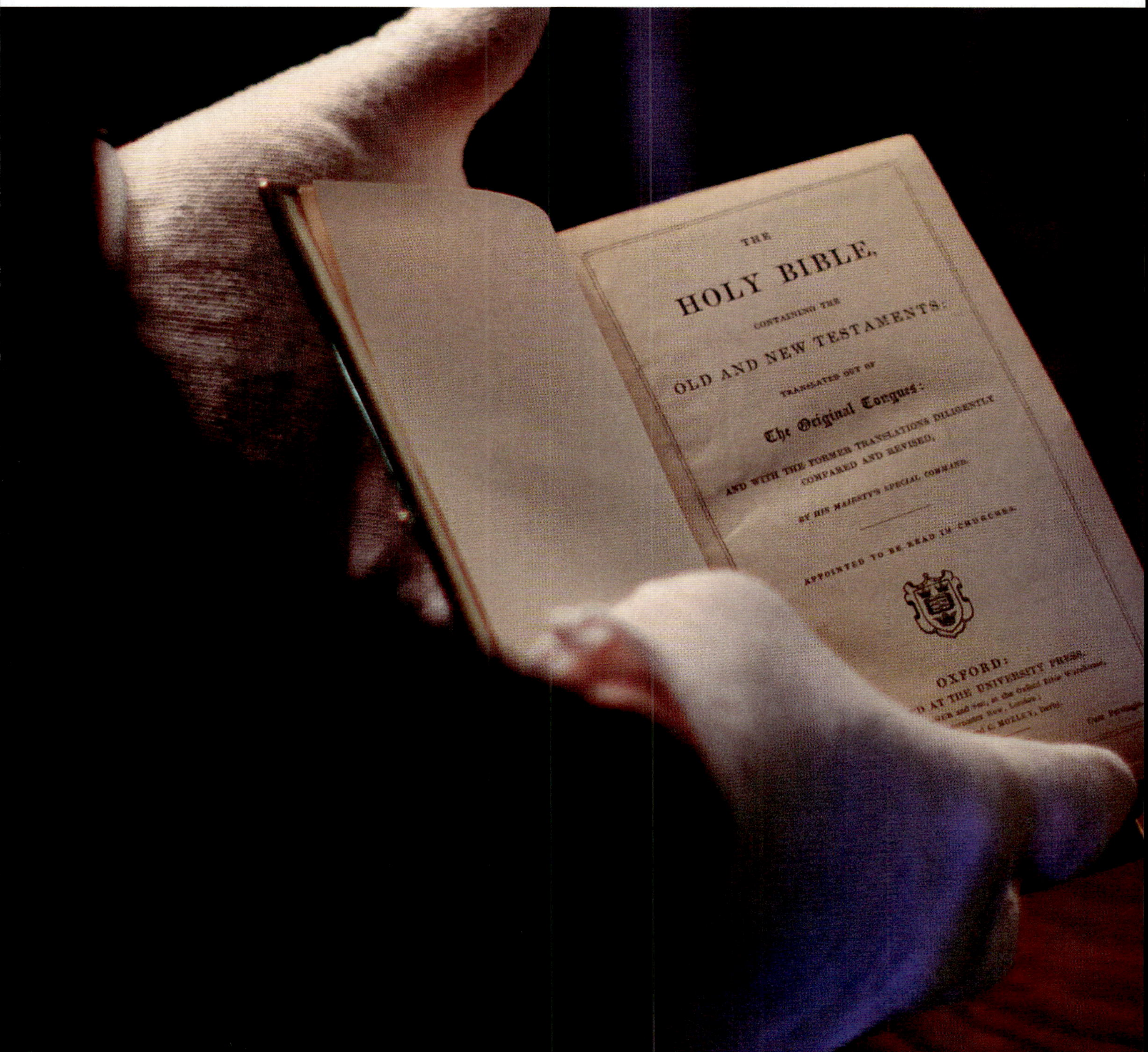

Civil Rights Leaders

In becoming the first African American president of the United States, Barack Obama fulfilled the dream that many Americans, of all backgrounds, fought for in the civil rights movement. Although his race was rarely mentioned within his own campaign, a quote was circulated that placed Obama in the lineage of those who came before him:

> *Rosa sat so Martin could march. Martin marched so Barack could run. Barack runs so our children can fly!*

Rosa Parks, the Rev. Dr. Martin Luther King Jr., and many other civil rights leaders did not live to see the historic day, but several of those who are still alive were asked to participate in the events of the inauguration.

The Rev. Dr. Joseph E. Lowery, who delivered the benediction following Obama's inaugural address, was one of the leaders of the Montgomery bus boycott following the arrest of Rosa Parks in 1955. The eventual victory in the boycott led Lowery, King, and many others to create the Southern Christian Leadership Conference in 1957. Eight years later, Lowery, who at the time was pastor of the Warren Street United Methodist Church, in Mobile, Alabama, led the marches from Selma to Montgomery to protest voter inequality.

Lowery served as president of the SCLC from 1977 until his retirement in 1997. He has received lifetime achievement awards from the National Urban League and from the NAACP, who named him the "dean of the civil rights movement." Lowery has a street named in his honor in Atlanta, Georgia.

The Rev. Dr. Otis Moss Jr. delivered the opening prayer at the National Prayer Service, at Washington's National Cathedral, on January 21, 2009. The

The Rev. Joseph E. Lowery gives the benediction at the end of the swearing-in ceremony.

service brought together 20 prominent leaders from all major religions. The tradition began with George Washington in 1791, and is considered to be the final event of the inaugural ceremonies.

In 1961, Moss became the regional director of the Cincinnati branch of the SCLC, where he worked to end job discrimination practices and organized an Operation Breadbasket program. He was an invited guest of President Bill Clinton's, witnessing the signing of the peace treaty between Israel and Jordan in 1994. Two years later he received a Leadership Award from the Cleveland chapter of the American Jewish Committee. Moss retired from Olivet Institutional Baptist Church in Cleveland in December 2008, after 33 years behind the pulpit. His son is the pastor at Trinity United Church of Christ in Chicago, which Obama attended for 20 years.

Two other major figures in the civil rights movement were given places of honor on the platform for Obama's inauguration. John Lewis was the chairman of the Student Nonviolent Coordinating Committee, which organized sit-ins, freedom rides, and voter registration drives. He spoke at the historic March on Washington and was a member of the "Big Six," the leading organizers of the movement. In 1965, he was beaten on "Bloody Sunday," the name given to the day when Alabama state troopers attacked those marching from Selma to Montgomery.

In the 1980s, Lewis moved into politics, first serving on the Atlanta City Council. Since 1986 he has represented Georgia's 5th District in the U.S.

President Obama embraces Rev. Lowery after the ceremony as Senator Dianne Feinstein and Vice President Biden look on.

House of Representatives, making him the second African American to represent Georgia since Reconstruction. In 2001 he received the Profile in Courage award from the John F. Kennedy Library Foundation.

In a career that has spanned eight decades, Dr. Dorothy Irene Height worked with every major civil rights figure of the 20th century. She was a friend and counselor of Eleanor Roosevelt's, and worked with presidents Dwight D. Eisenhower

and Lyndon B. Johnson. In 1964 she organized "Wednesdays in Mississippi," to create an open dialogue between women of different races and faiths to solve common problems.

Dr. Height is the chairwoman and president emerita of the National Council of Negro Women, the organization she ran from 1957 until 1997. She holds 36 honorary doctorate degrees, and has received the Congressional Gold Medal of Honor and the Presidential Medal of Freedom, the highest honor that can be bestowed on an American citizen.

Opposite: Dorothy Irene Height sits in front of her featured storyboard inside the Freedom's Sisters exhibition in Cincinnati. The 1,800-square-foot exhibit tells the story of 20 women who helped shape the civil rights movement.

Below: The Rev. Otis Moss gestures as he speaks during a service at Ebenezer Baptist Church in Atlanta, marking the 78th birthday of Rev. Martin Luther King Jr. in 2007.

Michelle and the Girls

Although the spotlight was focused brightly on the man of the Obama house during the inaugural festivities, there were also opportunities for the women of the family to shine.

On January 19, Michelle Obama, along with Dr. Jill Biden, co-hosted the "Kids Inaugural: We Are the Future" concert at Washington's Verizon Center. The concert, which honored military families, featured performances by Usher, Miley Cyrus, and the Jonas Brothers. Malia and Sasha Obama had front-row seats and danced throughout the show with Biden's four granddaughters.

The next day, the girls received an open letter in the *Wall Street Journal* from Jenna and Barbara Bush. The former first daughters gave Sasha and Malia tips for enjoying their time in the White House.

Opposite: U.S. service members and their families rock out during the "Kids Inaugural: We Are the Future" concert at the Verizon Center in downtown Washington.

Below: Michelle Obama and the girls rock along with the rest during the "Kids Inaugural" concert.

Past Presidents

The presidential inauguration of Barack Obama was an occasion to celebrate the dawn of a new day. But it was also an opportunity to recognize the achievements of the other living men who have worked in the Oval Office. Present on the steps of the Capitol that day were five past, present, and future presidents: Jimmy Carter, George H.W. Bush, Bill Clinton, George W. Bush, and Barack Obama.

Earlier in the month, on January 8, President-elect Obama had met with the four men at the White House. It was Obama's idea to bring everyone together for lunch. The White House did not comment on what was said during the meal, but Obama later revealed that he asked presidents Carter and Clinton for advice on raising children in the White House.

Former President Jimmy Carter and wife Rosalynn.

Former President Bill Clinton and wife, the soon-to-be secretary of state Hillary Clinton.

The most exclusive club in the world: men who have served as president of the United States. Left to right: George H.W. Bush, Barack Obama, George W. Bush, Bill Clinton, and Jimmy Carter.

The World Celebrates

Those who did not make the journey into Washington, D.C., for the weekend were still able to celebrate Barack Obama's inauguration. Across the country, and throughout the world, people came together united by their desire to witness the historic moment.

In the Windy City, restaurants, barber shops, and churches throughout Obama's South Side neighborhood of Hyde Park were filled to capacity as Chicagoans watched their neighbor become the president of the United States. Downtown, public viewings of the inauguration were set up in Daley Plaza and Pioneer Court; they attracted thousands of spectators despite a snowstorm.

In New York City, video screens were set up all around Times Square, and people packed the

Celebrating the inaugural in Kogelo, a village of dirt roads, tin-roofed huts, and maize fields in western Kenya that was home to Barack Obama Sr.

legendary intersection as if they were waiting for the ball to drop on New Year's Eve. On Wall Street, the New York Stock Exchange rang the opening bell from the steps of Federal Hall, the site of George Washington's inauguration in 1789. The Bible used by Washington that day was also on display.

As the scene of the first victory in Obama's improbable path to the White House, Iowa played an important role in the election. The Fort Des Moines Museum, located on the site of the first officer's training academy for African Americans, held a public viewing of the ceremony.

Despite a time differential that saw proceedings begin at 5:00 a.m., Obama's birth state of Hawaii was awake to celebrate. At Honolulu's Punahou Circle Apartments, where Madelyn Dunham, Obama's grandmother, lived, a potluck breakfast was held in the lobby as residents watched. Obama's sister, Maya Soetoro-Ng, contributed to the event two platters that belonged to her grandmother, while she attended the inauguration. That night at the Blaisdell Arena, singer Gloria Estefan honored the 50th state's favorite son from the stage.

In Jakarta, Indonesia, the U.S. ambassador to Indonesia, along with Obama's former classmates, attended a party at the SDN Menteng 01 school,

Front-page inaugural coverage in a display of French newspapers and the *International Herald Tribune*.

where young Obama spent three years. Children performed traditional dances and sang songs in honor of their school's most famous former student.

The inauguration ended a four-day celebration in Obama's father's hometown of Kogelo, Kenya. Money was raised to bring a generator and big-screen television to the primary school named after the new president. People chanted "Our son, our pride," and cheered when Obama referred to "the small village where my father was born" in his inaugural address.

In Paris, kiosks throughout the city displayed magazines and newspapers with the stylish first couple on the cover. Mayor Bertrand Delanoë invited more than 800 Americans to the Hôtel de Ville, Paris's city hall, to watch the inauguration. Shortly before Joe Biden was sworn in as vice president, Delanoë addressed the attendees, declaring that "the heart of Paris beats with the hearts of Americans."

At Camp Liberty, Iraq, troops watched the inauguration of their new commander-in-chief on televisions in mess halls, or over the Internet. When the ceremony was over, the base chaplain said a prayer and the soldiers returned to duty.

Children from the school Obama once attended in Jakarta, Indonesia, perform during the inauguration.

Moving In, Moving On

Shortly after the election in November, the Obama family met with the chief usher of the White House to arrange plans for life in their new residence. Everything from artwork to furniture to favorite foods was discussed to make the new first family as comfortable as possible on their first day in the White House. All decor used by previous administrations are stored in a warehouse in Maryland so that they can be requested by future residents.

When President George Bush and Barack Obama left together for the Capitol on inauguration day, the White House staff, comprised of 93 people, went into high gear. As the Obamas' belongings were transferred from Blair House and unpacked, the Bushes' items were moved out, placed on military cargo planes, and shipped to the Bush ranch in Crawford, Texas.

In keeping with tradition, President Bush left a note for his successor on his desk, wishing him the best in his position. Famously, President Ronald Reagan's message to Bush's father consisted solely of, "Don't let the turkeys get you down!"

The whole process, including any painting or carpentry work required by the Obamas, had to be completed by the time they entered the White House following the inaugural parade, approximately six hours later.

Former President George W. Bush and Laura Bush wave as they board a Marine helicopter at the Capitol in Washington after the swearing-in of Barack Obama as the 44th president of the United States.

After the ceremony, George and Laura Bush were flown via Marine One, the presidential helicopter, from the East Portico of the Capitol to Andrews Air Force Base. They then flew by Air Force One to George's hometown of Midland, Texas, where there was a rally in his honor.

As Obama was being sworn in, the White House's official Web site, whitehouse.gov, underwent a

The Obamas and Bidens bid the Bushes farewell.

complete makeover to reflect the new administration. Throughout the election season, Obama's campaign had received praise for understanding the power of the Internet in getting out the message, raising funds, and mobilizing voters.

The redesigned White House Web site is an extension of that vision, with a blog to communicate with the public, pages regarding Obama's agenda on every issue, and educational sections for children. (The Obama White House also plans to put videos of weekly addresses, briefings, and special events on YouTube.) To improve transparency in government, the new site contains a virtual "Briefing Room," featuring all executive orders, proclamations, public statements, and press releases.

In keeping with his campaign promise to increase public participation in government, all non-emergency legislation will be published on the Web site for five days before the president signs it. During this time, the public will be able to review and leave comments about the bill.

A folder for President Barack Obama, left by former president George W. Bush on the Resolute desk in the Oval Office of the White House.

Opposite: On a tour of the State Floor of the White House, President Barack Obama looks at a portrait of John F. Kennedy by Aaron Shikler.

The Inaugural Parade

Following the inaugural luncheon was the parade from the U.S. Capitol up Pennsylvania Avenue to the White House. The tradition of the inaugural parade began, like so many in American history, with George Washington in New York City in 1789. It wasn't until Thomas Jefferson's second inauguration in 1805 that the current parade route was first used.

After a ceremonial review of the military, the Obamas entered the new presidential limousine for

their first ride to their new home. Continuing the pattern begun by Jimmy and Rosalynn Carter in 1977, the new first couple exited their limousine to wave to the crowd. They left the car twice: at the halfway point by the National Archives building, and again as they neared the White House. The Bidens, who were behind the Obamas, followed suit.

After the Obamas and Bidens were on the reviewing stand, the second part of the parade began. Marching bands, drill teams, and drum-and-bugle

A U.S. military honor guard marches during the inaugural parade for President Barack Obama on Tuesday, January 20, 2009, in Washington.

corps from all 50 states and the District of Columbia walked the 1.5-mile route as thousands watched along Pennsylvania Avenue.

Another participant in the parade was Hollywood legend Mickey Rooney, who rode on the "Spirit of the Lincoln Way" fire truck, which was sponsored by the Lincoln Highway National Museum Archives in Galion, Ohio. The 88-year-old Rooney first participated in an inaugural parade in 1933.

The high schools of the president and first lady were represented in the parade. Chicago's Whitney Young Magnet High School, Michelle Obama's alma mater, sent their Naval Junior ROTC to perform their military drill routines in front of their most famous alum. The Punahou Academy in Honolulu, where Barack Obama spent eight years, sent their Junior ROTC and their marching band. As they passed the reviewing stand, Obama flashed the *shaka,* a traditional Hawaiian hand gesture that represents the essence of the laid-back style of the island.

The presidential limousine, which has the code name "Stagecoach," is a Cadillac with hand-stitched leather seats, and the presidential seal embroidered

into the center of the rear seat. It is believed to contain five inches of armor plating, bulletproof windows, run-flat tires, and a sealed interior to protect the president in case of chemical attack. For security purposes, neither the Secret Service nor General Motors have disclosed much information on the car. An identical model also travels with the president to act as a decoy.

All government vehicles used in the parade bore a special license plate for the occasion. The president's limousine license plate read "USA 1."

Opposite: President Barack Obama and first lady Michelle Obama walk the inaugural parade route.

The president shows a *shaka,* a traditional Hawaiian hand gesture, during the inaugural parade.

At the start of the inaugural parade, the president, the First Lady, Vice President Biden, and Mrs. Biden review the troops.

Inaugural Balls

Although parties were thrown across Washington, D.C., to celebrate the inauguration of President Barack Obama, only 10 were "official inaugural balls." Each ball featured appearances by the Obamas and the Bidens.

Their initial stop was the first-ever Neighborhood Ball. Tickets for the event were either free or available at an affordable price, and many were set aside for Washington residents. The ball was televised on ABC and featured performances by Mariah Carey, Stevie Wonder, Faith Hill, Sting, and Shakira. The Obamas danced for the crowd as Beyoncé Knowles sang the Etta James classic, "At Last."

The Youth Inaugural Ball was held for people between the ages of 18 and 35 to recognize the role that young people can play in their communities. The ball saw Kanyé West, Kid Rock, and Fall Out Boy rock the house, and was shown on MTV. Tickets were $75.

The armed forces were honored at the Commander-in-Chief 's Inaugural Ball. Tickets were free for guests, which included wounded soldiers and military families. American troops stationed around the world could watch the ball via the Pentagon Channel.

The two states each that Obama and Biden have lived in held their own events. The Obama Home States Ball was for the people of Hawaii and Illinois, and the Biden Home States Ball was for residents of Pennsylvania and Delaware. Others who came from out of town could attend a ball for their home state. Five regions of the country—the East, Mid-Atlantic, South, Midwest, and West—were represented. Tickets for the regional balls were $150.

President Obama and Michelle dance at the inaugural ball.

Michelle Obama, who as first lady is now seen as a symbol of fashion around the world, wore a floor-length, one-shoulder ivory chiffon gown by New York designer Jason Wu. Barack Obama's tuxedo, which he said was the first one he has bought in 15 years, was made by Chicago-based Hart Schaffner Marx. His white satin bow tie was made by J. Crew.

Five of the balls were held in the same building, the Washington Convention Center. The others took place at the National Building Museum, the D.C. Armory, the Washington Hilton, and Union Station.

While the president and first lady clearly enjoyed themselves during the celebrations, reality lingered around the festive edges. At the Commander-in-Chief Ball, Barack Obama addressed the nation's troops. "Please know that you are in our thoughts

President Barack Obama and First Lady Michelle Obama arrive at the Commander-in-Chief's Inaugural Ball.

and prayers today, every day, forever," he said. "Tonight we celebrate. Tomorrow, the work begins. Together, I am confident we will write the next great chapter in America's story."

A golf cart is a most informal means of transportation for the First Couple behind the scenes of the inaugural ball.

Wrapped in the president's tuxedo jacket for warmth, the First Lady shares a tender moment with her husband.

Down to Business

Many challenges faced the new president right from the start. In addition to trying to pass a major economic-stimulus bill, Obama scored two legislative victories in his first two weeks in office. The Lilly Ledbetter Fair Pay Restoration Act, which he had sponsored while a senator, extended the period in which equal-pay discrimination lawsuits can be filed. Another law reauthorized and expanded funding for the State Children's Health Insurance Program, which provides states with matching funds to give health insurance to working-class families.

Among Obama's first executive orders were those involving government ethics commitments; detention policy options; and the closing of the Guantanamo Bay (Cuba) prison, which held men from the Iraqi War, some with no specific charges preferred against them. His first memoranda included a salary freeze for senior members of the White House staff, as a signal to the nation "in a period of severe economic stress"; an updating and affirmation of the Freedom of Information Act; and a call for "transparent and open government."

On February 12, Obama delivered what would be an iconic speech at the 102nd annual dinner of the Abraham Lincoln Association in Springfield, Illinois. In the symbolic setting, Obama laid out—in typically eloquent and meaningful language—his vision of the relationship between our government and the people it serves.

On October 9 that year, Obama was awarded the 2009 Nobel Peace Prize for "his extraordinary efforts to strengthen international diplomacy and cooperation between peoples." The award drew equal parts applause and criticism. According to the rules, all nominations must be received by January 31 of the award year, meaning he'd been nominated after less than three weeks (at most) in office. Some pundits speculated that the award was more a rebuke to the Bush administration than a genuine measure of Obama's role in the world. The president's own camp may have been a bit uncomfortable with the situation, and did not seek to ballyhoo the prize in subsequent years.

President Barack Obama puts his hand to his heart during the Pledge of Allegiance at the 102nd Abraham Lincoln Association banquet in Springfield, Illinois, on February 12, 2009.

What Needs to be Done

by Barack Obama

Speech delivered at the 102nd annual dinner of the Abraham Lincoln Association in Springfield, Illinois, on February 12, 2009

It is wonderful to be back in Springfield, the city where I got my start in elected office, where I served for nearly a decade, and where I launched my candidacy for President two years ago, this week—on the steps of the Old State Capitol where Abraham Lincoln served and prepared for the presidency.

It was here, nearly one hundred and fifty years ago, that the man whose life we are celebrating today bid farewell to this city he had come to call his own. On a platform at a train station not far from where we're gathered, Lincoln turned to the crowd that had come to see him off, and said, "To this place, and the kindness of these people, I owe everything." Being here tonight, surrounded by all of you, I share his sentiments.

But looking out at this room, full of so many who did so much for me, I'm also reminded of what Lincoln once said to a favor-seeker who claimed it was his efforts that made the difference in the election. Lincoln asked him, "So you think you made me President?" "Yes," the man replied, "under Providence, I think I did." "Well," said Lincoln, "it's a pretty mess you've got me into. But I forgive you."

The spirit of Abraham Lincoln lives on through institutions like the Abraham Lincoln Association and memorials like the famous seated Lincoln sculpture by Daniel Chester French, shown here.

It is a humbling task, marking the bicentennial of our 16th President's birth—humbling for me in particular, I think, for the presidency of this singular figure in so many ways made my own story possible.

Here in Springfield, it is easier, perhaps, to reflect on Lincoln the man rather than the marble giant, before Gettysburg and Antietam, Fredericksburg and Bull Run, before emancipation was proclaimed and the captives were set free. In 1854, Lincoln was simply a Springfield lawyer, who'd served just a single term in Congress. Possibly in his law office, his feet on a cluttered desk, his sons playing around him, his clothes a bit too small to fit his uncommon frame, he put some thoughts on paper for what purpose we do not know:

"The legitimate object of government," he wrote, "is to do for the people what needs to be done, but which they can not, by individual effort, do at all, or do so well, by themselves."

To do for the people what needs to be done but which they cannot do on their own. It is a simple statement. But it answers a central question of Abraham Lincoln's life. Why did he land on the side of union? What was it that made him so unrelenting in pursuit of victory that he was willing to test the Constitution he ultimately preserved? What was it that led this man to give his last full measure of devotion so that our nation might endure?

These are not easy questions to answer, and I cannot know if I am right. But I suspect that his devotion to union came not from a belief that government always had the answer. It came not from a failure to understand our individual rights and responsibilities. This rugged rail-splitter, born in a log cabin of pioneer stock; who cleared a path through the woods as a boy; who lost a mother and a sister to the rigors of frontier life; who taught himself all he knew—this man, our first Republican President, knew, better than anyone, what it meant to pull yourself up by your bootstraps. He understood that strain of personal liberty and self-reliance at the heart of the American experience.

The legacy of Abraham Lincoln was felt during the opening inaugural ceremonies, when president-elect Barack Obama addressed the crowd from the Lincoln Memorial.

But he also understood something else. He recognized that while each of us must do our part, work as hard as we can, and be as responsible as we can—in the end, there are certain things we cannot do on our own. There are certain things we can only do together. There are certain things only a union can do.

Only a union could harness the courage of our pioneers to settle the American west, which is why he passed a Homestead Act giving a tract of land to anyone seeking a stake in our growing economy.

Only a union could foster the ingenuity of our farmers, which is why he set up land-grant colleges that taught them how to make the most of their land while giving their children an education that let them dream the American dream.

Only a union could speed our expansion and connect our coasts with a transcontinental railroad, and so, even in the midst of civil war, he built one. He fueled new enterprises with a national currency, spurred innovation, and ignited America's imagination with a national academy of sciences, believing we must, as he put it, add "the fuel of interest to the fire of genius in the discovery...of new and useful things." And on this day, that is also the bicentennial of Charles Darwin's birth, let us renew that commitment to science and innovation once more

Only a union could serve the hopes of every citizen—to knock down the barriers to opportunity and give each and every person the chance to pursue the American dream. Lincoln understood what Washington understood when he led farmers, craftsmen, and shopkeepers to rise up against an empire. What Roosevelt understood when he lifted us from Depression, built an arsenal of democracy, and created the largest middle-class in history with the GI Bill. It's what Kennedy understood when he sent us to the moon.

All these presidents recognized that America is—and always has been—more than a band of thirteen colonies, more than a bunch of Yankees and Confederates, more than a collection of Red States and Blue States. We are the United States of America and there isn't any dream beyond our reach, any obstacle

An aerial view of the imposing Lincoln Memorial in Washington, D.C., one of the most famous monuments to Abraham Lincoln.

that can stand in our way, when we recognize that our individual liberty is served, not negated, by a recognition of the common good.

That is the spirit we are called to show once more. The challenges we face are very different now. Two wars, and an economic crisis unlike any we have seen in our lifetime. Jobs have been lost. Pensions are gone. Families' dreams have been endangered. Health care costs are exploding. Schools are falling short. And we have an energy crisis that is hampering our economy, threatening our planet, and enriching our adversaries.

And yet, while our challenges may be new, they did not come about overnight. Ultimately, they result from a failure to meet the test that Lincoln set. To be sure, there have been times in our history when our government has misjudged what we can do by individual effort alone, and what we can only do together; when it has done things that people can—or should—do for themselves. Our welfare system, for example, too often dampened individual initiative, discouraging people from taking responsibility for their own upward mobility. With respect to education, we have all too frequently lost sight of the role of parents, rather than government, in cultivating a thirst for knowledge and instilling those qualities of a good character—hard work, discipline, and integrity—that are so important to educational achievement and professional success.

But in recent years, we've seen the pendulum swing too far in the opposite direction. It's a philosophy that says every problem can be solved if only government would step out of the way; that if government were just dismantled, divvied up into tax breaks, and handed out to the wealthiest among us, it would somehow benefit us all. Such knee-jerk disdain for government—this constant rejection of any common endeavor—cannot rebuild our levees or our roads or our bridges. It cannot refurbish our schools or modernize our health care system; lead to the next medical discovery or yield the research and technology that will spark a clean energy economy.

President Obama greets surprised tourists when he makes an unannounced visit to the Lincoln Memorial in April 2011.

Only a nation can do these things. Only by coming together, all of us, and expressing that sense of shared sacrifice and responsibility—for ourselves and one another—can we do the work that must be done in this country. That is the very definition of being American.

It is only by rebuilding our economy and fostering the conditions of growth that willing workers can find a job, companies can find capital, and the entrepreneurial spirit that is the key to our competitiveness can flourish. It is only by unleashing the potential of alternative fuels that we will lower our energy bills and raise our industries' sights, make our nation safer and our planet cleaner. It is only by remaking our schools for the 21st century that our children will get those good jobs so they can make of their lives what they will. It is only by coming together to do what people need done that we will, in Lincoln's words, "lift artificial weights from all shoulders [and give] all an unfettered start, and a fair chance, in the race of life."

That is what is required of us—now and in the years ahead. We will be remembered for what we choose to make of this moment. And when posterity looks back on our time, as we are looking back on Lincoln's, I do not want it said that we saw an economic crisis, but did not stem it. That we saw our schools decline and our bridges crumble, but did not rebuild them. That the world changed in the 21st century, but America did not lead it. That we were consumed with small things when we were called to do great things. Instead, let them say that this generation—our generation—of Americans rose to the moment and gave America a new birth of freedom and opportunity in our time.

These are trying days and they will grow tougher in the months to come. There will be moments when our doubts rise and our hopes recede. But let's always remember that we, as a people, have been here before. There were times when our revolution itself seemed altogether improbable, when the union was all but lost, and fascism seemed set to prevail. And yet, what earlier generations discovered—what we must rediscover right now—is that it is precisely when we are in the deepest valley, precisely when the climb is steepest, that Americans relearn how to take the mountaintop. Together. As one nation. As one people. That is how we will beat back our present dangers. That is how we will surpass what trials may come. And that is how we will do what Lincoln called on us to do, and "nobly save . . . the last best hope of earth."

Thank you, God Bless you, and may God Bless America.

This dramatic view of Daniel Chester French's statue captures the imposing presence of our 16th president.

A President, a Father, a Man

Barack Obama and his family, like the families of many presidents before them, make their personal home in a building that is a locus of power not only in the United States but in the world. They eat, sleep, brush their teeth, share hugs, argue, and do homework where some of the most powerful individuals make many of the most important decisions in the world. The imposing walls of the White House are an emblem of the strength of the United States of America—and behind those same imposing walls, surrounded by the Secret Service, lives an intelligent, athletic, middle-aged man with a wife, two daughters, a mother-in-law, and a dog named Bo.

President Obama reads briefing material in his cabin at Camp David in October 2012.

President Obama plays basketball with members of Congress and cabinet secretaries in fall 2009.

The president in another basketball game, this time with White House staffers while on vacation on Martha's Vineyard in summer 2009.

A moment of relaxation during a briefing in the Oval Office for a phone call to Prime Minister Taro Aso of Japan.

Family dog Bo receives a presidential pat.

The president and his then personal aide, Reggie Love, fill in as coaches for one of Sasha Obama's basketball games.

The president and guests watch the 2009 Super Bowl in the White House family theater.

President Obama warms up before he throws out the ceremonial first pitch on the opening day of baseball season at Nationals Park in Washington, D.C., on April 5, 2010.

On a presidential visit to Panama City Beach, Florida, Barack Obama and daughter Sasha go for a swim.

The president and First Lady get caught on the "kiss cam" while attending the U.S. Men's Olympic basketball team's game against Brazil at the Verizon Center in Washington, D.C., in July 2012.

During Sasha's birthday weekend celebration at Camp David, she and her dad have a water gun fight.

Ice cream is called for during a visit by the first couple and Sasha to Panama City Beach, Florida.

The president and First Lady enjoy watching the fireworks during the White House Independence Day celebration in 2012.

The First Term: A Retrospective

From day one, the economy continued to present problems. On February 17, 2009, Obama signed the American Recovery and Reinvestment Act, with a $787 billion stimulus package to revive commerce and unemployment. A large portion of this ended up going to Wall Street firms and big banks, and very little to citizens and small businesses. It was hoped that banks would lend money more freely to stimulating hiring, but the results were mixed. This episode would soon prove troublesome, providing ammunition for conservative opponents and disappointed liberals alike. Obama's supporters believed firmly that the stimulus bill had headed off a second Great Depression; detractors held that the money had simply appeared down a black hole, accomplishing nothing.

Conditions worsened. By the end of 2009 unemployment had reached a nationwide average of 10%. Although the mess was something Obama had inherited from his predecessor, by the time of the midterm elections in 2010, some voters felt his administration hadn't helped anyone except big business. When the ballots were counted, many Democrats had failed in their bids for election or reelection. The next House of Representatives, with a Republican majority, was at a stalemate with the Senate (which had a slight Democratic majority)—and utterly at odds with the White House. The result was a bitter stalemate that neither the Democrats nor the Republicans seemed willing to resolve.

Considering the intense challenges that marked his entire first term, Obama's main legislative accomplishments were surprisingly strong. The most dramatic were the repeal of the "Don't Ask, Don't Tell" policy regarding gays in the military, and the sweeping overhaul of the healthcare system that became known as "Obamacare." He also increased funding on stem-cell research, and when associate justice David Souter retired from the U.S. Supreme Court to return to his New Hampshire home, Obama appointed Sonia Sotomayor in his place. When associate justice John Paul Stevens retired, Obama appointed Elena Kagan. For the first time, three women were justices in the Supreme Court.

In foreign policy, he ended the war in Iraq, began the process for withdrawal from Afghanistan, and restored broken relationships with several allies, demonstrating that the praise of the Nobel committee, while perhaps premature, was nonetheless accurate. But the event for which he may be best remembered took place on May 1, 2011: al-Qaeda leader and 9/11 mastermind Osama bin Laden was killed by Navy SEALs at his compound in Pakistan, under Obama's orders. The president was quick to point out that the work of the SEALs was to their credit, not his. But it was Obama's ongoing decision that the hunt for bin Laden was worth the resources and not simply a lost cause; Obama's responsibility to guide the delicate relationship with Pakistan; and Obama's burden to take the heat of that nation's outrage in subsequent weeks.

Left: President Obama signs H.R. 2097, the Star-Spangled Banner Commemorative Coin Act, in the Oval Office on August 16, 2010. Opposite: President Obama speaks with Iraqi Prime Minister Nouri al-Maliki by telephone in February 2009.

Justices Sonia Sotomayor (left) and Ruth Bader Ginsburg (center) with Justice Elena Kagan in the justices' conference room prior to Justice Kagan's investiture ceremony.

U.S. Navy SEALs found this Osama Bin Laden propaganda poster located in an al Qaida classroom in the Zhawar Kili area.

D.C. resident Angela Botlicella and other Obamacare supporters celebrate the Supreme Court ruling on the Affordable Health Act on June 28, 2012.

A San Francisco woman holds a sign in support of the end of "don't ask, don't tell" on September 20, 2011.

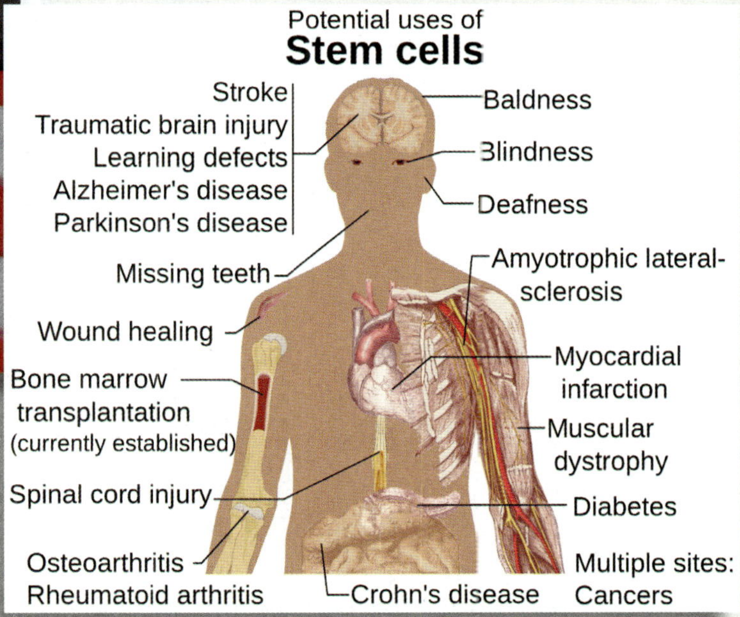

A diagram illustrates diseases and conditions for which stem cell treatment could potentially be beneficial.

A Gallery of Economic Policy Achievements

- The American Recovery and Reinvestment Act, the $787 billion stimulus signed on February 17, 2009, prevented a second Great Depression. By early 2010, the unemployment rate began to go down, and job growth continued every month through the rest of Obama's first term.
- The Dodd-Frank Wall Street Reform and Consumer Protection Act, which was passed in 2010, regulated the financial industry to protect consumers from the numerous practices that resulted in the economic collapse in 2008, ended taxpayer-funded bailouts of the banks, and improved transparency throughout the industry.
- President Obama loaned $62 billion to General Motors and Chrysler to prevent the struggling auto companies from going into bankruptcy. Since restructuring, the companies have become profitable again and created more than 100,000 jobs. Chrysler paid off its loans six years ahead of schedule.
- The Credit Card Accountability, Responsibility, and Disclosure Act of 2009 established fair and transparent practices for credit card companies, which included the ending of arbitrary interest rate increases, excessive fees, and double-cycle billing.
- During Obama's presidency the Dow Jones industrial average increased nearly 68%. This marks the fifth-highest percentage increase for a president's first term since 1900.

President Obama shakes hands with House Speaker Nancy Pelosi after signing the Dodd-Frank Wall Street Reform and Consumer Protection Act on July 21, 2010.

The president salutes while disembarking from Air Force One as he arrives in Youngstown, Ohio, to attend a roundtable event with auto workers at the General Motors Lordstown Assembly Plant on September 15, 2009.

During a tour of the General Motors Auto Plant in Hamtramck, Michigan, on July 30, 2010, Teri Quigley briefs the president on GM's Chevy Volt.

Remarks by the President at the Signing of the American Recovery and Reinvestment Act

Transcript of comments during signing at the Denver Museum of Nature and Science, Denver, Colorado, February 17, 2009

THE VICE PRESIDENT: You know, you don't need to be an economist to know that jobs are the engine of our economy. And without jobs, people can't earn. And when people can't earn, they can't spend. And if they don't spend, it means more jobs get lost. It's a vicious cycle. And that's the vicious cycle we're in today. And it's one of the reasons that this bill is so desperately needed. We have to reverse that cycle.

But everyone knows that jobs are more than just about a job. They're about dignity. They're about respect. They're about being able to get up in the morning, look your child in the eye and say, "Everything is going to be okay; everything is going to be okay."

Last year—last year our economy lost 3 million jobs; 600,000 more just this last month. There are an awful lot of mothers and father who had to walk up those stairs to the bedroom of their children and tell them that, "I'm out of work, honey. We may not be able to stay here. You may not be able to stay in this school. It's a tough, tough conversation. And many—too many times it's already occurred in this country. We're here today—we're here today to start to turn that around. (Applause.)

But folks, we're not just going to help the economy recover. We're going to start building the economy for the future. I'm particularly pleased that this bill includes investments in areas I've worked my whole political career. Thanks to the Recovery Act, thousands of additional police officers will go on the streets of America, and hundreds and hundreds of fire stations will be built, making the people of Denver and every other city in America safer.

Thanks to this act, we're going to see an unprecedented investment in improving America's rail system coast to coast. (Applause.) In Denver—right here in Denver, your light rail will be affected all the way to the Northeast Corridor where I come from. We should have the best transportation system in the world. (Applause.) And we don't.

But ladies and gentleman, it's not only that this will help create jobs in the rail sector—it's also good for the environment. So there's a double bang for the buck in a number of the investments we're making in this legislation.

Starting today, our administration will be working day and night to provide more aid for the unemployed, create immediate jobs, building our roads and our bridges, make long-term investments in a smarter energy grid, and so much more. And as we turn the economy around, we've got to make sure of one more thing. Last time an economic recovery occurred after a deep recession, the middle class got left behind—the middle class got left behind. And that's why the president has set up a White House Council on the Task Force on the Middle Class, which he's asking me to chair.

So as we go through this process, we're also going to make sure that America is—as we recover, that American middle class is not left behind. But before we start on the way, there is much more to be done in the weeks to come. I want to say something about what got us to this point. I remember having the meetings of the transition team with President-Elect Obama and Vice President–Elect Biden in Chicago, and meeting in those offices knowing we were about to inherit a very, very bad economic situation.

And we started to put together the president's leadership, the blueprint for our recovery. Faced with a swirl of options and uncertainties, then-President-Elect Obama was as clear and as firm then as he is today about what is needed. He said, and I quote: "We have to be bold . . . we have to act fast . . . and we have to think of the future that we wish to build." Well, I believe that's what the president delivered. He never lost sight of those goals that he set back in November and December of last year.

Opposite: As Vice President Joe Biden looks on, President Obama signs the American Recovery and Reinvestment Act.

Over the weeks that followed, I watched him reach out, asking senator and congressmen from both parties to put the good of the nation above the disagreement over one particular of this significant package.

The president showed a willingness to compromise on specifics, but he never compromised on the principles he set out in that room in Chicago back in November. And so, folks, he showed a willingness to work with others to get things done, but he never bent in his determination to put us on a road to recovery and reinvestment.

So today, less than a month—think of this, less than a month into his presidency, the president is about to sign into law what is I believe a landmark achievement. Because of what he did, America can take a first, very strong step leading us out of this very difficult road to recovery we find ourselves on.

So on behalf of our country and its people, Mr. President, let me presume to say, thank you. We owe you a great deal. (Applause.) . . .

THE PRESIDENT: Thank you, everybody. Please have a seat. You guys can sit down, too. (Laughter.) . . .

It is great to be back in Denver. (Applause.) I was here last summer—we had a good time—(laughter)—to accept the nomination of my party and to make a promise to people of all parties that I would do all that I could to give every American the chance to make of their lives what they will; to see their children climb higher than they did. And I'm back today to say that we have begun the difficult work of keeping that promise. We have begun the essential work of keeping the American Dream alive in our time. And that's why we're here today. (Applause.)

Now, I don't want to pretend that today marks the end of our economic problems. Nor does it constitute all of what we're going to have to do to turn our economy around. But today does mark the beginning of the end—the beginning of what we need to do to create jobs for Americans scrambling in the wake of layoffs; the beginning of what we need to do to provide relief for families worried they won't be able to pay next month's bills; the beginning of the first steps to set our economy on a firmer foundation, paving the way to long-term growth and prosperity.

The American Recovery and Reinvestment Act that I will sign today—a plan that meets the principles I laid out in January—is the most sweeping economic recovery package in our history. It's the product of broad consultation and the recipient of broad support—from business leaders, unions, public interest groups, from the Chamber of Commerce and the National Association of Manufacturers, as well as the AFL-CIO. (Applause.) From Democrats and Republicans, mayors as well as governors. It's a rare thing in Washington for people with such diverse and different viewpoints to come together and support the same bill. And on behalf of our nation, I want to thank all of them for it. . . .

Now, what makes this recovery plan so important is not just that it will create or save 3.5 million jobs over the next two years, including 60,000-plus here in Colorado. It's that we're putting Americans to work doing the work that America needs done—(applause)—in critical areas that have been neglected for too long; work that will bring real and lasting change for generations to come.

Because we know we can't build our economic future on the transportation and information networks of the past, we are remaking the American landscape with the largest new investment in our nation's infrastructure since Eisenhower built an interstate highway system in the 1950s. (Applause.) Because of this investment, nearly 400,000 men and women will go to work rebuilding our crumbling roads and bridges, repairing our faulty dams and levees, bringing critical broadband connections to businesses and homes in nearly every community in America, upgrading mass transit, building high-speed rail lines that will improve travel and commerce throughout our nation.

Because we know America can't out-compete the world tomorrow if our children are being out-educated today, we're making the largest investment in education in our nation's history. (Applause.) It's an investment that will create jobs building 21st century classrooms and libraries and labs for millions of children across America. It will provide funds to train a new generation of math and science teachers, while giving aid to states and school districts to stop teachers from being laid off and education programs from being cut.

In a place like New York City, 14,000 teachers who were set to be let go may now be able to continue pursuing their critical mission. It's an investment that will create a new $2,500 annual tax credit to put the dream of a college degree within reach for middle-class families and make college affordable for 7 million students—(applause)—helping more of our sons and daughters aim higher, reach further, fulfill their God-given potential. (Applause.)

Because we know that spiraling health care costs are crushing families and businesses alike, we're taking the most meaningful steps in years towards modernizing our health care system. It's an investment that will take the long overdue step of computerizing America's medical records to reduce the duplication and waste that costs billions of health care dollars, and medical errors that cost thousands of lives each year.

Further, thanks to the actions we've taken, 7 million Americans who lost their health care along the way will continue to get the coverage they need, and roughly 20 million more Americans can breathe a little easier knowing that their health care won't be cut due to a state budget shortfall. And a historic commitment to wellness initiatives will keep millions of Americans from setting foot in the doctor's office in the first place—because these are preventable diseases and we're going to invest in prevention. (Applause.)

So taken together with the enactment earlier this month of a long-delayed law to extend health care to millions more children of working families—(applause)—we have done more in 30 days to advance the cause of health care reform than this country has done in an entire decade. And that's something we should be proud of. (Applause.)

Because we know we can't power America's future on energy that's controlled by foreign dictators, we are taking big steps down the road to energy independence, laying the groundwork for new green energy economies that can create countless well-paying jobs. It's an investment that will double the amount of renewable energy produced over the next three years. Think about that—double the amount of renewable energy in three years. (Applause.) Provide tax credits and loan guarantees to companies like Namaste, a company that will be expanding, instead of laying people off, as a result of the plan that I'm about to sign.

And in the process, we will transform the way we use energy. Today, the electricity we use is carried along a grid of lines and wires that date back to Thomas Edison—a grid that can't support the

Delivering remarks at the groundbreaking of a road project funded by the act, June 18, 2010, in Columbus, Ohio.

demands of this economy. This means we're using 19th and 20th century technologies to battle 21st century problems like climate change and energy security. It also means that places like North Dakota can—that can produce a lot of wind energy can't deliver it to communities that want it, leading to a gap between how much clean energy we are using and how much we could be using.

The investment we're making today will create a newer, smarter electric grid that will allow for broader use of alternative energy. We will build on the work that's being done in places like Boulder—a community that's on its—that's on pace to be the world's first Smart Grid city. (Applause.) This investment will place Smart Meters in homes to make our energy bills lower, make outages less likely, and make it easier to use clean energy. It's an investment that will save taxpayers over $1 billion by slashing energy costs in our federal buildings by 25 percent; save working families hundreds of dollars a year on their energy bills by weatherizing over 1 million homes. And it's an investment that takes the important first step towards a national transmission superhighway that will connect our cities to the windy plains of the Dakotas and the sunny deserts of the Southwest.

Even beyond energy, from the National Institutes of Health to the National Science Foundation, this recovery act represents the biggest increase in basic research funding in the long history of America's noble endeavor to better understand our world. And just as President Kennedy sparked an explosion of innovation when he set America's sights on the moon, I hope this investment will ignite our imagination once more, spurring new discoveries and breakthroughs in science, in medicine, in energy, to make our economy stronger and our nation more secure and our planet safer for our children.

Now, while this package is composed mostly of critical investments, it also includes aid to state and local governments to prevent layoffs of firefighters or police recruits in—(applause)—recruits like the ones in Columbus, Ohio, who were told that instead of being sworn in as officers, they were about to be let go. It includes help for those hardest hit by our economic crisis like the nearly 18 million Americans who will get larger unemployment checks in the mail. About a third of this package comes in the forms of tax cuts—by the way, the most progressive in our history—(applause)—not only spurring job creation, but putting money in the pockets of 95 percent of hardworking families in America. (Applause.) So unlike the tax cuts that we've seen in recent years, the vast majority of these tax benefits will go not to the wealthiest Americans, but to the middle class—(applause)—with those workers who make the least benefiting the most.

And it's a plan that rewards responsibility, lifting two million Americans from poverty by ensuring that anyone who works hard does not have to raise a child below the poverty line. So as a whole, this plan will help poor and working Americans pull themselves into the middle class in a way we haven't seen in nearly 50 years.

What I'm signing, then, is a balanced plan with a mix of tax cuts and investments. It's a plan that's been put together without earmarks or the usual pork barrel spending. It's a plan that will be implemented with an unprecedented level of transparency and accountability.

With a recovery package of this size comes a responsibility to assure every taxpayer that we are being careful with the money they work so hard to earn. And that's why I'm assigning a team of managers to ensure that the precious dollars we've invested are being spent wisely and well. We will—(applause)—Governor Ritter, Mayor Hickenlooper, we're going to hold governors and local officials who receive the money to the same high standard. And we expect you, the American people, to hold us accountable for the results. And that's why we've created Recovery.gov—a web site so that every American can go online and see how this money is being spent and what kind of job is being created, where those jobs are being created. We want transparency and accountability throughout this process. (Applause.)

Now, as important as the step we take today is, this legislation represents only the first part of the broad strategy we need to address our economic crisis. In the coming days and weeks, I'll be launching other aspects of the plan. We will need to stabilize, repair, and reform our banking system, and get credit flowing again to families and businesses. We will need to end the culture where we ignore problems until they become full-blown crises instead of recognizing that the only way to build a thriving economy is to set and enforce firm rules of the road.

We must stem the spread of foreclosures and falling home values for all Americans, and do everything we can to help responsible homeowners stay in their homes—something I'll talk more about tomorrow. And we will need to do everything in the short term to get our economy moving again, while at the same time recognizing that we have inherited a trillion-dollar deficit, and we need to begin restoring fiscal discipline and taming our exploding deficits over the long term.

None of this will be easy. The road to recovery will not be straight. We will make progress and there may be some slippage along the way. It will demand courage and discipline. It will demand a new sense of responsibility that's been missing from Wall Street all the way to Washington. There will be hazards and reverses. But I have every confidence that if we are willing to continue doing the critical work that must be done—by each of us, by all of us—then we will leave this struggling economy behind us, and come out on the other side, more prosperous as a people.

For our American story is not—and has never been—about things coming easy. It's about rising to the moment when the moment is hard, and converting crisis into opportunity, and seeing to it that we emerge from whatever trials we face stronger than we were before. It's about rejecting the notion that our fate is somehow written for us, and instead laying claim to a destiny of our own making. That's what earlier generations of Americans have done, that's what we owe our children, that's what we are doing today.

Thank you, Colorado. Let's get to work. Thank you. (Applause.)

The president's signature on the act.

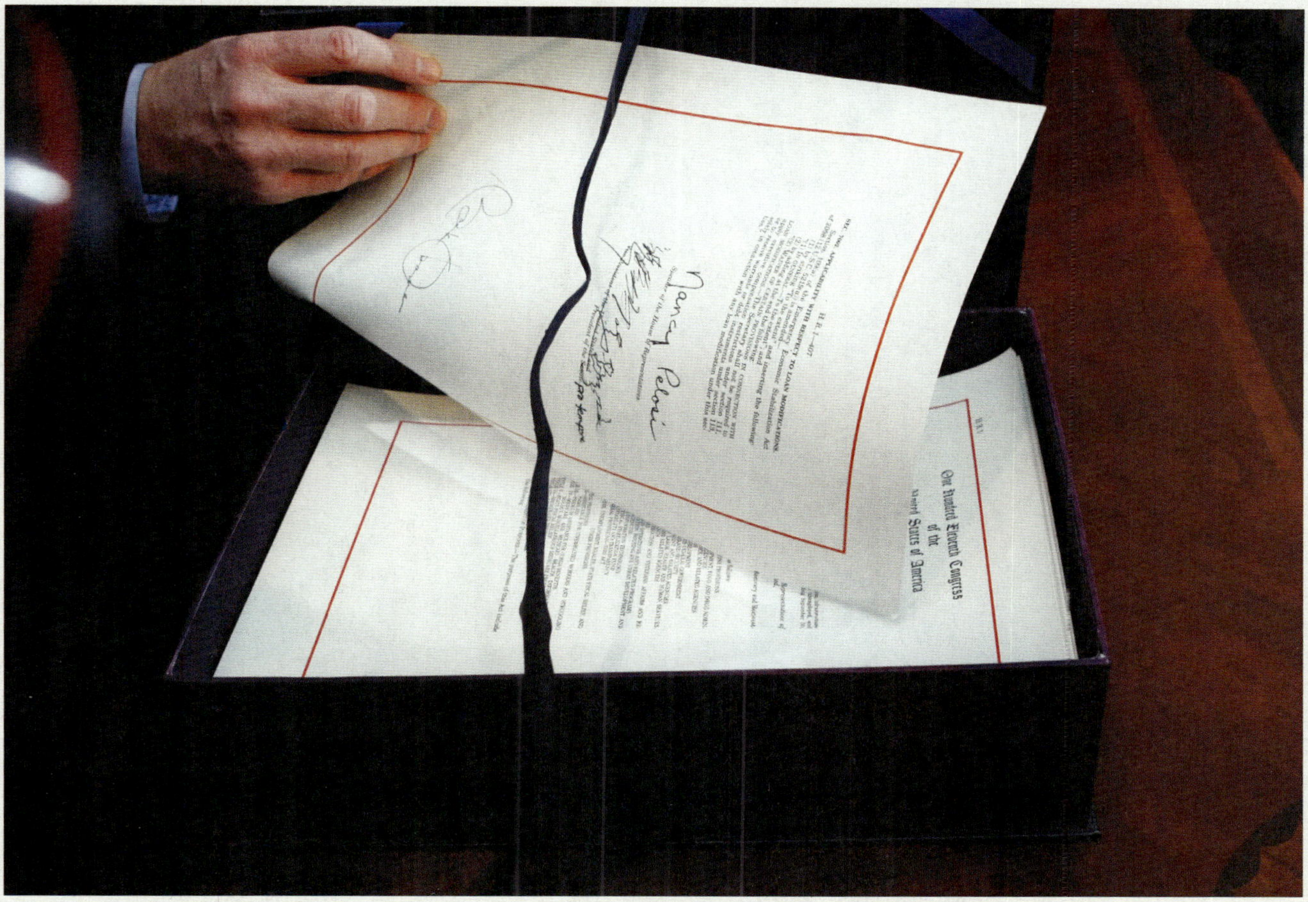

A Gallery of Domestic Policy Achievements

- The Lilly Ledbetter Fair Pay Act, the first bill signed into law by President Obama upon taking office in January 2009, extended the statute of limitations for filing equal-pay discrimination lawsuits.
- President Obama twice increased the budget for the Department of Veterans Affairs. The extra money would be used to treat physical and mental illnesses of the soldiers returning from combat. He also signed a new GI Bill for tuition assistance and offered tax incentives to businesses who hired veterans.
- The 2010 Patient Protection and Affordable Care Act, President Obama's overhaul of the healthcare system, gave coverage to 32 million Americans, allowed dependents up to the age of 26 to remain on their parents' plans, and made it illegal for insurers to deny coverage based on pre-existing conditions.
- In September 2011, "Don't Ask, Don't Tell," the policy that banned openly gay, lesbian, and transgendered Americans from serving in the military, was repealed by Congress on the president's instructions.
- The President expanded Pell Grants so that more lower-income students could attend college. He also reduced the rate by which a college graduate's disposable income could be used to repay student loans from 15% to 10%.

President Barack Obama walks with Lilly Ledbetter into the East Room of the White House to sign the Lilly Ledbetter Bill on January 29, 2009.

Remarks by the President at the Signing of the Lilly Ledbetter Bill

Transcript of comments during signing in the East Room of the White House, January 29, 2009

THE PRESIDENT: All right. Everybody please have a seat. Well, this is a wonderful day. (Applause.) First of all, it is fitting that the very first bill that I sign—the Lilly Ledbetter Fair Pay Restoration Act—(applause)—that it is upholding one of this nation's founding principles: that we are all created equal, and each deserve a chance to pursue our own version of happiness.

It's also fitting that we're joined today by the woman after whom this bill is named—someone who Michelle and I have had the privilege to get to know ourselves. And it is fitting that we are joined this morning by the first woman Speaker of the House of Representatives, Nancy Pelosi. (Applause.) It's appropriate that this is the first bill we do together. We could not have done it without her. Madam Speaker, thank you for your extraordinary work. And to all the sponsors and members of Congress and leadership who helped to make this day possible.

Lilly Ledbetter did not set out to be a trailblazer or a household name. She was just a good hard worker who did her job—and she did it well—for nearly two decades before discovering that for years, she was paid less than her male colleagues for doing the

Those present for the signing of the Lilly Ledbetter Act, from left, are Vice President Joe Biden, Secretary of State Hillary Rodham Clinton, Rep. Steny Hoyer, D-Md., Sen. Barbara Mikulski, D-Md. (left of Obama), and Lilly Ledbetter.

very same work. Over the course of her career, she lost more than $200,000 in salary, and even more in pension and Social Security benefits—losses that she still feels today.

Now, Lilly could have accepted her lot and moved on. She could have decided that it wasn't worth the hassle and the harassment that would inevitably come with speaking up for what she deserved. But instead, she decided that there was a principle at stake, something worth fighting for. So she set out on a journey that would take more than ten years, take her all the way to the Supreme Court of the United States, and lead to this day and this bill which will help others get the justice that she was denied.

Because while this bill bears her name, Lilly knows that this story isn't just about her. It's the story of women across this country still earning just 78 cents for every dollar men earn—women of color even less—which means that today, in the year 2009, countless women are still losing thousands of dollars in salary, income and retirement savings over the course of a lifetime.

Equal pay is by no means just a women's issue—it's a family issue. It's about parents who find themselves with less money for tuition and child care; couples who wind up with less to retire on; households where one breadwinner is paid less than she deserves; that's the difference between affording the mortgage—or not; between keeping the heat on, or paying the doctor bills—or not. And in this economy, when so many folks are already working harder for less and struggling to get by, the last thing they can afford is losing part of each month's paycheck to simple and plain discrimination.

So signing this bill today is to send a clear message: that making our economy work means making sure it works for everybody; that there are no second-class citizens in our workplaces; and that it's not just unfair and illegal, it's bad for business to pay somebody less because of their gender or their age or their race or their ethnicity, religion or disability; and that justice isn't about some abstract legal theory, or footnote in a casebook. It's about how our laws affect the daily lives and the daily realities of people: their ability to make a living and care for their families and achieve their goals.

Ultimately, equal pay isn't just an economic issue for millions of Americans and their families, it's a question of who we are—and whether we're truly living up to our fundamental ideals; whether we'll do our part, as generations before us, to ensure those words put on paper some 200 years ago really mean something—to breathe new life into them with a more enlightened understanding that is appropriate for our time.

That is what Lilly Ledbetter challenged us to do. And today, I sign this bill not just in her honor, but in the honor of those who came before—women like my grandmother, who worked in a bank all her life, and even after she hit that glass ceiling, kept getting up and giving her best every day, without complaint, because she wanted something better for me and my sister.

And I sign this bill for my daughters, and all those who will come after us, because I want them to grow up in a nation that values their contributions, where there are no limits to their dreams and they have opportunities their mothers and grandmothers never could have imagined.

In the end, that's why Lilly stayed the course. She knew it was too late for her—that this bill wouldn't undo the years of injustice she faced or restore the earnings she was denied. But this grandmother from Alabama kept on fighting, because she was thinking about the next generation. It's what we've always done in America—set our sights high for ourselves, but even higher for our children and our grandchildren.

And now it's up to us to continue this work. This bill is an important step—a simple fix to ensure fundamental fairness for American workers—and I want to thank this remarkable and bipartisan group of legislators who worked so hard to get it passed. And I want to thank all the advocates who are in the audience who worked so hard to get it passed. This is only the beginning. I know that if we stay focused, as Lilly did—and keep standing for what's right, as Lilly did—we will close that pay gap and we will make sure that our daughters have the same rights, the same chances, and the same freedoms to pursue their dreams as our sons.

So thank you, Lilly Ledbetter. (Applause.)

Remarks by the President and Vice President at the Signing of the Health Insurance Reform Bill ("Obamacare")

Transcript of comments during signing in the East Room of the White House, March 23, 2010

THE VICE PRESIDENT: Thank you all. (Applause.)

AUDIENCE: Fired up! Ready to go! Fired up! Ready to go!

THE VICE PRESIDENT: Thank you.

Mr. President, I think we got a happy room here. (Laughter.) It seems ridiculous to say thank you all for being here. (Laughter.) Ladies and gentlemen, to state the obvious, this is a historic day. (Applause.)

In our business you use that phrase a lot, but I can't think of a day in the 37 years that I've been a United States senator and the short time I've been Vice President that it is more appropriately stated. This is a historic day.

And history—history is not merely what is printed in textbooks. It doesn't begin or end with the stroke of a pen. History is made. History is made when men and women decide that there is a greater risk in accepting a situation that we cannot bear than in steeling our spine and embracing the promise of change. That's when history is made. (Applause.)

History is made when you all assembled here today, members of Congress, take charge to change the lives of tens of millions of Americans. Through the efforts of those of us lucky enough to serve here in this town, that's exactly what you've done. You've made history.

President Obama greets the Gramajo family, participants with the Make-A-Wish Foundation, in the Oval Office on July 15, 2009.

President Barack Obama welcomes Make-A-Wish child Kennedy Alexander to the Oval Office on March 15, 2011.

The president greets Halle Major and members of her family during a Make-A-Wish visit on March 29, 2011.

Accompanied by her family, Janiya Penny, an eight-year old Make-A-Wish child from Ft. Lauderdale, Florida, visits the Oval Office on August 8, 2012.

History is made when a leader steps up, stays true to his values, and charts a fundamentally different course for the country. History is made when a leader's passion—passion—is matched with principle to set a new course. Well, ladies and gentlemen, Mr. President, you are that leader. (Applause.)

Mr. President, your fierce advocacy, the clarity of purpose that you showed, your perseverance—these are in fact—it is not hyperbole to say—these are the reasons why we're assembled in this room together, today. But for those attributes we would not be here. Many, many men and women are going to feel the pride that I feel in watching you shortly, watching you sign this bill, knowing that their work—their work has helped make this day possible. But, Mr. President, you're the guy that made it happen. (Applause.)

And so, Mr. President, all of us, press and elected officials, assembled in this town over the years, we've seen some incredible things happen. But you know, Mr. President, you've done what generations of not just ordinary, but great men and women, have attempted to do. Republicans as well as Democrats, they've tried before. Everybody knows the story, starting with Teddy Roosevelt. They've tried. They were real bold leaders. But, Mr. President, they fell short. You have turned, Mr. President, the right of every American to have access to decent health care into reality for the first time in American history. (Applause.)

Mr. President, I've gotten to know you well enough. You want me to stop because I'm embarrassing you. (Laughter.) But I'm not going to stop for another minute, Mr. President, because you delivered on a promise—a promise you made to all Americans when we moved into this building.

Mr. President, you are—to repeat myself—literally about to make history. Our children and our grandchildren, they're going to grow up knowing that a man named Barack Obama put the final girder in the framework for a social network in this country to provide the single most important element of what people need—and that is access to good health—(applause)—and that every American from this day forward will be treated with simple fairness and basic justice.

Look, the classic poet, Virgil, once said that "The greatest wealth is health." The greatest wealth is health. Well, today, America becomes a whole lot wealthier because tens of millions of Americans will be a whole lot healthier from this moment on.

Ladies and gentlemen, the President of the United States of America, Barack Obama. (Applause.)

THE PRESIDENT: Thank you, everybody. Thank you. (Applause.) Thank you so much. Thank you. (Applause.) Thank you, everybody. Please, have a seat. Thank you, Joe. (Laughter.)

THE VICE PRESIDENT: Good to be with you, Mr. President. (Laughter.)

THE PRESIDENT: Today, after almost a century of trying; today, after over a year of debate; today, after all the votes have been tallied—health insurance reform becomes law in the United States of America. (Applause.) Today.

It is fitting that Congress passed this historic legislation this week. For as we mark the turning of spring, we also mark a new season in America. In a few moments, when I sign this bill, all of the overheated rhetoric over reform will finally confront the reality of reform. (Applause.)

And while the Senate still has a last round of improvements to make on this historic legislation—and these are improvements I'm confident they will make swiftly—(applause)—the bill I'm signing will set in motion reforms that generations of Americans have fought for, and marched for, and hungered to see.

It will take four years to implement fully many of these reforms, because we need to implement them responsibly. We need to get this right. But a host of desperately needed reforms will take effect right away. (Applause.)

This year, we'll start offering tax credits to about 4 million small businessmen and women to help them cover the cost of insurance for their employees. (Applause.) That happens this year.

This year, tens of thousands of uninsured Americans with preexisting conditions, the parents of children who have a preexisting condition, will finally be able to purchase the coverage they need. That happens this year. (Applause.)

This year, insurance companies will no longer be able to drop people's coverage when they get sick.

(Applause.) They won't be able to place lifetime limits or restrictive annual limits on the amount of care they can receive. (Applause.)

This year, all new insurance plans will be required to offer free preventive care. And this year, young adults will be able to stay on their parents' policies until they're 26 years old. That happens this year. (Applause.)

And this year, seniors who fall in the coverage gap known as the doughnut hole will start getting some help. They'll receive $250 to help pay for prescriptions, and that will, over time, fill in the doughnut hole. And I want seniors to know, despite what some have said, these reforms will not cut your guaranteed benefits. (Applause.) In fact, under this law, Americans on Medicare will receive free preventive care without co-payments or deductibles. That begins this year. (Applause.)

Once this reform is implemented, health insurance exchanges will be created, a competitive marketplace where uninsured people and small businesses will finally be able to purchase affordable, quality insurance. They will be able to be part of a big pool and get the same good deal that members of Congress get. That's what's going to happen under this reform. (Applause.) And when this exchange is up and running, millions of people will get tax breaks to help them afford coverage, which represents the largest middle-class tax cut for health care in history. That's what this reform is about. (Applause.)

This legislation will also lower costs for families and for businesses and for the federal government, reducing our deficit by over $1 trillion in the next two decades. It is paid for. It is fiscally responsible. And it will help lift a decades-long drag on our economy. That's part of what all of you together worked on and made happen. (Applause.)

That our generation is able to succeed in passing this reform is a testament to the persistence—and the character—of the American people, who championed this cause; who mobilized; who organized; who believed that people who love this country can change it.

It's also a testament to the historic leadership—and uncommon courage—of the men and women of the United States Congress, who've taken their lumps during this difficult debate. (Laughter.)

AUDIENCE MEMBER: Yes, we did. (Laughter.)

THE PRESIDENT: You know, there are few tougher jobs in politics or government than leading one of our legislative chambers. In each chamber, there are men and women who come from different places and face different pressures, who reach different conclusions about the same things and feel deeply concerned about different things.

By necessity, leaders have to speak to those different concerns. It isn't always tidy; it is almost never easy. But perhaps the greatest—and most difficult—challenge is to cobble together out of those differences the sense of common interest and common purpose that's required to advance the dreams of all people—especially in a country as large and diverse as ours.

And we are blessed by leaders in each chamber who not only do their jobs very well but who never lost sight of that larger mission. They didn't play for the short term; they didn't play to the polls or to politics. . . .

Today, I'm signing this reform bill into law on behalf of my mother, who argued with insurance companies even as she battled cancer in her final days.

I'm signing it for Ryan Smith, who's here today. He runs a small business with five employees. He's trying to do the right thing, paying half the cost of coverage for his workers. This bill will help him afford that coverage.

I'm signing it for 11-year-old Marcelas Owens, who's also here. (Applause.) Marcelas lost his mom to an illness. And she didn't have insurance and couldn't afford the care that she needed. So in her memory he has told her story across America so that no other children have to go through what his family has experienced. (Applause.)

I'm signing it for Natoma Canfield. Natoma had to give up her health coverage after her rates were jacked up by more than 40 percent. She was terrified that an illness would mean she'd lose the house that her parents built, so she gave up her insurance. Now she's lying in a hospital bed, as we speak, faced with just such an illness, praying that she can somehow afford to get well without insurance. Natoma's family is here today because Natoma can't be. And her sister Connie is here. Connie, stand up. (Applause.)

President Obama greets Landon Still on the South Lawn of the White House, July 4, 2012.

Little Sarah Froman, daughter of Nancy Goodman and Mike Froman, Deputy National Security Advisor for International Economics, chases the president around the Oval Office in July 2012.

The president says goodbye to visitors to the Oval Office, including Jon Wolfsthal, Special Advisor to the Vice President for Nonproliferation and Nuclear Security, in July 2012.

I'm signing this bill for all the leaders who took up this cause through the generations—from Teddy Roosevelt to Franklin Roosevelt, from Harry Truman, to Lyndon Johnson, from Bill and Hillary Clinton, to one of the deans who's been fighting this so long, John Dingell. (Applause.) To Senator Ted Kennedy. (Applause.) And it's fitting that Ted's widow, Vicki, is here—it's fitting that Teddy's widow, Vicki, is here; and his niece Caroline; his son Patrick, whose vote helped make this reform a reality. (Applause.)

I remember seeing Ted walk through that door in a summit in this room a year ago—one of his last public appearances. And it was hard for him to make it. But he was confident that we would do the right thing.

Our presence here today is remarkable and improbable. With all the punditry, all of the lobbying, all of the game-playing that passes for governing in Washington, it's been easy at times to doubt our ability to do such a big thing, such a complicated thing; to wonder if there are limits to what we, as a people, can still achieve. It's easy to succumb to the sense of cynicism about what's possible in this country.

But today, we are affirming that essential truth—a truth every generation is called to rediscover for itself—that we are not a nation that scales back its aspirations. (Applause.) We are not a nation that falls prey to doubt or mistrust. We don't fall prey to fear. We are not a nation that does what's easy. That's not who we are. That's not how we got here.

We are a nation that faces its challenges and accepts its responsibilities. We are a nation that does what is hard. What is necessary. What is right. Here, in this country, we shape our own destiny. That is what we do. That is who we are. That is what makes us the United States of America.

And we have now just enshrined, as soon as I sign this bill, the core principle that everybody should have some basic security when it comes to their

A sleepy visitor catches the president's eye during afternoon meetings in May 2009.

An informal moment during a drop-by with Sen. Jack Reed, D-R.I., and family in the Oval Office, July 22, 2010.

health care. (Applause.) And it is an extraordinary achievement that has happened because of all of you and all the advocates all across the country.

So, thank you. Thank you. God bless you, and may God bless the United States. (Applause.) Thank you. Thank you.

All right, I would now like to call up to stage some of the members of Congress who helped make this day possible, and some of the Americans who will benefit from these reforms. And we're going to sign this bill.

This is going to take a little while. I've got to use every pen, so it's going to take a really long time. (Laughter.) I didn't practice. (Laughter.)

(The bill is signed.)

THE PRESIDENT: We are done. (Applause.)

President Obama cheers on a young participant in the 2009 White House Easter Egg Roll.

Remarks by the President and Vice President at the Signing of the Don't Ask, Don't Tell Repeal Act of 2010

Transcript of comments during signing at the Department of Interior, Washington, D.C., December 27, 2010

THE VICE PRESIDENT: Hey, folks, how are you? (Applause.) It's a good day. (Applause.) It's a real good day. As some of my colleagues can tell you, this is a long time in coming. But I am happy it's here.

Ladies and gentlemen, welcome. Please be seated.

It was a great five-star general and President, Dwight D. Eisenhower, who once said, "Though force can protect in emergency, only justice, fairness and consideration, and cooperation can finally lead men to the dawn of eternal peace."

By repealing "Don't Ask, Don't Tell" today, we take a big step toward fostering justice, fairness and consideration, and that real cooperation President Eisenhower spoke of.

This fulfills an important campaign promise the President and I made, and many here on this stage made, and many of you have fought for, for a long time, in repealing a policy that actually weakens our national security, diminished our ability to have military readiness, and violates the fundamental American principle of fairness and equality—that exact same set of principles that brave gay men and women will now be able to openly defend around the world. (Applause.)

It is both morally and militarily simply the right thing to do. And it's particularly important that this result was fully supported by those within the military who are charged with implementing it. And I want to pay particular respect, just as a personal note—as we used to say, I used to be allowed to say in the Senate, a point of personal privilege—Admiral Mullen, you're a stand-up guy. (Applause.) . . . And it couldn't have been done without these men and women leading our military. And certainly it could not have been done without the steady, dedicated and persistent leadership of the President of the United States. (Applause.)

Mr. President, by signing this bill, you will be linking military might with an abiding sense of justice. You'll be projecting power by promoting fairness, and making the United States military as strong as they can be at a time we need it to be the strongest.

Ladies and gentlemen, the president of the United States of America, the Commander-in-Chief, Barack Obama. (Applause.)

AUDIENCE: Yes, we did! Yes, we did! Yes, we did!

THE PRESIDENT: Thank you! Yes, we did.

AUDIENCE MEMBER: Thank you, Mr. President!

THE PRESIDENT: You are welcome. (Applause.) This is a good day.

AUDIENCE MEMBER: Yes, it is!

AUDIENCE MEMBER: You rock, President Obama!

THE PRESIDENT: Thank you, thank you, thank you. (Laughter.)

You know, I am just overwhelmed. This is a very good day. (Applause.) And I want to thank all of you, especially the people on this stage, but each and every one of you who have been working so hard on this, members of my staff who worked so hard on this. I couldn't be prouder.

Sixty-six years ago, in the dense, snow-covered forests of Western Europe, Allied Forces were beating back a massive assault in what would become known as the Battle of the Bulge. And in the final days of fighting, a regiment in the 80th Division of Patton's Third Army came under fire. The men were traveling along a narrow trail. They were exposed and they were vulnerable. Hundreds of soldiers were cut down by the enemy.

And during the firefight, a private named Lloyd Corwin tumbled 40 feet down the deep side of a ravine. And dazed and trapped, he was as good as dead. But one soldier, a friend, turned back. And with shells landing around him, amid smoke and chaos and the screams of wounded men, this soldier, this friend, scaled down the icy slope, risking his own life to bring Private Corwin to safer ground.

For the rest of his years, Lloyd credited this soldier, this friend, named Andy Lee, with saving his life, knowing he would never have made it out alone. It was a full four decades after the war, when the two friends reunited in their golden years, that

Lloyd learned that the man who saved his life, his friend Andy, was gay. He had no idea. And he didn't much care. Lloyd knew what mattered. He knew what had kept him alive; what made it possible for him to come home and start a family and live the rest of his life. It was his friend.

And Lloyd's son is with us today. And he knew that valor and sacrifice are no more limited by sexual orientation than they are by race or by gender or by religion or by creed; that what made it possible for him to survive the battlefields of Europe is the reason that we are here today. (Applause.) That's the reason we are here today. (Applause.)

So this morning, I am proud to sign a law that will bring an end to "Don't Ask, Don't Tell." (Applause.) It is a law—this law I'm about to sign will strengthen our national security and uphold the ideals that our fighting men and women risk their lives to defend.

No longer will our country be denied the service of thousands of patriotic Americans who were forced to leave the military—regardless of their skills, no matter their bravery or their zeal, no matter their

The signing of the Don't Ask, Don't Tell Repeal Act of 2010 at the U.S. Department of Interior in Washington, D.C.

years of exemplary performance—because they happen to be gay. No longer will tens of thousands of Americans in uniform be asked to live a lie, or look over their shoulder, in order to serve the country that they love. (Applause.)

As Admiral Mike Mullen has said, "Our people sacrifice a lot for their country, including their lives. None of them should have to sacrifice their integrity as well." (Applause.)

That's why I believe this is the right thing to do for our military. That's why I believe it is the right thing to do, period.

Now, many fought long and hard to reach this day. I want to thank the Democrats and Republicans who put conviction ahead of politics to get this done together. . . .

I also want to commend our military leadership. Ending "Don't Ask, Don't Tell" was a topic in my first meeting with Secretary Gates, Admiral Mullen, and the Joint Chiefs. (Applause.) We talked about how to end this policy. We talked about how success in both passing and implementing this change depended on working closely with the Pentagon. And that's what we did.

And two years later, I'm confident that history will remember well the courage and the vision of Secretary Gates—(applause)—of Admiral Mike Mullen, who spoke from the heart and said what he believed was right—(applause)—of General James Cartwright, the Vice Chairman of the Joint Chiefs; and Deputy Secretary William Lynn, who is here. (Applause.) Also, the authors of the Pentagon's review, Jeh Johnson and General Carter Ham, who did outstanding and meticulous work—(applause)—and all those who laid the groundwork for this transition.

And finally, I want to express my gratitude to the men and women in this room who have worn the uniform of the United States Armed Services. (Applause.) I want to thank all the patriots who are here today, all of them who were forced to hang up their uniforms as a result of "Don't Ask, Don't Tell"—but who never stopped fighting for this country, and who rallied and who marched and fought for change. I want to thank everyone here who stood with them in that fight.

An audience member is moved by the president's remarks at the bill-signing ceremony.

Because of these efforts, in the coming days we will begin the process laid out by this law. Now, the old policy remains in effect until Secretary Gates, Admiral Mullen and I certify the military's readiness to implement the repeal. And it's especially important for service members to remember that. But I have spoken to every one of the service chiefs and they are all committed to implementing this change swiftly and efficiently. We are not going to be dragging our feet to get this done. (Applause.)

Now, with any change, there's some apprehension. That's natural. But as Commander-in-Chief, I am certain that we can effect this transition in a way that only strengthens our military readiness; that people will look back on this moment and wonder why it was ever a source of controversy in the first place.

I have every confidence in the professionalism and patriotism of our service members. Just as they have adapted and grown stronger with each of the other changes, I know they will do so again. I know that Secretary Gates, Admiral Mullen, as well as the vast majority of service members themselves, share this view. And they share it based on their own experiences, including the experience of serving with dedicated, duty-bound service members who were also gay.

Chairman of the Joint Chiefs of Staff Admiral Mike Mullen is applauded during the bill-signing ceremony.

As one special operations warfighter said during the Pentagon's review—this was one of my favorites—it echoes the experience of Lloyd Corwin decades earlier: "We have a gay guy in the unit. He's big, he's mean, he kills lots of bad guys." (Laughter.) "No one cared that he was gay." (Laughter.) And I think that sums up perfectly the situation. (Applause.)

Finally, I want to speak directly to the gay men and women currently serving in our military. For a long time your service has demanded a particular kind of sacrifice. You've been asked to carry the added burden of secrecy and isolation. And all the while, you've put your lives on the line for the freedoms and privileges of citizenship that are not fully granted to you.

You're not the first to have carried this burden, for while today marks the end of a particular struggle that has lasted almost two decades, this is a moment more than two centuries in the making.

There will never be a full accounting of the heroism demonstrated by gay Americans in service to this country; their service has been obscured in history. It's been lost to prejudices that have waned in our own lifetimes. But at every turn, every crossroads in our past, we know gay Americans fought just as hard, gave just as much to protect this nation and the ideals for which it stands.

There can be little doubt there were gay soldiers who fought for American independence, who consecrated the ground at Gettysburg, who manned the trenches along the Western Front, who stormed the beaches of Iwo Jima. Their names are etched into the walls of our memorials. Their headstones dot the grounds at Arlington.

And so, as the first generation to serve openly in our Armed Forces, you will stand for all those who came before you, and you will serve as role models to all who come after. And I know that you will fulfill this responsibility with integrity and honor, just as you have every other mission with which you've been charged.

And you need to look no further than the servicemen and women in this room—distinguished officers like former Navy Commander Zoe Dunning. (Applause.) Marines like Eric Alva, one of the first Americans to be injured in Iraq. (Applause.) Leaders like Captain Jonathan Hopkins, who led a platoon into northern Iraq during the initial invasion, quelling an ethnic riot, earning a Bronze Star with valor. (Applause.) He was discharged, only to receive emails and letters from his soldiers saying they had known he was gay all along—(laughter)—and thought that he was the best commander they ever had. (Applause.)

There are a lot of stories like these—stories that only underscore the importance of enlisting the service of all who are willing to fight for this country. That's why I hope those soldiers, sailors, airmen, Marines and Coast Guardsmen who have been discharged under this discriminatory policy will seek to reenlist once the repeal is implemented. (Applause.)

That is why I say to all Americans, gay or straight, who want nothing more than to defend this country in uniform: Your country needs you, your country wants you, and we will be honored to welcome you into the ranks of the finest military the world has ever known. (Applause.)

Some of you remembered I visited Afghanistan just a few weeks ago. And while I was walking along the rope line—it was a big crowd, about 3,000—a young woman in uniform was shaking my hand and other people were grabbing and taking pictures. And she pulled me into a hug and she whispered in my ear, "Get 'Don't Ask, Don't Tell' done." (Laughter and applause.) And I said to her, "I promise you I will." (Applause.)

For we are not a nation that says, "don't ask, don't tell." We are a nation that says, "Out of many, we are one." (Applause.) We are a nation that welcomes the service of every patriot. We are a nation that believes that all men and women are created equal. (Applause.) Those are the ideals that generations have fought for. Those are the ideals that we uphold today. And now, it is my honor to sign this bill into law. (Applause.)

AUDIENCE MEMBER: Thank you, Mr. President!

THE PRESIDENT: Thank you!

AUDIENCE MEMBER: We're here, Mr. President. Enlist us now. (Laughter.)

(The bill is signed.)

THE PRESIDENT: This is done. (Applause.)

A Gallery of Foreign Policy Achievements

- Obama re-focused the U.S. intelligence efforts on finding Osama bin Laden, who orchestrated the terrorist attacks of September 11, 2001. On May 1, 2011, on the president's orders, a team of Navy SEALs raided his compound in Abbottabad, Pakistan. Bin Laden and four others living in the compound were killed during the operation.
- Almost immediately upon taking office, Obama signed an executive order that reversed the Bush administration's policy on torturing detainees. Practices such as waterboarding, physical abuse, and stress positions. Going forward, only interrogation techniques outlined in the U.S. Army Field Manual were to be followed.
- On December 18, 2011, the Iraq war officially ended when the last group of U.S. soldiers left the country. The war, which began in March 2003, claimed 4,500 American and more than 100,000 Iraqi lives, and cost an estimated $800 billion.
- In 2011, the president began the process for withdrawal from Afghanistan. It is expected that, by 2014, combat operations in Afghanistan will end.
- President Obama tightened sanctions on Iran, and worked with American allies to impose their own sanctions and cut back on their oil purchases from Iran.

The president and vice president, along with members of the national security team, receive an update on the mission against Osama bin Laden in the Situation Room of the White House, May 1, 2011.

On the Death of Osama bin Laden

by Barack Obama

Speech delivered from the East Room of the White House on May 2, 2011

Good evening. Tonight, I can report to the American people and to the world that the United States has conducted an operation that killed Osama bin Laden, the leader of al Qaeda, and a terrorist who's responsible for the murder of thousands of innocent men, women, and children.

It was nearly 10 years ago that a bright September day was darkened by the worst attack on the American people in our history. The images of Nine-Eleven are seared into our national memory—hijacked planes cutting through a cloudless September sky; the Twin Towers collapsing to the ground; black smoke billowing up from the Pentagon; the wreckage of Flight 93 in Shanksville, Pennsylvania, where the actions of heroic citizens saved even more heartbreak and destruction.

And yet we know that the worst images are those that were unseen to the world—the empty seat at the

A composite of images of the president and his national security team during a series of meetings in the Situation Room of the White House discussing the mission against Osama bin Laden on Sunday, May 1, 2011.

dinner table; children who were forced to grow up without their mother or their father; parents who would never know the feeling of their child's embrace; Nearly 3,000 citizens taken from us, leaving a gaping hole in our hearts.

On September 11, 2001, in our time of grief, the American people came together. We offered our neighbors a hand, and we offered the wounded our blood. We reaffirmed our ties to each other, and our love of community and country. On that day, no matter where we came from, what God we prayed to, or what race or ethnicity we were, we were united as one American family.

We were also united in our resolve to protect our nation and to bring those who committed this vicious attack to justice. We quickly learned that the Nine-Eleven attacks were carried out by al Qaeda—an organization headed by Osama bin Laden, which had openly declared war on the United States and was committed to killing innocents in our country and around the globe. And so we went to war against al Qaeda to protect our citizens, our friends, and our allies.

Over the last ten years, thanks to the tireless and heroic work of our military and our counterterrorism professionals, we've made great strides in that effort. We've disrupted terrorist attacks and strengthened our homeland defense. In Afghanistan, we removed the Taliban government, which had given bin Laden and al Qaeda safe haven and support. And around the

globe, we worked with our friends and allies to capture or kill scores of al Qaeda terrorists, including several who were a part of the Nine-Eleven plot.

Yet Osama bin Laden avoided capture and escaped across the Afghan border into Pakistan. Meanwhile, al Qaeda continued to operate from along that border and operate through its affiliates across the world.

And so shortly after taking office, I directed Leon Panetta, the director of the CIA, to make the killing or capture of bin Laden the top priority of our war against al Qaeda, even as we continued our broader efforts to disrupt, dismantle, and defeat his network.

Then, last August, after years of painstaking work by our intelligence community, I was briefed on a possible lead to bin Laden. It was far from certain, and it took many months to run this thread to ground. I met repeatedly with my national security team as we developed more information about the possibility that we had located bin Laden hiding within a compound deep inside Pakistan. And finally, last week, I determined that we had enough intelligence to take action, and authorized an operation to get Osama bin Laden and bring him to justice.

Today, at my direction, the United States launched a targeted operation against that compound in Abbottabad, Pakistan. A small team of Americans carried out the operation with extraordinary courage and capability. No Americans were harmed. They took care to

The internal structure of the Pentagon is exposed after one of the planes hijacked on 9/11 crashed into it.

United Airlines Flight 175 crashes into the south tower of the World Trade Center complex in New York City during the September 11 attacks.

The ruins of the World Trade Center after the events of 9/11.

avoid civilian casualties. After a firefight, they killed Osama bin Laden and took custody of his body.

For over two decades, bin Laden has been al Qaeda's leader and symbol, and has continued to plot attacks against our country and our friends and allies. The death of bin Laden marks the most significant achievement to date in our nation's effort to defeat al Qaeda.

Yet his death does not mark the end of our effort. There's no doubt that al Qaeda will continue to pursue attacks against us. We must—and we will—remain vigilant at home and abroad.

As we do, we must also reaffirm that the United States is not—and never will be—at war with Islam. I've made clear, just as President Bush did shortly after Nine-Eleven, that our war is not against Islam. Bin Laden was not a Muslim leader; he was a mass murderer of Muslims. Indeed, al Qaeda has slaughtered scores of Muslims in many countries, including our own. So his demise should be welcomed by all who believe in peace and human dignity.

Over the years, I've repeatedly made clear that we would take action within Pakistan if we knew where bin Laden was. That is what we've done. But it's important to note that our counterterrorism cooperation with Pakistan helped lead us to bin Laden and the compound where he was hiding. Indeed, bin Laden had declared war against Pakistan as well, and ordered attacks against the Pakistani people.

Tonight, I called President Zardari, and my team has also spoken with their Pakistani counterparts. They agree that this is a good and historic day for both of our nations. And going forward, it is essential

Osama bin Laden watches himself on the news in his hideout.

Navy SEALs explore the entrance to one of 70 caves they discovered in the Zhawar Kili area.

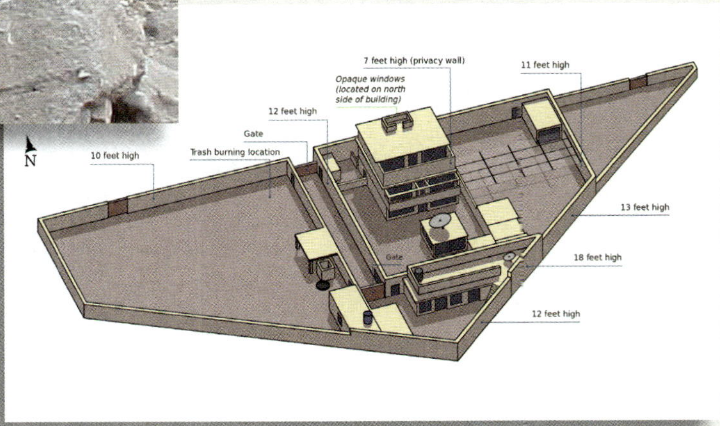

Diagram of the dwelling where bin Laden was finally found.

that Pakistan continue to join us in the fight against al Qaeda and its affiliates.

The American people did not choose this fight. It came to our shores, and started with the senseless slaughter of our citizens. After nearly ten years of service, struggle, and sacrifice, we know well the costs of war. These efforts weigh on me every time I, as Commander-in-Chief, have to sign a letter to a family that has lost a loved one, or look into the eyes of a service member who's been gravely wounded.

So Americans understand the costs of war. Yet as a country, we will never tolerate our security being threatened, nor stand idly by when our people have been killed. We will be relentless in defense of our citizens and our friends and allies. We will be true to the values that make us who we are. And on nights like this one, we can say to those families who have lost loved ones to al Qaeda's terror: justice has been done.

Tonight, we give thanks to the countless intelligence and counterterrorism professionals who've worked tirelessly to achieve this outcome. The American people do not see their work, nor know their names. But tonight, they feel the satisfaction of their work and the result of their pursuit of justice.

We give thanks for the men who carried out this operation, for they exemplify the professionalism, patriotism, and unparalleled courage of those who serve our country. And they are part of a generation that has borne the heaviest share of the burden since that September day.

Finally, let me say to the families who lost loved ones on 9/11 that we have never forgotten your loss, nor wavered in our commitment to see that we do whatever it takes to prevent another attack on our shores.

And tonight, let us think back to the sense of unity that prevailed on 9/11. I know that it has, at times, frayed. Yet today's achievement is a testament to the greatness of our country and the determination of the American people.

The cause of securing our country is not complete. But tonight, we are once again reminded that America can do whatever we set our mind to. That is the story of our history, whether it's the pursuit of prosperity for our people, or the struggle for equality for all our citizens; our commitment to stand up for our values abroad, and our sacrifices to make the world a safer place.

Let us remember that we can do these things not just because of wealth or power, but because of who we are: one nation, under God, indivisible, with liberty and justice for all.

Thank you. May God bless you. And may God bless the United States of America.

President Barack Obama talks on the phone in the Oval Office before making a statement to the media about the mission against Osama bin Laden, May 1, 2011.

At Kandahar Airfield, Afghanistan,U.S. service members watch on television as President Obama talks on May 2 about the details of the death of bin Laden.

President Obama shakes hands with Admiral Mike Mullen, Chairman of the Joint Chiefs of Staff, following his statement detailing the mission against Osama bin Laden, May 1, 2011.

On the End of Combat Operations in Iraq

by Barack Obama

Speech delivered from the Oval Office on August 31, 2010

Good evening. Tonight, I'd like to talk to you about the end of our combat mission in Iraq, the ongoing security challenges we face, and the need to rebuild our nation here at home.

I know this historic moment comes at a time of great uncertainty for many Americans. We've now been through nearly a decade of war. We've endured a long and painful recession. And sometimes in the midst of these storms, the future that we're trying to build for our nation—a future of lasting peace and long-term prosperity—may seem beyond our reach.

But this milestone should serve as a reminder to all Americans that the future is ours to shape if we move forward with confidence and commitment. It should also serve as a message to the world that the United States of America intends to sustain and strengthen our leadership in this young century.

From this desk, seven and a half years ago, President Bush announced the beginning of military operations in Iraq. Much has changed since that night. A war to disarm a state became a fight against an insurgency. Terrorism and sectarian warfare threatened to tear Iraq apart. Thousands of Americans gave their lives; tens of thousands have been wounded. Our relations abroad were strained. Our unity at home was tested.

These are the rough waters encountered during the course of one of America's longest wars. Yet there has been one constant amidst these shifting tides. At every turn, America's men and women in uniform have served with courage and resolve. As Commander-in-Chief, I am incredibly proud of their service. And like all Americans, I'm awed by their sacrifice, and by the sacrifices of their families.

The Americans who have served in Iraq completed every mission they were given. They defeated a regime that had terrorized its people. Together with Iraqis and coalition partners who made huge sacrifices of their own, our troops fought block by block to help Iraq seize the chance for a better future. They shifted tactics to protect the Iraqi people, trained Iraqi Security Forces, and took out terrorist leaders. Because of our troops and civilians—and because of the resilience of the Iraqi people—Iraq has the opportunity to embrace a new destiny, even though many challenges remain.

So tonight, I am announcing that the American combat mission in Iraq has ended. Operation Iraqi Freedom is over, and the Iraqi people now have lead responsibility for the security of their country.

This was my pledge to the American people as a candidate for this office. Last February, I announced a plan that would bring our combat brigades out of Iraq, while redoubling our efforts to strengthen Iraq's Security Forces and support its government and people.

That's what we've done. We've removed nearly 100,000 U.S. troops from Iraq. We've closed or transferred to the Iraqis hundreds of bases. And we have moved millions of pieces of equipment out of Iraq.

This completes a transition to Iraqi responsibility for their own security. U.S. troops pulled out of Iraq's cities last summer, and Iraqi forces have moved into the lead with considerable skill and commitment to their fellow citizens. Even as Iraq continues to suffer terrorist attacks, security incidents have been near the lowest on record since the war began. And Iraqi forces have taken the fight to al Qaeda, removing much of its leadership in Iraqi-led operations.

This year also saw Iraq hold credible elections that drew a strong turnout. A caretaker administration is in place as Iraqis form a government based on the results of that election. Tonight, I encourage Iraq's leaders to move forward with a sense of urgency to form an inclusive government that is just, representative, and accountable to the Iraqi people. And when that government is in place, there should be no doubt: The Iraqi people will have a strong partner in the United States. Our combat mission is ending, but our commitment to Iraq's future is not.

Going forward, a transitional force of U.S. troops will remain in Iraq with a different mission: advising and assisting Iraq's Security Forces, supporting Iraqi troops in targeted counterterrorism missions, and protecting our civilians. Consistent with our agreement with the Iraqi government, all U.S. troops will leave by the end of next year. As our military draws down, our dedicated civilians—diplomats, aid workers, and advisors—are moving into the lead to support Iraq as it strengthens its government, resolves political disputes, resettles those displaced by war, and builds ties with the region and the world. That's a message that Vice President Biden is delivering to the Iraqi people through his visit there today.

This new approach reflects our long-term partnership with Iraq—one based upon mutual interest and mutual respect. Of course, violence will not end with our combat mission. Extremists will continue to set off bombs, attack Iraqi civilians and try to spark sectarian strife. But ultimately, these terrorists will fail to achieve their goals. Iraqis are a proud people. They have rejected sectarian war, and they have no interest in endless destruction. They understand that, in the end, only Iraqis can resolve their differences and police their streets. Only Iraqis can build a democracy within their borders. What America can do, and will do, is provide support for the Iraqi people as both a friend and a partner.

Ending this war is not only in Iraq's interest—it's in our own. The United States has paid a huge price to put the future of Iraq in the hands of its people. We have sent our young men and women to make enormous sacrifices in Iraq, and spent vast resources abroad at a time of tight budgets at home. We've persevered because of a belief we share with the Iraqi people—a belief that out of the ashes of war, a new beginning could be born in this cradle of civilization. Through this remarkable chapter in the history of the United States and Iraq, we have met our responsibility. Now, it's time to turn the page.

As we do, I'm mindful that the Iraq war has been a contentious issue at home. Here, too, it's time to turn the page. This afternoon, I spoke to former President George W. Bush. It's well known that he and I disagreed about the war from its outset. Yet no one can doubt President Bush's support for our troops, or his love of country and commitment to

President Barack Obama addresses the nation from Bagram Air Field, Afghanistan, May 1, 2012.

our security. As I've said, there were patriots who supported this war, and patriots who opposed it. And all of us are united in appreciation for our servicemen and women, and our hopes for Iraqis' future.

The greatness of our democracy is grounded in our ability to move beyond our differences, and to learn from our experience as we confront the many challenges ahead. And no challenge is more essential to our security than our fight against al Qaeda.

Americans across the political spectrum supported the use of force against those who attacked us on 9/11. Now, as we approach our 10th year of combat in Afghanistan, there are those who are understandably asking tough questions about our mission there. But we must never lose sight of what's at stake. As we speak, al Qaeda continues to plot against us, and its leadership remains anchored in the border regions of Afghanistan and Pakistan. We will disrupt, dismantle and defeat al Qaeda, while preventing Afghanistan from again serving as a base for terrorists. And because of our drawdown in Iraq, we are now able to apply the resources necessary to go on offense. In fact, over the last 19 months, nearly a dozen al Qaeda leaders—and hundreds of al Qaeda's extremist allies—have been killed or captured around the world.

Within Afghanistan, I've ordered the deployment of additional troops who—under the command of General David Petraeus—are fighting to break the Taliban's momentum. As with the surge in Iraq, these forces will be in place for a limited time to provide space for the Afghans to build their capacity and secure their own future. But, as was the case in Iraq, we can't do for Afghans what they must ultimately do for themselves. That's why we're training Afghan Security Forces and supporting a political resolution to Afghanistan's problems. And next August, we will begin a transition to Afghan responsibility. The pace of our troop reductions will be determined by conditions on the ground, and our support for Afghanistan will endure. But make no mistake: This transition will begin—because open-ended war serves neither our interests nor the Afghan people's.

Indeed, one of the lessons of our effort in Iraq is that American influence around the world is not a function of military force alone. We must use all elements of our power—including our diplomacy, our

economic strength, and the power of America's example—to secure our interests and stand by our allies. And we must project a vision of the future that's based not just on our fears, but also on our hopes—a vision that recognizes the real dangers that exist around the world, but also the limitless possibilities of our time.

Today, old adversaries are at peace, and emerging democracies are potential partners. New markets for our goods stretch from Asia to the Americas. A new push for peace in the Middle East will begin here tomorrow. Billions of young people want to move beyond the shackles of poverty and conflict. As the leader of the free world, America will do more than just defeat on the battlefield those who offer hatred and destruction—we will also lead among those who are willing to work together to expand freedom and opportunity for all people.

Now, that effort must begin within our own borders. Throughout our history, America has been willing to bear the burden of promoting liberty and human dignity overseas, understanding its links to our own liberty and security. But we have also understood that our nation's strength and influence abroad must be firmly anchored in our prosperity at home. And the bedrock of that prosperity must be a growing middle class.

Unfortunately, over the last decade, we've not done what's necessary to shore up the foundations of our own prosperity. We spent a trillion dollars at war, often financed by borrowing from overseas. This, in turn, has short-changed investments in our own people, and contributed to record deficits. For too long, we have put off tough decisions on everything from our manufacturing base to our energy policy to education reform. As a result, too many middle-class families find themselves working harder for less, while our nation's long-term competitiveness is put at risk.

And so at this moment, as we wind down the war in Iraq, we must tackle those challenges at home with as much energy, and grit, and sense of common purpose as our men and women in uniform who have served abroad. They have met every test that they

Opposite: Thousands of vehicles and other pieces of equipment have been returned from Iraq and wait to be retrograded at Camp Arifjan, Kuwait.

Below: At Sather Air Base, Iraq, soldiers are shown redeploying as Operation Iraqi Freedom ends and Operation New Dawn begins.

faced. Now, it's our turn. Now, it's our responsibility to honor them by coming together, all of us, and working to secure the dream that so many generations have fought for—the dream that a better life awaits anyone who is willing to work for it and reach for it.

Our most urgent task is to restore our economy, and put the millions of Americans who have lost their jobs back to work. To strengthen our middle class, we must give all our children the education they deserve, and all our workers the skills that they need to compete in a global economy. We must jumpstart industries that create jobs, and end our dependence on foreign oil. We must unleash the innovation that allows new products to roll off our assembly lines, and nurture the ideas that spring from our entrepreneurs. This will be difficult. But in the days to come, it must be our central mission as a people, and my central responsibility as President.

Part of that responsibility is making sure that we honor our commitments to those who have served our country with such valor. As long as I am President, we will maintain the finest fighting force that the world has ever known, and we will do whatever it takes to serve our veterans as well as they have served us. This is a sacred trust. That's why we've already made one of the largest increases in funding for veterans in decades. We're treating the signature wounds of today's wars—post-traumatic stress disorder and traumatic brain injury—while providing the health care and benefits that all of our veterans have earned. And we're funding a Post-9/11 GI Bill that helps our veterans and their families pursue the dream of a college education. Just as the GI Bill helped those who fought World War II—including my grandfather—become the backbone of our middle class, so today's servicemen and women must have the chance to apply their gifts to expand the American economy. Because part of ending a war responsibly is standing by those who have fought it.

Two weeks ago, America's final combat brigade in Iraq—the Army's Fourth Stryker Brigade—journeyed home in the pre-dawn darkness. Thousands of soldiers and hundreds of vehicles made the trip from Baghdad, the last of them passing into Kuwait in the early morning hours. Over seven years before, American troops and coalition partners had fought their way across similar highways, but this time no shots were fired. It was just a convoy of brave Americans, making their way home.

Of course, the soldiers left much behind. Some were teenagers when the war began. Many have served multiple tours of duty, far from families who bore a heroic burden of their own, enduring the absence of a husband's embrace or a mother's kiss.

Most pain-fully, since the war began, 55 members of the Fourth Stryker Brigade made the ultimate sacrifice—part of over 4,400 Americans who have given their lives in Iraq. As one staff sergeant said, "I know that to my brothers in arms who fought and died, this day would probably mean a lot."

Those Americans gave their lives for the values that have lived in the hearts of our people for over two centuries. Along with nearly 1.5 million Americans who have served in Iraq, they fought in a faraway place for people they never knew. They stared into the darkest of human creations—war—and helped the Iraqi people seek the light of peace.

In an age without surrender ceremonies, we must earn victory through the success of our partners and the strength of our own nation. Every American who serves joins an unbroken line of heroes that stretches from Lexington to Gettysburg; from Iwo Jima to Inchon; from Khe Sanh to Kandahar—Americans who have fought to see that the lives of our children are better than our own. Our troops are the steel in our ship of state. And though our nation may be travelling through rough waters, they give us confidence that our course is true, and that beyond the pre-dawn darkness, better days lie ahead.

Thank you. May God bless you. And may God bless the United States of America, and all who serve her.

Opposite: One of the last few convoys of service members crosses over the border into Kuwait from Iraq on December 18, 2011.

Below: U.S. and Kuwaiti service members unite to close the gate here between Kuwait and Iraq following the final convoy of Operation New Dawn passing through on December 18.

Barack Obama: Candidate All Over Again

The Teams Are Chosen

In contrast to their victory in 2008, President Barack Obama and Vice President Joe Biden didn't have to go through an ugly, lengthy challenge for the nomination. On April 4, 2011, Obama filed the appropriate paperwork and officially declared his intention to seek a second term with a video titled "It Begins With Us." Democratic primaries and caucuses took place in 2012, but they were essentially formalities held without serious opposition, and Obama officially sewed up the nomination almost one year to the day after he announced his candidacy.

Meanwhile, the many Republican hopefuls, who ranged from seasoned politicians like former speaker of the house Newt Gingrich to businessman Herman Cain, fought for the other side of the ballot. During the long campaign, each of them had spells when they gained momentum, but none were able to mount a sustained challenge to former Massachusetts governor Mitt Romney.

By the end of April 2012, Romney, who had been considered the frontrunner by the establishment ever since his second-place finish in the 2008 primaries, had become the presumptive Republican nominee.

The Obama-Biden campaign began in earnest on May 5, with two events at colleges, first in Columbus, Ohio, and later that day in Richmond, Virginia. The symbolism of the locations was clear: Obama was targeting young people in key battleground states. With a new campaign slogan, "Forward," the president took little time in stating his case for reelection.

Clockwise from top left: Mitt Romney, Newt Gingrich, Ron Paul, and Rick Santorum.

For Obama, the difference between himself and Romney was clear. Although the economy had not bounced back as quickly as everyone had hoped, conditions were nonetheless improving. His policies would continue the recovery, while Romney's economic plans, with tax cuts that favored the wealthiest Americans, were a return to the same mindset that brought about the crisis in the first place.

SuperPACs Control the Discussion

There was a very important third player throughout the electoral season. In 2010, the Supreme Court, in their decision *Citizens United v. Federal Election Commission,* struck down vital portions of the 2002 McCain-Feingold campaign finance reform law. The court declared that regulating the campaign contributions of corporations, associations, and unions was a violation of the First Amendment.

The decision paved the way for "SuperPACs"—political action committees on steroids—to raise and spend unlimited funds in advocacy of their preferred candidates. The result was a nonstop barrage of advertisements, many of them negative, all over the media throughout the summer and fall. It was estimated that 1,115 SuperPACs raised more than $650 million and spent more than $630 million during the 2012 election cycle.

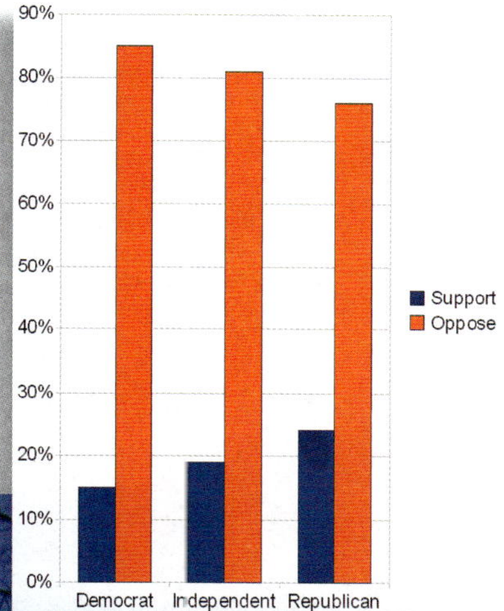

An ABC–*Washington Post* poll conducted February 4–8, 2010, showed that 80% of those surveyed opposed (and 65% strongly opposed) the Citizens United ruling.

A flash rally at the Supreme Court to protest the Citizens United decision.

Obama on the Attack

Contrary to his 2008 campaign, in which he ran on a platform of hope and change, Obama's 2012 campaign seemed to run on a platform of the status quo. He proposed no new legislation that was significantly different from that during his first term. Instead, he attacked Romney's professional and personal record and character.

The president frequently went after his opponent for his shifting opinions. Romney governed the famously liberal Massachusetts as a moderate Republican, and boasted of his record during his unsuccessful run for the presidency four years earlier. But during the 2012 primaries, he shifted to the right, running as a staunch conservative, and either ignored or distorted his accomplishments as governor to try to avoid the politically deadly term "flip-flopper."

On economic issues, Obama said that a Romney presidency would kill, rather than speed up, the slow recovery that had been taking place since the recession officially ended in June 2009. Obama's most effective strategy was to criticize Romney for his tenure as the chief executive officer of Bain Capital, a private equity investment firm. At Bain, Romney had accumulated a personal fortune estimated

Political activists wear flip-flop costumes as they protest outside an event where GOP presidential candidate Mitt Romney is scheduled to receive an award from an anti-abortion group in Agawam, Massachusetts.

at close to $200 million, and much of his wealth was stored in offshore bank accounts, which were shielded from U.S. tax law.

Obama had long fought for the repeal of the tax cuts on the wealthiest Americans that had been passed during the George W. Bush administration, only to come up against strong opposition by congressional Republicans. The added revenue caused by a return to the rates during the Clinton years, he said, would help ease the nation's record deficits and allow the recovery to continue at a faster rate. He used Romney as an example of those who had financially benefited the most from the American system but were not willing to pay their fair share.

Romney's candidacy also brought Bain's business practices into the public discussion. Bain and similar firms collected millions for their shareholders at minimal risk by taking over struggling companies, driving them into bankruptcy, and laying off employees or outsourcing jobs. With the unemployment rate hovering around 8.2%, Obama said, America could not afford a president who had so greatly profited at the expense of the middle class.

The Republican candidate had been a sharp critic of Obama's decision to bail out General Motors and Chrysler shortly after taking office, and had penned an op-ed for the *New York Times* called "Let Detroit Go Bankrupt." But the bailout proved profitable for the auto industry in the long run and saved countless American jobs. Obama repeatedly used his opponent's own words to show how Romney's business expertise did not mean that he was more qualified to run the world's largest economy.

In addition, Romney had, against precedent for presidential candidates, refused to release all but his two most recent tax returns. This led to accusations from the left that there was information in those returns that could prove fatal to his campaign if made public.

As one of Obama's most potent ads said, Romney wasn't the solution to the nation's economic woes, he was the problem.

Mitt Romney shares a laugh with supporters at a Nashua, New Hampshire, rally for Romney Ryan 2012.

"Obamacare" Upheld

On June 28, the Supreme Court, by a 5-4 vote, upheld Obama's signature piece of legislation, the Patient Protection and Affordable Care Act that came to be known as "Obamacare." In a surprise move, Chief Justice John Roberts, a conservative, sided with the court's liberal wing and cast the deciding vote, saying that its most controversial provision, the individual mandate, was constitutional. Ironically, Obama, as a senator, had voted against Roberts's appointment to the nation's highest court in 2005.

Even though Romney had signed a similar bill into law as governor of Massachusetts in 2006, he pledged throughout the campaign that he would take steps to get the bill repealed on his first day in office. The decision put the question of the federal government's responsibility to all of its citizens into sharp focus, and was used by Obama as definitive proof that Romney would adopt any position that could be politically beneficial.

Below: The president at an America Forward! grassroots event, Las Vegas, Nevada, October 24, 2012. Opposite: President Obama speaks during his grassroots event at the Kissimmee Civic Center in Kissimmee, Florida, on September 8, 2012.

FORWARD.
BARACKOBAMA.COM
FORWARD

Democratic National Convention

The campaign moved to Charlotte, North Carolina, for the Democratic National Convention, which was held September 3 through 6. A week earlier, the Republicans had held their convention, where Romney and his running mate, Rep. Paul Ryan of Wisconsin (a rising GOP star for his budget expertise), received the official nomination.

The opening night of the DNC began with a rousing keynote address by San Antonio mayor Julian Castro. As Obama had done eight years earlier, the 37-year-old told his uniquely American story, as a Mexican American who had achieved success through hard work and dedication, and was committed to a life of public service.

Castro then assailed the Romney-Ryan budget, saying that it would "dismantle" the middle class his family had struggled so hard to enter. "He just has no idea how good he's had it," Castro said, referring to the candidate's privileged upbringing.

But the night belonged to First Lady Michelle Obama, who wowed the audience with her eloquence and grace as she spoke of her life with her husband, and how his upbringing had shaped the man she fell in love with. She admitted that, four years ago, she was worried that the presidency would change him. However, she said, "after so many struggles and triumphs and moments that have tested my husband in ways I never could have imagined, I have seen firsthand that being president doesn't change who you are—it *reveals* who you are."

That character, she continued, was why he had fought throughout his first term for such important issues as women's rights, affordable healthcare, and a stronger middle class. She closed by speaking from the heart about their daughters, and said

Below: President Obama and his daughters, Malia and Sasha, watch on television as First Lady Michelle Obama begins her speech at the Democratic National Convention on September 4, 2012.

Opposite: Michelle Obama speaking at the convention.

that of all her duties as first lady, she was, foremost, "mom-in-chief."

On the second night, President Bill Clinton brought the house down with his nomination speech. Using his trademark wit and charm, he praised Obama's temperament and judgment, defended the president's record on the economy, and took aim at the Republican Party for being too ideologically rigid to work with the president.

He also drew from his own experience to explain why the Republican's tax cut–heavy budget was economically unfeasible and would not, as Romney claimed, reduce the deficit. In what was possibly the most quoted line of the convention, he laid out the secret of his own success. "People ask me all the time how we got four surplus budgets in a row," he said. "What new ideas did we bring to Washington? I always give a one-word answer: Arithmetic."

The stage was set for the final night and the appearance of the candidates. Vice President Joe Biden said that Romney's career in business had left him too focused on the bottom line to understand the devastating effect his positions would have on the American worker.

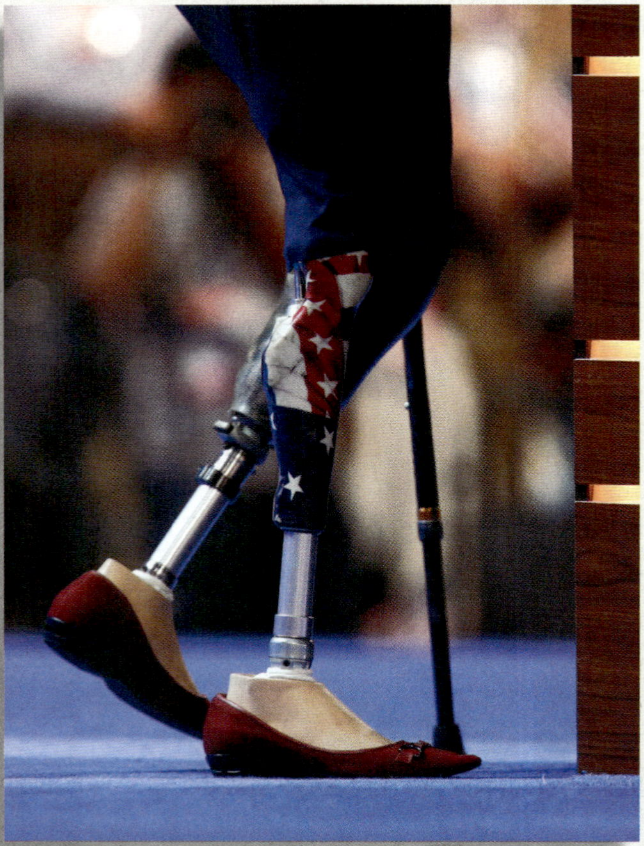

Former assistant secretary of the U.S. Department of Veterans Affairs Tammy Duckworth stands at the podium as she addresses the convention.

San Antonio mayor Julian Castro gives the convention's keynote address.

Former president Bill Clinton addresses the convention on September 5, 2012.

He also spoke with passion about how he'd witnessed the president's character firsthand on a daily basis. "This man has courage in his soul, compassion in his heart, and a spine of steel," Biden said. "And because of all the actions he took . . . we can now proudly say what you've heard me say the last six months: Osama bin Laden is dead, and General Motors is alive!"

President Obama closed the convention by speaking of how citizenship means that all members of society, from the wealthiest to the poorest, and the government and the churches, are dependent upon each other. Our shared desire to leave a better country for future generations, he said, ties our destinies together.

As opposed to his inspiring speeches in 2004 and 2008, he struck a more reflective tone. "I recognize that times have changed since I first spoke to this convention," he told the crowd. "Times have changed, and so have I. I'm no longer just a candidate. I'm the president." But his four years in office, he said, have strengthened his optimism because he has seen the resiliency and spirit of the American people throughout these difficult times.

Colorado delegate Tracy Ducharme from Colorado Springs attends the convention wearing cowboy boots and bringing a bag showing President Obama.

On the final day of the convention, President Obama and Vice President Biden wave to the crowd after accepting the nomination.

Debates

Following the conventions, the candidates returned to the campaign trail with Obama holding a small, but steady, lead in most polls. A month later, on October 3—which happened to be the Obamas' 20th wedding anniversary—the debate season began in Denver. The consensus for the first debate was that Obama did not perform well. To many of the 67 million people watching on television, the president appeared removed from the proceedings. He seemed to lose focus while speaking, was often found looking down at his notes, and allowed many of Romney's attacks to go unchallenged.

The talk was that only one candidate looked presidential, and it wasn't the president. Almost immediately, Obama began to lose hold on his small lead. In a debate between Biden and Ryan a week later, the vice president won points by hammering on the inconsistencies in the Romney-Ryan economic plan and Ryan's inexperience in foreign policy, but he failed to stem the tide of public opinion.

But Obama bounced back for the last two debates. He was considerably more engaged, and he took strong and forceful shots at Romney's positions on foreign policy and women's issues, and on Romney's record of outsourcing jobs in his own businesses. In later public events Obama would poke fun at his poor showing in the first debate, saying, for example, that "millions of Americans focused on the second debate who didn't focus on the first debate—and I happen to be one of them."

In his closing statement in the final debate, he criticized Romney for his comments in a video where he told wealthy donors that 47% of the population lived off government handouts and had no incentive to work. Although it was a not a true "knockout blow" and the race was still tight, Obama's performances on those last two nights had many of his supporters wondering where *this* Obama had been hiding in the first debate.

President Obama, right, and Mitt Romney participate in a presidential debate at the University of Denver in Denver, Colorado, on October 3, 2012.

President Barack Obama answers a question during a town hall style debate at Hofstra University, Hempstead, New York, on October 16, 2012.

The final presidential debate before the election took place on October 22, 2012, in Boca Raton, Florida

Vice President Joe Biden and his daughter Ashley Biden watch the third presidential debate from a hotel room in Toledo, Ohio, on October 22, 2012.

Employment Rising

A few days after the first presidential debate, the Bureau of Labor and Statistics gave the Obama campaign some much-needed good news: The unemployment rate had dropped a surprising 0.3%, to 7.8%, the lowest it had been since Obama had taken office. No incumbent since Franklin Delano Roosevelt in 1936 had won reelection with an unemployment rate above 8.0%. Obama saw the numbers as vindication that his policies were working.

Changes in Voting Practices

For the 2012 presidential election, 38 states and the District of Columbia enacted early voting policies, with polls open for as long as six weeks before election day in some states. The practice made it easier for citizens to participate in the democratic process due to the convenience and shorter lines. More than 30 million Americans took advantage of early voting, which was seen as crucial to the Democrats' "Get Out the Vote" initiatives.

On October 25, President Obama became the first president to vote before election day when he cast his vote at the Martin Luther King Community Center on the South Side of Chicago.

Voters stand in line during early voting in Miami, Florida

Supporters wave as President Barack Obama leaves the Martin Luther King Community Center after casting his ballot during early voting on October 25, 2012 in Chicago, Illinois.

Sandy and Final Rallies

With two weeks until election day, the Obama campaign went into overdrive, with their efforts focused almost exclusively in swing states, notably Iowa, Ohio, Pennsylvania, and Virginia. But the president was forced to temporarily suspend his campaign on October 29, when Hurricane Sandy ravaged the East Coast, in particular New Jersey and New York City.

During the crisis, New Jersey governor Chris Christie, who was one of Romney's chief surrogates, acted without partisanship in praising Obama's hands-on approach, leadership, and compassion. Christie's words inadvertently nullified some of the main charges that had been leveled at the president throughout the campaign.

Obama and Christie toured the damage together a couple of days after the storm hit. To many, the presence of the commander-in-chief also proved a need for disaster relief at the federal level, something that Romney had spoken out against during the Republican primaries. Obama's poll numbers began to rise again.

In its final days, Obama brought out the star power. Bruce Springsteen, who campaigned for the president in 2008 but had decided to stay on the sidelines this time around, changed his mind and performed at five rallies down the stretch. Stevie Wonder, Jay-Z, Alicia Keys, and Katy Perry also made appearances at events, while A-list actors like Eva Longoria, Jake Gyllenhaal, Julianne Moore, and Jon Hamm worked on behalf of the Obama campaign.

Cathy O'Hanlon stands in front of the charred remains of her home in the borough of Queens New York, after a fire started during Superstorm Sandy destroyed more than 50 homes in her oceanfront community.

President Barack Obama and New Jersey governor Chris Christie talk with local residents at the Brigantine Beach Community Center in Brigantine, New Jersey, on October 31, 2012.

An Obama campaign sign rises above the floodwaters in a neighborhood as rain continues to fall in Norfolk, Virginia during Superstorm Sandy.

"Four More Years"

After nearly two years of campaigning, it all came down to one night, November 6, 2012, as nearly 120 million people cast their ballots. Most of the focus centered on the swing states where the race was the closest. As the results came in, it became clear that most of them were leaning toward Obama.

At approximately 11:12 p.m. Eastern, the networks called Ohio for Obama, which gave him the necessary 270 electoral votes needed to win a second term. Although he won the popular vote by a fairly small majority of 50.5% to 47.9%, Obama's victories in eight of the nine most hotly contested states gave him a massive 332-206 decision in the Electoral College.

Romney conceded nearly two hours later when the remaining incoming results proved too conclusive to work out in his favor. In his gracious concession speech, he called for the nation to put partisanship aside and work together to solve the nation's problems.

Shortly thereafter, the now two-term president took to the stage at McCormick Place in Chicago. He congratulated the Romney-Ryan campaign and praised his family, Vice President Biden, and his staff. Then he turned his focus to the American people, reminding them that, for all of its messiness, the democratic process is vital to our growth as a nation because it shines a spotlight on our shared values. He closed by echoing his words that struck such a chord during the 2004 Democratic National Convention.

"I believe we can seize this future together because we are not as divided as our politics suggests," he said. "We're not as cynical as the pundits believe. We are greater than the sum of our individual ambitions, and we remain more than a collection of red states and blue states. We are and forever will be the United States of America."

In Chicago, Illinois, President Barack Obama claps as he arrives on stage to deliver his acceptance speech on November 7, 2012.

President Barack Obama and First Lady Michelle Obama embrace Vice President Joe Biden and Dr. Jill Biden moments after the television networks called the election in their favor.

2012 Victory Speech

Delivered from McCormick Place, Chicago, Illinois, November 7, 2012 as 12:38 a.m. CST

Tonight, more than 200 years after a former colony won the right to determine its own destiny, the task of perfecting our union moves forward.

It moves forward because of you. It moves forward because you reaffirmed the spirit that has triumphed over war and depression; the spirit that has lifted this country from the depths of despair to the great heights of hope—the belief that while each of us will pursue our own individual dreams, we are an American family, and we rise or fall together, as one nation, and as one people.

Tonight, in this election, you, the American people, reminded us that while our road has been hard, while our journey has been long, we have picked ourselves up, we have fought our way back, and we know in our hearts that for the United States of America, the best is yet to come.

I want to thank every American who participated in this election. Whether you voted for the very first time or waited in line for a very long time—by the way, we have to fix that. Whether you pounded the pavement or picked up the phone, whether you held an Obama sign or a Romney sign, you made your voice heard, and you made a difference.

I just spoke with Governor Romney, and I congratulated him and Paul Ryan on a hard-fought campaign. We may have battled fiercely, but it's only because we love this country deeply, and we care so strongly about its future. From George to Lenore to their son Mitt, the Romney family has chosen to give back to America through public service, and that is a legacy that we honor and applaud tonight.

Below: Confetti falls over supporters at the end of President Barack Obama remarks during an election night party in Chicago.

Opposite: President Barack Obama celebrates on stage after delivering his acceptance speech.

In the weeks ahead, I also look forward to sitting down with Governor Romney to talk about where we can work together to move this country forward.

I want to thank my friend and partner of the last four years, America's happy warrior—the best vice president anybody could ever hope for—Joe Biden.

And I wouldn't be the man I am today without the woman who agreed to marry me 20 years ago. Let me say this publicly—Michelle, I have never loved you more. I have never been prouder to watch the rest of America fall in love with you, too, as our nation's first lady. Sasha and Malia, before our very eyes, you're growing up to become two strong, smart, beautiful young women, just like your mom. And I'm so proud of you guys. But I will say that for now, one dog is probably enough.

To the best campaign team and volunteers in the history of politics—the best. The best ever. Some of you were new this time around, and some of you have been at my side since the very beginning. But all of you are family. No matter what you do or where you go from here, you will carry the memory of the history we made together, and you will have the lifelong appreciation of a grateful President. Thank you for believing all the way, through every hill, through every valley. You lifted me up the whole way. And I will always be grateful for everything that you've done and all the incredible work that you put in.

I know that political campaigns can sometimes seem small, even silly. And that provides plenty of fodder for the cynics who tell us that politics is nothing more than a contest of egos, or the domain of special interests. But if you ever get the chance to talk to folks who turned out at our rallies, and crowded along a rope line in a high school gym, or saw folks working late at a campaign office in some tiny county far away from home, you'll discover something else.

You'll hear the determination in the voice of a young field organizer who's worked his way through college, and wants to make sure every child has that same opportunity. You'll hear the pride in the voice of a volunteer who's going door to door because her

Below left: President-elect Barack Obama and Michelle Obama at their night victory rally at Grant Park on November 4, 2008 in Chicago, Illinois; Below right: The couple celebrating on stage after Obama delivered his acceptance speech on November 7, 2012.

Opposite: President Barack Obama waves to supporters at the election night party, November 7, 2012, in Chicago, proclaiming victory in the presidential election.

brother was finally hired when the local auto plant added another shift. You'll hear the deep patriotism in the voice of a military spouse who's working the phones late at night to make sure that no one who fights for this country ever has to fight for a job, or a roof over their head when they come home.

That's why we do this. That's what politics can be. That's why elections matter. It's not small; it's big. It's important.

Democracy in a nation of 300 million can be noisy and messy and complicated. We have our own opinions. Each of us has deeply held beliefs. And when we go through tough times, when we make big decisions as a country, it necessarily stirs passions, stirs up controversy. That won't change after tonight—and it shouldn't. These arguments we have are a mark of our liberty, and we can never forget that as we speak, people in distant nations are risking their lives right now just for a chance to argue about the issues that matter, the chance to cast their ballots like we did today.

But despite all our differences, most of us share certain hopes for America's future. We want our kids to grow up in a country where they have access to the best schools and the best teachers—a country that lives up to its legacy as the global leader in technology and discovery and innovation, with all the good jobs and new businesses that follow.

We want our children to live in an America that isn't burdened by debt; that isn't weakened by inequality; that isn't threatened by the destructive power of a warming planet.

We want to pass on a country that's safe and respected and admired around the world; a nation that is defended by the strongest military on Earth and the best troops this world has ever known but also a

Below: Sarah Obama, step-grandmother of President Barack Obama, speaks to the media about her reaction to Obama's re-election, in her village of Kogelo, western Kenya.

Opposite: First Lady Michelle Obama hugs President Barack Obama as they celebrate on election night, November 7, 2012.

country that moves with confidence beyond this time of war to shape a peace that is built on the promise of freedom and dignity for every human being.

We believe in a generous America; in a compassionate America; in a tolerant America, open to the dreams of an immigrant's daughter who studies in our schools and pledges to our flag. To the young boy on the South Side of Chicago who sees a life beyond the nearest street corner. To the furniture worker's child in North Carolina who wants to become a doctor or a scientist, an engineer or entrepreneur, a diplomat or even a President. That's the future we hope for. That's the vision we share. That's where we need to go. Forward. That's where we need to go.

Now, we will disagree, sometimes fiercely, about how to get there. As it has for more than two centuries, progress will come in fits and starts. It's not always a straight line. It's not always a smooth path. By itself, the recognition that we have common hopes and dreams won't end all the gridlock, or solve all our problems, or substitute for the painstaking work of building consensus, and making the difficult compromises needed to move this country forward. But that common bond is where we must begin.

Our economy is recovering. A decade of war is ending. A long campaign is now over. And whether I earned your vote or not, I have listened to you. I have learned from you. And you've made me a better President. With your stories and your struggles, I return to the White House more determined and more inspired than ever about the work there is to do, and the future that lies ahead.

Tonight, you voted for action, not politics as usual. You elected us to focus on your jobs, not ours. And in the coming weeks and months, I am looking forward to reaching out and working with leaders

Staff of the American Chamber of Commerce in Singapore carry cutouts of presidential candidates Barack Obama and Mitt Romney, for a gathering at the American Club to watch the live coverage of the U.S. presidential election.

of both parties to meet the challenges we can only solve together: reducing our deficit; reforming our tax code; fixing our immigration system; freeing ourselves from foreign oil. We've got more work to do.

But that doesn't mean your work is done. The role of citizen in our democracy does not end with your vote. America has never been about what can be done for us. It's about what can be done by us, together, through the hard and frustrating but necessary work of self-government. That's the principle we were founded on.

This country has more wealth than any nation, but that's not what makes us rich. We have the most powerful military in history, but that's not what makes us strong. Our university, culture are the envy of the world, but that's not what keeps the world coming to our shores.

What makes America exceptional are the bonds that hold together the most diverse nation on Earth—the belief that our destiny is shared; that this country only works when we accept certain obligations to one another, and to future generations; that the freedom which so many Americans have fought for and died for comes with responsibilities as well as rights, and among those are love and charity and duty and patriotism. That's what makes America great.

I am hopeful tonight because I have seen this spirit at work in America. I've seen it in the family business whose owners would rather cut their own pay than lay off their neighbors, and in the workers who would rather cut back their hours than see a friend lose a job.

I've seen it in the soldiers who re-enlist after losing a limb, and in those SEALs who charged up the stairs into darkness and danger because they knew there was a buddy behind them, watching their back.

I've seen it on the shores of New Jersey and New York, where leaders from every party and level of

Chicago supporters of President Barack Obama cheer after networks project Obama as reelected.

government have swept aside their differences to help a community rebuild from the wreckage of a terrible storm.

And I saw it just the other day in Mentor, Ohio, where a father told the story of his eight-year-old daughter, whose long battle with leukemia nearly cost their family everything, had it not been for health care reform passing just a few months before the insurance company was about to stop paying for her care. I had an opportunity to not just talk to the father, but meet this incredible daughter of his. And when he spoke to the crowd, listening to that father's story, every parent in that room had tears in their eyes, because we knew that little girl could be our own. And I know that every American wants her future to be just as bright.

That's who we are. That's the country I'm so proud to lead as your president. And tonight, despite all the hardship we've been through, despite all the frustrations of Washington, I've never been more hopeful about our future. I have never been more hopeful about America. And I ask you to sustain that hope.

I'm not talking about blind optimism—the kind of hope that just ignores the enormity of the tasks ahead or the roadblocks that stand in our path. I'm not talking about the wishful idealism that allows us to just sit on the sidelines or shirk from a fight. I have always believed that hope is that stubborn thing inside us that insists, despite all the evidence to the contrary, that something better awaits us, so long as we have the courage to keep reaching, to keep working, to keep fighting.

America, I believe we can build on the progress we've made, and continue to fight for new jobs, and new opportunity, and new security for the middle class. I believe we can keep the promise of our

Below: President Barack Obama takes the stage to give his victory speech after winning the 2012 presidential election.

Opposite: Shauna Harry, left, and Alana Hearn celebrate Obama's victory by leaping in the air at New York State Democratic Headquarters following election day.

founding—the idea that if you're willing to work hard, it doesn't matter who you are, or where you come from, or what you look like, or where you love—it doesn't matter whether you're black or white, or Hispanic or Asian, or Native American, or young or old, or rich or poor, abled, disabled, gay, or straight—you can make it here in America if you're willing to try.

I believe we can seize this future together—because we are not as divided as our politics suggest; we're not as cynical as the pundits believe; we are greater than the sum of our individual ambitions; and we remain more than a collection of red states and blue states. We are, and forever will be, the United States of America. And together, with your help, and God's grace, we will continue our journey forward, and remind the world just why it is that we live in the greatest nation on Earth.

Thank you, America. God bless you. God bless these United States.

Below: President Obama making one of 10 calls made to U.S. military service members on Thanksgiving Day, 2011, to thank them for their service in Iraq and Afghanistan and wish them a Happy Thanksgiving.

Opposite: President Barack Obama looks out the Green Room window.

Obama's Plan for the Future: Domestic Policy

Since the first day of his first term, President Obama has pursued an ambitious program designed to encourage a thriving and resilient economy. There is no predicting what events, be they national disasters or other uncontrollable factors, the next four years will hold, or what adaptations will be needed to overcome the results. But with a balanced and flexible plan, the Obama administration intends to handle the unexpected while at the same time furthering its first-term goals.

In keeping with his vow to keep the public informed and involved, the Obama administration has published its domestic-policy agenda online as a series of "Policy Snapshots," which (with some adaptations) follow. On this framework are woven the details of a more complex plan—also freely available to the public at all times—to keep America safe, secure, and competitive, now and in the future.

Jobs Creation, Trade/Exports, and the Manufacturing Base

The rationale: Investing in education, clean energy, manufacturing, and infrastructure will help create jobs and restore middle-class security. Building an economy that will last means making things the world buys.

The basic plan:

- Reward companies that bring jobs back to America with lower taxes, and offset the revenue loss by eliminating tax incentives for companies that ship jobs overseas.

President Barack Obama jogs past boxes on his way to deliver remarks at a Small Business Administration event at the Metropolitan Archives in Hyattsville, Maryland.

- Jumpstart small-business hiring by cutting taxes for businesses that hire new workers or pay higher wages.
- Prepare workers with the skills and credentials employers need. Support programs that train workers for jobs in growing industries like high-tech manufacturing and information technology.
- Open new export markets, stay tough on trade enforcement to protect U.S. companies selling products overseas, and provide U.S. businesses the tools they need to export goods.
- Put construction workers back to work with good jobs—that can't be outsourced—building the tools and transportation network our businesses need to compete globally.
- Invest in a domestic clean-energy economy powered by sources like wind, solar, and clean coal. Renew successful bipartisan tax incentives that create American jobs and reduce our reliance on foreign oil (see the "Energy" section).
- Streamline government services by consolidating six agencies (the U.S. Department of Commerce's core business and trade functions, the Small Business Administration, the Office of the U.S. Trade Representative, the Export-Import Bank, the Overseas Private Investment Corporation, and the U.S. Trade and Development Agency) and several other programs into a single department focused on helping American businesses grow and export.

In support of this ambitious agenda, in May 2012 the president outlined a "job-creation to-do list" for Congress: reward American jobs, not outsourcing; expand refinancing for responsible homeowners; invest in tax credits for small-business jobs; invest in clean-energy manufacturing; and create a veterans' jobs corps.

People line the motorcade route as President Barack Obama makes his way to the Mount Holly Truck Manufacturing Plant in Charlotte, North Carolina, on March 7, 2012.

President Barack Obama tours the Automotive Training Facility and the General Motors Automotive Service Program at Northern Virginia Community College in Alexandria, Virginia.

Small Businesses

The rationale: Small businesses are the engines of job growth and innovation in America.

The basic plan:

- Keep taxes low for 97% of small businesses by extending tax credits that will expire in 2013.
- Jumpstart small-business hiring by cutting taxes for businesses that hire new workers or pay higher wages.
- Renew tax breaks that allow companies to immediately write off the total cost of certain purchases, like computers and machinery, to encourage investment.
- Ensure that in 2014, small business will be able to shop for affordable health insurance plans through state-based marketplaces, and be eligible for tax credits that cover up to 50% of the cost of providing health care for employees.
- Permanently eliminate capital gains taxes on certain small business stock held for more than five years to encourage investment that provides crucial funding for small businesses.

Middle-Class Tax Cuts

The rationale: America prospers when the middle class is secure, everyone does their fair share, and everyone plays by the same rules.

The basic plan:

- Keep taxes low for 98% of Americans and nearly every small business by preventing a $2,200 tax increase for the typical family of four on January 1, 2013.
- Ensure the wealthiest Americans do their fair share by paying at least the same tax rate as middle-class

President Barack Obama, with Professor Vladimir Bulovic, tours an alternative energy research laboratory at Massachusetts Institute of Technology in Cambridge, Massachusetts.

families so we can reduce the deficit in a balanced way while preserving investments in education, clean energy, manufacturing, and small businesses (see "On the Buffett Rule").

- Make the American Opportunity Tax Credit permanent to give more students a fair shot at an affordable higher education.
- Extend the expansions of the Child Tax Credit and the Earned Income Tax Credit to help hardworking families with children become a part of the middle class.

Financial Reform

The rationale: Everyone should play by the same rules, from Main Street to Wall Street.

The basic plan:

- Eliminate confusing financial forms by simplifying credit-card agreements and consolidating two complex mortgage disclosure forms into one plain-language document.
- Supervise and regulate previously unregulated financial-services providers, such as payday lenders, debt collectors, credit bureaus, and money-transmitting services.
- Impose a Financial Crisis Responsibility Fee on the largest financial institutions to compensate taxpayers for the extraordinary support they provided to stabilize the financial sector.
- Make Wall Street play by the same rules as Main Street. Continue implementing Wall Street reform to prevent practices that helped lead to the financial crisis.
- Crack down on fraud. Investigate large-scale financial fraud, and make the penalties for fraud *count* rather than being viewed by banks and financial firms as the price of doing business.

President Barack Obama talks with a patron at Reid's House Restaurant in Reidsville, N.C., during a lunch stop on the American Jobs Act bus tour.

Health Care

The rationale: The health-care law gives middle-class families the security of affordable coverage they deserve and protects every American from the worst insurance company abuses.

The basic plan:

- Establish new health-insurance marketplaces where people can compare premiums and benefits across plans. Require state-based exchanges to be in place by 2014 to help people shop for affordable insurance.

President Barack Obama and Jon Favreau, head speechwriter, edit a speech on health care.

President Barack Obama's signature on a wall in a health classroom at Southwest High School in Green Bay, Wisconsin, left there by request after attending a town hall meeting on health care at the school.

- Help families with the cost of health care. In 2014, 18 million middle-class people and families will get a tax cut averaging $4,000 to help cover the cost of care.
- Lower Medicare costs and close the donut hole. Seniors with traditional Medicare will save nearly $4,200 by 2021, and those with high prescription drug costs will save even more.

Energy

The rationale: Controlling our energy future through an "all-of-the-above" approach will create good middle-class jobs and reduce our reliance on foreign oil.

The basic plan:

- Take control of our energy future by expanding domestic oil and gas production to create 600,000 new jobs and using more renewable energy like wind and solar power.
- Invest in a domestic clean-energy economy powered by sources like wind, solar, and clean coal. Renew successful bipartisan tax incentives that create American jobs and reduce our reliance on foreign oil.
- Reduce building-energy use. Create jobs, save money, and cut pollution by improving energy efficiency in our nonresidential building space.
- Make more than 75% of our potential offshore oil and gas resources available for exploration and development, and permit clean-energy projects on public lands that will generate enough renewable energy to power 3 million homes.

President Barack Obama tours the DeSoto Next Generation Solar Energy Center with executives of FPL Groupin Arcadia, Florida.

Higher Education

The rationale: Education is critical to strengthening the middle class and preparing our young people with the skills they need to find good jobs and to compete in the global economy.

The basic plan:

- Make the American Opportunity Tax Credit permanent to give more of our hardworking students a fair shot at an affordable higher education and the skills they need to find good jobs.
- Rein in college costs by reforming student aid to colleges. Reward schools that set tuition prices responsibly. Schools that do the most to provide students with good long-term value should receive more money to help students attend than schools that don't.
- Provide better information about college costs. Develop tools that compare costs, graduation rates, and graduate earnings among schools to inform student decisions.
- Improve college quality and value through competition. Invest $1 billion in a competition to provide incentives for colleges to keep costs under control and graduate students on time.
- Prepare workers with the skills and credentials employers need. Support programs that train workers for jobs in growing industries like high-tech manufacturing and information technology.

Pre-K–12 Education

The rationale: Education is an economic imperative, and every child should have the opportunity to rise as far as their hard work and initiative will take them.

The basic plan:

- Reform K-12 education funding by encouraging states to adopt higher standards, and improving teaching and learning assessments.

First Lady Michelle Obama has lunch with students at Parklawn Elementary School in Alexandria, Virginia, to sample a healthy meal that meets the United States Department of Agriculture's new and improved nutrition standards for school lunches.

- Encourage innovation in education. Continue funding competitions that increase student success and prepare students for college and careers.
- Invest in the next generation of scientists and engineers. Improve science, technology, engineering, and math (STEM) education, and expand programs that expose kids to opportunities in those fields.
- Put a great teacher in every classroom. Attract, prepare, support, and reward effective teachers and school leaders, and reduce teacher shortages in STEM subject areas.

Above: First Lady Michelle Obama greets students following a flash mob dance at Alice Deal Middle School in Washington, D.C.

Below: President Barack Obama congratulates Google Science Fair winners, from left, Naomi Shah, Shree Bose, and Lauren Hodge in the Oval Office.

On the Buffett Rule

by Barack Obama

Speech delivered from the Eisenhower Executive Office Building, Washington, D.C., on April 11, 2012

THE PRESIDENT: Thank you. (Applause.) Everybody, please have a seat. Thank you. It is wonderful to see you. Lately, we've been talking about the fundamental choice that we face as a country. We can settle for an economy where a shrinking number of people do very, very well and everybody else is struggling to get by, or we can build an economy where we're rewarding hard work and responsibility—an economy where everybody has a fair shot, and everybody is doing their fair share, and everybody is playing by the same set of rules.

The people who have joined me here today are extremely successful. They've created jobs and opportunity for thousands of Americans. They're rightly proud of their success. They love the country that made their success possible, and most importantly, they want to make sure that the next generation, people coming up behind them, have the same opportunities that they had.

They understand, though, that for some time now, when compared to the middle class, they haven't been asked to do their fair share. And they are here because they believe there is something deeply wrong and irresponsible about that.

At a time when the share of national income flowing to the top 1 percent of people in this country has climbed to levels we haven't seen since the 1920s, these same folks are paying taxes at one of the lowest rates in 50 years. In fact, one in four millionaires pays a lower tax rate than millions of hardworking middle-class households. And while many millionaires do pay their fair share, some take advantage of loopholes and shelters that let them get away with paying no income taxes whatsoever—and that's all perfectly legal under the system that we currently have.

You've heard that my friend Warren Buffett pays a lower tax rate than his secretary—because he's the one who's been pointing that out and saying we should fix it. The executives who are with me here today, not just behind me but in the audience, agree with me. They agree with Warren—they should be fixed. They, in fact, have brought some of their own assistants to prove that same point—that it is just plain wrong that middle-class Americans pay a higher share of their income in taxes than some millionaires and billionaires.

Now, it's not that these folks are excited about the idea of paying more taxes. This thing I've always made clear. (Laughter.) I have yet to meet people who just love taxes. Nobody loves paying taxes. In a perfect world, none of us would have to pay any taxes. We'd have no deficits to pay down. And schools and bridges and roads and national defense and caring for our veterans would all happen magically.

We'd all have the money we need to make investments in the things that help us grow—investments, by the way, that have always been essential to the private sector's success, as well, not just—they're not just important in terms of the people that directly benefit from these programs, but historically, those investments that we've made in infrastructure, in education, in science, in technology, in transportation, that's part of what has made us an economic superpower.

And it would be nice if we didn't have to pay for them, but this is the real world that we live in. We have real choices and real consequences. Right now, we've got significant deficits that are going to have to be closed. Right now, we have significant needs if we want to continue to grow this economy and compete in this 21st-century, hyper-competitive, technologically-integrated economy. That means we can't afford to keep spending more money on tax cuts for wealthy Americans who don't need them and weren't even asking for them. And it's time we did something about it.

Now, I want to emphasize, this is not simply an issue of redistributing wealth. That's what you'll hear from those who object to a tax plan that is fair. This is not just about fairness. This is also about growth. This is also about being able to make the investments we need to succeed. And it's about we as a country being willing to pay for those investments and closing our deficits. That's what this is about.

Now, next week, members of Congress are going to have a chance to vote on what we call the Buffett

Rule. And it's simple: If you make more money—more than $1 million a year, not if you have $1 million, but if you make more than $1 million a year, you should pay at least the same percentage of your income in taxes as middle-class families do. If on the other hand, you make less than $250,000 a year—like 98 percent of American families do—your taxes shouldn't go up.

That's all there is to it. That's pretty sensible. Most Americans agree with me, so do most millionaires. One survey found that two-thirds of millionaires support this idea. So do nearly half of all Republicans across America.

So we just need some of the Republican politicians here in Washington to get on board with where the country is. I know that some prefer to run around using the same reflexive, false claims about wanting to raise people's taxes. What they won't tell you is the truth—that I've cut taxes for middle-class families each year that I've been in office. I've cut taxes for small business owners not once or twice, but 17 times.

As I said, for most of the folks in this room, taxes are lower than they've been, or as low as they've been, in 50 years. There are others who are saying, well, this is just a gimmick. Just taxing millionaires and billionaires, just imposing the Buffett Rule won't do enough to close the deficit. Well, I agree. That's not all we have to do to close the deficit. But the notion that it doesn't solve the entire problem doesn't mean that we shouldn't do it at all.

There are enough excuses for inaction in Washington. We certainly don't need more excuses. I'd just point out that the Buffett Rule is something that will get us moving in the right direction towards fairness, towards economic growth. It will help us close

President Barack Obama meets with Warren Buffett, the chairman of Berkshire Hathaway, in the Oval Office, on July 18, 2011.

our deficit and it's a lot more specific than anything that the other side has proposed so far. And if Republicans in Congress were truly concerned with deficits and debt, then I'm assuming they wouldn't have just proposed to spend an additional $4.6 trillion on lower tax rates, including an average tax cut of at least $150,000 for every millionaire in America.

They want to go in the opposite direction. They want to double down on some of the inequities that already exist in the tax code. If we're going to keep giving somebody like me or some of the people in this room tax breaks that we don't need and we can't afford, then one of two things happens: Either you've got to borrow more money to pay down a deeper deficit, or you've got to demand deeper sacrifices from the middle class, and you've got to cut investments that help us grow as an economy.

You've got to tell seniors to pay a little bit more for their Medicare. You've got to tell the college student, we're going to have to charge you higher interest rates on your student loan or you're just going to get smaller student loans. You're going to have to tell that working family that's scraping by that they're going to have to do more because the wealthiest of Americans are doing less.

That's not right. The middle class has seen enough of its security erode over the past few decades that we shouldn't let that happen. And we're not going to stop investing in the things that create real and lasting growth in this country just so folks like me can get an additional tax cut. We're not going to stop building first-class schools and making sure that they've got science labs in them. We're not going to fail to make investments in basic science and research that could cure diseases that harm people, or create the new technology that ends up creating entire jobs and industries that we haven't seen before. In America, prosperity has never just trickled down from a wealthy few. Prosperity has always been built from the bottom up and from the heart of the middle class outward. And so it's time for Congress to stand up for the middle class and make our tax system fairer by passing this Buffett Rule.

Let me just close by saying this. I'm not the first President to call for this idea that everybody has got to do their fair share. Some years ago, one of my predecessors traveled across the country pushing for the same concept. He gave a speech where he talked about a letter he had received from a wealthy executive who paid lower tax rates than his secretary, and wanted to come to Washington and tell Congress why that was wrong. So this President gave another speech where he said it was "crazy"—that's a quote—that certain tax loopholes make it possible for multimillionaires to pay nothing, while a bus driver was paying 10 percent of his salary. That wild-eyed, socialist, tax-hiking class warrior was Ronald Reagan.

He thought that, in America, the wealthiest should pay their fair share, and he said so. I know that position might disqualify him from the Republican primaries these days—(laughter)—but what Ronald Reagan was calling for then is the same thing that we're calling for now: a return to basic fairness and responsibility; everybody doing their part. And if it will help convince folks in Congress to make the right choice, we could call it the Reagan Rule instead of the Buffett Rule.

But the choice is clear. This vote is coming up. I'm asking every American who agrees with me to call your member of Congress, or write them an email, tweet them. Tell them to stop giving tax breaks to the wealthiest Americans who don't need them and aren't asking for them. Tell them to start asking everybody to do their fair share and play by the same rules, so that every American who's willing to work hard has a chance at similar success, so that we're making the investments that help this economy grow, so that we're able to bring down our deficits in a fair and balanced and sensible way. Tell them to pass the Buffett Rule.

I'm going to keep on making this case across the country because I believe that this rule is consistent with those principles and those values that have helped make us this remarkable place where everybody has opportunity.

Now, each of us is only here because somebody, somewhere, felt responsibility not only for themselves, but also for their community and for their country. They felt a responsibility to us, to future generations. And now it's our turn to be similarly responsible. Now it's our turn to preserve that American Dream for future generations.

So I want to thank those of you who are here with me today. I want to thank everybody who is in the audience. And I want to appeal to the American people: Let's make sure that we keep the pressure on Congress to do the right thing.

Thank you very much, everybody. (Applause.)

Obama's Plan for the Future: Foreign Policy

The administration's foreign policy is underpinned by a "whole-of-government" approach, under which integrating and coordinating all parts of government—not just the military, which must nonetheless remain superior—will strengthen the nation as a whole. This means that defense, diplomacy, economic capacity, development, homeland security, intelligence, strategic communications, the American citizenry, and the private sector must no longer exist as islands, but must share their information and strengths for the greater good of all.

The "National Security Strategy" of the Obama administration, published in May 2010, involves "adapt[ing] to advance our interests and sustain our leadership." American interests are defined as

- the *security* of the United States, its citizens, and U.S. allies and partners,
- a strong, innovative, and growing U.S. economy in an open international economic system that promotes opportunity and *prosperity,*
- respect for universal *values* at home and around the world, and
- an *international order,* advanced by U.S. leadership, that promotes peace, security, and opportunity through stronger cooperation to meet global challenges.

The following outlines the Obama strategy for advancing America's interests in an increasingly volatile and competitive world.

Security

"We will not apologize for our way of life, nor will we waver in its defense. And for those who seek to advance their aims by inducing terror and slaughtering innocents, we say to you now that our spirit is stronger and cannot

President Obama and Secretary of State Hillary Rodham Clinton participate in a round table meeting of the North Atlantic Council during a NATO summit in Lisbon in November 2010.

be broken—you cannot outlast us, and we will defeat you."—President Barack Obama, Inaugural Address, January 20, 2009

Strengthen security and resilience at home. We are pursuing a strategy capable of meeting the full range of threats and hazards to our communities, including terrorism, natural disasters, large-scale cyber attacks, and pandemics. We must not only prevent these events, we must enhance our ability to adapt to changing conditions and prepare for, withstand, and rapidly recover from disruption. This involves enhancing domestic security, effectively managing emergencies, empowering communities to counter radicalization, improving resilience through increased public-private partnerships, and engaging with communities and citizens.

Disrupt, dismantle, and defeat Al Qaeda and its violent extremist affiliates in Afghanistan, Pakistan, and around the world. Success requires a broad, sustained, and integrated campaign that judiciously applies every tool of American power—both military and civilian—as well as the concerted efforts of like-minded states and multilateral institutions. We must prevent attacks on and in the homeland; strengthen aviation security; deny terrorists weapons of mass destruction; deny Al Qaeda the ability to threaten the American people and our allies, partners, and interests; prevent the spread of Al Qaeda in Afghanistan and Pakistan; deny safe havens and strengthen at-risk states; deliver swift and sure justice; resist fear and overreaction; and contrast Al Qaeda's intent to destroy with our own constructive vision.

Reverse the spread of nuclear and biological weapons and secure nuclear materials. The American people face no greater or more urgent danger than a terrorist attack with a nuclear weapon. To ensure our security, we must pursue the goal of a world without nuclear weapons, strengthen the nuclear non-proliferation treaty, and present a clear choice to Iran and North Korea. We must also secure vulnerable nuclear weapons and material, support peaceful nuclear energy, and counter biological threats.

Advance peace, security, and opportunity in the greater Middle East. Protecting our interests in the Middle East involves broad cooperation on a wide range of issues with our close friend, Israel, and an unshakable commitment to its security; the achievement of the Palestinian people's legitimate aspirations for statehood, opportunity, and the realization of their extraordinary potential; the unity and security of Iraq and the fostering of its democracy and reintegration into the region; the transformation of Iranian policy away from its pursuit of nuclear weapons, support for terrorism, and threats against its neighbors; nuclear nonproliferation; and counterterrorism cooperation, access to energy, and integration of the region into global markets.

In 2009, President Obama welcomed China's President Hu Jintao for the G-20 summit dinner in Pittsburgh.

Invest in the capacity of strong and capable partners. Where governments are incapable of meeting their citizens' basic needs and fulfilling their responsibilities to provide security within their borders, the consequences are often global and may directly threaten the American people. To advance our common security, we must address the underlying political and economic deficits that foster instability, enable radicalization and extremism, and ultimately undermine the ability of governments to manage threats within their borders and to be our partners in addressing common challenges. To invest in the capacity of strong and capable partners, we must work hard to foster security and reconstruction in the aftermath of conflict, to pursue sustainable and responsible security systems in at-risk states, and to prevent the emergence of conflict.

Secure cyberspace. Cybersecurity threats represent one of the most serious national security, public safety, and economic challenges we face as a nation. Our digital infrastructure is a strategic national asset, and protecting it—while safeguarding privacy and civil liberties—is a national security priority. We will deter, prevent, detect, defend against, and quickly recover from cyber intrusions and attacks by investing in people and technology, and by strengthening partnerships among all levels of government and the private sector, both nationally and internationally.

A note on the use of force: Before entering war, we will exhaust other options whenever we can, and carefully weigh the costs and risks of action against the costs and risks of inaction. When force is necessary, its use will reflect our values and strengthen our legitimacy, and we will seek broad international support, working with such institutions as NATO and the U.N. Security Council. We must reserve the right to act unilaterally if necessary to defend our nation and our interests, yet we will also seek to adhere to standards that govern the use of force. Doing so strengthens those who act in line with international standards, while isolating and weakening those who do not. We will also outline a clear mandate and specific objectives and thoroughly consider the consequences—intended and unintended—of our actions. And the United States will take care when sending the men and women of our Armed Forces into harm's way to ensure they have the leadership, training, and equipment they require to accomplish their mission.

President Barack Obama talks with Ambassador Ryan Crocker aboard Marine One en route to the Afghan Presidential Palace in Kabul, Afghanistan on May 1, 2012.

President Barack Obama leading a moment of silence at a meeting of the Nuclear Security Summit in Washington, D.C., on April 13, 2010, in memory of the lives lost when the plane carrying President Lech Kaczynski of Poland crashed in Russia.

President Barack Obama speaking at a meeting of the Nuclear Security Summit in Washington, D.C., on April 12, 2010.

Prosperity

"The answers to our problems don't lie beyond our reach. They exist in our laboratories and universities; in our fields and our factories; in the imaginations of our entrepreneurs and the pride of the hardest-working people on Earth. Those qualities that have made America the greatest force of progress and prosperity in human history we still possess in ample measure. What is required now is for this country to pull together, confront boldly the challenges we face, and take responsibility for our future once more."—President Barack Obama, Address to Joint Session of Congress, February 24, 2009

Strengthen education and human capital. In a global economy of vastly increased mobility and interdependence, our own prosperity and leadership depend increasingly on our ability to provide our citizens with the education that they need to succeed, while attracting the premier human capital for our workforce. We must ensure that the most innovative ideas take root in America, while providing our people with the skills that they need to compete. That means we must improve education at all levels; invest in science, technology, engineering, and math education (STEM); increase international education and exchange; and pursue comprehensive immigration reform.

Enhance science, technology, and innovation. Reaffirming America's role as the global engine of scientific discovery and technological innovation has never been more critical. Challenges like climate change, pandemic disease, and resource scarcity demand new innovation. Meanwhile, the nation that leads the world in building a clean energy economy will enjoy a substantial economic and security advantage. This will involve transforming our energy economy; investing in research; expanding international science partnerships; employing technology to protect our nation; and leveraging and expanding our space capabilities.

Achieve balanced and sustainable growth. Balanced and sustainable growth, at home and throughout the global economy, drives the momentum of the U.S. economy and underpins our prosperity. A steadily growing global economy means an expanding market for exports of our goods and services. To promote prosperity for all Americans, we will need to prevent renewed instability in the global economy; save more and export more; shift to greater domestic demand abroad; open foreign markets to our products and services; build cooperation with our international partners; and deter threats to the international financial system.

Accelerate sustainable development. The growth of emerging economies in recent decades has lifted people out of poverty and forged a more

The National Medal of Science, as well as Medal of Technology and Innovation, medals prior to presentation.

interconnected and vibrant global economy. But while some countries are growing, many are mired in insecurity, constrained by poor governance, or overly dependent upon commodity prices. We are pursuing a range of specific initiatives in areas such as food security and global health that will be essential to the future security and prosperity of nations and peoples around the globe: increasing investments in development, investing in the foundations of long-term development, and exercising leadership in the provision of global public goods.

Spend taxpayers' dollars wisely. The U.S. government has an obligation to make the best use of taxpayer money, and our ability to achieve long-term goals depends upon our fiscal responsibility. Our national security goals can be reached only if we make hard choices and work with international partners to share burdens. This means reducing the deficit; reforming acquisition and contracting processes to eliminate wasteful spending, duplicative programs, and contracts with poor oversight; and increasing transparency.

Values

"We uphold our most cherished values not only because doing so is right, but because it strengthens our country and keeps us safe. Time and again, our values have been our best national security asset—in war and peace, in times of ease, and in eras of upheaval. Fidelity to our values is the reason why the United States of America grew from a small string of colonies under the writ of an empire to the strongest nation in the world."—President Barack Obama, National Archives, May 21, 2009

Strengthen the power of our example. This means prohibiting torture without exception or equivocation; determining legal aspects of countering terrorism; balancing the imperatives of secrecy and transparency; protecting civil liberties, privacy, and oversight; upholding the rule of law; and drawing strength from diversity.

Promote democracy and human rights abroad. We will achieve this by ensuring that new and fragile democracies deliver tangible improvements for their

A model energy-efficient greenhouse operated by Metrolina Greenhouses.

citizens; practicing principled engagement with non-democratic regimes; recognizing the legitimacy of all peaceful democratic movements; supporting the rights of women and girls; strengthening international norms against corruption; building a broader coalition of actors to advance universal values; and marshalling new technologies and promoting the right to access information.

Promote dignity by meeting basic needs. We will continue to promote the dignity that comes through development efforts such as pursuing a comprehensive global health strategy, promoting food security, and leading efforts to address humanitarian crises.

International Order

"As President of the United States, I will work tirelessly to protect America's security and to advance our interests. But no one nation can meet the challenges of the 21st century on its own, nor dictate its terms to the world. That is why America seeks an international system that lets nations pursue their interests peacefully, especially when those interests diverge; a system where the universal rights of human beings are respected, and violations of those rights are opposed; a system where we hold ourselves to the same standards that we apply to other nations, with clear rights and responsibilities for all."—President Barack Obama, Moscow, Russia, July 7, 2009

Ensure strong alliances. The foundation of U.S., regional, and global security will remain America's relations with our allies, and our commitment to their security is unshakable. These relationships are indispensable for U.S. interests and national security objectives, and are fundamental to our collective security. Alliances are force multipliers: through multinational cooperation and coordination, the sum of our actions is always greater than if we act alone. We will continue to maintain the capacity to defend our allies against old and new threats. We will also continue to closely consult with our allies as well as newly emerging partners and organizations so that we revitalize and expand our cooperation to achieve common objectives. And we will continue to mutually benefit from the collective security provided by strong alliances.

Build cooperation with other 21st-century centers of influence. The United States is part of a dynamic international environment, in which different nations are exerting greater influence, and advancing our interests will require expanding spheres of cooperation around the word. Certain bilateral relationships—such as U.S. relations with China, India, and Russia—will be critical to building broader cooperation on areas of mutual interest. And emerging powers in every region of the world are increasingly asserting themselves, raising partnership opportunities for the United States.

Strengthen institutions and mechanisms for cooperation. Our ability to advance peace, security, and opportunity will turn on our ability to strengthen both our national and our multilateral capabilities. To solve problems, we will pursue modes of cooperation that reflect evolving distributions of power and responsibility. We need to assist existing institutions to perform effectively. When they come up short, we must seek meaningful changes and develop alternative mechanisms.

Sustain broad cooperation on key global challenges. Many of today's challenges cannot be solved by one nation or even a group of nations. The test of our international order, therefore, will be its ability to facilitate the broad and effective global cooperation necessary to meet 21st-century challenges. In addition to violent extremism, nuclear proliferation, and promotion of global prosperity, other key challenges requiring broad global cooperation include climate change, peacekeeping and armed conflict, pandemics and infectious disease, transnational criminal threats and threats to governance, security of the global commons, and security of our Arctic interests.

II.
OUR PRESIDENTS

JAMES MONROE.
JOHN Q. ADAMS.
GEORGE WASHINGTON
ANDREW JACKSON.
MARTIN VAN BUREN
JAMES K. POLK.
ULYSSES S. GRANT.
RUTHERFORD B. HAYES.
ANDREW JOHNSON.
ABRAHAM LINCOLN.
INDIANA
MICHIGAN
ILLINOIS
NEW YORK
VIRGINIA
PENNSYLVANIA
N. HAMPSHIRE
RHODE ISLAND
N. CAROLINA
MAINE
S. CAROLINA
DELAWARE
TENNESSEE
KANSAS
NEBRASKA
TEXAS
IOWA
MINNESOTA
WISCONSIN
NEVADA
COLORADO

1st President (1789–1797)

GEORGE WASHINGTON

February 22, 1732–December 14, 1799

Political party: None

Vice president: John Adams, 1789 to 1797

First Lady and family: Married widow Martha Dandridge Custis in 1759. The couple raised two children by Martha's first marriage: John "Jack" Parke Custis and Martha "Patsy" Custis.

Especially remembered for: Leadership during the Revolutionary War. Defining the duties of the office of president. "The Father of Our Country." His sterling character, which served as a shining example of integrity. Most popular president in terms of the number of different coins, tokens, medals, and currency notes with his portrait. One of four presidents honored on Mount Rushmore.

The Earlier Life of George Washington

George Washington, our first and most famous president, was born in Virginia in 1732 to a well-to-do family. He learned surveying, and then served with British forces in the French and Indian War. During this time, and continuing into the early 1770s, there was a rising sentiment in the American colonies that England was exploiting their resources. On March 5, 1770, British soldiers confronted civilian demonstrators in Boston and killed five of them. This event, known as the Boston Massacre, was illustrated on a popular print by patriot, silversmith, and engraver Paul Revere. On the other side of the Atlantic, the British called the event the Boston Riot, implying that it necessarily had to be quelled.

The fires of discontent grew hotter, and in 1775 the Battle of Lexington and Concord pitted American militiamen against British soldiers. The Revolutionary War had begun. The Continental Congress, meeting in Philadelphia, selected George Washington as commander in chief of the Continental Army. Despite almost overwhelming odds at the outset, he and his men persevered. His forcing of the British to evacuate Boston, the privations of winter camp in Valley Forge, the crossing of the icy Delaware River, and other difficulties and triumphs he faced became part of history. In 1781, with the aid of French allies and the assistance of the Marquis de Lafayette, he forced the surrender of British general Lord Charles Cornwallis at Yorktown. The actions and accomplishments of Washington in the Revolutionary War could fill a large book.

His home, Mount Vernon, was an estate on the banks of the Potomac River near what would later become the District of Columbia. He hoped to return there after the war and enjoy plantation life. Today, Mount Vernon is a National Historic Site.

Opposite: The so-called Lansdowne portrait of George Washington was painted by Gilbert Stuart in 1796. Washington is shown renouncing a third term as president. The "constrained" expression, said Stuart, was caused by the 64-year-old president's new false teeth.

Opposite: Another portrait of Washington by Gilbert Stuart; this painting dates from 1795. Above: Martha Washington, the first First Lady of the United States.

Washington's Presidency

Washington was chairman of the Constitutional Convention in 1787 and 1788. After the ratification of the Constitution, the Electoral College named him as our first president. It was his task and challenge to develop the first cabinet, to work with Congress and the Supreme Court, and to establish procedures for the presidency. At the time, the seat of the federal government was in New York City. His first State of the Union Address took place on January 9, 1790.

There were many diverse factions as the new federal government sought to define itself. It was viewed by some as a glorious experiment, with no model anywhere else in the world. The rights and privileges of states were delineated, refined, and adjusted, and plans were made for other aspects. Prior to the Revolution, the various British colonies had acted independently of each other. There was no connection between, for example, New York and Pennsylvania, or South Carolina and Virginia. Each state had its own laws, monetary regulations, and commercial procedures. The idea of surrendering anything to a central government became a political focal point. States' rights, as they were called, would continue to be a hot political issue until the Civil War broke out in the early 1860s.

Washington endorsed the plans of Alexander Hamilton for the federal government to pay off debts incurred by the states and also the nation. Vast quantities of Continental currency had been issued—paper notes of face value up to $80—which had become nearly worthless. It took $720 in such bills to buy what $10 in silver or gold coins could buy. Hamilton also proposed to create a national bank (in keeping with the practice in certain other countries) and to lay the groundwork for a system of taxation. Thomas Jefferson opposed much of this. However, Jefferson joined the Washington administration and became important in financial and other matters.

In 1792, George Washington was elected for a second term. On September 18, 1793, he laid the first foundation stone for the United States Capitol building in what was to be called Federal City, in the District of Columbia, carved out of Maryland and Washington not far from his Mount Vernon estate.

In 1794 the Whiskey Rebellion reached its climax in western Pennsylvania when more than 500 armed men attacked the home of tax inspector John Neville to protest a federal tax on whiskey. At the time, liquor was both a medium of exchange and a store of value, as corn distilled into whiskey could be more easily shipped, stored, and traded than grain. Federal troops were called in to quell the uprising, the first test of a government power to enforce a law enacted by Congress. On March 22, 1794, Congress forbade the states to engage in slave trade with foreign nations. However, the law was widely ignored, and ships continued to bring unfortunate souls from Africa to ports in the southern United States, where

United States and Great Britain. Some provisions of this treaty were widely criticized in the United States, including allowing British to stop American vessels on the high seas and take as prisoners any British citizens. The treaty was opposed by Thomas Jefferson and his followers but set the plan for peace in ensuing years, a necessary condition as the different elements of the American government were put in place.

President Washington's famous farewell address, still remembered today, warned the nation against participation in foreign wars, sectionalism, and divisive influences, and reliance on political party programs—in a phrase, to "avoid entangling alliances."

they were bought and sold in markets, often at public auction.

When the French Revolution was followed by war between England and France, Washington ignored the recommendations of the secretary of state, Thomas Jefferson, and the secretary of the Treasury, Alexander Hamilton, and insisted upon a neutral stance. On February 29, 1796, Jay's Treaty took effect, settling certain disputes between the

Opposite: This 1776 portrait of Washington by Charles Willson Peale was commissioned as a reward to the military leader for liberating Boston from the British in that year. Above, top and left: Mount Vernon, Washington's plantation home in Virginia.

Washington's Later Life

In 1797, when John Adams took office as president, Washington went back to Mount Vernon to retire. He and Martha envisioned enjoying the ensuing years in comfort, in an area that he had known since childhood. He received visitors and contemplated with satisfaction the success of the new American government. In December 1799, he took chill while riding, became ill, and was confined to bed. Despite—or because of—the application of leeches (to remove "bad blood"), he weakened, and on December 14 he passed away, leaving Martha a widow for a second time.

The nation went into mourning, and within the next two weeks, as word spread, memorial parades were held, sermons were preached, and other recognitions given, including the distribution of a medal with the sentimental inscription HE IS IN GLORY, THE WORLD IN TEARS.

Mason Locke Weems, an Episcopal clergyman, published *The Life and Memorable Actions of George Washington,* which went into multiple editions, the fifth of which (published in 1806) included the fanciful tale of young Washington, the mysteriously cut-down cherry tree, and the statement "Father, I cannot tell a lie." Much of Weems's fiction passed into popular history. Admiration for Washington continued into later years, , including his being remembered as the Father of Our Country. Today, his image is seen on coins and paper money and in many other places, including on the Purple Heart award.

THE AMERICAN SCENE

On May 29, 1790, Rhode Island ratified the Constitution, being the last of the original 13 colonies to do so. In the same year the Supreme Court of the United States met for the first time, and the U.S. patent system was established. Vermont was admitted as the 14th state on March 4, 1791. The Bill of Rights (the first 10 amendments to the Constitution) was ratified on December 15 of the same year.

The Coinage Act of April 2, 1792, set in motion the establishment of the Philadelphia Mint and, eventually, the establishment of mints in other locations (beginning in 1838). Up to this time, coins of foreign countries were the only ones used in American commerce, especially those of Europe, Mexico, Central America, and South America.

Kentucky became the 15th state on June 15 of the same year. Also in 1792, the new state provided money to upgrade the Wilderness Road, which had been carved out in 1775 by pioneer explorer Daniel Boone; this route made it possible for future settlers to move west. Tennessee, earlier a part of North Carolina, was admitted to the Union as the 16th state in 1796.

Opposite: Washington's likeness on Mount Rushmore. The first of the four presidential likenesses to be completed, it was dedicated on July 4, 1934.

NOTABLE SAYINGS

"To be prepared for war is the most effective means of preserving peace." (From the first State of the Union address, on January 8, 1790)

"Few men have virtue to withstand the highest bidder."

"Associate with men of good quality if you esteem your own reputation, for it is better to be alone than in bad company."

"It is better to offer no excuse than a bad one."

2nd President (1797–1801)

JOHN ADAMS

October 30, 1735–July 4, 1826

Political party: Federalist

Vice president: Thomas Jefferson

First Lady and family: Married Abigail Smith on October 25, 1764. The couple had five surviving children: Abigail Amelia Adams (1765–1813); John Quincy Adams (who became president; 1767–1848); Susanna Adams (1768–1770); Charles Adams (1770–1800); and Thomas Boylston Adams (1772–1832). A stillborn daughter, Elizabeth, was born and died in 1777.

Especially remembered for: First president to compete in a national election. The XYZ Affair.

The Life and Presidency of John Adams

John Adams was born in what is now Quincy, Massachusetts, son of John and Susanna Boylston Adams. He studied law and graduated from Harvard in 1755. Inspired by patriotic fervor, he served in the Continental Congress from 1774 to 1778. He was commissioner to France in 1778, minister to the Netherlands in 1780, and chief negotiator in the 1783 peace treaty that ended the American Revolution. Later, he was minister to England from 1785 to 1788 and vice president of the United States under George Washington from 1789 to 1797.

In the 1796 election, his rival, Thomas Jefferson, came within three Electoral College votes of being named president. Due to a flaw in the Constitution (later corrected), the loser became his vice president, creating much friction.

When Adams became president, the war between the French and British was causing great difficulties for the United States on the high seas and sparking intense differences among political factions within America. Adams sent three commissioners to France to try to quiet matters, but in spring 1798 it was learned that French foreign minister Charles de Talleyrand and the Directory refused to negotiate unless the United States paid a bribe. Adams reported the dire matter to Congress. Correspondence was made public, in which the Frenchmen seeking bribes were named only as "X," "Y," and "Z." The XYZ Affair became the cause of the day, and Adams's stance against the extortion made him a popular hero. This gave rise to a slogan first used by Robert Goodloe Harper in a toast at a banquet on June 18, 1798: "Millions for defense, but not one cent for tribute."

In 1798, over the objections of vice president Thomas Jefferson, the first of four pieces of legislation known collectively as the Alien and Sedition

Opposite: This portrait of John Adams was painted circa 1792 or 1793 by John Trumbull, who would go on to create the famous painting *The Declaration of Independence.*

Act was adopted, amending the Naturalization Act of 1795 with a new requirement of 14 years of residence in America and an oath of allegiance five years before citizenship. The most offensive provision allowed for the arrest and imprisonment of anyone who attempted to speak or publish any false statement about the government, Congress, or the president. Much of this was sparked by resentment against the French government and the Federalist Party's fear that the opposing Democratic Republican Party was increasing in power. Ultimately, the Alien and Sedition Act resulted in the dissolution of the Federalist Party.

In the summer of 1800, the capital of the United States was moved to Washington, D.C., with 123 federal clerks making the transfer; previously, Congress had met in various locations, most recently spending 10 years in Philadelphia. Congressmen held their first session in Washington, D.C., on November 17, 1800. President Adams had moved into the White House on November 1, 1800, just before the next presidential election. In a letter to his wife, he stated, "I pray Heaven to bestow the best of Blessings on this House and all that shall hereafter inhabit it. May none but honest and wise men ever rule under this roof." His new residence had no plumbing: water needed to be carried from five blocks away.

By the time of the 1800 election, his Federalist Party was on the ropes, while the opposing Republicans were united in their stance. President Adams ran against Jefferson, but lost in a contest decided by the Electoral College. After his presidency, Adams retired to his farm in Quincy, Massachusetts. He died the same day as his old political rival, Thomas Jefferson: the fourth of July, 1826.

Below: A commemorative pottery pitcher depicts President Adams with figures representing Prosperity, Liberty, and Justice. Opposite: Adams's birthplace in Quincy, Massachusetts, is now part of the Adams National Historical Park.

THE AMERICAN SCENE

In 1797, the City of Brotherly Love experienced an epidemic of yellow fever. Mosquitoes carrying the disease were the cause; doctors didn't realize this at the time, however. Those citizens who could afford to flee to the countryside did so during the warm months, in order to avoid the fever.

The Library of Congress was established in 1800 with a $5,000 appropriation to purchase 990 books.

The federal census of 1800 showed that 2,464 free residents and 623 slaves lived in Washington. Slave auctions were held regularly in the nation's capital. Nationwide, there were 5,308,483 citizens, including 896,849 slaves.

Indiana Territory was carved out of the Northwest Territory on May 7, 1800. The Louisiana Territory, comprising much of what would later become the central part of the United States, which had been ceded to Spain by the Treaty of Paris in 1783, was returned to France on October 1, 1800, under a secret agreement. France agreed not to transfer the territory to any country other than back to Spain if the matter should come up.

NOTABLE SAYINGS

"Old minds are like old horses, you must exercise them if you want to keep them in working order."

"Facts are stubborn things."

3rd President (1801–1809)

THOMAS JEFFERSON

April 13, 1743–July 4, 1826

Especially remembered for: Drafting the Declaration of Independence. Work on finance during the Washington administration. The Louisiana Purchase of 1803, which more than doubled the size of the United States. His Embargo Act of 1807, which was widely considered to be a failure. His design for his home (Monticello) and other buildings considered to be high examples of architecture. Nicknames: "Man of the People," "Sage of Monticello." One of four presidents honored on Mount Rushmore. The Jefferson Memorial is a prime attraction today in Washington, D.C.

Political party: Democrat-Republican

Vice president: Aaron Burr, 1801 to 1805; George Clinton, 1805 to 1809

First Lady and family: Married 22-year-old widow Martha Wayles Skelton on January 1, 1772. The couple had six children: Martha Washington Jefferson (called "Patsy"; 1772–1836); Jane Randolph Jefferson (1774–1775); an unnamed infant son (1777); Mary Jefferson (called "Polly"; 1778–1804); Lucy Elizabeth Jefferson (who died in infancy); and Lucy Elizabeth Jefferson (the second daughter with that name; 1782–1785). Mrs. Jefferson died in 1782. There was no spousal First Lady in the Jefferson White House, although his daughter, Patsy—by then Mrs. Thomas Mann Randolph—stayed there for protracted periods and helped with entertaining. She gave birth to a son there. Jefferson formed an intimate relationship with one of his slaves who was a half-sister of his wife, Sarah ("Sally") Hemings, who sometimes traveled with him and became the mother of six of his children.

The Early Life of Thomas Jefferson

Thomas Jefferson was born in Shadwell, Virginia, to a prosperous family. His father, Peter Jefferson, owned a plantation of 5,000 acres, which eventually passed to his son. His mother, Jane Randolph Jefferson, was well known in society. Thomas graduated from the College of William and Mary in 1762, and afterward studied law. Of a literary turn of mind, Jefferson read widely and built a memorable library (later to become a part of the Library of Congress).

Jefferson was talented as a writer, less so as an orator. Most of his contributions as member of the Virginia House of Burgesses and the Continental Congress were letters and documents, including many with astute recommendations of policy. In 1776 he drafted the Declaration of Independence. After the Revolutionary War he was governor of

Opposite: This portrait of Thomas Jefferson was painted by Rembrandt Peale in 1800, the year he was elected president. The so-called Revolution of 1800 saw Jefferson defeat then-president John Adams and began what would be a generation of Democratic-Republican Party rule.

Virginia and, later, minister to France. In 1786 his draft of an act allowing religious freedom was signed into law. His sympathy for the French Revolution led him into conflict with Alexander Hamilton when Jefferson was the first secretary of state in Washington's cabinet, a post he resigned in 1793. In 1796 Jefferson ran for president, but lost by three Electoral College votes to John Adams. Due to a flaw in the Constitution (later corrected), Jefferson as runner up became vice president.

In the November 1800 presidential election, Democratic-Republican Thomas Jefferson won 73 Electoral College votes, as did Aaron Burr, followed by 65 for the president, John Adams, and 64 for Charles Pinckney. The House of Representatives broke the tie between Jefferson and Burr, choosing Jefferson as president. Once again the Constitution provided for the runner-up to be vice president. Burr, who took that secondary office, never forgave Hamilton.

The Jefferson Administration and Later Years

Jefferson took the oath of office on March 4, 1801. He was sworn in by chief justice John Marshall at the new capitol building in the Federal City, now named Washington, D.C. To American citizens, the president promised "peace, commerce and honest friendship with all nations—and tangling alliances with none." Jefferson opposed a strong centralized government and advocated the rights of states for most matters, bringing decisions closer to the people.

By this time, earlier political conflict with France had ceased, but there were new problems to face. In 1801 the United States entered a state of war—in this case undeclared—when the pasha of Tripoli ordered his soldiers to cut down the American flag after the United States refused to pay tribute to Barbary Coast pirates who were making depredations in the Mediterranean Sea. Several years later, on February 16, 1804, U.S. troops led by Lt. Stephen Decatur sneaked aboard the captured American ship *Philadelphia* in Tripoli harbor, attacked the guards, and set the ship afire before rowing away to safety. In 1805, the U.S. consul in Tunis assembled a ragtag army in Egypt, which crossed 600 miles of desert to attack Tripoli from the rear. The phrase "to the shores of Tripoli" in the "Marines' Hymn" refers to this conflict.

The United States more than doubled in size under Jefferson's Louisiana Purchase in 1803, acquiring essentially the American Midwest and most of the Mississippi River basin, including the important seaport of New Orleans. This was probably the most significant accomplishment of his time in office. During his administration Jefferson also reduced the federal debt by a third and made many internal improvements.

On December 5, 1804, Thomas Jefferson was reelected president, and George Clinton, the first governor of New York, was elected vice president. The election was the first to offer separate ballots for each office. Seeking to keep American vessels from depredations during the Napoleonic Wars between England and France, Jefferson signed the Embargo Act in 1807. This proved to be a disaster for American commerce and precipitated many difficulties.

In John Trumbull's famous painting *The Declaration of Independence,* Jefferson and the other members of the so-called Committee of Five present their draft of the declaration to the Second Continental Congress. To some viewers, it appears that Jefferson is stepping on John Adams's foot.

In the same year, Congress, at Jefferson's request, passed an act prohibiting the importation of slaves, which went into effect on January 1, 1808. This had no effect on existing slavery in America, and was widely flouted by pirates and others, who continued bringing slaves into Southern ports. In an era in which Southern plantation owners, including Jefferson, held slaves, his actions were inconsistent. As president he signed a bill that segregated the United States Postal Service and forbade African Americans to carry the mail.

After his presidency, Jefferson retired to Monticello, where he became an active correspondent with government leaders, participated in the design of buildings for the University of Virginia, and spent time in cultural and leisure activities. Jefferson became ill in July 1825, and by June 1826 he was confined to bed. He died on July 4, 1826, a few hours before president John Adams died. It was on the 50th anniversary of the signing of the Declaration of Independence. Today he is remembered as one of the greatest American presidents.

THE AMERICAN SCENE

The U.S. Military Academy at West Point was opened on July 4, 1802. In the same year, the Library of Congress issued what is believed to be the first catalog of books printed in America. Ohio became the 17th state in the Union on February 19, 1803, and the first new state to abolish slavery from the beginning of statehood; earlier, Vermont, which joined the Union in 1791, had abolished slavery under its constitution of July 1777. The Louisiana Purchase was completed at a cost of about $15 million and added about 828,000 square miles of land to the United States.

Fort Dearborn was established on the western shore of the lower part of Lake Michigan in the area that would later be known as Chicago, Illinois.

Buffalo, New York, was founded where the Niagara River meets Lake Erie. In May 1803, official U.S. architect Benjamin Latrobe addressed the American Philosophical Society on the subject of steam power, but was not enthusiastic about its prospects. In April 1803, John James Audubon arrived from France and began banding the feet of phoebes to study their habits; later, Audubon's studies would become famous, and an elephant-folio-size collection of his bird paintings would be published.

In 1804 the Lewis and Clark Expedition set out from St. Louis, Missouri, and went to the Pacific Northwest, reaching the Columbia River, then the Pacific Ocean, and then returning in 1806. This opened the gates to great expansion of that area, beginning with the well-established city of New Orleans, continuing up the Mississippi River to St. Louis and elsewhere, and later in the century providing the area for the creation of new states.

On July 11, 1804, Alexander Hamilton was killed in a pistol duel with Aaron Burr. The two had been adversaries ever since Hamilton opposed Burr's effort to become president in 1800. Hamilton, a gentleman, deliberately misfired, while Burr shot with the intent to kill. After this incident, Burr became one of the scoundrels of American history.

On November 15, 1806, Zebulon Pike sighted the Colorado peak that now bears his name during an expedition in the Southwest. He did not climb it, however. On February 23, 1809, the Illinois Territory was created. On February 20, 1809, the Supreme Court of the United States stated that the power of the federal government is greater than that of any individual state. In time, the philosophy of states' rights was diminished in many areas, but not without seemingly endless controversy in the halls of Congress. On March 1, 1809, the Embargo Act was repealed and replaced by the Non-Intercourse Act.

Opposite: The Jefferson Memorial in Washington, D.C. Above: Jefferson was honored on this 1993 commemorative silver dollar, which marked Jefferson's 250th birthday. The reverse depicts Jefferson's Virginia home, Monticello, which he designed.

NOTABLE SAYINGS

"Banking establishments are more dangerous than standing armies."

"That government is best which governs the least, because its people discipline themselves."

"The price of freedom is eternal vigilance."

"Delay is preferable to error."

"Do you want to know who you are? Don't ask. Act. Action will delineate and define you."

"I cannot live without books."

"The harder I work, the more luck I seem to have."

"Never spend your money before you've earned it."

4th President (1809–1817)

JAMES MADISON

March 16, 1751–June 28, 1836

Political party: Democrat-Republican

Vice president: George Clinton, 1809 to 1812; none 1812 and 1813; Elbridge Gerry, 1813 and 1814; none 1814 to 1817

First Lady and family: Married Dolley Payne Todd on September 15, 1794. The couple had no children.

Especially remembered for: Making a major contribution to the ratification of the Constitution by writing, with Alexander Hamilton and John Jay, the Federalist essays. Strong proponent of the Bill of Rights. Many historians view the War of 1812 as a tragic blunder by the president. It had far-reaching negative effects on the economy of America. Nickname: "Father of the Constitution." His wife Dolley became one of the best-remembered first ladies.

The Life of James Madison

James Madison was born in Port Conway, King George County, Virginia, son of James and Nelly Conway Madison. He spent his youth in the same state, entered Princeton (then the College of New Jersey), and took his degree in 1771. Madison studied history and law. When the Virginia Constitution was framed in 1776, he helped with its provisions.

From 1780 to 1783 he was a member of the Continental Congress. This was followed by service in the Virginia legislature. Madison was a delegate to the Constitutional Convention in 1787. As a representative to Congress he helped frame the Bill of Rights and the first federal revenue bill. He was outspoken concerning Alexander Hamilton's financial proposals, which he felt would concentrate wealth in the hands of Northern interests. From this opposition the Republican Party arose. Under Thomas Jefferson, Madison was secretary of state from 1801 to 1809—a particularly trying time in international relations, especially after the 1807 Embargo Act became law.

James Madison was elected president in 1808. During the first year of his administration, the United States prohibited trade with warring Britain and France; in May 1810, Congress authorized trade with both, directing the president, if either nation accepted America's view of neutral rights, to forbid trade with the other nation. Napoleon acceded, and in late 1810 Madison proclaimed non-intercourse with Great Britain. Relations worsened as British ships seized American cargoes and kidnapped ("impressed") American sailors. On June 1, 1812, at Madison's request, Congress declared war.

On March 4, 1813, Madison was sworn in for his second term. The War of 1812 saw military engagements at sea, on the Great Lakes, and in the British invasions of Maryland and Washington, where the

Opposite: President Madison in 1816, in a portrait by John Vanderlyn. Madison drafted the first 10 amendments to the Constitution, and for that reason is sometimes called the "Father of the Bill of Rights."

This memorial ribbon was released in 1836 to commemorate Madison's death.

White House, the Capitol, and other buildings were burned. The tide turned with the unsuccessful bombardment of Baltimore (inspiring Francis Scott Key to write "The Star-Spangled Banner"), and the enemy troops went home. Peace was declared in December 1814, but before the news reached America, the Battle of New Orleans was fought in January 1815, with General Andrew Jackson scoring a sound victory.

When Madison left office he retired to Montpelier, his tobacco plantation in Virginia. The estate had sustained difficulties, and he was saddled with debt. His retirement in many aspects was anything but enjoyable. He sought to strengthen his legacy, and he rewrote history, changing dates on certain documents and letters in his possession, adding and deleting characters, and changing words. The final six years of his life were distressed, including nearly two years bedridden. He died at Montpelier on June 28, 1836, the last of the Founding Fathers to pass away. By that time he was scarcely noticed, having indeed been almost forgotten by his contemporaries.

THE AMERICAN SCENE

In 1810 the third federal census gave the population as 7,239,881, including 1,211,364 slaves, 186,746 "free Negroes," and an estimated 60,000 immigrants.

On September 23, 1810, the Republic of West Florida declared its independence from Spain. On October 27 of that year, the United States annexed the Republic of West Florida.

It was anticipated that great prosperity would occur after the War of 1812 ended in early 1815, but economic problems became endemic, currency and paper money were in disorder, and difficulties extended for the next several years.

1816 was known as "the year without a summer." In sections of the Northeast there was snow on the ground for at least one day in each summer month. Farmers had a very difficult time, with many of their crops failing.

NOTABLE SAYINGS

"The truth is that all men having power ought to be mistrusted."

The Life of James Monroe

James Monroe was born in Westmoreland County, Virginia, to Spence and Elizabeth Jones Monroe. In 1776 he graduated from the College of William and Mary, after which he joined the Continental Army, distinguishing himself in the Revolution. He then practiced law in Virginia. A member of the Continental Congress from 1783 to 1786, he was also prominent in state politics and was among those who ratified the Constitution. In 1790 he was elected as a United States senator, serving until 1794, after which he was minister to France until 1796. Continuing in public service, he was governor of Virginia from 1799 to 1802, minister to France and England from 1803 to 1807 (participating in the 1803 Louisiana Purchase negotiations), secretary of state from 1811 to 1817, and for part of the time (1814 and 1815), concurrently the secretary of war.

With the endorsement of incumbent president James Madison, Monroe was named as the Republican candidate for president in 1816, and in November he won handily. On March 4, 1817, James Monroe was inaugurated president.

After entering the White House, he started on a goodwill tour that wound through the Northeast. The nation was weary from the War of 1812 and from depressed economic conditions, and Monroe's administration was viewed as ushering in the "Era of Good Feelings." His tour had very little pomp and circumstance. At each stop he was greeted by state and local dignitaries and made to feel welcome, but without fanfare.

Unfortunately, economic conditions took a downturn in 1818 and 1819, causing much rancor in Congress and elsewhere, although Monroe himself remained popular. Matters improved, however, and on December 3, 1820, James Monroe was reelected president in a landslide.

On December 2, 1823, the president issued this statement: "The American continents are henceforth not to be considered as subjects for future colonization by any European powers." This became

5th President (1817–1825)

JAMES MONROE

April 28, 1758–July 4, 1831

Political party: Democrat-Republican

Vice president: Daniel D. Tompkins, 1817 to 1825

First Lady and family: Married Elizabeth "Eliza" Kortright on February 16, 1786. The couple had three children: Eliza Kortright Monroe (1786–1835); James Spence Monroe (1799–1800); and Maria Hester Monroe (1803–1850).

Especially remembered for: The Era of Good Feelings. The Missouri Compromise bill. The Monroe Doctrine (whose name was assigned years later). In 1923 the latter was commemorated with a special commemorative half dollar.

Opposite: James Monroe as depicted by portraitist Gilbert Stuart circa 1818 to 1820. Left top: Monroe's Virginia estate, now known as Ash Lawn–Highland. Left bottom: This statue of Monroe stands on the grounds of Ash Lawn–Highland.

known as the Monroe Doctrine, and it would be his most famous legacy.

Monroe left the White House in 1825. He died in New York City in 1831 on the fourth of July.

THE AMERICAN SCENE

On July 4, 1817, construction of the Erie Canal began in Rome, New York. This would be completed in 1825 and would make shipping possible from the port of New York to Lake Erie, greatly facilitating trade to the American West. On April 4, 1818, Congress adopted the flag of the United States with 13 red and white stripes and one star for each state—20 at the time—with the provision to add another star when a new state was added to the Union.

In 1819 Missouri Territory's application to join the Union as a slave-holding state failed, setting off two years of controversy. The result was the Missouri Compromise of 1820, which kept the North-South political balance by admitting Missouri as a slavery state and at the same time admitting Maine as a free state. Under the provisions of the agreement, slavery was prohibited to the west and north of Missouri.

On August 15, 1824, the Marquis de Lafayette, French hero of the American Revolution, arrived in the United States as "the Nation's Guest" (as Congress named him in its letter of invitation). He toured the nation and was received with enthusiasm and cheering crowds. Before his departure on September 7, 1825, he had visited all 24 states.

NOTABLE SAYINGS

"A little flattery will support a man through great fatigue."

6th President (1825–1829)

JOHN QUINCY ADAMS

July 11, 1767–February 23, 1848

Political party: Democrat-Republican

Vice president: John C. Calhoun, 1825 to 1829

First Lady and family: Married Louisa Catherine Johnson on July 26, 1797. The couple had four children: George Washington Adams (1801–1829); John Adams (1803–1834); Charles Francis Adams (1807–1886); and Louisa Catherine Adams (1811–1812).

Especially remembered for: His foreign ministry, development of the country's infrastructure, and support of literature, art, and science.

The Life of John Quincy Adams

John Quincy Adams was born in Braintree, Massachusetts, to John and Abigail Smith Adams, eventually becoming the first son of a president to be elected to the same office. As a youth he watched the 1775 Battle of Bunker Hill from a vantage point above the family farm. He grew into a man of literary talent, widely read and fluent in several languages. He accompanied his father to Europe, acting as his secretary and keeping a particularly detailed diary.

In 1787 Adams graduated from Harvard College, after which he practiced law. In 1794 he was named as minister to the Netherlands, after which he served as minister to Prussia through 1801. Elected to the United States Senate in 1802, he served until 1808. He was minister to Russia from 1809 to 1811, and was the peace commissioner at Ghent, Belgium, in 1814 at the settlement of the War of 1812. Under James Monroe he was secretary of state through 1825, serving with great distinction: among his actions were arranging the cession of Florida from Spain in 1821, negotiating with Great Britain for the joint control of the Oregon Territory, and helping formulate what became known as the Monroe Doctrine.

In 1824 he was one of several candidates for president. The field also included War of 1812 hero Andrew Jackson, William H. Crawford, and Henry Clay. None attained a majority of Electoral College votes, and the matter was put before the House of Representatives, which decided for Adams, largely through the influence of Henry Clay. Adams named Clay as secretary of state, provoking great antagonism from Jackson backers, who called it a "corrupt bargain." As president, Adams faced much opposition from Congress, but was able to institute important programs, including setting up a network of roads and canals. He strongly supported education, art, and science.

Opposite: This portrait of John Quincy Adams was painted in 1858, a decade after his death, by American portraitist G.P.A. Healy.

The presidential contest of 1828 pitted Adams against Jackson. The election was hard fought, with Jacksonians accusing Adams of widespread corruption, although most of these charges did not stand up to close scrutiny. Nevertheless, Jackson won, and Adams went back to Massachusetts, intending to spend time farming and reading. Supporters persuaded him to run for Congress in 1830, which he did with success: he went on to serve from 1831 to 1848. Among his accomplishments in Congress was helping with the repeal of the 1836 "gag rule" mandating that any petitions against slavery be automatically tabled. In 1848 he had a stroke on the House floor, and died two days later, on February 23.

The first photograph ever taken of an American president is this daguerreotype from 1843, taken by Philip Haas.

THE AMERICAN SCENE

During the mid-1820s there was a great expansion of private banks and insurance companies. However, the situation was short lived, and in 1825 many prices fell, causing an economic crisis in the United States. The controversial Bank of the United States was beset with many problems; it had a shortage of gold and silver coins, and could not redeem its own notes. There was a business recession in 1826, but by 1827 conditions had improved.

In one of the great coincidences in American history, on July 4, 1826, former presidents Thomas Jefferson and John Adams both died; this date was the 50th anniversary of the signing of the Declaration of Independence.

The Baltimore & Ohio Railroad was incorporated in 1827, soon to become the first rail line in America offering commercial transportation of people and freight.

NOTABLE SAYINGS

"May our country always be successful, but whether successful or otherwise, always right."

"If your action inspires others to dream more, learn more, do more, and become more, you are a leader."

Two unusual keepsakes of the president: an ivory snuffbox (left) and a campaign pin with engraved portrait (above).

The Early Life of Andrew Jackson

Andrew Jackson was born in Waxhaw, Carolina, son of Andrew and Elizabeth Hutchinson Jackson. His education was intermittent, causing many later critics to call him illiterate. No matter; he read law for about two years, and then entered practice in Tennessee, where he was viewed as very competent. He became well-to-do and built a mansion, the Hermitage, near Nashville, and was a slave owner. He was a ready debater and quickly rose to challenges. In a duel with a man who had insulted his wife, Jackson was the winner.

In 1796 and 1797 Jackson served as a congressman, then as a senator for the next two years, after which he held a judicial position on the Tennessee Supreme Court until 1804. As a major general in the War of 1812 he became known as the "Hero of New Orleans." In January 1815 his forces devastated a large corps of British soldiers—even though, unbeknownst to the combatants, the war had ended by a peace settlement in December 1814. He was appointed governor of the newly acquired Florida Territory in 1821, and served as a U.S. senator from 1823 to 1825. In 1824 Andrew Jackson ran for president, but lost to John Quincy Adams.

The Administration and Later Life of Jackson

In 1828 Jackson and incumbent president John Quincy Adams squared off again in a particularly vitriolic contest. Jackson won, was inaugurated on March 4, 1829, and went to the White House. Contrary to the policy of his predecessors, the doors of the Executive Mansion (as it was called in those days) were opened to everyday citizens—much to the dismay of certain elements of Washington society, who considered the new president to be without finesse or manners.

The country became very polarized, with Democrats following Jackson's every step, while the National Republicans or Whigs opposed just about everything he did. A major clash arose with Senator

7th President (1829–1837)

Andrew Jackson

March 15, 1767–June 8, 1845

Political party: Democratic

Vice president: John C. Calhoun, 1829 to 1832; none 1832 to 1833; Martin Van Buren, 1833 to 1837

First Lady and family: Married Rachel Donelson Robards in August 1791, and in a second ceremony on January 17, 1794, after it was learned that Rachel's earlier divorce had been invalid. They had one child, Andrew Jackson Jr., who was adopted. Although Rachel did not live long enough to become First Lady, during Jackson's tenure Rachel's niece Emily Donelson lived at the White House with her husband and served as hostess.

Especially remembered for: Greatest plurality of popular votes gained by any president to date. "The Union must and shall be preserved," a statement made during the political conflict with Senator John C. Calhoun. Veto of the charter renewal for the Second Bank of the United States and his conflict with backers of the bank. "Kitchen Cabinet" of political cronies. Great U.S. prosperity during the early 1830s, including a Treasury surplus. Construction and occupation of the second Philadelphia Mint. Nickname: "Old Hickory."

John C. Calhoun and the state of South Carolina, which threatened to nullify federal import tariffs and was considering seceding from the Union. A compromise was negotiated by Henry Clay.

In 1832 the main contender in Jackson's bid for reelection was Clay. At the polls Jackson overwhelmed him with 56% of the popular vote and nearly five times as many Electoral College votes. Jackson had opposed the Second Bank of the United States, a private corporation in which the federal government held a stake and dictated much policy. The charter, up for renewal in 1836, was brought before Congress in 1832 and passed, only to be vetoed by Jackson. This caused a great uproar, as did his moving federal funds to selected state institutions, called "pet banks" by his opponents.

On March 4, 1833, Jackson was inaugurated for his second presidential term. In the meantime, the economy experienced great prosperity from the development of the West and the sale of public lands, as well as expansion of railroads, canals, and domestic works. The president had many detractors, and on March 27, 1834, Andrew Jackson was censured by Congress. Some years later, in 1837, this censure was expunged from the record, causing uproar. On January 8, 1835, the United States public debt was officially reduced to zero dollars, for the first and only time in the history of our country. The Treasury had a surplus that year and returned money to each state. On January 30, 1835, there was an assassination attempt against Jackson in the Capitol, the first such attempt against an American president.

The year 1836 saw the record purchase of 24.8 million dollars' worth of public lands, up sharply from $14.7 in 1835 and from only $4.8 million in 1834. To slow the rampant speculation, on July 11, 1836, Jackson issued his Specie Circular, stating that henceforth public lands could be purchased only by paying in gold and silver coin, no longer in bank bills or promissory notes. This set the scene for a chill in the American economy.

After his presidency, Jackson retired to the Hermitage, where he died in 1845.

Opposite: Andrew Jackson was dubbed "Old Hickory" due to his tough, no-nonsense character. Below: A satirical 1836 cartoon imagines Jackson hosting French dancer Madame Celeste in a White House parlor.

THE AMERICAN SCENE

From January 12 to January 27, 1830, Robert V. Hayne of South Carolina and Daniel Webster of Massachusetts debated in Congress the burning issue of states' rights and federal authority.

North Carolina and Georgia were the scenes of early gold discoveries in the United States. Native Americans in those regions were an inconvenience for whites who wanted to explore and mine for gold. They pressured Congress to pass the Indian Removal Act (May 28, 1830), which forced them from their homes and into the Midwest.

Meanwhile, in the White House, President Jackson's first-term cabinet was in turmoil, with

Above: The inaugural medal marking the start of Jackson's second term in 1833. Below: A political cartoon depicts President Jackson in a power struggle with Congress.

some members opposing his interests. Jackson began to rely more on unofficial advisors, called his "Kitchen Cabinet" because they were said to meet in the White House kitchen.

On November 14, 1832, Charles Carroll, the last signer of the Declaration of the Independence, passed away at his home in Maryland, at age 96.

Texas erupted into revolution on October 20, 1835, with the Battle of Gonzales, when Mexican soldiers were challenged by a group of local armed men. Several weeks of conflict followed, including the famous Battle of the Alamo. Finally, on December 9, Texas was declared an independent nation, free from Mexico's government. (It would become part of the United States the following year.)

Top: Critics of Jackson sometimes portrayed him as a vainglorious despot, as in this cartoon from circa 1832. Right: This plate was produced for Jackson's presidential campaign of 1824. It reads, "Gen'l Jackson, Hero of America."

NOTABLE SAYINGS

"The individual who refuses to defend his rights when called by his government deserves to be a slave, and must be punished as an enemy of the country and a friend to her foe."

"Internal improvement and the diffusion of knowledge, so far as they can be promoted by the constitutional acts of the federal government, are of high importance."

8th President (1837–1841)

MARTIN VAN BUREN

December 5, 1782–July 24, 1862

Political party: Democratic

Vice president: Richard M. Johnson, 1837 to 1841

First Lady and family: Married Hannah Hoes on February 21, 1807. They had four children: Abraham Van Buren (1807–1873); John Van Buren (1810–1866); Martin Van Buren (1812–1855); and Smith Thompson Van Buren (1817–1876).

Especially remembered for: His loyalty to President Jackson while serving as secretary of state and as vice president. The Panic of 1837, an economic disaster that occurred under his watch. Lack of popularity throughout his presidency.

The Life of Martin Van Buren

Martin Van Buren was born in Kinderhook, New York, to Abraham and Maria Hoes Van Buren. He completed his education in 1796 with a degree from Kinderhook Academy. He entered law and became involved in state politics in nearby Albany. As a favorite of the political organization, Van Buren dispensed patronage in a manner intended to generate loyalty and votes. He went up the ladder as a state senator (1813 to 1815), state attorney general (1815 to 1819), U.S. senator (1821 to 1829), governor of New York state (1829), secretary of state under Jackson (1829 to 1831), minister to England (1831), and vice president (1833 to 1837).

Although the Jackson administration had been one of great prosperity, storm clouds gathered in the summer of 1836 when Jackson issued the Specie Circular, seeking to bridle speculation in Western land by making purchases payable only in gold or silver coin instead of paper money and debt instruments. Riding on Jackson's coattails and the still-strong economy, Van Buren was elected president in 1836. He was inaugurated on March 4, 1837, the same day the city of Chicago, Illinois, was officially incorporated.

Soon the economy experienced problems, and there was a tightening of credit. In May 1837, two months after Van Buren's inauguration, most banks suspended payment of silver and gold coins in exchange for paper money. The Hard Times era was on, and it did not end until after he left the White House. Thousands of businesses and hundreds of banks closed their doors. The economy did not recover until early 1843.

In the presidential election of 1840, the incumbent Van Buren was trounced by William Henry Harrison, the hero of the Battle of Tippecanoe, who

Opposite: Martin Van Buren as photographed by Mathew Brady, who was known for his portraits until he achieved greater fame by documenting the Civil War in photographs.

This Free Soil Party campaign poster from Van Buren's unsuccessful 1848 bid for the presidency depicts him alongside the vice-presidential candidate, Charles F. Adams, son of John Quincy Adams.

captured 234 electoral votes to Van Buren's 60. The rallying campaign cry was "Tippecanoe and Tyler, too" (in reference to John Tyler, who became vice president).

In 1848 Van Buren ran again, on the new Free Soil ticket, and lost. He died in Kinderhook in 1862.

THE AMERICAN SCENE

The American scene during Van Buren's presidency was dominated by the Hard Times era. When the leading banks suspended payments in gold and silver on May 10, 1837, this precipitated the Panic of 1837, which quickly spread across the nation.

In 1837, slavery was a hot topic in Congress, which enacted a gag rule to suppress debate. In a lighter vein, also in 1837, P.T. Barnum hoaxed more than 10,000 visitors to Niblo's Garden in New York City with his exhibition of Joice Heth, a frail "161-year-old" former slave whom he claimed was the midwife who had assisted in the delivery of baby George Washington in 1732.

In 1838 the so-called Underground Railroad was in operation, helping slaves in the South to escape to the Northern states or to Canada. Secret way stations were set up in the North, but the network was most active in Ohio, through which a stream of slaves came up from Kentucky.

In the government's continuing exploitation of Native Americans, more than 14,000 Cherokees were forced by federal troops under the command of General Winfield Scott ("Old Fuss and Feathers") to walk the "Trail of Tears" from their native territories in Alabama, Tennessee, and Georgia to a resettlement area 800 miles distant in Indian Territory west of the Red River. About 4,000 Cherokee people died en route.

NOTABLE SAYINGS

"It is easier to do a job right than to explain why you didn't."

"I tread in the footsteps of illustrious men . . . in receiving from the people the sacred trust confided to my illustrious predecessor."

"As to the presidency, the two happiest days of my life were those of my entrance upon the office and my surrender of it."

The Life of William Henry Harrison

William Henry Harrison was born in Berkeley, Virginia, son of Benjamin and Elizabeth Bassett Harrison. He took courses in history and classics at Hampden-Sydney College, and in 1791 began the study of medicine in Richmond. He quickly had a change of heart, however, and decided to enter the military. Obtaining a commission as an ensign in the First Infantry of the army, he went to the Western frontier in the prairie states.

Resigning from the army in 1798, Harrison was appointed as secretary of the Northwest Territory and served as its first delegate to Congress. He was important in legislation to separate the Indiana Territory from the rest of the Northwest Territory. Named as governor of Indiana in 1801, he sought to obtain the title to Native American land so that settlers from the eastern states could set up homesteads and so that those already living in the area could have peace of mind. The landowners would have none of this, and it fell to Harrison to attack the confederacy formed by the Indians under Chief Tecumseh and his religiously oriented brother, the Prophet. As the settlers became increasingly endangered, Harrison received permission to attack. The Indians struck first, at the Army camp on the Tippecanoe River, before daybreak on November 7, 1811. Harrison was the victor, but with 190 casualties. His routing of the Native Americans was widely hailed as a triumph. He remained governor until 1813. In the War of 1812 he was given command of the army in the Northwest, where he vanquished British forces and their Indian allies, killing Tecumseh. From 1816 to 1819 he was a congressman from Ohio, then a U.S. senator from the same state (1825–1828), then minister to Columbia in 1828 and 1829.

Harrison went back to civilian life, but in 1840 answered the call of the Whig party as nominee for president. Harrison and vice presidential candidate John Tyler, the duo nicknamed "Tippecanoe and Tyler too," ran against incumbent Martin Van

9th President (1841)

WILLIAM HENRY HARRISON

February 9, 1773–April 4, 1841

Political party: Whig

Vice president: John Tyler, 1841

First Lady and family: Married Anna Tuthill Symmes on November 25, 1795. They had 10 children: Elizabeth Bassett Harrison (1796–1846); John Cleves Symmes Harrison (1798–1830); Lucy Singleton Harrison (1800–1826); William Henry Harrison (1802–1838); John Scott Harrison (1804–1878), whose son Benjamin served as president from 1889 to 1893; Benjamin Harrison (1806–1840); Mary Symmes Harrison (1809–1842); Carter Bassett Harrison (1811–1839); Anna Tuthill Harrison (1813–1865); and James Findlay Harrison (1814–1817).

Especially remembered for: Victor at the Battle of Tippecanoe against Native Americans in 1811. First president to die in office. Shortest presidential term (one month). Nickname: "Old Tippecanoe." The campaign slogan "Tippecanoe and Tyler too."

Buren. Harrison won by a popular plurality of less than 150,000 votes, but carried the day in the Electoral College with 234 votes to Van Buren's 60. In March 1841 his inaugural address, edited by Daniel Webster, had elegant touches of the classic and promised to advance the cause of the average citizen. Unfortunately he caught pneumonia, and he died on April 4, after a single month in office.

THE AMERICAN SCENE

In the month-long presidency of Harrison there were no notable changes. The economy was improving steadily. Following the trend, the funds of the United States, as shown by a surplus in the Treasury, continued to build up. On January 1, 1841, the amount of excess funds stood at $13.5 million, up sharply from $5.2 million a year earlier. This was an era of fiscal responsibility by the federal government.

Opposite: This portrait by James Reid Lambdin depicts William Henry Harrison in 1835, six years before his death. Right: A campaign ribbon from the 1840 presidential race dubs Harrison the "Poor Man's Friend."

NOTABLE SAYINGS

"The prudent capitalist will never venture his capital . . . if there exists a state of uncertainty as to whether the government will repeal tomorrow what it has enacted today."

"A decent and manly examination of the acts of the government should be not only tolerated but encouraged."

10th President (1841–1845)

JOHN TYLER

March 29, 1790–January 18, 1862

Political party: Whig

Vice president: None

First Lady and family: Married Letitia Christian on March 29, 1813; his second wife was Julia Gardiner, whom he married on June 26, 1844. Over the course of his two marriages he fathered 15 children: Mary Tyler (1815–1848); Robert Tyler (1816–1877); John Tyler (1819–1896); Letitia Tyler (1821–1907); Elizabeth Tyler (1823–1850); Anne Contesse Tyler (1825); Alice Tyler (1827–1854); Tazewell Tyler (1830–1874); David Gardiner Tyler (1846–1927); John Alexander Tyler (1848–1883); Julia Gardiner Tyler (1849–1871); Lachlan Tyler (1851–1902); Lyon Gardiner Tyler (1853–1935); Robert Fitzwalter Tyler (1856–1927); and Pearl Tyler (1860–1947).

Especially remembered for: Being the first vice president to be elevated to the office of president by the death of his predecessor—the "accidental president," as some opponents nicknamed him.

The Life of John Tyler

John Tyler was born in Greenway, Virginia, son of John and Mary Marot Armistead Tyler. He graduated from the College of William and Mary in 1807. He practiced law and became involved in politics: as a congressman from 1816 to 1821, Virginia state legislator (1823 to 1835) and governor (1825 and 1826), and U.S. senator (1827 to 1836). An early supporter of Jackson, Tyler changed his philosophy and took up the advocacy of states' rights, believing that less power should be given to the federal government.

Although in the 1840 presidential election Tyler took up the "Tippecanoe and Tyler too" banner, he felt that the slogan was nationalistic. Prominent Whigs Henry Clay and Daniel Webster carried considerable weight with newly elected president William Henry Harrison. After Harrison's unexpected death, Clay and Webster believed that Tyler would promote Whig ideas as well. This did not happen, and in a pivotal move Tyler vetoed a new plan for a national bank brought forward by Clay. Matters went from bad to worse, and the entire cabinet, inherited from Harrison, resigned save for secretary of state Daniel Webster. Tyler was ejected from the Whig party, which controlled Congress. The first impeachment bill against a president was introduced into the House of Representatives after he vetoed a tariff bill, but failed.

States' rights advocacy was the rallying call of the South, and relations between North and South were strained under Tyler. Despite political problems, however, his administration had several achievements, including an act to enable settlers to take possession of 160 acres of public land for farming before it was put up for public sale. The Webster-Ashburton Treaty resolved a border dispute with Canada. In 1842 a protective tariff bill aided Northern manufacturers and helped speed the end of the Hard Times era.

Opposite: G.P.A. Healy's portrait of John Tyler dates from 1859, when the former president was nearing the age of 70.

On February 20, 1844, President Tyler and other dignitaries were on board the steam frigate *Princeton* on the Potomac River to see the action of a powerful new gun, the Peacemaker, which could fire a 212-pound load the remarkable distance of three miles. Without warning, the gun exploded on deck, and eight people were killed, including the secretary of state. In that year Tyler sought reelection. However, the Democrats, his former party, favored Martin Van Buren, and the Whigs, still alienated by his activities early in his presidency, were for Henry Clay. In August 1844, realizing that starting a third party was not feasible, Tyler gave up the idea. The Democrats switched their backing from Van Buren to James Knox Polk, who was soon supported by Tyler.

After South Carolina seceded from the Union in December 1860, followed by other Southern states, Tyler helped form the government of the Confederate States of America. He died in 1862 in the Confederate capital of Richmond, while a member of the Confederate House of Representatives. His dying words were "I am going now. Perhaps it is for the best."

Below: A satirical cartoon depicts President Tyler performing on stilts as Daniel Webster attempts to collect money from onlookers.

THE AMERICAN SCENE

In New York City on April 10, 1841, Horace Greeley, age 30, launched the *New York Tribune* with $1,000 in borrowed capital. The Webster-Ashburton Treaty, signed August 9, 1842, finalized the Maine-Canada border. Abolition remained the most compelling and divisive issue on the American scene, a situation greatly aggravated when in March the Supreme Court upheld the 1793 Fugitive Slave Act, but interpreted it by saying while slave owners could recover runaways, the states had no legal obligation to render assistance to the slaveholder.

In Massachusetts, children under the age of 12 were limited to working no more than 10 hours

per day. This was the era of great expansion and prosperity of textile mills in New England towns, and young children were among those employed to tend the looms.

P.T. Barnum and Edgar Allan Poe were among Americans active in the fields of entertainment.

About 1,000 settlers followed the Oregon Trail in 1843 with missionary Marcus Whitman to settle in the Columbia River Valley. At the Bowery Amphitheatre in New York City the Virginia Minstrels launched a branch of entertainment that would become wildly popular in ensuing decades.

President Tyler's Indian peace medal (below) and commemorative ribbon (right) both showcase the president's distinctive aquiline nose. Indian peace medals were given to prominent Native Americans as a goodwill gesture from U.S. presidents or their representatives.

NOTABLE SAYINGS

"Popularity, I have always thought, may aptly be compared to a coquette—the more you woo her, the more apt she is to elude your embrace."

"Wealth can only be accumulated by the earnings of industry and the savings of frugality."

11th President (1845–1849)

JAMES KNOX POLK

November 2, 1795–June 15, 1849

Political party: Democratic

Vice president: George M. Dallas, 1845 to 1849

First Lady and family: Married Sarah Childress on January 1, 1824. The union was a happy one, and Sarah worked closely with her husband, serving as his secretary in the White House. The couple had no children.

Especially remembered for: His dynamic administration, which included expansion of the boundaries of the United States, reflecting imperialism and also adding acrimony to the long-standing differences between the North and the South concerning slavery in new states. The War with Mexico. New boundaries for the Oregon Territory. The beginning of the California Gold Rush. During Polk's administration, dancing and drinking were not allowed in the White House, in deference to Mrs. Polk's religious convictions.

The Life of James Knox Polk

James Knox Polk was born in Mecklenburg County, North Carolina, the son of Samuel and Jane Knox Polk. In 1818 he graduated with honors from the University of North Carolina, after which he practiced law. He soon became absorbed in politics, became a friend of Andrew Jackson, and ran for public office. From 1823 to 1825 he was a state representative, then a representative to the U.S. Congress from 1825 to 1839, serving as speaker from 1835 onward. During the early part of the decade he supported Jackson in his conflict with the Second Bank of the United States. Afterward he was governor of Tennessee from 1829 to 1841.

In 1844 he was considered to be a strong possibility for vice president, with Martin Van Buren expected to get the nod for presidential nominee at the Democratic nominating convention. Polk aired his expansionist views, stating that Texas, California, and the Oregon Territory should come under federal control, upstaging what Van Buren (who had been defeated in 1840) had to offer. Jackson admired Polk's views as a part of the "manifest destiny" to enlarge the United States, and influenced attendees to nominate him as president, which happened on the ninth ballot. In the general election in November he beat Henry Clay, the Whig candidate.

To secure California as additional territory for the United States, Polk sent an envoy to Mexico with an offer of $20 million plus cancellation of damage claims owed. The thought of selling such a vast district was not interesting to the authorities to the south, and they declined to discuss the matter. To force attention, Polk sent General Zachary Taylor and troops to the Rio Grande area. This was perceived by the Mexicans as aggression, and they attacked the American forces. Thus was launched the Mexican-American War of 1846 and 1847. Mexico acknowledged defeat after a series of decisive battles. California and New Mexico were ceded

Opposite: James Knox Polk as depicted in 1858 by G.P.A. Healy.

to the United States for $15 million and settlement of damage claims. Soon afterward, on January 24, 1848, gold nuggets were found in the American River at Sutter's Mill, in California, launching the Gold Rush.

The acquisition of the vast new districts precipitated bitter arguments in Congress as to whether new states and territories should permit slavery. In the next decade this would become the main focus of debates in the nation's capital, while differences

between the North and the South continued to grow. After he left the White House, Polk went back to Tennessee, where he died a few months later on June 15, 1849.

THE AMERICAN SCENE

On March 3, 1845, Florida joined the Union as the 27th state, and on December 29 the Republic of Texas (established the year before after splitting from Mexico) became the 28th.

The clipper ship *Rainbow* was launched in New York City. It was of the "extreme" variety (a new, high-speed design). These fast sailing vessels would grow in number over the next 20 years, even though they saw increasing competition worldwide from iron ships powered by steam.

In 1845, the U.S. Naval Academy was opened in Annapolis, Maryland.

The Walter Tariff Act enacted on July 30, 1845, helped the United States come close to free trade. During the next decade, exports would double to $306 million and imports would triple to $361 million. Many imports consisted of manufactured goods from Europe and (particularly) England, while food was a major export item.

The Oregon boundary dispute with Britain was resolved on June 15, 1846, when the United States accepted the territory below the 49th parallel, while Britain retained the northern side mainland and Vancouver Island. In Washington, D.C., Congress utilized a bequest of £100,000 from James Smithson (an Englishman who knew relatively little about America) to found the Smithsonian Institution "for the diffusion of knowledge."

Richard Hoe patented his rotary "lightning press" in 1846, which soon made obsolete the flatbed presses used in print shops and newspaper offices everywhere. In 1847, military engagements in a war with Mexico concluded with a string of U.S. victories at Vera Cruz, Cerro Gordo, Contreras, Churubusco, and Molina del Rey, capped by General Winfield Scott's triumph at Chapultepec on September 13.

This was a time of great immigration from Europe to the United States, with hundreds of thousands of people leaving Ireland, the Netherlands, and other countries, traveling with their families and belongings to make a new life in the land of opportunity.

In late January, 1848, in California, John Marshall glimpsed shiny flakes of gold. With his discovery the California Gold Rush erupted, and by 1849 it was going full-steam. Tens of thousands of Americans packed up and headed west to try to make a fortune.

Opposite: Polk circa 1849, photographed by Mathew Brady. Right: Polk's inaugural medal from 1845 and a campaign ribbon from 1844, which dubs the presidential candidate "Young Hickory of Tennessee."

NOTABLE SAYINGS

"I am heartily rejoiced that my term is so near its close. I will soon cease to be a servant and will become a sovereign."

12th President (1849–1850)

ZACHARY TAYLOR

November 24, 1784–July 9, 1850

Political party: Whig

Vice president: Millard Fillmore, 1849 and 1850

First Lady and family: Married Margaret Mackall Smith on June 21, 1810. In the White House Margaret was ill much of the time and did not attend most functions. The couple had six children: Ann Mackall Taylor (1811–1875); Sarah Knox Taylor (1814–1835); Octavia P. Taylor (1816–1820); Margaret Smith Taylor (1819–1820); Mary Elizabeth Taylor (1824–1909); and Richard Taylor (1826–1879).

Especially remembered for: As the hero of the Mexican-American War he was admired by both the North and the South, while Southerners appreciated him as an owner of slaves. His brief presidency did not accomplish much in the way of national progress. Nickname: "Old Rough and Ready."

The Life of Zachary Taylor

Zachary Taylor was born near Barboursville, Virginia, son of Lieutenant Colonel Richard and Sarah Dabney Strother Taylor. He was a second cousin of James Madison. Zachary spent his youth on a plantation in Kentucky. With but a meager formal education, he pursued a military career while maintaining his own plantation in Mississippi, complete with a large retinue of slaves to plant and pick cotton. Taylor had no advanced schooling. In the army he gained fame by slaughtering Native Americans. In the war with Mexico, he shared heroic honors with General Winfield Scott. Taylor had little interest in politics, and never voted in a presidential election.

For the contest of 1848 the Whigs nominated Taylor, while the choice of the Democrats was Lewis Cass. In protest against both Taylor, who owned slaves, and Cass, who wanted to allow states to decide for themselves if they wanted slavery, the Free Soil Party arose. The new party became strong in the North and chose Van Buren as its presidential candidate. He took votes away from Cass, propelling Taylor into the White House, although Taylor had not campaigned actively.

America continued to be torn by the slavery question. Taylor suggested that the territories of California and New Mexico (including what is today Arizona) draft their own constitutions and apply for statehood, making their own provisions regarding the issue. Southern politicians were incensed, claiming that it was the right of Congress to determine the status of slaves. Some threatened secession. Taylor was firm, stating in 1850 that if need be he would personally command the army in the suppression of such a notion. Ironically, when the Civil War broke out a decade later, his only son Richard was appointed as a general in the army of the Confederate States of America.

Opposite: The official White House portrait of Zachary Taylor was painted by Joseph Henry Bush in 1848, the year before Taylor took office.

Above: Taylor in a daguerreotype from circa 1843 to 1845. Right: A ribbon was issued to commemorate Taylor's inauguration.

Unforeseen events intervened when Taylor became ill on July 4, 1850, in ceremonies at the Washington Monument (under construction since 1836, with work dragging on until 1888). He died a few days later on July 9. Vice President Millard Fillmore succeeded him as chief executive.

THE AMERICAN SCENE

The California Gold Rush expanded, and as Taylor was spending his first months in the White House, tens of thousands of adventurers were heading to the land of seemingly unlimited opportunities. Most traveled overland by wagon, starting from Missouri or another jumping-off spot and continuing west to lands now a part of Wyoming, Utah, and Nevada; they then went over the Sierra Nevada into California. Others came by sea, taking a steamship to Panama, crossing about 50 miles of river and jungle, and then taking passage on another steamer on the Pacific side, traveling from there north to San Francisco. This was the fastest way, but the journey still took a few weeks. Still others sailed around the Cape Horn at the tip of South America, then north via the Pacific to California. San Francisco was the focal point of commerce, but towns and gold camps were scattered over a wide area. Other gold seekers arrived from Europe, Australia, the Orient, and other places.

In 1850 just over 23 million people lived in the United States. About a million of them had arrived from European countries over the past six years—about 40 percent from Ireland. Most Americans—about 21 million—lived east of the Mississippi River. Railroads had tripled in the United States since 1840, from about 3,000 miles of tracks to about 9,000.

NOTABLE SAYINGS

"For more than half a century during which kingdoms and empires have fallen, the Union has stood unshaken. The patriots who formed it have long since descended to the grave; yet it still remains, the proudest monument to their memory."

The Life of Millard Fillmore

Millard Fillmore was born in Locke Township, Cayuga County, New York, son of Nathaniel and Phoebe Millard Fillmore. He grew up on the family farm in what was at the time part of the western frontier. His early education was sparse, and at the age of 15 he was apprenticed to a wool carder. Imbued with ambition, he pursued further studies when he was 19 years old, read law, and in 1823 was admitted to the bar. In 1830 he set up his office in Buffalo, by which time he had been a member of the New York State Assembly for two years, as he would continue to be through 1831. Well-known politician Thurlow Weed was a friend and mentor. From 1833 to 1835 and again from 1837 to 1845 Fillmore served in the U.S. House of Representatives. In 1848, while he was the comptroller of the state of New York, he joined Zachary Taylor as running mate on the Whig ticket.

When Fillmore unexpectedly became president after Taylor's death, the question of slavery in the new territories was still being fiercely debated in the halls of Congress, with the North against the South. Taylor's cabinet resigned, and Fillmore filled the vacancies with his own choices, including Daniel Webster as secretary of state. Under senator Stephen A. Douglas, the Compromise of 1850 was worked out, providing that California be admitted to the Union as a free state, slavery be abolished in the District of Columbia, boundary disputes between Texas and New Mexico be resolved, and slaveholders be given the right to pursue and capture escaped slaves in the North (the Fugitive Slave Act).

The Whig party became ineffective, as many Northerners would not forgive Fillmore for not vetoing the Fugitive Slave Act. The plight of Southern slaves looked worse than ever. In 1856 Fillmore was invited to become a part of the newly formed Republican Party, but declined and instead became the presidential candidate for the American Party, more popularly known as the "Know Nothing" Party. This bid failed, and Fillmore left public service.

13th President (1850–1853)

MILLARD FILLMORE

January 7, 1800–March 8, 1874

Political party: Whig

Vice president: None

First Lady and family: Married Abigail Powers on February 5, 1826. The union was blissful. The couple had two children: Millard Powers Fillmore (1828–1889) and Mary Abigail Fillmore (1832–1854). Fillmore's second wife was Caroline Carmichael McIntosh, a wealthy widow whom he married on February 10, 1858.

Especially remembered for: Debates over the Compromise of 1850, which he favored. Signing the unfortunate Fugitive Slave Act. Good economy fueled by the Gold Rush. The slavery question dominated Fillmore's administration, as it would his successors'. He was faithful to his duties and trust, but undistinguished in the annals of the presidency.

In later years he was a critic of president Abraham Lincoln, but during Reconstruction he supported President Johnson. Fillmore died in Buffalo, New York, in 1874.

THE AMERICAN SCENE

P.T. Barnum continued to entertain Americans through the Fillmore years, with his shows and attractions. This was a time of invention and innovation in American business and society. The *New York Times* was founded, writers like Nathaniel Hawthorne, Herman Melville, and Harriet Beecher Stowe were publishing great works, and the entertainment scene saw popular new songs and traveling minstrel shows.

The Gold Rush continued in California, though by 1851 most of the easily accessible streamside deposits had been played out, and large corporations were more and more active in gold mining.

NOTABLE SAYINGS

"An honorable defeat is better than a dishonorable victory."

"The man who can look upon a crisis without being willing to offer himself upon the altar of his country is not for public trust."

Opposite: President Fillmore's portrait was painted by G.P.A. Healy. Below: An 1856 cartoon depicts Fillmore, the Know-Nothing Party's presidential candidate, as a vigilant farmer protecting the "government crib."

FANCIED SECURITY, OR THE RATS ON A BENDER.

14th President (1853–1857)

FRANKLIN PIERCE

November 23, 1804–October 8, 1869

Political party: Democratic

Vice president: William King, March 4 to April 18, 1853; none 1853 to 1857

First Lady and family: Married Jane Means Appleton on November 10, 1834. The couple had three children: Franklin Pierce (1836; died when three days old); Frank Robert Pierce (1839–1843); and Benjamin Pierce (1841–1853). Two months before he took office, he and his wife saw 11-year-old Benjamin killed when their train was wrecked. Jane dressed in black thereafter, and as First Lady was consumed with grief and delusions, including writing letters to her dead son.

Especially remembered for: Being undistinguished as a leader—a minor presidential figure, as were his two predecessors. The continuation of Gold Rush prosperity.

The Life of Franklin Pierce

Franklin Pierce was born in Hillsborough, New Hampshire, son of General Benjamin Pierce and Ann Kendrick Pierce. In 1824 he graduated from Bowdoin College, after which he studied law, then entered the political arena. At the age of 24 he was elected to the New Hampshire Legislature, becoming speaker of that body two years later. Then followed service in the U.S. House of Representatives from 1833 to 1837, then in the Senate from 1837 to 1842. He then returned to New Hampshire, as his wife Jane disliked living in Washington and the couple had suffered the loss of an infant son (in 1836). Later, Pierce served in the Mexican-American War.

In 1852 at the Democratic convention the delegates decided upon a platform to support the Compromise of 1850 and to resist any further stirring of the slavery question, which by this time had dominated American politics for many years and had rendered ineffectual the two most recent presidents (Taylor and Fillmore). There was no unanimity on a nominee for president, and after an exhausting 48 ballots Pierce was selected, one of the most obscure "dark horse" candidates ever.

Elected that November, Pierce in his inaugural address in March 1853 promised an era of peace and prosperity. Moving into the White House was a somber event, as he and his wife had suffered the loss of another son, Benjamin, in a train accident two months earlier. There were few festivities and no inaugural ball.

Despite the continuing animosity between the North and the South, the economy had been sound since the end of the Hard Times era in 1843, and was still growing. Railroads were a particularly dynamic part of the equation. Soon the new president was viewed with suspicion by many Northerners, who felt he was soft on slavery and was working

Opposite: Franklin Pierce in a portrait by G.P.A. Healy, as he appeared in 1858, one year after the end of his presidency.

for the interests of the South. His administration was wracked by this continuing question, which came to a head with the Kansas-Nebraska Act, engineered by senator Stephen A. Douglas, which repealed the Missouri Compromise of 1820 and threw open the possibility of slavery beyond the boundaries of that state. Douglas was an advocate of building railroads in the West and sought to organize governments in the districts through which the main line toward California would run. The $10 million Gadsden Purchase of land from Mexico (at the southern border of New Mexico) was made to facilitate the route. Douglas felt that citizens of the western areas should decide the slavery question for themselves. "Bleeding Kansas" saw widespread destruction and killing as renegades from both the North and the South rushed there to gain control.

After his presidency, Pierce returned to his native state. His wife died in 1863, after which alcohol became his companion. He died of cirrhosis of the liver in Concord, New Hampshire, in 1869.

THE AMERICAN SCENE

Manufacturing continued to increase in the United States during Pierce's presidency. By this time fewer than half of Americans were employed in agriculture, down from 80% a generation earlier. European immigration continued as well. Many families were leaving Germany's kingdoms and principalities, seeking to escape political and social unrest, to settle in Ohio, Wisconsin, and other states with large German population centers.

Left: The Currier firm's depiction of Pierce as the Democratic presidential candidate in 1852. Below: President Pierce's portrait on his Indian peace medal from the following year.

NOTABLE SAYINGS

"We have nothing in our history or position to invite aggression; have everything to beckon us to the cultivation of relations of peace and amity with all relations."

"The revenue of the country, levied almost insensibly to the tax payer, goes on from year to year, increasing beyond either the interest or prospective wants of the government."

15th President (1857–1861)

JAMES BUCHANAN

April 23, 1791–June 1, 1868

Political party: Democratic

Vice president: John C. Breckinridge, 1857 to 1861

First Lady and family: The only president never to marry, Buchanan had been engaged at age 28, but his fiancée committed suicide. A niece, Harriet Lane (1830–1904), orphaned at age 11 and his ward since that time, served as hostess at the White House.

Especially remembered for: Trying to appease both the North and the South and pleasing neither. Known as "Old Buck," he pronounced his name similar to "buck-cannon"; indeed, both these items were shown on an 1856 campaign medal.

The Life of James Buchanan

James Buchanan was born in Cove Gap, Pennsylvania, son of James and Elizabeth Speer Buchanan. Scion of a prosperous family, he was raised with the trappings of the good life. In 1809 he graduated from Dickinson College. Buchanan was well studied in law and a talented debater. He went from one success to another. He gravitated into politics as state representative in 1815 and 1816, then as a U.S. congressman from 1821 to 1821, minister to Russia (1832 to 1834), and U.S. senator (1834 to 1845). Under president James Knox Polk he was secretary of state from 1845 to 1849, then minister to England for most of the Pierce administration from 1853 to 1856.

In 1856 Buchanan was the candidate for president on the Democratic ticket. Having been overseas in recent years, he was unscarred by controversy over the slavery question. The fourth time was the charm, as he had sought the candidacy unsuccessfully in 1844, 1848, and 1852. He was elected handily in a three-way contest with Millard Fillmore and John C. Frémont, and in March 1857 he went to the White House. In his inaugural address he dismissed the question of slavery in the territories, stating that the Supreme Court would soon decide the matter. Two days later, chief justice Roger B. Taney ruled that Congress had no power to deprive holders of slaves in the territories of their right of ownership. Northerners were outraged, while Southerners rejoiced. Buchanan was aware of the worsening differences between the North and the South, and sought to quiet the matter by making cabinet and other appointments from both sides, although his bias toward the South was obvious.

To stop the conflict in "Bleeding Kansas" he recommended that the district be admitted as a slave state, which turned some members of his own Democratic Party against him, although many members were oriented toward Southern views. The matter was set aside, and statehood would not occur until years later. The Panic of 1857 caused widespread financial hardship from autumn of that year through

1858. In the latter year the House of Representatives was under Republican control, and Democrats ruled the Senate. Neither party would support the other, and much legislation reached an impasse.

The Democrats divided into Northern and Southern factions, strengthening the position of the Republicans. Buchanan did not seek a second term. When Abraham Lincoln won the presidential election of November 1860, tempers broke in the South. South Carolina seceded on December 20, followed in early 1861 by the formation of the Confederate States of America. The Buchanan administration, never strong to begin with, fell into shambles as many key appointees and other government officials left Washington and joined the Confederacy.

In March 1861, Buchanan left the capital and went to his mansion, Wheatland, near Lancaster, Pennsylvania. He died in 1868.

THE AMERICAN SCENE

The population of the United States in 1860 was 31.4 million people, having doubled in just 40 years. New York City was the nation's largest urban center, with just over 800,000 citizens. Other major cities included Philadelphia, Brooklyn, Baltimore, Boston, New Orleans, Cincinnati, St. Louis, and Chicago.

Slavery continued to be a source of national anxiety during James Buchanan's presidency. The State of Wisconsin judged that the Fugitive Slave Act of 1850—which allowed slaves who had escaped to the North to be captured and returned to their masters—was unconstitutional. However, the federal Supreme Court struck down that ruling, upholding the act. John Brown, an abolitionist, attempted to start a slave rebellion in Virginia (and throughout the South, he hoped), but the effort failed, Brown was arrested, and he ultimately was hanged for treason. Slave labor continued to be a cornerstone of Southern production.

A young John D. Rockefeller entered the oil business during Buchanan's tenure. The Pony Express was started in 1860 as a fast way to deliver mail. Daily newspapers were out in force, with nearly 400 on the scene nationwide. About a third of those had started within the past 10 years. Cotton was big business, accounting for nearly 60 percent of U.S. export value.

NOTABLE SAYINGS

"There is nothing stable but heaven and the Constitution."

Opposite: President Buchanan as portrayed in the Currier firm's lithograph. Right: Buchanan's memorial in Meridian Hill Park, Washington, D.C. Sculpted by Hans Schuler, it is the only public memorial to Buchanan.

Left: The new president's likeness is featured on this invitation to the inaugural ball held on March 4, 1857, in honor of President Buchanan and Vice President Breckenridge. Below: This medal bearing Buchanan's image was presented by the Japanese Embassy on the occasion of an 1860 visit to America.

The Early Life of Abraham Lincoln

Abraham Lincoln was born on February 12, 1809, in Hodgenville, Kentucky, son of Thomas and Nancy Hanks Lincoln. He grew up in the semi-wilderness of the frontier, where his family had to work hard, and many efforts were a struggle. When he was eight, he moved with his family to Indiana. When he was 10 his mother died, and in time he gained a stepmother, Sarah Bush Johnston Lincoln. With ambition and perseverance, young Abe gained an education largely on his own, learning to read, write, and do mathematics. He worked hard on a farm, split rails to make fences, and kept a store in New Salem, Illinois, his adopted state.

Lincoln was a captain in the Black Hawk War, after which he practiced law, riding the circuit of courts in his district. Elected to the Illinois State Legislature in 1834, he served for eight years. In 1847 and 1849 he was a representative to Congress. In Illinois in 1858, Lincoln accepted the nomination as Republican candidate for senator, stating in reference to the divide between the North and the South that "A house divided against itself cannot stand." Though defeated by Stephen A. Douglas, Lincoln would go on to greater things.

His debates in that campaign gained national attention and brought him the fame that secured the Republican nomination for president in 1860. With four candidates in the running and with the Democrats divided into North–South factions, Lincoln won the November election.

The president-elect's stance against slavery was intolerable to the South, and in December 1860 the state of South Carolina seceded from the Union, followed by six others, and these states soon formed the Confederate States of America.

Lincoln's Presidency

Abraham Lincoln in his inaugural address on March 4, 1861, offered this commentary on the Confederacy: "This country, with its institutions, belongs

16th President (1861–1865)

Abraham Lincoln

February 12, 1809–April 15, 1865

Political party: Republican

Vice president: Hannibal Hamlin, 1861 to 1865; Andrew Johnson, 1865

First Lady and family: Married Mary Todd on November 4, 1842. The couple had four boys, only one of whom lived to maturity: Robert Todd Lincoln (1843–1926); Edward Baker Lincoln (1846–1850); William Wallace Lincoln (1850–1862); and Thomas "Tad" Lincoln (1853–1871).

Especially remembered for: "Log cabin" childhood. Illinois railsplitter. Leadership in the Civil War. Emancipation Proclamation. Viewed as a hero by the North, a scoundrel by the South. Assassination. Nicknames: "Honest Abe," "the Great Emancipator." One of four presidents honored on Mount Rushmore.

to the people who inhabit it. Whenever they shall grow weary of the existing government they can exercise their constitutional right of amending it, or their revolutionary right to dismember or overthrow it."

Many politicians (both federal and Confederate) still held out hope that the North and South could live in harmony—as two separate nations. The South, they felt, could maintain slave labor as a foundation of its production, being entitled to make such decisions as a sovereign nation; meanwhile, both countries would benefit from international commerce. Many companies had offices in both North and South, and the CSA even had its first paper money and bonds printed in New York City.

The social and political scenes weren't all rosy, however. The separation of nearly a dozen states from the Union brought unavoidable turmoil—many high-level federal officials, for example, left their positions and went South, where their sympathies lay, to take office with the new Confederate government. Many Americans in the border states found themselves between North and South not only geographically, but philosophically as well, uncertain where their best interests lay. In the meantime, complications arose from large parts of infrastructure and government (railroad lines, the postal system, banks, federal offices, etc.) now being in a foreign nation.

Those who hoped for friendly relations between the two countries were soon disappointed. Several weeks into his presidency, on April 11, Lincoln received the news that the Confederacy was shelling Fort Sumter, a federal fort in Charleston's harbor, in South Carolina. On April 15, the president called for volunteers to defend the nation. The American Civil War had begun.

On the day of Lincoln's inauguration, there were 13,024 officers and men in the U.S. Army. After war was declared, the president called for 42,034 volunteers to enlist for a three-month term. Northerners predicted an easy victory—the North had vast industrial resources, especially compared to the largely agricultural South. They hosted parties and parades to send off the troops, expecting that they would be back in a month or two to celebrate victory. By July there were 30,000 new soldiers in the Washington area, commanded by General Winfield Scott, a hero of the Mexican-American War.

The Confederacy's July 21 victory at Manassas, Virginia, evaporated any illusions of a quick and easy end to the war. The Union's soldiers scattered in retreat. After several more losses, President Lincoln put General George B. McClellan in command of all Union forces. This would prove to be one of his worst mistakes.

Opposite: An 1869 painting of the late President Lincoln by William F. Cogswell. Right: Lincoln in 1864 with his youngest son, Thomas, nicknamed Tad by his father because he was "as wriggly as a tadpole" as a baby.

Opposite: G.P.A. Healy depicts a pensive Lincoln. Above: An 1864 campaign pin. Below: David G. Blythe's fanciful depiction of the writing of the Emancipation Proclamation.

The president was faced with daunting challenges: financing the war, reorganizing many of the federal government's departments, supervising the army and navy, and trying to manage the monetary disorder caused by the war.

While Lincoln's main objective was to save the Union, the institution of slavery was on his mind, as well. On September 22, 1862, he issued one of the defining executive orders of his presidency: the Emancipation Proclamation, which announced the freedom of 3.1 million slaves in bondage in the Confederate states. He took this step as "a necessary war measure."

Both North and South saw major military victories in 1862, with action on land and on the water. Lincoln dismissed and appointed generals in an attempt to find the commander who could bring final victory. That November, he relieved

General McClellan of his command and put General Ambrose Everett Burnside in charge of the Army of the Potomac. The next month, Burnside was defeated by Confederate general Robert E. Lee at the Battle of Fredericksburg, and he too was relieved of command.

The bloody war continued through 1863, finally reaching a turning point with the Battle of Gettysburg in early July. Both sides were hit with terrifying losses, but the Confederacy's soldiers were routed in Pickett's Charge. That November, while the war still raged, the federal government would consecrate Gettysburg National Cemetery so that more than 3,500 fallen Union soldiers could be transferred from shallow temporary graves to a more dignified resting ground. President Lincoln spoke for slightly more than two minutes, giving history what would become known as his Gettysburg Address—one of the most famous speeches in American history. He urged the nation to resolve that "government of the people, by the people, for the people, shall not perish from the earth."

A draft was authorized for the Union army by the Conscription Act of March 3, and selections got under way that July. Angry riots broke out in New York, Buffalo, and other Northern cities. Rioters were angry that the congressional act allowed a $300 fee to avoid being drafted, unfairly protecting the wealthy.

In March 1864, Lincoln put General Ulysses S. Grant in command of all Union armies. That June saw Grant defeated by Confederate general Robert E. Lee at the Battle of Cold Harbor (Virginia); after

A Currier & Ives print depicting the assassination of Lincoln at Ford's Theater on April 14, 1865. After shooting the president, Booth leapt to the stage and shouted "Sic semper tyrannus (Thus be it always for tyrants)!" Less than two weeks later, he was apprehended and killed. Lincoln was the first American president to be assassinated.

Above: Mourning ribbons were created to honor the memory of the assassinated president. Right: A bronze statuette depicts Lincoln holding the Emancipation Proclamation.

that, Union general William Tecumseh Sherman was defeated at the Battle of Kennesaw Mountain in Georgia. Sherman was victorious in the Battle of Atlanta, however, and in November and December he led 60,000 soldiers on a "total war" march of destruction, 30 to 60 miles wide, from Atlanta to the sea. On December 26, Lincoln wrote to Sherman: "Many, many thanks for your Christmas gift—the capture of Savannah."

Abraham Lincoln faced an opponent in the 1864 election: General George B. McClellan. The president retained his office with 55 percent of the popular vote. The following year, 1865, saw a string of military victories for the Union. Northern troops occupied Columbia, South Carolina, on February 17, and Charleston surrendered to the Union fleet the next day. Petersburg, Virginia, was taken on April 2, the same day that General Grant captured the Confederate capital of Richmond. Finally, on

THE MEMORY OF ABRAHAM LINCOLN
IS ENSHRINED FOREVER

April 9, General Robert E. Lee surrendered to Grant at Appomattox Court House in Virginia.

With Lee's surrender, the American Civil War was over—but not before more than a million men had been killed or injured, making it the nation's bloodiest conflict.

On April 14, 1865, less than a week after Lee's surrender, Abraham Lincoln and his wife, Mary, attended a performance of *Our American Cousin* at Ford's Theatre in Washington, D.C. Lurking in the theater was John Wilkes Booth, a well-known stage actor sympathetic to the defeated Confederacy's cause. Angry at Lincoln's policies, Booth was determined to kill the president and avenge the South. He waited for the laughter he knew would come from a certain scene. As the audience loudly laughed, Booth approached the president from behind, shot him in the head, and fled the theater.

Lincoln was rushed to a nearby boarding house and doctors attempted to care for him, but his wound proved fatal. He died in the early hours of April 15. Secretary of War Edwin M. Stanton had taken charge of the scene. After the president passed away, Stanton made a lament that would become famous: "Now he belongs to the ages. There lies the most perfect ruler of men the world has ever seen."

THE AMERICAN SCENE

The American scene during the Lincoln administration was mainly preoccupied with the Civil War. This dominated all aspects of life and commerce.

The economy was strengthened by the production of war goods and by economic inflation. There was employment for anyone who wanted to work. In the field of literature, Edward Everett Hale's short story "The Man Without a Country" was published and would go on to become an American classic. Samuel L. Clemens (Mark Twain) was on the staff of the *Territorial Enterprise* in Virginia City, Nevada, a town that was experiencing great prosperity from the Comstock gold and silver lode. Popular songs included "Clementine," "The Battle Cry of Freedom," "Lorena" (which moved soldiers to tears as it told of a faraway sweetheart), "When Johnny Comes Marching Home," and "The Rock Island Line."

On May 26, 1864, Montana Territory was created from part of Idaho Territory. Gold explorations and discoveries had been made there in Virginia City, a town with the same name as that at the center of silver-mining activity in Nevada. Congress voted to set aside Yosemite Valley as the first national scenic reserve.

Opposite: The Lincoln Memorial in Washington, D.C. Since its dedication in 1922, the memorial has been the setting for a number of famous speeches, including Martin Luther King Jr.'s "I Have a Dream" speech.

NOTABLE SAYINGS

"You can fool some of the people all the time and all the people some of the time, but you can't fool all the people all the time."

"If slavery is not wrong, nothing is wrong."

"Do I not destroy my enemies when I make them my friends?"

"Be sure to put your feet in the right place, then stand firm."

"No man has a good enough memory to be a successful liar."

"We can complain that rose bushes have thorns, or can rejoice that thorn bushes have roses."

"Better to remain silent and be thought a fool than to speak out and remove all doubt."

"Most folks are about as happy as they make up their minds to be."

"How many legs does a dog have if you call the tail a leg? Four. Calling a tail a leg doesn't make it a leg."

17th President (1865–1869)

ANDREW JOHNSON

December 29, 1808–July 31, 1875

Political party: Democratic

Vice president: None

First Lady and family: Married Eliza McCardle on May 5, 1827. The couple had five children: Martha Johnson (1828–1901); Charles Johnson (1830–1863); Mary Johnson (1832–1883); Robert Johnson (1834–1869); and Andrew Johnson (1852–1879).

Especially remembered for: Efforts at reconstruction of the South after the Civil War. Impeachment and acquittal. The purchase of Alaska from Russia.

The Life of Andrew Johnson

Andrew Johnson was born in Raleigh, North Carolina, son of Jacob and Mary McDonough Johnson, who struggled in poverty. Young Andrew never attended school, but as a child was apprenticed to a tailor. He fled this position, and in time he opened his own tailor shop in Greeneville, Tennessee. For the rest of his life he made most of his own clothes. He learned to read and write through instruction from his wife Eliza, and at the local academy was recognized for his talents as a debater. Entering politics, he became an alderman in Greeneville in 1830 and was elected mayor in 1834. From there it was to the Tennessee State Legislature from 1835 to 1843, then to the U.S. House of Representatives from 1843 to 1853. In the House he championed the rights of poor people and supported legislation to provide farms to people who would work on and manage them.

Next, he served as governor of his state until 1857, then as a U.S. senator until 1862. From the latter year to 1865 he remained in the Senate, although Tennessee had seceded. This made him a traitor in the view of most Southerners and a hero to Northerners. At the 1864 Republican nominating convention, the party stated that it welcomed all loyal men regardless of prior political affiliation. Johnson, although both a Southerner and Democrat, was selected as the candidate for vice president, running with incumbent president Abraham Lincoln.

After Lincoln's death, Johnson moved quickly into the complex problems of the presidency in the aftermath of the Civil War. Although Congress was not in session and would not be until December, he set about reconstructing the Union. An automatic pardon was given to all who would swear an oath of allegiance, except former leaders and wealthy supporters of the Confederacy, who had to apply for a presidential pardon.

Opposite: President Andrew Johnson in his later years, as photographed by Mathew Brady.

When Congress convened, there was much debate and dissention about the condition of the South. Many of Johnson's moves were criticized. Matters were not going well in many districts, as former leaders during the Confederacy were holding new offices, and although former slaves were legally free, many restrictions were made to regulate them. Clearly, many Southerners did not want to see African Americans achieve the same status as whites or hold elective office.

Congress refused to seat any representative or senator who had held a significant office in the Confederacy. The rights of black Americans were increased, at least in theory, with the Civil Rights Act of 1866 and with the 14th amendment to the Constitution, which provided that no state could "deprive any person of life, liberty, or property, without due process of law." In the South, all state legislatures except that of Tennessee refused to ratify the amendment.

In March 1867, Congress took Reconstruction efforts a step further, placing Southern states under military rule and setting restrictions on the president's actions. President Johnson dismissed his secretary of war, Edwin M. Stanton, on February 18, 1868, because Stanton had supported Republicans who favored retribution for the South and felt that properties there were fair game as the spoils of war. The House of Representatives voted on February

A political cartoon of 1865, released before Abraham Lincoln's assassination, depicts Johnson and Lincoln attempting together to repair the Union.

THE "RAIL SPLITTER" AT WORK REPAIRING THE UNION.

21 to impeach Johnson of "high crimes and misdemeanors." A lengthy trial ensued. Benjamin Wade, the president pro tempore of the Senate, and the person in line to be president if Johnson was ousted, was so sure that Johnson would lose that he had already selected the members of his cabinet. On May 16, a ballot in the Senate failed by one vote to achieve the necessary two-thirds majority needed for impeachment.

Throughout Johnson's term, which ended in March 1869, Reconstruction had been very difficult. The transition of former slaves into society had seen many setbacks, caused in no small part by Congress's resistance to many of the president's policies.

In 1875, Andrew Johnson returned to the U.S. Senate—a vindication of his career by citizens of his state—but served only briefly before dying that summer in Carter's Station, Tennessee.

A souvenir handkerchief features a portrait of President Johnson in the center, over a scene from the Battle of Richmond, surrounded by portraits of prominent Union generals: Sherman, Grant, Sheridan, and Meade.

THE AMERICAN SCENE

As the Reconstruction era began in the South, so-called carpetbaggers arrived from the North to become involved in local and state governments and to help the former slaves. White Southerners who befriended blacks and aided them in their new-found independence were called "scalawags."

On April 27, 1865, 1,600 people were killed when the sidewheel steamer *Sultana* exploded on the Mississippi River. In the same year the Ku Klux Klan was founded in Tennessee, and the Salvation Army was organized in England, later to become prominent and much appreciated in America.

Congress passed the Civil Rights Act on April 9, 1866, overriding President Johnson's veto. The act meant that all native-born American people automatically became citizens, Indians excepted.

In New York City, "Boss" Tweed and the Tammany Hall political machine were hugely influential in city and state politics, with Tweed manipulating the state legislature through illegal payments.

Over papal objections, the American Society for the Prevention of Cruelty to Animals was established in New York City, primarily to prevent the mistreatment of horses. (Pope Pius IX's argument cited the passage in Genesis where Adam is given dominion over all other species, and deduced from this that humans have no ethical obligations toward lower animals.)

After the Civil War, the American economy had a solid foundation, but in 1866 a decline in prices set in and a recession started.

In 1867 Secretary of State William Henry Seward negotiated the purchase of Alaska (nearly 600,000 square miles) from the Russian Empire for $7,200,000—about two cents per acre. Critics sarcastically called the purchase "Seward's Icebox."

The directors of the Union Pacific Railroad were making unconscionable personal profits on the construction of the rail link with the West. To avoid a government investigation they gave shares to congressmen and sold shares at low prices in the Crédit Mobilier Company, a newly formed enterprise intended to capture some of the profits from the construction. Cornelius Vanderbilt acquired control of the New York Central Railroad. The Pullman Palace Car Company was formed by George Pullman and Andrew Carnegie, the latter being well on his way to becoming one of America's wealthiest industrialists. Jay Gould and Jim Fisk printed and sold counterfeit Erie Railroad stock certificates, and then fled to New Jersey with $6 million in illicit profits.

In June 1868, Congress voted to readmit the seven states that formerly comprised the Confederate States of America, provided that African Americans be allowed to vote.

In 1867 William Cody began an eighteen-month hunt in which he killed some 4,300 bison, giving rise to his nickname, Buffalo Bill. He was contracted to supply workers of the Kansas Pacific Railroad with buffalo meat.

Left: An assortment of passes admitting the public to Johnson's impeachment proceedings. The attempt to impeach Johnson was ultimately unsuccessful. Above: A carte de visite bearing a photograph of Johnson.

NOTABLE SAYINGS

"If the rabble were lopped at one end and the aristocrat at the other, all would be well with the country."

"The goal to strive for is a poor government but a rich people."

The Life of Ulysses S. Grant

U.S. Grant (as he was generally known) was born in Point Pleasant, Ohio, son of Jesse Root and Hannah Simpson Grant. His father was a tanner, and the family was of average financial circumstances. At his father's insistence but against his own preference, he was sent to West Point, where he graduated near the bottom of his class. He received an army commission and embarked on a military career, but resigned (according to some rumors, after being caught drinking on duty).

At the outset of the Civil War in the spring of 1861, Grant was clerking for his father in a leather shop in Galena, Illinois. He was tapped by the governor to head a disorganized regiment of volunteer soldiers. He performed with distinction, turning the unit into a dynamic company. His achievement was recognized, and by September 1861 he was a brigadier general.

Grant was sent to gain federal control of the Mississippi River. In February 1862 he captured Fort Henry and mounted an attack against Fort Donelson. The Confederate general in charge asked for terms to be negotiated, to which Grant replied that the only option was unconditional surrender. President Lincoln advanced Grant to major general. At the Battle of Shiloh he suffered a setback, and some suggested that Lincoln remove him from command. The president, however, kept his faith in Grant, who went on to take Vicksburg, Mississippi, after a long and bitter siege, thus dividing the Confederacy into two parts. From there he vanquished the Confederates at Chattanooga. Lincoln appointed him general-in-chief in March, and Grant directed much of the rest of the war, sending General William Tecumseh Sherman on this march through Georgia and the South, defeating General Robert E. Lee's Army of Northern Virginia. On April 9, 1865, General Lee surrendered at Appomattox Court House in Virginia. Grant formulated terms of surrender that prevented treason trials and were intended to smooth the return of Confederate soldiers to civilian life.

18th President (1869–1877)

ULYSSES S. GRANT

April 27, 1822–July 23, 1885

Political party: Republican

Vice president: Schuyler Colfax, 1869 to 1873; Henry Wilson, 1873 to 1875; none 1875 to 1877

First Lady and family: Married Julia Boggs Dent on August 22, 1848. The couple had four children: Frederick Dent Grant (1850–1912); Ulysses Simpson Grant (1852–1929); Ellen Wrenshall Grant (1855–1922); and Jesse Root Grant (1858–1934).

Especially remembered for: Military service during the Civil War. Being a great general but a below-average president. Allowing himself to be used by others. Depiction on several types of paper money (most famously the $50 bill) and on commemorative coins.

In the 1868 presidential contest, military hero Grant, running on the Republican ticket, was elected by the support of bankers and creditors who held bonds and wanted them repaid in gold, as opposed to the Democratic platform, which provided for payment in paper money (of lesser value).

Citizens hoped that the turmoil of Reconstruction under the Johnson administration would come to a satisfactory conclusion. This did not happen, however. Grant seemed to be overwhelmed by the intricacies of the government and the problems confronting it. Unwisely, he accepted gifts from those seeking government favors. In one memorable gaffe he warmly met two notorious stock-market speculators and manipulators, James Fisk and Jay Gould, who later conspired to corner the market in gold.

Despite many problems, including alcoholism, Grant persevered, and in the 1872 presidential contest he was reelected in a contest against Democratic challenger Horace Greeley, famous New York newspaper publisher. His second term ran its course without distinction, as Reconstruction problems continued, with many eventually worked out

Opposite: A portrait of General Grant in uniform. Upper left: An assortment of campaign pins and a ribbon endorsing Grant for president. Below: A cigar box with a fanciful political cartoon depicting the presidential race of 1880. Former president Grant and Democratic candidate Thomas Bayard appear to be holding their own, while Democratic vice-presidential nominee Thomas Hendricks, Democrat Samuel Tilden, and Republican John Sherman have hit a rough patch.

through actions in the South rather than by presidential leadership.

After he left office in 1877 he joined a financial firm as a partner. The company went bankrupt. In desperate financial straits and with cancer of the throat, Grant began to write his memoirs. The project was completed shortly before his death at a resort in Mount Gregor, New York, on July 23, 1885. Upon publication, the book became a best-seller and earned his family nearly $450,000.

Below: This 1885 bust of Grant in his military uniform is actually an advertisement for the Empire Soap Company. Opposite: Grant is depicted in the laurel wreath of martial victory on the invitation to the inaugural reception of March 4, 1969.

THE AMERICAN SCENE

On May 10, 1869, at Promontory Summit, Utah, railroad tracks from the East met those from the West, and the Union Pacific and Central Pacific railroads joined to complete the transcontinental rail link. To get from New York to California, it was no longer necessary to travel south by ship, cross Panama, and then head back north. By rail the trip from New York City to San Francisco could be made in only eight days.

On the American grocery scene, the H.J. Heinz Company and the Campbell Soup Company were both founded during Grant's presidency, in 1869.

The first of several notable "black days" in financial history occurred on Wall Street on "Black Friday," September 24, 1869, which saw many speculators ruined. Jay Gould, James Fisk, and others, one of whom was President Grant's brother-in-law, attempted to corner the market on gold. They drove the price up to $162 per ounce, at which point Secretary of the Treasury George Boutwell began to sell government gold holdings to drive down the price.

The Cincinnati Red Stockings, the first professional baseball team, had an undefeated season, winning 56 games and tying one. The first intercollegiate football game, with 25 men per team, was held on November 6 between Rutgers and Princeton, with Rutgers the winner.

Gypsy moths were imported into the United States by a well-meaning entrepreneur who hoped they would be the nucleus for a native silk industry. As with many importations of foreign species, the results were disastrous, with the moths being destructive to native hardwood trees.

In 1870 the federal census reported the United States population as 38,558,371, including about three million immigrants who had arrived in the preceding decade. In this year the first black members of Congress were seated, one in the House and one in the Senate. The 15th Amendment to the U.S. Constitution was ratified, forbidding Americans to be denied the right to vote "on account

of race, color, or previous condition of servitude." Women were not included, and African Americans still had a difficult time registering to vote in certain Southern areas.

The Great Chicago Fire, popularly said to have been started when Mrs. O'Leary's cow kicked over a lantern, raged on October 8 and 9, 1871, destroying nearly four square miles of the city. Damages were estimated at $222 million, and about 250 people died.

In 1875 Alexander Graham Bell conducted experiments that would lead to the creation of the telephone. On March 1, Congress passed a civil rights act that guaranteed African Americans equal rights in public places and forbade their exclusion from juries, but for the next 80 years in many areas of the South, black people still had to use separate restrooms, drinking fountains, bus seating sections, waiting rooms, educational facilities, and so on.

On June 25, 1876, General George Armstrong Custer and more than 250 of his men engaged a coalition of Indians led by Sioux chief Sitting Bull, in the Battle of the Little Bighorn. It was an overwhelming victory for the Indians; Custer was killed in his "last stand," and all of his soldiers died in the battle, as well.

The nation's Centennial Exhibition was held in Fairmount Park in Philadelphia on a 236-acre site. On opening day, May 10, President Grant addressed the assembled throng, with a celebrated visitor, Dom Pedro, emperor of Brazil, at his side. Exhibits of art, industries, agriculture, and other accomplishments were mounted by 37 nations and 26 states during the celebration of the 100th anniversary of American independence.

NOTABLE SAYINGS

"I have never advocated war as a means of peace."

"My failures have been errors of judgment, not of intent."

"In every battle there comes a time when both sides consider themselves beaten. Then he who continues the attack wins."

19th President (1877–1881)

RUTHERFORD B. HAYES

October 4, 1822–January 17, 1893

Political party: Republican

Vice president: William Wheeler, 1877 to 1881

First Lady and family: Married Lucy Ware Webb on December 30, 1852. The couple had eight children: Birchard Austin Hayes (1853–1926); James Webb Cook Hayes (1856–1934); Rutherford Platt Hayes (1858–1927); Joseph Thompson Hayes (1861–1863); George Crook Hayes (1864–1866); Fanny Hayes (1867–1950); Scott Russell Hayes (1871–1923); and Manning Force Hayes (1873–1874). In the White House the First Lady was known as Lemonade Lucy, as she forbade the serving of alcohol.

Especially remembered for: The most contested, controversial election results up to that time in history. Integrity and temperance, seemingly a contrast to the previous administration. Presidency marked by lack of cooperation between Northern and Southern factions.

The Life of Rutherford B. Hayes

Rutherford B. Hayes was born in Delaware, Ohio, to Rutherford and Sophia Birchard Hayes. He graduated from Kenyon College in 1842 and Harvard Law School in 1845, after which he practiced law for five years in Lower Sandusky, Ohio, then went to Cincinnati, where he continued in the profession and also became involved in politics in the Whig Party. Hayes served in the Civil War, rose to become brevet major general, and was wounded in action. Afterward he went to the U.S. House of Representatives from 1865 to 1867. As a House member, he was disturbed at the direction Reconstruction had taken, and felt that the Andrew Johnson administration was overly influenced by former Confederates. He then served as governor of his home state from 1868 to 1872 and again in 1876 and 1877.

In 1876 Hayes was nominated as the Republican candidate for president, opposing Samuel J. Tilden, governor of New York State. Although Hayes had many supporters—popular writer Mark Twain among them—he had no illusions about his chances of victory. After the popular votes were counted, the score was 4,300,000 for Tilden and 4,036,000 for Hayes. At the Electoral College, votes from Florida, Louisiana, and South Carolina were disputed. Tilden would be the winner if just one of these votes went to him, but for Hayes to be elected he would need all the votes that were in contention. The matter was hotly disputed. In January 1877, with no winner declared, Congress established a commission to decide. Made up of eight Republicans and seven Democrats, the commission voted down party lines, and every disputed vote was given to Hayes. The final count was 185 to 184.

President Hayes took office on March 4, in place of the popular-vote winner, Samuel Tilden.

Opposite: President Hayes as captured by Mathew Brady's camera. A passionate advocate of education, Hayes believed that the divisions in American society could be eradicated through vocational and academic education.

The editor of the *Washington Post,* which was founded later in the year (December 6, 1877), would call Hayes "His Fraudulency" and refer to "President Tilden" in discussions about "the crime of 1876."

Hayes endeavored to appoint cabinet members and other key officials on the basis of merit, causing problems for members of his party who had promised patronage for certain interests in the South, including at least one cabinet post and the assurance that federal troops would be withdrawn from Louisiana and South Carolina. Hayes did not carry out these promises, and as a result his administration lost influence in the South, weakening its effectiveness. Hayes did not seek reelection in 1880 but retired to Spiegel Grove, his estate in Fremont, Ohio, where he lived until his death early in 1893.

THE AMERICAN SCENE

As Hayes entered the White House in 1877 the United States continued in an economic slump that had commenced in 1873. There was a further dip in that year, what some called the Panic of 1877.

In Hartford, Connecticut, Augustus Pope opened the first bicycle factory in the United States, manufacturing the Columbia brand bicycle. Bicycling would catch on as a fad in America. It was a boon for people who didn't own horses and were dependent on streetcars or other public transportation.

They year 1877 saw an explosion of telephone use: six Bell telephones were put into commercial use in May, and by August nearly 800 were being used nationwide. Thomas Edison continued his prolific inventions, demonstrating a hand-cranked phonograph in November 1877 (originally envisioned as a business machine, it would finally take off as home entertainment in the 1890s).

In 1879 crop failure in Europe caused a great demand for American wheat exports, bringing prosperity to farms in the Midwest, with influence on other areas as well, changing the economic outlook from negative to positive. The silver mining industry was booming in Colorado, and such towns as Central City, Black Hawk, Georgetown, and, further to the west, Leadville, were enjoying good times. Silverites (politicians and others who promoted silver) were temporarily happy, as under the 1878 Bland-Allison Act the government continued to buy millions of ounces of unwanted metal. However, during the next two decades silver would become the burning political question of the age. By 1879, it was already a standard political issue.

On October 21, 1879, Thomas Alva Edison claimed success in his search for a suitable material from which to make a filament for an incandescent lamp. This idea of lighting was not new, and others had demonstrated such lamps earlier, but none had lasted for an appreciable length of time. Frank Winfield Woolworth laid the foundation for a fortune made in five-and-dime stores when he set up a counter at which all merchandise cost five cents. "Twenty nickels make a dollar, you know," he reportedly said. He then borrowed $400 to open a store in Utica, New York, which failed in three months. Undaunted, he opened a similar store in Lancaster, Pennsylvania. What happened changed the face of retailing in America.

NOTABLE SAYINGS

Of the telephone: "Amazing invention, who would ever want to use one of them?"

"Nothing brings out the lower traits of human nature like office seeking."

"It is now true that this is God's country if equal rights—a fair start and an equal chance at the race of life—are everywhere secured to all."

"Conscience is the authentic voice of God to you."

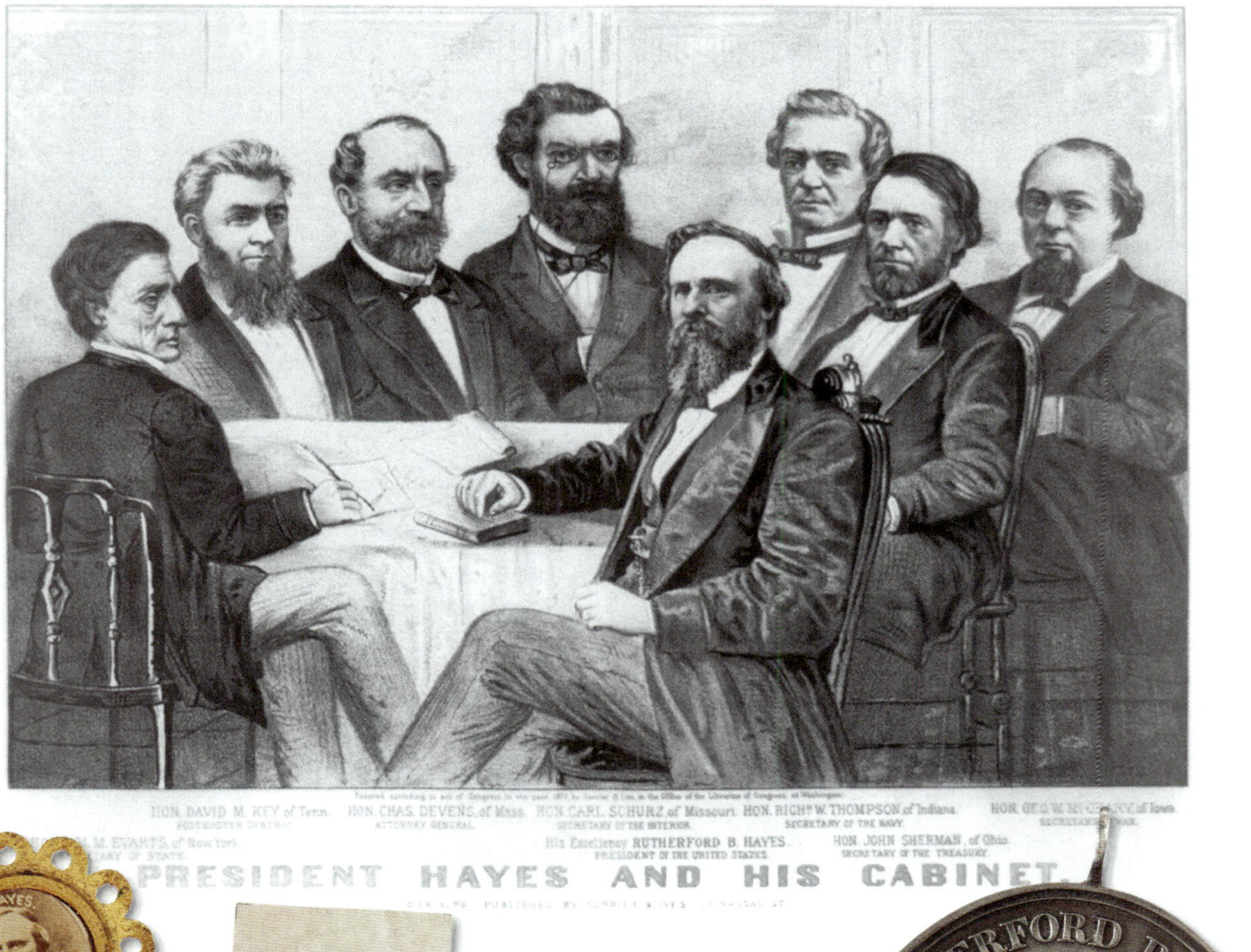

Top: A Currier & Ives lithograph depicting President Hayes and his cabinet, circa 1877. Left: Ribbons and a portrait pin showed support for Hayes's presidential campaign. Above: President Hayes's Indian peace medal.

20th President (1881)

JAMES A. GARFIELD

November 19, 1831–September 19, 1881

Political party: Republican

Vice president: Chester Alan Arthur, 1881

First Lady and family: Married Lucretia Rudolph on November 11, 1858. She was well read in the classics, designed the family's mansion, and was a devout adherent of the Disciples of Christ. The couple had seven children: Eliza A. Garfield (1860–1863); Harry A. Garfield (1863–1942); James R. Garfield (1865–1950); Mary Garfield (1867–1947); Irvin M. Garfield (1870–1951); Abram Garfield (1872–1958); and Edward Garfield (1874–1876).

Especially remembered for: Brief presidency terminated by his assassination. He was widely mourned, and his portrait soon appeared on paper money.

The Life of James A. Garfield

James A. Garfield was born in Orange, Ohio, son of Abram and Eliza Ballou Garfield. When James was two years old his father died. As a youth he worked at various occupations including driving mule teams that towed canal boats. In 1856 he graduated from Williams College in Massachusetts. He joined the faculty of the Western Reserve Eclectic Institute (later known as Hiram College) as a professor in the classics, and within a year was named president of the institution.

In 1859 Garfield was elected to the Ohio State Senate on the Republican ticket. In the Civil War he distinguished himself in action in 1862 when he led a brigade against Confederate soldiers at Middle Creek, Kentucky. He was made a brigadier general, and two years later a general. In the meantime, in 1862 he was elected as an Ohio representative to the U.S. Congress. On the advice of President Lincoln he resigned his military commission. For 18 years he was in the House of Representatives, later becoming the leading Republican in that body. Then in 1880 he was elected to the Senate.

For the 1880 presidential nomination many Republican Party supporters wanted Ulysses S. Grant to come out of retirement to run for a third term. Garfield endorsed John Sherman, but the effort was a failure. The convention was deadlocked. Finally, on the 36th ballot Garfield himself was chosen, the first true dark horse candidate since Franklin Pierce in 1852. In the popular vote he bested his Democratic opponent (General Winfield Scott Hancock) by just 10,000 votes.

After his inauguration, certain of his appointments had to be ratified by the Senate. The spoils went to the victor, and presidents of this era gained many advantages by dispensing patronage. Senator Roscoe Conkling of New York, one of the most powerful men in the Senate, insisted that many of his

Opposite: President Garfield as depicted by artist Lawrence Williams. A self-made man known for his oratorical skill, Garfield would hold the office of president only 200 days.

favorites be appointed. Garfield complied in most cases, but a contretemps arose when the president ignored Conkling's preference for the collector of the Port of New York, America's main port of entry. The two sparred, but Garfield secured the necessary votes to confirm his choice.

On July 2, 1881, Charles J. Guiteau, a disappointed office seeker, shot the president in a Washington railroad station. Despite a brief hope of recovery, Garfield died painfully from internal hemorrhage and infection on September 19 at the New Jersey seaside, where he had been taken to recuperate.

THE AMERICAN SCENE

In 1881 the Supreme Court ruled the Federal Income Tax Law of 1862 unconstitutional. The American National Red Cross was founded by Clara Barton in Washington, D.C.

The Wharton School of Finance was established at the University of Pennsylvania with a gift from nickel baron Joseph Wharton, who for years had been the sole U.S. refiner of nickel (and a close friend of politicians and Mint interests). The Barnum & Bailey Circus was created by a merger between P.T. Barnum's traveling show and that of James Anthony Bailey. Circuses were big businesses in the United States, and usually traveled from city to city in special railroad cars.

Above: The assassination as depicted in *Frank Leslie's Illustrated Newspaper*, July 16, 1881.

NOTABLE SAYINGS

"I have many troubles in my life, but the worst of them never came."

"Whoever controls the volume of money in any country is absolute master of all industrial commerce."

"A brave man is a man who dares to look the devil in the face and tell him he is a devil."

21st President (1881–1885)

CHESTER ALAN ARTHUR

October 5, 1829–November 18, 1886

The Life of Chester Alan Arthur

Chester Alan Arthur was born in Fairfield, Vermont, son of William and Malvina Stone Arthur. His father, who had come to America from Ireland, was a Baptist minister. Chester Arthur graduated from Union College a Phi Beta Kappa in 1848, then taught school while studying law. After being admitted to the bar, he practiced law in New York City. After the Civil War commenced he served for a time as quartermaster general for New York State.

In 1871 President Grant appointed him collector of the Port of New York, a position that was one of the most prized political plums and controlled by Roscoe Conkling and his Republican cronies. Arthur dutifully made his nearly 1,000 employees beholden to Conkling's interests. In 1878, President Hayes ousted Arthur from the post. As vice president to James Garfield starting in March 1881, Arthur supported Conkling in his sparring with President Garfield over the latest nomination for this desirable political post.

When Arthur succeeded to the presidency following the death of Garfield, he took full advantage of his ability to dispense patronage to his own friends and supporters, although he did so without dishonesty. He personally enjoyed the good life, dressed well, and enjoyed the company of those prominent in society.

In seeming contradiction to his own past actions, he advocated civil service reform. The Pendleton Act of 1883 set up the Civil Service Commission, which prohibited politicians from extracting money from appointees and made certain positions available to the best-qualified applicants.

A supporter of tariff reform, he advocated lowering rates so that the government would not have surpluses and at the same time imported goods would be cheaper. The effort was partially successful in that it led to the Tariff Act of 1883. Arthur worked to establish a general immigration law that

Political party: Republican

Vice president: None

First Lady and family: Married Ellen Lewis Herndon (only child of Captain William Lewis Herndon of the United States Navy, who went down with the SS *Central America* in 1857) on October 25, 1859. She died of pneumonia on January 12, 1880. The couple had three children: William Lewis Herndon Arthur (1860–1863); Chester Alan Arthur (1864–1937); and Ellen Herndon Arthur (1871–1915). At the White House his sister Mary (Mrs. John E. McElroy) served as hostess and helped care for his daughter Ellen.

Especially remembered for: The first significant federal immigration law, enacted during his administration. His dislike of the furnishings of the White House; he did not move in until it was redecorated in the Victorian style with everything new. (The old furniture was sold at auction.) Change of his reception from one of distrust when he became president to respect when he left office.

Opposite: Chester Alan Arthur in his official White House portrait, painted by Daniel Huntington in 1885. Left: A newspaper's depiction of Arthur taking the oath as president after the assassination of President Garfield. Top: Like many presidents before him, Arthur was depicted on cigar labels. Bottom: An 1882 photograph of Arthur.

excluded criminals, paupers, and the mentally ill from coming to America.

By the end of his term, Arthur had earned the respect of many legislators and the public. In 1884, he sought reelection on the Republican ticket, although he was suffering from a fatal kidney disease that he had not disclosed to the public. He was not nominated.

Chester Alan Arthur died in New York City in November 1886.

THE AMERICAN SCENE

During President Arthur's term, a congressional committee reported that adulteration of food had caused many deaths and had constituted a fraud upon the people. However, little would be accomplished until the Pure Food and Drug Act of 1906. Advertising for patent medicines and drugs was unregulated and was full of preposterous, unfounded claims.

On September 4, 1882, electricity was used for the first time to illuminate large sections of New

York City. Power was generated by the Edison Illuminating Company, financed by J.P. Morgan. However, conditions would remain primitive for years to come. In 1882, only 2% of the homes in New York were connected to a water main, and nearly all private houses had privies in the backyard.

Popular criticism of industrial "robber barons" was widespread in this era. As an example of a corporate monopoly, the Standard Oil Trust was incorporated by John D. Rockefeller and his associates. This brought more than 80% of the American petroleum industry under a single management.

Jesse James, the notorious outlaw who was then living under the name ofThomas Howard, was shot and killed by a friend who sought to claim a large cash reward for James "dead or alive."

On March 3, 1883, Congress voted to build three new warships, the first to be constructed since the Civil War. Since that conflict, America had fallen to 12th place among sea powers of the world. William Cody's traveling entourage, "Buffalo Bill's Wild West," opened in Omaha, Nebraska, in 1883 and went on to achieve great fame, thrilling Americans (and audiences in Europe) with dramatizations of the rough-and-ready cowboy life.

The Brooklyn Bridge opened in 1883, connecting Brooklyn to Manhattan. Robert Louis Stevenson and Mark Twain were among the popular writers of the day. In other diversions, the roller coaster, a new attraction, debuted at Coney Island.

NOTABLE SAYINGS

"Good ballplayers will make good citizens."

"If it were not for the reporters I would tell you the truth."

In 1883, President Arthur and companions went on an expedition to Yellowstone National Park and northwestern Wyoming. Second from the right is Robert Todd Lincoln, the only surviving son of Abraham Lincoln.

22nd President (first term: 1885–1889)

GROVER CLEVELAND

March 18, 1837–June 24, 1908

Political party: Democratic

Vice president: Thomas Hendricks, March 4 to November 25, 1885; none November 26, 1885 to 1889

First Lady and family: Married Frances Folsom on June 2, 1886. She was the daughter of Cleveland's late law partner, and he had been her legal guardian since she was 11. Although he had fathered a child earlier, he did not marry the mother. He was the only president to have his wedding ceremony in the White House. The Clevelands had five children: Ruth Cleveland (1891–1904); Esther Cleveland (1893–1980); Marion Cleveland (1895–1977); Richard Folsom Cleveland (1897–1974); and Francis Grover Cleveland (1903–1995).

Especially remembered for: Objective evaluation of legislative proposals with a desire to be fair and to benefit the citizenry. Action against scandals involving railroads. Passage of the Interstate Commerce Act.

The Life of Grover Cleveland

Grover Cleveland was born in Caldwell, New Jersey, on March 18, 1837, son of Richard Falley Cleveland (a Presbyterian minister) and Anne Neal Cleveland. He was raised in upstate New York with no advanced education, but read law and set up practice in Buffalo.

Cleveland served as sheriff of Erie County, New York, from 1870 to 1873; as mayor of Buffalo on a platform of reform in 1882; and as governor of New York from 1883 to 1885. As the Democratic presidential candidate in 1884 he faced Republican candidate James G. Blaine of Maine, who was nicknamed "the Plumed Knight" and widely considered to be the favorite. The tide turned when a well-meaning supporter of Blaine chastised the Democratic Party as one of "rum, Romanism, and rebellion," the "Romanism" referring to members of the Catholic Church. This aroused many citizens who had been sitting on the sidelines and moved them to vote for Cleveland, making him the victor. He was the first Democrat to reach the White House since James Buchanan was elected in 1856.

With a dislike of social functions and formal dinners, Cleveland was seemingly a dedicated bachelor. That ended on June 2, 1886, when he took as his bride the 21-year-old Frances Folsom in a ceremony performed at the White House.

The president endeavored to be impartial to groups seeking to gain influence; likewise, he tried to promote legislation that he considered to be in the public good. He aided farmers in Texas crippled by drought, vetoed fraudulent applications for Civil War veterans' pensions, and probed irregularities in the granting of vast tracts of Western land to railroads that had bribed legislators, resulting in 81 million acres' being returned to the government. He also endorsed the Interstate Commerce Act, which regulated railroads.

In 1887 Cleveland called for Congress to reduce certain import tariffs that he felt remained unnecessarily high. This angered many Northern supporters,

FOR PRESIDENT

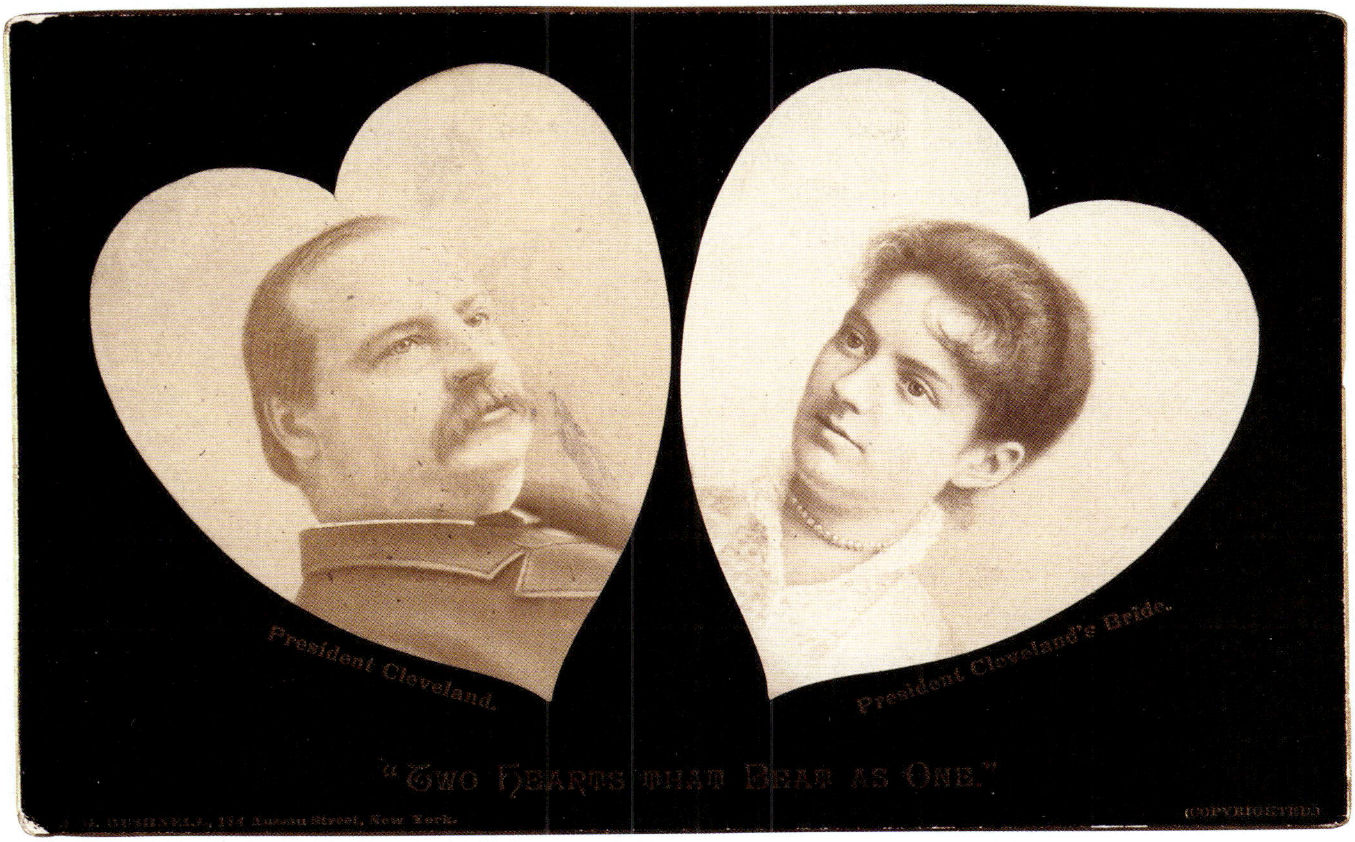

who desired to protect domestic industry. In 1888 he ran for reelection against Republican Benjamin Harrison. Although Cleveland won more popular votes, Harrison was the winner of the deciding Electoral College vote. Cleveland left Washington to reside in New York City, where his wife gave birth to their first child, known as Baby Ruth (the namesake of the candy bar). He would run for president again—and win—in 1892.

THE AMERICAN SCENE

In Salem, Massachusetts, Parker Brothers was founded in 1885; its first game was called Banking. Fifty years later another game, Monopoly, would make the company a fortune. The Audubon Society was formed.

The labor movement in the United States, which had an uncertain status and future up to this point and had been largely at the mercy of industrialists, received worldwide attention and gained its first martyrs in 1886 in Chicago's Haymarket Massacre. This disaster had its beginnings when police fired into a crowd of striking laborers on May 1, killing four and wounding others. Three days later, a peaceful mass meeting was held to protest police brutality; when an unidentified person threw a bomb, police

Opposite: Presidential candidate Grover Cleveland on a campaign poster from 1884. Top: The American public was delighted by Cleveland's wedding. This dual portrait of Cleveland and his bride was one keepsake created to commemorate the event. Left: An illustration of the wedding ceremony.

fired into the crowd, and more casualties were added to the list.

Aluminum, which had been known for many years but was difficult to refine, lost its status as a semi-valuable metal in 1886 when Charles M. Hall devised a practical method of extracting it from bauxite ore by the use of electricity.

On October 28, 1886, a gift from France, the Statue of Liberty (more formally known as *Liberty Enlightening the World*) was dedicated on Bedloe's Island in New York Harbor.

Richard Warren Sears entered the merchandising business in Minnesota by buying a group of watches that had been refused by a local jeweler, thus sowing the seed for Sears, Roebuck & Co. On the beverage scene, Coca-Cola was sold for the first time in Atlanta, Georgia.

The Interstate Commerce Act, approved by Congress, became effective on February 4, 1887, and regulated the rates of railroads. By the end of this year there were 200,000 telephone subscribers in America.

George Eastman, of Rochester, New York, introduced the Kodak box camera, which made it possible for amateurs to take satisfactory photographs. For $25 a shutterbug could buy a Kodak loaded with enough roll film to snap 100 shots. He could then send the camera and film with $10 to Kodak headquarters in Rochester; Kodak would develop the film, make prints, and load a new roll of film into his camera.

The economy had been strengthening ever since the early 1880s. During Cleveland's time in office it went into overdrive, fueled by vast investments in the Midwestern states.

Above right: Mrs. Frances Cleveland, née Frances Folsom, as depicted by prominent Swedish artist Anders Zorn in 1899. Zorn's subjects included three American presidents, including President Cleveland.

NOTABLE SAYINGS

"It is the responsibility of the citizens to support their government. It is not the responsibility of the government to support its citizens."

"Sensible and responsible women do not want to vote. The relative positions to be assumed by man and woman and the working out of our civilization were assigned long ago by a higher intelligence than ours."

"A man is known by the company he keeps, and also by the company from which he is kept out."

23rd President (1889–1893)

BENJAMIN HARRISON

August 20, 1833–March 13, 1901

Political party: Republican

Vice president: Levi P. Morton, 1889 to 1893

First Lady and family: Married Caroline Lavinia Scott on October 20, 1853. After an extended illness she died in October 1892, near the end of Harrison's presidency. While serving as First Lady she had the White House renovated and improved its appointments. Harrison's second wife was his wife's niece, the much younger widow Mary Scott Lord Dimmick (1858–1948), whom he married on April 6, 1896, much to the dismay of her three children, who refused to attend the wedding. Harrison had three children: Russell Benjamin Harrison (1854–1936); Mary Scott Harrison (1858–1930); and Elizabeth Harrison (1897–1955)

Especially remembered for: Successful foreign policy. Robust economy and a Treasury surplus in the beginning of his administration. Being a staunch Presbyterian, who often quoted the Bible and felt that God shepherded his presidency.

The Life of Benjamin Harrison

Benjamin Harrison was born in North Bend, Ohio, son of John Scott and Elizabeth Ramsey Irwin Harrison. His grandfather was President William Henry Harrison (in office in 1841). He graduated in 1852 from Miami University in Oxford, Ohio, and went to Cincinnati, where he studied law. Afterward he moved to Indianapolis and set up practice. With Republican leanings he was a vigorous campaigner for the party's candidates. In the Civil War he was commissioned as a second lieutenant, rising to the rank of general, more by exercising political influence than any accomplishments on the battlefield. After the war he served as colonel of the 70th Indiana Volunteer Infantry.

Harrison ran twice for the office of governor of Indiana but was defeated each time. Opponents belittled him as "Kid Gloves" Harrison. From 1881 to 1887 he served in the United States Senate, where he took up causes he thought worthy, such as aid to Native Americans, Civil War veterans, and homesteaders on the frontier. He lost his 1886 bid for reelection.

With an endorsement from the Republicans' 1884 nominee, James G. Blaine, Harrison entered the 1888 presidential contest. He faced incumbent Grover Cleveland. Harrison engaged in what was called a "front porch" campaign—a seemingly casual effort in which he greeted those who cared to visit him in Indianapolis—but did little on a national scale. Short, stout, and often seen with a cigar in his mouth, Harrison was viewed as having a colorless personality.

In the election Cleveland carried the popular vote, 5,540,309 to Harrison's 5,444,337, but in the Electoral College Harrison won 233 to 168. Primaries held in Maine in the weeks prior to the national election gave Harrison the lead, giving rise to the popular axiom "As Maine goes, so goes the nation." Harrison's cabinet and patronage appointments were largely determined by Republican Party

bosses, whose promises to supporters and favor seekers Harrison felt obliged to honor.

During his administration Harrison had a successful foreign policy capped by the meeting of the first Pan-American Congress in Washington in 1889, a prelude to what became the Pan-American Union. He worked on the expansion of the navy, the improvement of commercial steamship lines through subsidies, and many domestic improvements. He signed the Sherman Anti-Trust Act into law, although it proved largely ineffective through corporate manipulations and evasions (years later, Theodore Roosevelt would gain fame as the "Trust Buster").

Harrison ran for reelection but lost to Grover Cleveland. He went back to Indianapolis, where he was often consulted on government policies. In 1896 he married widow Mary Dimmick. He died in Indianapolis in 1901.

Opposite: Benjamin Harrison as depicted by Lawrence Williams. Right: A humorous piece of political ephemera, this ribbon was worn by a voter who could boast of voting for Harrison, the winning presidential candidate. Below: Another political keepsake is this mug bearing Harrison's likeness.

Above: A photograph of Harrison predating his presidency. Below right: Despite Harrison's dour visage, he, like many of his predecessors, appeared on a cigar label of the era.

THE AMERICAN SCENE

At the outset of the Harrison administration the national economy continued to be in overdrive. It was known as the Gilded Age (from the title of a Mark Twain book of the preceding decade). Six weeks after his inauguration, on April 22, 1889, President Harrison made 1,900,000 acres of former Indian lands available to white homesteaders. The lands were to be distributed starting at noon that day. However, by that morning, many homesteaders who had come earlier—"sooners," as they were called—had already rushed into the "Unassigned Lands" and staked their claims. By nightfall, communities were established at Guthrie, Oklahoma City, and elsewhere. In the same year, North Dakota, South Dakota, Montana, and Washington were admitted to the Union.

On July 8 a new American publication started: the *Wall Street Journal* was an expansion of a daily financial newsletter issued by Dow Jones & Company, owned by Charles Henry Dow and Edward D. Jones.

Congress passed the Sherman Anti-Trust Act on July 2, 1890, seeking to curtail "restraint of trade or commerce" and limit the powers of monopolies, which at the time had a stranglehold on certain sectors of the American economy. The McKinley Tariff Act, passed on October 1, 1890, increased certain tariffs to record high levels but provided for reciprocal agreements with certain other countries. William Jennings Bryan was elected a congressman from Nebraska, his first public office. The one-sided Battle of Wounded Knee in South Dakota saw about 350 Sioux killed by nearly 500 government soldiers; it effectively ended the resistance of Native Americans to the encroachments of white men.

Steel baron Andrew Carnegie gave a gift to New York City in May of 1891: the building that would later become known as Carnegie Hall. In Springfield, Massachusetts, physical-education instructor James Naismith invented the sport of basketball.

NOTABLE SAYINGS

"We Americans have no commission from God to police the world."

24th President (second term: 1893 to 1897)

GROVER CLEVELAND

March 18, 1837–June 24, 1908

Political party: Democratic

Vice president: Adlai E. Stevenson, 1893 to 1897

First Lady and family: Frances Folsom Cleveland (see details under 22nd presidency)

Especially remembered for: Being the only president to serve two nonconsecutive terms (a State Department ruling held that as his terms were not consecutive, he should be considered as both the 22nd and 24th president). His work to repeal the Sherman Silver Purchase Act. Maintaining financial stability while gold reserves were being drained to overseas.

The Second Administration of Grover Cleveland

In the presidential election year of 1892, the groundswell of popular support was with the Democratic candidate, Grover Cleveland, who had served a term from 1885 to 1889. Adlai E. Stevenson was his running mate. President Benjamin Harrison, the incumbent, lost the election because of widespread dissatisfaction with the economy and, in particular, the perceived ill effects of the McKinley Tariff Act, which diminished exports of agricultural products.

Cleveland returned to the White House in March 1893 with the country in deep trouble, a complete turnaround from the prosperity of his first term. Business failures were spreading widely, and there was particular distress in the prairie states, where a decade of runaway inflation and prosperity had ended. Cleveland was able to maintain the integrity of the Treasury reserves, and the American financial system began to improve. In Chicago, railroad workers went on strike against a federal injunction. The president threatened to send federal troops as enforcement. Certain of his policies and actions proved unpopular with fellow Democrats, including his repeal of the Sherman Silver Purchase Act of 1890. Accordingly, in 1896 he was not nominated again for president.

In retirement, Grover Cleveland lived in Princeton, New Jersey, and was a frequent visitor to New Hampshire, where he enjoyed relaxing in his summer home on an estate in Tamworth. He died in Princeton in 1908.

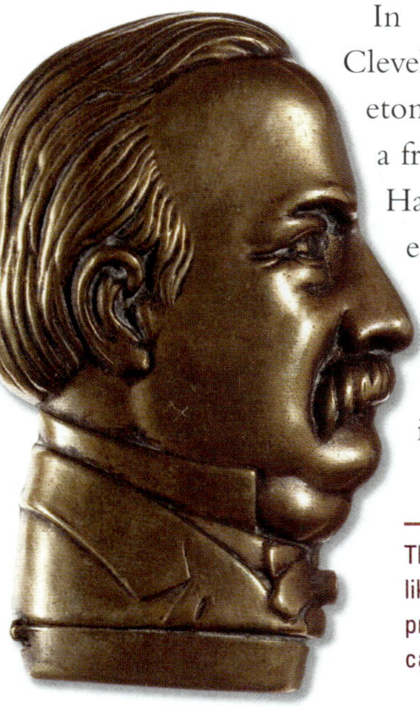

This match safe made in the likeness of Cleveland was produced for his presidential campaign.

THE AMERICAN SCENE

Grover Cleveland's second term started with the American economy in a slump that accelerated into the Panic of '93. The stock market dropped sharply on May 5, and June 27 brought a collapse followed by depression. By the end of the year, hundreds of U.S. banks had failed, thousands of businesses had closed, and nearly a hundred railroads went bankrupt. The hard times would last through Cleveland's entire second presidency.

Henry Ford, age 30, tested his first gasoline-powered automobile, a step that would lead to the founding of one of America's greatest industrial empires.

Western expansion had been part of American life in the 19th century, but the first to widely publicize its importance was historian Frederick Jackson Turner, who delivered the paper "The Significance of the Frontier in American History" to the American Historical Association at the 1893 World's Columbian Exposition in Chicago. Turner suggested that the challenges of the frontier were responsible for developing the American spirit of self-reliance, energy, inventiveness, and realism.

There wasn't much open land left, but among the remainder was a six-million-acre tract bought by the government from the Cherokees. This was opened to homesteaders on September 16, 1893. It was estimated that fewer than 1,100 bison survived in the United States—a far cry from the countless millions of a few decades earlier.

On June 18, 1894, Congress passed an act establishing the first Monday of every September as Labor Day.

No one knows when or where the first motion picture was projected to a paying audience, but tradition maintains that it occurred in Paris in December 1895. Another contender is a display said to have taken place on May 20 of that year in a converted New York store at 153 Broadway, where viewers saw a four-minute film of a boxing match.

"America the Beautiful," by Katherine Lee Bates, was published.

On August 17, 1896, gold was discovered in the Klondike region of Alaska, setting off a new gold rush that began early in 1897 and would last for the next several years. In Athens, Greece, the first modern Olympic Games were held, with the U.S. team taking the top prize in 11 of the 43 athletic contests.

Opposite: Artist Lawrence Williams's depiction of President Cleveland. Below top: One of the souvenirs produced to mark Cleveland's presidency was this flag bearing his likeness. Below bottom: Cleveland makes a magisterial appearance on a cigar label.

25th President (1897–1901)

WILLIAM McKINLEY

January 29, 1843–September 14, 1901

Political party: Republican

Vice president: Garret Hobart, 1897 to 1901; Theodore Roosevelt, 1901

First Lady and family: Married Ida Saxton on January 25, 1871. The couple had two children, both of whom lived only a short time: Katherine McKinley (1871–1875); and Ida McKinley (1873). After the death of her children, Ida led an emotionally distressed life, punctuated by seizures. Despite travails, the couple remained close.

Especially remembered for: Tariff reform and changes. The Spanish-American War of 1898, which many felt was initiated without real cause. First president in office to be photographed for motion pictures.

The Life of William McKinley

William McKinley was born in Niles, Ohio, son of William and Nancy Campbell Allison McKinley. He attended Allegheny College for a short time, then gained a position as a teacher in a country school. At the outset of the Civil War he enlisted in the Union Army, where he served for the duration, finally being mustered out with the rank of brevet major. Afterward he studied law and went into practice in Canton, Ohio.

From 1877 to 1891 he served as a representative to the U.S. Congress, where his name was attached to the tariff bill of 1890. His peers considered him to be intelligent, personable, and mindful of the interests of citizens when making decisions. From 1892 to 1896 he was governor of Ohio. At the Republican convention in June 1896, McKinley was nominated for president by his close friend, Cleveland magnate Marcus Alonzo Hanna, who cast him as "the advance agent of prosperity." The country was recovering from the depression or panic of 1893, but there were still many hardships.

At the Democratic National Foundation meeting held on July 8, 1896, William Jennings Bryan gave his famous "Cross of Gold" speech, stating that if cities were torn down they would spring up again as if by magic, but if farms were torn down, grass would grow in the city streets. His speech concluded with the ringing statement "You shall not press down upon the brow of labor this crown of thorns, you shall not crucify mankind upon a cross of gold." Riding on a platform of free and unlimited coinage of silver, Bryan was swept into the Democratic nomination for president.

Notwithstanding the popular passion for Bryan, in November McKinley carried the day with a wide margin of votes. By the time he was inaugurated in March 1897 the economy was in recovery and was experiencing growth in some sectors, aided by high protective tariffs.

Opposite: President McKinley as portrayed by Lawrence Williams.

In 1898, soldiers from Spain fought revolutionaries who were seeking to achieve independence for Spain. Under circumstances that were never explained, the USS *Maine,* anchored in the harbor of Havana, exploded and sank. Newspaper publisher William Randolph Hearst and others blamed the explosion on Spain and called for immediate war, keeping up a strong and incessant call for action. Congress voted to go to war, and in slightly more than three months the Spanish were defeated, the pivotal engagement being the triumph of Admiral George Dewey in the Battle of Manila Bay in the Spanish-held Philippine Islands. Imperialism became the order of the day, and the United States annexed the Philippines, Guam, and Puerto Rico, while separately during the McKinley administration Hawaii was also added to the Union.

In the summer of 1899 President McKinley became the first American president to ride in an automobile when he took a spin in a Stanley Steamer at his Canton, Ohio, home. The use of horsepower in the literal sense for transportation was set to fade, and rapidly.

In the summer of 1900 the Populist and the Democratic parties both selected William Jennings Bryan as their presidential candidate, and the Republicans named President McKinley for reelection. Governor Theodore Roosevelt of New York was nominated for the vice presidency on the Republican ticket. By that time, Roosevelt was well known as an author and politician and for his accomplishments in the Spanish-American War. On November 6, McKinley, who campaigned with the promise of a "full dinner pail," was reelected by an overwhelming majority. The Electoral College gave McKinley 292 votes against Bryan's 155. The "silver question," key once again to the Bryan campaign, had faded from widespread public interest in an America that was now quite prosperous.

In September 1901, while in a receiving line at the Temple of Music at the Pan-American Exposition in Buffalo, President McKinley was shot by anarchist Leon Czolgolz. The president hovered at the brink of death while news of his condition was sent to the world by young telegrapher Thomas L. Elder. Eight days after the attack, on September 14, he died. His vice president, Theodore Roosevelt, became chief executive.

Numerous colorful items marked McKinley's presidential campaign. Opposite and lower left: This poster and button promise prosperity under McKinley's auspices. Upper left: Produced during President McKinley's time in office, this poster asserts that "the administration's promises have been kept."

PROSPERITY
AT HOME, PRESTIGE ABROAD.
COMMERCE.
CIVILIZATION.
SOUND MONEY
GAR
NORTHWESTERN LITHO CO. MILWAUKEE

THE AMERICAN SCENE

Early in McKinley's presidency, enthusiasm from the discovery of gold in the Klondike and Cripple Creek, plus normal market-cycle behavior, combined to ease the economic depression that had gripped the nation since 1893.

The Spanish-American War was the nation's defining event of 1898.

Ragtime was the popular new style in American music; Scott Joplin's "Maple Leaf Rag" was registered for copyright in 1899. The song was an instant hit.

In 1900 the U.S. population stood at just under 76 million. In the 1890s, nearly 3.7 million immigrants had made their journey to the United States. Only 10.7% of Americans couldn't read and write—a new low for the nation. The number of telephones in use was 1,335,911. There were 8,000 automobiles registered in the United States, puttering along on about 10 miles of paved roads nationwide (in addition to unpaved lanes).

In Beaumont, Texas, the Lucas gusher was struck on Spindletop Hill in Beaumont, Texas, on January 10, 1901, and spouted up to 110,000 barrels of oil daily for nine days, until it was capped. Texas was thus established as an oil-producing center, and in coming years vast reserves would be found. The United States Steel Corporation was organized on March 3, 1901, and was capitalized at $1,402,846,000 under the auspices of J.P. Morgan, who consolidated the Carnegie Steel Company and other firms in a transaction valued at $492 million. Carnegie was personally paid in 5% gold bonds with a par value of $225 million.

The International Ladies' Garment Workers Union (ILGWU) was established. At the time the typical work week was 70 hours. The garment industry employed many people to do piecework in their homes, at an average wage of about 30 cents a day, according to social reformer Jacob A. Riis. Pipes, cigars, and chewing tobacco were the most popular forms of consuming tobacco. Cigarettes were considered to be unmanly; nevertheless, some four billion were produced in 1901.

Among the books published in this year was L. Frank Baum's *The Wonderful Wizard of Oz*. Frank Norris's novel *The Octopus* told of the struggles of California farmers against the merciless Southern Pacific Railroad. George Barr McCutcheon's novel *Graustark,* a romance centered on a mythical European kingdom, became a bestseller and was followed by numerous other novels of the same genre, a number of which told of American girls marrying wealthy Europeans and living the life of royalty. The American League was formed in Chicago on January 29.

Top right: A keepsake memorial photograph displays "our martyred president's" likeness surrounded by flowers and draped with the Stars and Stripes.

NOTABLE SAYINGS

"That's all a man can hope for during his lifetime—to set an example—and when he is dead, be an inspiration for history."

"In the times of darkest defeat victory may be nearest."

The Early Life of "Teddy" Roosevelt

Theodore Roosevelt was born in New York City, son of Theodore and Martha Bulloch Roosevelt, a well-to-do family firmly situated in social circles. As a youth he suffered from ill health but overcame it with exercise and outdoor activities, making him an advocate of what he called "the strenuous life." He studied intensely, developed skills as a writer and speaker, and graduated from Harvard in 1880, a Phi Beta Kappa. He then studied law at Columbia.

At age 23 Roosevelt entered politics as a Republican, and he served in the New York State Assembly from 1882 to 1884. In the latter year his first wife, Alice, died in childbirth, and his mother died on the same day, leaving him a widower with an infant daughter, also named Alice. He went to the Dakota Territory to recover from his grief and spent two years on his ranch, driving cattle, hunting game, and experiencing the "Wild West." Among other things, he captured an outlaw.

In 1886 he married Edith Kermit Carow, who had been a friend since childhood and during his teenage years a frequent companion on outings. She had attended his first wedding. The couple would have five children.

Returning to the East, he served on the Civil Service Commission from 1889 to 1895 as assistant secretary of the navy from 1895 to 1897, and as New York police commissioner. Famously, during the Spanish-American War he was lieutenant colonel of the Rough Riders, leading them on a charge against the enemy in Cuba in the Battle of San Juan Hill. After the war he was elected governor of New York State. In 1900 he was named as running mate to President McKinley on the Republican ticket. They won, and Roosevelt became vice president in March 1901.

26th President (1901–1909)

THEODORE ROOSEVELT

October 27, 1858–January 6, 1919

Political party: Republican

Vice president: None 1901 to early 1905; Charles Fairbanks, March 4, 1905 to 1909

First Lady and family: Married Alice Hathaway Lee on October 27, 1880. She died in childbirth. His second wife was Edith Kermit Carow (1861–1948), a friend since childhood, whom he married on December 2, 1886. Roosevelt had six children: Alice Lee Roosevelt (1884–1980); Theodore Roosevelt Jr. (1887–1944); Kermit Roosevelt (1889–1943); Ethel Carow Roosevelt (1891–1977); Archibald Bulloch Roosevelt (1894–1979); and Quentin Roosevelt (1897–1918).

Especially remembered for: One of the most interesting and admired presidencies from the viewpoint of the public. Trust busting. "Speak softly, but carry a big stick." The teddy bear, so called after his nickname, "Teddy." Accomplishments as an author, including his multi-volume *Winning of the West*. Originator of the terms "muckraker," "lunatic fringe," and "my hat is in the ring," among many others. One of four presidents honored on Mount Rushmore. The only president who has ever worked closely on coin designs; curiously, he has been sadly neglected as a portrait figure on coins and currency.

Roosevelt in the White House

On September 6, President McKinley, visiting the Pan-American Exposition in Buffalo, was shot twice by anarchist Leon Czolgosz, who was in a greeting line. The president died on September 14 and was succeeded by Vice President Roosevelt.

On October 16, 1901, President Roosevelt dined with well-known black educator Booker T. Washington, causing an uproar among numerous white people in the South who felt that this was beneath the president's station. This set the scene for the new chief executive to do and say what he thought was right, regardless of the dictates of conventional wisdom and political correctness.

During Roosevelt's presidency the White House was the brilliant social center of Washington. His daughter Alice, born in 1884, was a free spirit and an independent young woman ahead of her time, who smoked cigarettes (heaven forbid!) and flirted with distinguished visitors. Her father once remarked that he could either manage Alice or conduct the presidency, but could not do both. In time such humor, plus extensive media coverage of his family activities, made him one of the most popular of American presidents—with no serious competitors in history until the John F. Kennedy administration decades later.

During Roosevelt's presidency, which included a second term from 1905 to 1909 (defeating Democrat Alton B. Parker in a landslide), he took an interest in nearly every national and world situation. Attacking combines of big business that were strangling competition and raising prices for the public, he went on a trust-busting campaign under the previously little-used Sherman Anti-Trust Act, with great success.

In 1904, the Japanese navy attacked Port Arthur in Southern Manchuria and trapped a Russian squadron, launching the largest and most mechanized war at that point in history. On September 5, 1905, the Treaty of Portsmouth was mediated by President Roosevelt and signed by Japan and Russia. Roosevelt was awarded a Nobel Peace Prize.

The Pure Food and Drug Act of 1906 (effective January 1, 1907) ended the sale of toxic patent medicines, the adulteration and mislabeling of food, and other abuses. Roosevelt furthered the development of the Panama Canal and proclaimed the United States the protector of Latin American countries against foreign interference or domination. As a show of strength he sent the "Great White Fleet" of battleships on a world tour, in accordance with his often-stated philosophy "Speak softly, but carry a big stick."

Roosevelt was a lover of nature, literature, and the arts. He achieved much in the development of national forests and parks, land conservation, and public works projects. Working with America's most acclaimed sculptor, Augustus Saint-Gaudens, he embarked on a program to elevate the artistry of circulating U.S. coinage to a high level, over the opposition of the chief engraver at the Mint.

One of Roosevelt's most famous legacies arose from a hunting trip in the South in 1902. After a day of unsuccessful hunting, on returning to camp

Opposite: Famous portraitist John Singer Sargent created this striking study of President Roosevelt in 1903. Top right: Two posters from the 1904 campaign depict Roosevelt as presidential candidate and Charles Fairbanks as vice presidential candidate.

he was led to a captured bear that his staff had tied to a tree, ready for him to shoot. He spared the creature, earning national acclaim for his sportsmanlike choice and spawning stuffed toys known as "teddy bears," which proved to be of enduring appeal to generations of children.

Roosevelt's Later Life

In 1908 Roosevelt did not seek a third term. With an entourage he soon left for a big-game hunting expedition in Africa, accompanied by a photographer from *National Geographic* magazine. This excited the public, the Selig-Polyscope Company of Chicago tapped into the interest by creating a film, *Hunting Big Game in Africa,* with faked shots of the jungle. This was a great success at the box office, preceding by a year *Roosevelt in Africa,* filmed on location by an official photographer, which was also a sensation.

In 1912 Roosevelt decided to make another run for the White House, but the Republican Party endorsed his successor, William Howard Taft, for reelection. Undaunted, Roosevelt joined with his allies to create the Progressive Party and stated that

A NEW UNIFORM AND NEW RESPONSIBILITIES.

Below left: A 1901 cartoon panel titled "A New Uniform and New Responsibilities" shows Roosevelt taking up the role of president after McKinley's assassination. His discarded Rough Rider outfit hangs on the wall behind him. Opposite: Colonel Roosevelt in his Rough Rider uniform during his time with the 1st United States Volunteer Cavalry.

he was as "fit as a bull moose" for another term, giving rise to the party's popular nickname, "the Bull Moose Party." On a campaign stop in Milwaukee he was shot in the chest by a lunatic, but recovered quickly. Commenting at the time, he said, "No man has had a happier life than I have led; a happier life in every way." Roosevelt's bid split the Republican votes, and Democrat Woodrow Wilson was elected.

Teddy Roosevelt stayed active in private life, writing copiously, reading in multiple languages, and adventuring. When the United States entered World War I in Europe in 1917, the old Rough Rider volunteered to raise and lead an infantry division, but President Wilson refused the offer. Roosevelt died in 1919 at his Sagamore Hill mansion in Oyster Bay, New York.

THE AMERICAN SCENE

President Roosevelt was very interested in natural resources, and during his term the United States added nearly 150 million acres to its reserves, primarily in the Western states. The Department of the Interior was established in 1902, as was the U.S. Bureau of Reformation. On May 20, 1902, Cuba became independent, ending its status as a U.S. protectorate, which had been established at the conclusion of the Spanish-American War. On June 28, 1902, Congress passed the Isthmian Canal Act to authorize building a canal across Panama or an alternative route across Nicaragua if proper arrangements could not be made with Colombia (which owned the land in question) and the Panama Canal Company of France (which had the concession). Later, the Panama Canal Company was paid $40 million, and the difficulties with Colombia were settled by a rebellion and the separation of Panama in November 1903. The newly formed country

A souvenir tray depicts Rough Rider Roosevelt with saber held aloft, charging up San Juan Hill.

granted the United States a strip 10 miles wide for the canal.

The International Harvester Company was incorporated in New Jersey on August 12, 1902, with a capital of $120 million. Combining several other firms, it controlled the output of 85% of the farm machinery in the United States. The International Nickel Company was created by a merger of the Canadian Copper Company and the Orford Copper Company. Business trusts were becoming an increasing concern, and one against which President Roosevelt would take action. On March 10, 1902, he stated that the government would proceed under the Sherman Anti-Trust Act against the National Securities Company, a firm controlled by J.P. Morgan. The average wage of shopgirls in Boston was about $5 to $6 a week, and the pay of factory workers in New England mills was in the same range. On May 12 of that year, 147,000 United Mine Workers union members went on strike, refusing to work the anthracite coal mines. The price of coal rose from $5 in May to about $30 in October. Many schools closed to save fuel costs.

Travel time on the New York Central Railroad from New York to Chicago was 20 hours. In Pasadena, California, on January 1, 1903, the first Tournament of Roses Association football game was held; Michigan bested Stanford 49–0 (in 1923 the contest would become known as the Rose Bowl game).

On February 19, 1903, the Elkins Act endeavored to end price discrimination by railroads that were giving certain customers preferential rates. The legislation was ineffective, and in 1906 the Hepburn Act would give the Interstate Commerce Commission the power to regulate the rates charged by railroads and pipelines. The Department of Commerce and Labor was created on February 14, 1903, with its secretary holding a cabinet position. In this year the Ford Motor Company was established by Henry Ford. On May 23 two automobilists in a 20-horsepower Winston began a trip across the United States, completing it on July 26—achieving what was probably the first transcontinental automobile trip. On December 17, 1903, Orville Wright made man's first powered flight in a heavier-than-air self-propelled machine. The event took place on the beach near Kitty Hawk, North Carolina, lasted for about 12 seconds, and covered 120 feet. Later in the day, Wilbur Wright stayed aloft for 59 seconds and traversed 852 feet. The world would never be the same. The Harley-Davidson motorcycle was introduced in 1903; by 1917, production had risen to an annual rate of 18,000 vehicles.

On January 19, Guglielmo Marconi sent a wireless radio message from President Roosevelt to Britain's King Edward VII, transmitting from four 250-foot wooden towers at South Wellfleet, Massachusetts.

Sanka decaffeinated coffee (from the French *sans caféine*) was first sold by a tradesman who found that a consignment of coffee had been exposed to sea water and the beans had lost their caffeine.

The first World Series game was played when the American League and National League champions met in a post-season playoff in a best-of-nine contest in November 1903. The winners were the Boston Red Sox (originally called the Boston Americans).

On January 4, 1904, the Supreme Court ruled that citizens of Puerto Rico could come to the United States mainland and were not aliens, but neither were they U.S. citizens. On February 7 and 8, 1904, some 2,600 buildings were destroyed in downtown Baltimore, Maryland, in the largest urban fire since the Chicago conflagration of 1871.

Ida M. Tarbell's book *The History of the Standard Oil Company* told of profits made by the Rockefeller family at the expense of American citizens, and helped arouse passions against monopolies, trusts,

Below: A 1906 cartoon from *Puck* portrays Roosevelt conducting an orchestra with his "Big Stick"; the musicians are Elihu Root and William Taft. Right: An assortment of campaign pins from Roosevelt's political career.

and big business in general. Readers learned that John D. Rockefeller had a personal income of $45 million per year and that his firms now controlled 90% of the oil business in America. In terms of effecting business reform, this book became one of the most pivotal in history. On March 14, 1904, the Supreme Court ordered that the Northern Securities Company, a railroad holding company, be dissolved.

On October 27, 1904, the first section of the New York City subway system was opened, consisting of a conduit from Brooklyn Bridge extending north to 145th Street and Broadway. Opening a year late to celebrate the 1903 centennial, the Louisiana Purchase Exposition was held in St. Louis and attracted visitors from all over the world. The Inside Inn, with 2,257 rooms, was a stunning success at the fair and netted a $361,000 profit to its owner, Ellsworth M. Statler, who would later build a chain of hotels with its flagship facility in Buffalo, New York.

Women could not vote in 1904, were rarely seen in business circles, and were frowned upon if they engaged in "men's" activities such as smoking. On September 28, 1904, a woman who was smoking a

A family portrait from circa 1903 shows Roosevelt and his wife, Edith, among their children: Quentin, Theodore Jr., Archie, Alice (the child of Roosevelt's first wife), Kermit, and Ethel. Opposite: Two books that Roosevelt wrote about frontier life.

cigarette while riding in an open automobile in New York City was arrested.

W.A. Clark, who earned millions of dollars in copper mining in Montana, moved into his 130-room mansion at Fifth Avenue and 77th Street in New York City. The residence set a new standard for opulence.

In 1905, Albert Einstein presented his doctoral dissertation, *A New Determination of Molecular Dimensions,* and four other important papers, propelling him into prominence that lasted for the rest of his life.

On May 15, Las Vegas, Nevada, was founded after 110 acres of land were auctioned in a district that later became part of the city's downtown area.

On April 18, 1906, the San Francisco earthquake and ensuing fire destroyed much of the city. The earthquake's intensity was later estimated as magnitude 7.9 on the Richter scale. At least 3,000 people died, and well over 200,000 were left homeless; the property damage amounted to upward of $350 million. This became the most costly natural disaster in the United States up to that time.

In 1907 Lee DeForest invented the triode amplifying tube, paving the way for the electronics industry. In the autumn the Panic of 1907 rippled through the stock market, then the entire economy, casting gloom that lasted for several years as banks and businesses failed.

In 1908 Robert Baden-Powell of England began the Boy Scout movement. Soon the Boy Scouts of America would capture the enthusiasm of youths across the country.

On September 17, Thomas Selfridge died in an air crash at Fort Meyer, Virginia, becoming the first known fatality of this means of transportation. On September 27, Henry Ford, after having worked in the automotive industry for several years in Detroit, produced his first Model T.

NOTABLE SAYINGS

"It is hard to fail, but it is worse never to have tried to succeed. In this life we get nothing save by effort."

"Get action. Seize the moment. Man was never intended to become an oyster."

"To announce that there must be no criticism of the president, or that we are to stand by the president, right or wrong, is not only unpatriotic and servile, but is morally treasonable to the American public."

"Speak softly and carry a big stick."

"The only man who makes no mistake is the man who does nothing."

"It is common sense to take a method and try it. If it fails, admit it frankly and try another. But above all, try something."

"Believe you can and you're halfway there."

"There's never yet been a man in our history that has led a life of ease whose name is worth remembering."

"Keep your eyes on the stars, and your feet on the ground."

"People ask the difference between a leader and a boss. The leader leads and the boss drives."

27th President (1909–1913)

WILLIAM HOWARD TAFT

September 15, 1857–March 8, 1930

Political party: Republican

Vice president: James S. Sherman, 1909 to 1912; none for the remainder of his term

First Lady and family: Married Helen Herron, on June 19, 1886. The couple had three children: Robert Alphonso Taft (1889–1953); Helen Herron Taft (1891–1987); and Charles Phelps Taft (1897–1983).

Especially remembered for: Continuing trust-busting and certain other of Roosevelt's policies. As his predecessor was a difficult act to follow in terms of public acclaim, Taft never achieved notable recognition in his own right.

The Life of William Howard Taft

William Howard Taft was born in Cincinnati, Ohio, son of Alphonso (a former United States attorney and famous judge) and Louisa Maria Torrey Taft. He graduated from Yale in 1878 and Cincinnati Law School in 1880, after which he entered law practice in his hometown. He went into politics as a Republican and gained important judiciary appointments, in which positions he acquitted himself well. He was a judge in the Ohio Superior Court from 1887 to 1890, then solicitor-general of the United States until 1892, following this with a post as judge in the U.S. Circuit Court until 1900. From 1901 to 1904 he was governor of the Philippine Islands, which had been annexed by the United States in 1898. President Theodore Roosevelt appointed him secretary of war in 1904.

When President Roosevelt decided not to run for reelection in 1908 he championed Taft as his successor in the White House, although Taft was reluctant at first. Finally, his wife Nellie convinced him that he should run. Taft's opponent in the November contest was William Jennings Bryan, the unsuccessful Democratic candidate in 1896 and 1900. Taft won handily, with the popular vote in his favor and the Electoral College votes numbering 322 to Bryan's 162.

Tipping the scales at 325 pounds, Taft was the largest president in history and required special furniture to sit upon. He suffered from sleep apnea, which robbed him of restful nights, and it was not unusual for him to fall asleep in the middle of a meeting or even a conversation.

Taft set about following Roosevelt's policies, but he was not as inventive in the use of executive power. Anti-trust actions were pursued, but Taft did

Opposite: In 1908, photographer George Harris captured Taft in a candid photograph as the then secretary of war learned via the telephone that he had just been selected as Republican presidential nominee.

not lead in matters of conservation. In time, he disappointed many of his backers, including Roosevelt. The Republican Party became divided when the president supported the Payne-Aldrich Act, which furthered high tariffs at a time when the economy was still suffering from the Panic of 1907.

In 1912 Taft ran for reelection. Roosevelt left the Republican Party, joined the new Progressive Party, and entered the contest as well. Democrats put Woodrow Wilson forward. In the election, Wilson won as the Republican vote was split between Roosevelt and Taft, with the incumbent president finishing a sorry third.

After leaving the White House, Taft became a law professor at Yale. In 1921, then president Warren G. Harding appointed him as chief justice of the U.S. Supreme Court, a position he held until shortly before his death in 1930.

Appointed chief justice by President Warren Harding, Taft sits at the center of this photograph of the U.S. Supreme Court in 1921. He was the only person ever to serve as both president and chief justice.

THE AMERICAN SCENE

On April 21, 1908, Frederick Cook claimed to be the first to reach the North Pole, causing a sensation. On July 6, 1909, Edward Peary, skeptical of Cook's claim, set sail toward the North Pole, traveled overland, and definitely reached it. This inaugurated a great controversy as to whether Cook had ever been successful in his earlier attempt.

On August 2, 1909, the United States Signal Corps acquired the world's first military airplane, a Wright Military flyer. Flight was becoming increasingly popular during Taft's presidency, and Americans closely followed its progress. On January 10, 1910, the Los Angeles International Air Meet was held in California, the first such aviation gathering. "Barnstormers" (private pilots who took their planes to country fairs and places where such machines were unfamiliar) were very popular in the next several years. On January 18, 1911, Eugene Ely landed his plane on the deck of the USS *Pennsylvania* in San Francisco harbor; the first instance of an aircraft landing on a ship, this event would eventually inspire the creation of the aircraft carrier.

In April 1910, Halley's Comet was visible in the skies, creating much excitement, many predictions of doomsday, and other accounts that appeared in the media. In May the earth passed harmlessly through the tail of the comet.

On March 25, 1911, 146 people were killed in a fire at the Triangle Shirtwaist factory in New York City. This brought attention and criticism to current labor practices and the lack of safety procedures. To the south, the Mexican Revolution began, with various rebels attacking government forces. The revolution would last for the rest of the decade and occupy the attention of the world. In time, American troops would become involved.

On April 14, 1912, the RMS *Titanic,* the world's latest and largest ocean liner, struck an iceberg in the northern Atlantic Ocean. At first, the ship's officers and crew were unalarmed, but that changed as water filled the lower compartments. Less than six hours later, in the early morning of the 15th, the vessel sank, taking more than 1,500 people with it and leaving some 700 survivors floundering at sea.

In May of the same year, the women's suffrage movement saw more than 10,000 women and more than 1,000 men on parade in New York City. This, along with temperance, was one of the great social movements of Taft's presidency and beyond.

Below, two pieces of Taft political ephemera: a button and ribbon from the 1912 campaign, and a paper fan from the 1908 presidential race showing Uncle Sam undecided between the two candidates, William Jennings Bryan and Taft.

NOTABLE SAYINGS

"Politics, when I am in it, makes me sick."

"Next to the right of liberty, the right of property is the most important individual right guaranteed by the Constitution."

28th President (1913–1921)

WOODROW WILSON

December 28, 1856–February 3, 1924

Political party: Democratic

Vice president: Thomas R. Marshall, 1913 to 1921

First Lady and family: Married Ellen Louise Axson on June 24, 1885. As First Lady she entertained effectively but without pretense, and was admired by all. Interested in art, she installed a studio in the White House, complete with a skylight. Ellen died in the White House, of Bright's disease, on August 6, 1914. The couple had three children: Margaret Woodrow Wilson (1886–1944); Jessie Woodrow Wilson (1887–1933); and Eleanor Randolph Wilson (1889–1967). Wilson's second wife was Edith Bolling Galt, a Washington widow, whom he married on December 18, 1915, amid criticism that such a brief mourning period might impair his chances for reelection. It didn't. Edith was a highly talented woman who added much to his presidency.

Especially remembered for: His academic knowledge. The Federal Reserve Act and the establishment of the Federal Trade Commission. His leadership during the Great War and his subsequent unsuccessful bid to have the United States join the League of Nations.

The Life of Woodrow Wilson

Woodrow Wilson was born in Staunton, Virginia, on December 28, 1856, son of Joseph Ruggles and Jessie Janet Woodrow Wilson. His father later served as a Presbyterian minister in Augusta, Georgia, in the Civil War, and still later as a professor in Columbia, South Carolina. Wilson graduated from the College of New Jersey (today's Princeton) and the University of Virginia Law School, then went on to earn a doctorate at the Johns Hopkins University. He entered academia as a professor of political science, teaching at Bryn Mawr College, Wesleyan University, and, starting in 1890, Princeton, where in 1902 he became president.

In 1910 admirers in the Democratic Party suggested that Wilson run for governor of New Jersey, which he did with success, serving from 1911 to 1913. In the 1912 election he was the party's candidate for president, mounting a platform called the "New Freedom," which emphasized states' rights and those of individual citizens. In the meantime, Theodore Roosevelt, who had exited the White House in 1909 and did not seek reelection at that time, went on to enjoy other aspects of life, including a well-publicized safari in Africa. In 1912, dissatisfied with President Taft's actions, Roosevelt decided to throw his hat in the ring once again. As the Republican nomination was locked up in the hands of incumbent Taft, Roosevelt and other dissident party members formed the Progressive Party, popularly known as the Bull Moose, nominating Roosevelt as the candidate. In the election on November 5, the Republican votes were divided, and Wilson won in a landslide. (Roosevelt finished second—still ahead of Taft.)

In office, President Wilson backed many important and far-reaching pieces of legislation, including the Federal Reserve Act, which set up the Federal

Opposite: Woodrow Wilson circa 1919 in a portrait photograph by Harris & Ewing, Inc. His pince-nez were one of his distinguishing characteristics; along with former president Teddy Roosevelt, Wilson helped to popularize these armless spectacles.

Reserve System of 12 banks and helped regulate the monetary system; the Federal Trade Commission, which dealt with anti-trust complaints and encouraged good business practices; and laws regulating child labor, among others. Meanwhile, the Great War ignited in Europe in August 1914. While America provided supplies and munitions to England and France in their war against Germany, the United States did not yet have direct involvement.

In March of 1916, Mexican revolutionist Pancho Villa led about 500 raiders in an attack on the town of Columbus in New Mexico, killing 12 American soldiers. A unit of the United States 13th Cavalry Regiment drove them back across the border. On March 15, President Wilson ordered 12,000 U.S. troops to pursue Pancho Villa into Mexican territory.

Left: Campaign buttons promoting Wilson as presidential candidate. Below: To mark the start of the baseball season, President Wilson throws out the first ball on opening day in 1916. Opposite: A 1915 poster demonstrates the president's support of women's fight for the vote.

In that year Wilson sought reelection, campaigning with the slogan "He kept us out of war," against Republican contender Charles Evans Hughes. The contest was a close one, and would have gone to Hughes had 2,000 more Californians voted Republican. Wilson took both the popular and Electoral College tallies, the latter 277 to 254. On March 14, 1917, he began his second term. On the same day, Jeannette Rankin of Montana became the first woman to become a member of the U.S. House of Representatives.

Contrary to his campaign platform, President Wilson requested on April 2, 1917, that war be declared against Germany. By that time German interference in shipping, including the sinking of the passenger ship *Lusitania,* had become intolerable. Many American volunteers had gone to France and England to help in the war effort. Still, many others had mixed emotions and loyalties to both sides. On May 18, the Selective Service Act set up the power of conscription or draft into the army.

After the United States helped turn the tide of the war, a peace treaty was signed in November 1918. The League of Nations was proposed as a way to promote harmony and, hopefully, to prevent future large-scale wars. On December 14, 1918, President Woodrow Wilson left by ship for the Paris Peace Conference, becoming the first U.S. president to travel to a foreign country during his term in office. On October 2, 1919, he suffered a stroke in a strenuous road campaign to promote the League of Nations, but recovered with partial paralysis. His wife Edith nursed him and helped with many decisions in the last two years of his presidency. By the time the League of Nations came up for vote in Congress, the power balance had shifted to the Republicans, and the United States' membership application failed.

Wilson left the White House in March 1921, still an invalid, with no thought of seeking reelection. By that time the country was tired of the president and his policies. In 1924, his health never having recovered, he died in Washington, D.C.

THE AMERICAN SCENE

In March, the month Wilson was inaugurated, great floods ravaged Ohio, with the city of Dayton in particular being hard hit. On April 24 the Woolworth Building, the world's tallest, opened in New York City, becoming an icon.

On October 13, 1913, the United States Revenue Act of 1913 enacted a revision of earlier laws, extending the federal income tax to many people. In this year the first specifically designated transcontinental automobile road opened: the Lincoln highway, going from New York City to Manhattan Beach, California, also known as Route 40.

In a way, the year 1914 marked the end of the "gilded" age in America, which had been characterized by the building of mansions, the development of elegant cars, and similar extravagance during

Above: A 1920 portrait of the president with his wife, the former Edith Bolling Galt, at his side. Right: Another view of the Wilsons, this time on a celluloid badge. After Wilson's stroke in 1919, Edith took on many of the responsibilities of the presidency.

the early 20th century. Now, attention turned to the war in Europe.

In Seattle, Washington, in July 1915, William Boeing incorporated the Pacific Aero Products Company, later renamed Boeing. On November 1, 1916, the first 40-hour work week was put in place at the Endicott-Johnson shoe factories in Johnson City, New York.

On January 25, 1917, the Danish West Indies group of islands was sold to the United States for $25 million. Possession of the Danish West Indies was taken on March 31.

On January 31, Germany announced that its submarines (U-boats) would engage in unrestricted submarine warfare against any and all ships found to be of interest. On February 3 the United States severed diplomatic relations with Germany. In the same month, the so-called Zimmermann telegram was intercepted, which revealed that Germany offered to give the southwestern section of the United States to Mexico if Mexico would declare war against the United States.

On March 2, residents of Puerto Rico were granted U.S. citizenship.

On May 15, 1918, the first regular air mail postal service in the United States began; flights connected Washington, D.C., Philadelphia, and New York City. In August the Spanish influenza became a pandemic, eventually closing down much of America in the autumn (such as movie theaters and other places of public gathering); it would kill more than 50 million people worldwide by the time it abated in December 1920.

On October 28, 1919, nationwide Prohibition was authorized through the Volstead Act, which went into effect in January 1920, under the 19th Amendment to the United States Constitution.

NOTABLE SAYINGS

"Some people call me an idealist. Well, that is the way I know I am an American. America is the only idealistic nation in the world."

"We grow great by dreams. All big men are dreamers."

"If you want to make enemies, try to change something."

29th President (1921–1923)

WARREN G. HARDING

November 2, 1865–August 2, 1923

Political party: Republican

Vice president: Calvin Coolidge, 1921 to 1923

First Lady and family: Married divorcée Florence Kling De Wolfe on July 8, 1891. Florence had a son from her first marriage, Marshall Eugene DeWolfe. Warren Harding fathered one illegitimate child, Elizabeth Ann Christian (born in 1919); the mother was Nan Britton, one of several women with whom he had affairs.

Especially remembered for: The economic recession of 1921. Cronyism in the White House. The Teapot Dome and other scandals, most of which surfaced after his death. Generally viewed as one of the poorest performing presidents.

The Life of Warren G. Harding

Warren Gamaliel Harding was born in Corsica (later known as Blooming Grove), Ohio, son of George Tyron and Phoebe Elizabeth Dickerson Harding. His schooling concluded with a degree from Ohio Central College in 1882. Harding became involved in newspaper publishing, organized the town band, and was interested in several businesses in and around Marion, Ohio.

A tool of the powerful Ohio political machine, he rose rapidly in state politics, eventually serving in the Ohio Senate from 1900 to 1904 and then as lieutenant governor until 1906, but failed in a try at the governorship. At the Republican convention in 1912 he gave the nominating address for William Howard Taft. In 1914 Harding was elected to the United States Senate, where he remained in office until 1921.

At the 1920 nominating convention, delegates were deadlocked, with none of the leading candidates moving forward. A group of powerful senators took charge and nominated Harding, and he was chosen. In the general election in November he took an unprecedented 60.3% of the popular vote (16,152,200), wiping out Democratic contender James M. Cox (9,139,661 or 34.1% of the popular vote, with the rest going to minor candidates). He went on to carry the Electoral College 404 to 127. Also in the contest was Socialist Eugene V. Debs, then serving time in federal prison, who captured about a million votes.

Once Harding was in the White House, Republican legislators found him to be nearly a puppet of powerful figures in Washington and willing to endorse about any proposal. Changes enacted by Harding were both positive and negative, depending upon one's viewpoint, and included eliminating wartime controls and restrictions, restoring a high protective tariff, establishing tight quotas on immigration, and setting up a federal budget system.

On May 19, 1921, Harding signed legislation limiting yearly immigration to 3% of the number of a given nationality recorded in the 1910 federal

census, with a total of all immigrants not to exceed 357,000; this was done to counter the widespread notion that large-scale immigration was a prime cause of unemployment. The economy was going through a recession. This proved to be relatively short-lived, and business turned upward by 1923.

Certain of Harding's appointees engaged in illegal and corrupt practices, causing rumors of scandal to swirl through Washington. The most famous of these appointees was the secretary of the interior, Albert Fall, who accepted a bribe to lease federal oil lands at Teapot Dome, Wyoming, to private interests. Harding, whose personal life had its own scandals, was at a loss as to what to do.

Opposite: President Harding as portrayed by Lawrence Williams. Above: Keepsakes from Harding's political career commemorate his terms as governor and president.

In the summer of 1923, in company with his honest and helpful secretary of commerce, Herbert Hoover, he took a trip to Alaska. Depressed and weary, he discussed the brewing scandals with Hoover, who advised that investigations should be made and the findings publicized, after which the matters might be laid to rest. No such opportunity occurred, however: in San Francisco, on his way back from Alaska, on August 2, the president collapsed and died. He was succeeded in the office by vice president Calvin Coolidge.

Immediately, rumors swirled as to the cause of his death. Suicide? Not likely, as he had stated his intention to seek a second term. Poisoning by his wife, who refused to allow an autopsy and burned most of his personal papers? This, too, was unlikely. Today, historians generally agree that Harding died of congestive heart failure.

THE AMERICAN SCENE

Prohibition defined society during the Harding administration. The Volstead Act gave rise to legions of bootleggers who smuggled liquor from foreign countries, especially Canada. Countless thousands of druggists obtained licenses to sell alcohol for "medicinal purposes," prompting one songwriter to compose "The Drugstore Cabaret." The government went to great expense and effort during the 1920s to enforce Prohibition, and by 1930 an estimated 500,000 people had been arrested for liquor-related violations.

General William "Billy" Mitchell, in a controversial test in the ocean off the Virginia coast, staged

a demonstration of air power and sunk the German battleship *Ostfriesland* (transferred to the U.S. Navy after the Great War); eventually air strikes changed the strategy of naval warfare.

A congressional committee heard George Washington Carver of the Tuskegee Institute tell of the dozens of commercial uses for peanuts, which were becoming an increasingly important commercial crop in the South.

General Motors produced several makes of automobiles and controlled about 12% of that market.

In Pittsburgh, pioneer radio station KDKA, which had begun broadcasting in autumn 1920, saw its first full year of operation. Among popular songs and melodies of the year 1921 were "Kitten on the Keys," "Blue Moon"," "Look for the Silver Lining," "Down in Chinatown," "There'll Be Some Changes Made," "I'm Nobody's Baby," "All By Myself," "Ain't We Got Fun," "The Sheik of Araby," and "My Mammy."

In 1922 Rebecca Latimer Felton of Georgia was appointed to fill a vacant seat in the Senate, becoming the first woman U.S. senator. The Lincoln Memorial was dedicated on May 30 in Washington, D.C. Although business improved in some areas of the United States with a sharp upturn in automobile sales, an economic recession continued in other areas, notably agriculture.

In protest to wage cuts, coal miners went on strike for many months. This action by United Mine Workers had far-reaching effects on U.S. industry. A 13% wage cut was announced on May 28, 1922, affecting 400,000 workers, who went on strike from July 1 through the rest of the summer.

The stage comedy *Abie's Irish Rose* opened in New York City on May 23, 1922, and would see a record run of 2,327 performances. The magazines *True Confessions* and *Better Homes and Gardens* began publication in 1922, with the first issue of *Reader's Digest* appearing in February of that year.

Above left: In 1922 President Harding speaks into a recording device that will preserve his voice on phonograph records. Above right: Harding's dog, Laddie, shows his enthusiasm during a White House photo session.

NOTABLE SAYINGS

"My god, this is a hell of a job. I have no trouble with my enemies . . . but my damn friends, they are the ones that keep me walking the floor nights."

"The most dangerous tendency is to expect too much of government, and at the same time do for it too little."

The Life of Calvin Coolidge

Calvin Coolidge was born in Plymouth, Vermont, son of John Calvin and Victoria Josephine Moor Coolidge. His father kept a general store in the village. Calvin graduated with honors from Amherst College (in Northampton, Massachusetts) in 1895, and set up a law practice in the same city. In 1899 he was elected as a city councilman, launching a political career that would see him elected to the State Legislature and then elected mayor of Northampton, lieutenant governor of the state, and in 1919 and 1920 governor. In 1920 he was vice president on the winning Harding ticket.

In the wee hours of the morning on August 3, 1923, while visiting in Vermont, he received a message of Harding's death. By the light of a kerosene lamp his father, a notary public, administrated the oath of office, and Coolidge became president. Immediately afterward, as legend has it, he went to his father's store for a glass of Moxie soda.

Although he was of unquestioned character, Coolidge was faced with a rapidly unfolding scenario of scandals and other wrongdoings surfacing from the Harding administration. Alfred E. Smith, a leading Democrat prominent in New York, commented that the presidency had "reached the lowest ebb in our history" under Harding and that it was Coolidge's challenge to restore dignity and prestige to the nation's highest office.

Coolidge was readily accessible to friends, politicians of both parties, and others who sought to visit. Most of the time he let others do the talking. Famous for his quiet nature and lack of expression, he was known as "Silent Cal" and "the Great Stone Face," a reference to the famous natural icon in the White Mountains of New Hampshire. Theodore Roosevelt's daughter Alice suggested that he had been "weaned on a pickle." At a dinner party a guest seated nearby told him that she had bet that she could get him to say at least three words. "You lose!" he replied.

30th President (1923–1929)

CALVIN COOLIDGE

July 4, 1872–January 5, 1933

Political party: Republican

Vice president: None 1923 to 1925; Charles Dawes, 1925 to 1929

First Lady and family: Married Grace Anna Goodhue on October 4, 1905. During her stint as First Lady, the White House was no longer a social center for lavish parties and dinners. The couple had two children: John Coolidge (1906–2000) and Calvin Coolidge Jr. (1908–1924).

Especially remembered for: An era of prosperity, the "Roaring Twenties." A "do-nothing" president. Nickname: "Silent Cal."

Wisely, Coolidge let the ongoing scandal investigations take their course without interference. In the meantime, the nation had recovered from the economic depression of 1921 and 1922 and was enjoying unprecedented "Coolidge prosperity." The "Roaring Twenties" was an age replete with speakeasies and Prohibition bathtub gin, finely appointed luxury automobiles, the Charleston, jazz, and other good times. This was the era of *The Great Gatsby,* the 1925 novel by F. Scott Fitzgerald whose title character epitomized the times by living life to its fullest excess.

In the 1924 presidential election, using the theme "Coolidge Prosperity," Coolidge as the Republican candidate gained more than 54% of the popular vote and handily defeated his opponent, Democrat John W. Davis.

In his second administration the economy went onward and upward. The Florida land boom quieted in 1925, then went silent, but was more than

Opposite: His New England reserve resulted in President Coolidge's nickname "the Great Stone Face." Below: Campaign pins offer puns on Coolidge's name and reference another of his nicknames, "Silent Cal." Right: Photo postcards attempt to portray the reserved Coolidge as a man of the people.

Above: Sheet music composed for Coolidge's 1924 presidential campaign. Below and below opposite: Pro-Coolidge license plates from the same campaign. Opposite top: President Coolidge met with famous speaker and activist Helen Keller in 1926.

made up for by a heightened pitch in the value of investment securities. It was an era of expansion and continuing good times. In 1926 political pundit Walter Lippmann commented that Coolidge had a talent for "effectively doing nothing." Perhaps that was ideal for his era, when America was recovering from the Great War, an economic recession, and political scandals.

On August 2, 1927, when asked if he would seek the presidential nomination in 1928, Coolidge said, "I do not choose to run." After leaving the White House, he led a quiet life in retirement. He died in Northampton, Massachusetts, in January 1933.

THE AMERICAN SCENE

The Coolidge administration was one of enthusiasm, happiness, and changes on the American Scene—a pivotal era in many ways.

While repercussions from the recent recession were still felt, business trends turned upward with increased corporate profits and greater prosperity. In Chicago, the Zenith Radio Corporation was founded, and John D. Hertz established the Hertz Drive-Urself system. Milky Way and Butterfinger candy bars and the Popsicle made their debut in 1923.

Among songs popular that year were "Yes, We Have No Bananas" by Frank Silver and Irving Cohen, "Barney Google," "Linger Awhile," "Who's Sorry Now," "Mexicali Rose," and "Sonny Boy." The Silver-Cohen song, which set a record for sheet-music sales, was inspired by the visit of one of the songwriters to a fruit stand operated by a Greek immigrant, who in response to a request for a certain fruit gave the reply used for the title.

In 1924 most immigrants to the United States came from Canada, Mexico, and South America.

International Business Machines Corporation was formed in New York. In due course IBM data-processing cards would become popular; they were made the size of American currency notes, to facilitate the public's becoming used to handling them.

The first Chrysler automobile was made. More than half of the world's cars were Model T Fords,

priced then as low as $290. An entire sub-industry arose to supply accessories such as radiator caps, car tops, and other items to Model T owners.

Radio became a national fascination, with more than 3 million Americans owning sets, mostly of the crystal set variety. In Chicago, Al Capone and other gangsters raked in untold profits from bootleg liquor and other activities made possible by Prohibition and by lax law enforcement.

Metro-Goldwyn-Mayer and Columbia Pictures were formed in 1924, and would go on to many accomplishments. The Music Corporation of America (MCA) was founded; over the years it would book many musical, theatrical, and film personalities.

More and more zeppelins (with metal frame) and dirigibles (without frame) were seen in the skies around the world. The *ZR-3,* made in Germany, flew from Friedrichshafen to Lakehurst, New Jersey. The United States Navy acquired the craft and renamed it the *Los Angeles.*

In Florida in 1923 and 1924 there was wild speculation in real estate. Salesmen, including William Jennings Bryan, extolled the virtues of buying land in the Sunshine State. Most purchasers wrote checks without ever visiting their properties. Values multiplied.

Nellie Tayloe Ross was inaugurated as the governor of Wyoming on January 5, 1925, becoming the first woman governor in the United States.

Nashville radio station WSM's program *Barn Dance,* later to become the *Grand Ole Opry,* first aired in November 1925. The season's best-known stage musical was *No, No, Nanette.* Movie theaters in 1925 showed *The Big Parade, The Phantom of the Opera* (with Lon Chaney), *Ben Hur, The Freshman* (starring Harold Lloyd), and *The Gold Rush* (with Charlie Chaplin). Books published that year included Theodore Dreiser's *An American Tragedy,* Sinclair Lewis's *Arrowsmith,* Anita Loos's *Gentlemen Prefer Blondes,* and *The Great Gatsby* by F. Scott Fitzgerald. Persistence paid off for another writer that year: after his first 20 submissions received rejection slips, James T. Thurber finally became a regular contributor to *The New Yorker* magazine, which had premiered on August 21, 1925.

Robert H. Goddard successfully launched the world's first liquid-fueled rocket on a farm near

Auburn, Massachusetts, on March 16, 1926. Rear Admiral Richard Byrd and Floyd Bennett made the first successful flight over the North Pole on May 9. The Army Air Corps was established on July 2. Later, it would become known as the United States Air Force.

Charles Lindbergh left Long Island's Roosevelt Field alone in his Ryan monoplane, the *Spirit of St. Louis,* at 7:55 a.m. on May 20, 1927, and arrived in Paris 33 hours and 29 minutes later, making headlines all over the world and winning a $25,000 prize as the first pilot to fly solo across the Atlantic.

After 15 million Model T Fords had exited the assembly lines, the Model A Ford was introduced after six months of retooling the assembly lines. In 1927 more than 20 million automobiles were registered in the United States. Television was first demonstrated on April 7, 1927, by the Bell Telephone Company. John Willard Marriott opened a food stand in Washington, D.C., laying the foundation for the family's vast hotel and restaurant empire.

Radio's popularity continued, with programs being played in public places. The 15-minute *Amos 'n' Andy Show* made its debut on March 19, 1928, in Chicago. The next year the show would be broadcast nationally, and it soon captured about two-thirds of the available radio audience, or 40 million listeners. Movie theaters, seeking to maintain their trade, interrupted their programs to broadcast *Amos 'n' Andy* each evening. On May 11, the first scheduled television program was broadcast by WGY in Schenectady, New York. William S. Paley took over what would become the Columbia Broadcasting System (CBS) under his ownership.

Although films had been coordinated with sound for many years, none had achieved technical success or popularity until *The Jazz Singer,* starring Al Jolson, captured the imagination of Americans with its limited singing and dialogue sections. The Academy of Motion Picture Arts and Sciences was founded on May 11, 1927. The 1927 film *Wings* would be the first film awarded the statuette, later nicknamed "the Oscar." Walt Disney introduced Mickey Mouse in *Plane Crazy,* a black-and-white cartoon, Disney Productions' first release. *Galloping Gaucho* and *Steamboat Willie* soon followed, the latter featuring sound. George Gershwin composed *An American in Paris.* Babe Ruth, who began his major league career as a pitcher for the Boston Red Sox in 1914, was the year's leading hitter.

On August 27, 1928, the Kellogg-Briand Pact was signed by world leaders, denouncing war. The German *Graf Zeppelin* arrived at Lakehurst, New Jersey, on October 15, 1928 from Friedrichshafen, Germany, completing a 6,630-mile flight in 121 hours. The antibacterial property of penicillin was discovered, and it soon caused a revolution in the medical treatment of infection.

Throughout Coolidge's presidency the American economy was booming, and soaring stock prices led the way. Pledging their assets and buying on margin, many citizens contemplated their paper profits. The Bank of America (formerly called the Bank of Italy) was the country's largest banking institution, and the Continental-Illinois Bank & Trust Company, created in the merger of two large banks in Chicago, dominated in the Midwest.

NOTABLE SAYINGS

"Don't expect to build up the weak by pulling down the strong."

"Nothing in the world can take the place of persistence. Talent will not; nothing is more common than unsuccessful men with talent. Genius will not; unrewarded genius is almost a proverb. Education will not; the world is full of educated derelicts. Persistence and determination are omnipotent. The slogan, 'press on,' solved and always will solve the problems of the human race. No person was ever been honored for what he received. Honor has been the reward for what he gave."

The Life of Herbert Hoover

Herbert Hoover was born in West Branch, Iowa, son of Jesse Clark and Hulda Randall Minthorn Hoover. His father was a blacksmith, and the family was affiliated with the Society of Friends (Quakers). Much of his youth was spent in Oregon. He enrolled in the Leland Stanford Jr. University (today's Stanford University) in 1891, the year it opened, graduating with a degree in mining engineering in 1895.

Hoover married Lou Henry in 1899, after which the couple went to China, where he became the most important engineer in that rapidly developing country. In pursuit of the mining business they went to Europe, Asia, Africa, and elsewhere, accompanied by their sons. By the 1910s Hoover was a multimillionaire.

In the summer of 1914 he was in London when the Great War broke out. The American consul sought his help in facilitating the return of more than 100,000 American tourists to the United States. That done, he aided in the feeding of starving citizens of Belgium, which had been occupied by German troops. When America entered the war in 1917, Hoover was put in charge of the Food Administration to supply military and relief needs overseas without hardships or rationing on the home front. Conservation and careful management worked well, and his efforts brought him great praise. After the war he headed the American Relief Administration to feed starving millions in Europe, and, amid criticism, people suffering under the Bolshevik regime in Soviet Russia. Next, he served as secretary of commerce under President Harding and was continued in the post by Harding's successor, Coolidge.

In the 1928 presidential election Hoover became the Republican candidate, riding on a wave of economic prosperity. He wiped out his Democratic opponent, Albert E. Smith, by 444 electoral votes to 87.

Due to excessive speculation and securities prices unsupported by any reasonable expectations

31st President (1929–1933)

HERBERT HOOVER

August 10, 1874–October 20, 1964

Political party: Republican

Vice president: Charles Curtis, 1929 to 1933

First Lady and family: Married Lou Henry on February 10, 1899. The couple had two children: Herbert Clark Hoover (1903–1969) and Allan Henry Hoover (1907–1993).

Especially remembered for: Aiding in the recovery of Europe after the Great War. Establishing the Reconstruction Finance Corporation in an unsuccessful attempt to end the economic depression, for which many held him responsible.

of earnings, the stock market collapsed in October 1929, just eight months after Hoover entered the White House. President Hoover signed the Smoot-Hawley Tariff Act into law on June 17, 1930, which later generations of historians felt was responsible for deepening what became known as the Great Depression.

The good times were over, and the remainder of Hoover's term was spent trying to solve unemployment, business failures, banking crises, and other ever-increasing problems. As the economy was becoming worse, President Hoover went to Congress and asked for $150 million to be invested in a public works program to increase employment and to stimulate business activity.

His critics stated that he enjoyed gala dinners at the White House while citizens were starving. Temporary settlements of shacks and tents were often called Hoovervilles, and a newspaper used for warmth was called a Hoover blanket. Without question, the president managed many things poorly, including directing the destruction of a temporary camp set up by veterans of the Great War who came to the capital to seek pension funds. "Prosperity cannot be restored by raids upon the public Treasury," he stated, in defense of his position that people should help themselves with the aid of private business, and that relief was not the government's responsibility.

Opposite: Herbert Hoover circa 1928 with his dog King Tut. This photograph, widely circulated, helped to establish Hoover as a warm, friendly presidential candidate, and King Tut is sometimes credited with getting his master elected. Below left: Hoover's inaugurat on medal from 1929. Above: Caricaturist Jack Rosen's portrait of the president.

In 1932 Hoover sought reelection, opposed by Franklin D. Roosevelt on the Democratic ticket. Roosevelt and many others blamed Hoover for the continuing effects of the deepening depression, and Roosevelt won in a landslide.

Hoover was a sharp critic of the Roosevelt administration. Afterward, he was respected as an elder statesman. In 1947 President Truman named him to a commission, which he chaired, to reorganize the executive branch of government and its departments. Hoover wrote extensively and was often consulted on matters of national interest. He died in New York City in 1964, highly honored.

THE AMERICAN SCENE

On May 16, 1929, the first Academy Awards were presented at the Hollywood Roosevelt Hotel. The stock market was breaking records, but some saw storm clouds gathering on the horizon. There had been some slowing of business expansion, but few dared to speak or write of it. On September 3 the Dow Jones Industrial average peaked at 381.17, an

Below left: An assortment of campaign pins boosting Hoover. Below right: Hoover circa 1960. After leaving the White House, Hoover enjoyed road trips and fishing vacations. Among the more than a dozen books he authored during his life was the guide *Fishing for Fun—And to Wash Your Soul*. He also wrote a biography of Woodrow Wilson, the first biography of one president to be written by another. The book was a best seller.

all-time high. Not until November 23, 1954, would it surpass that point! Reality struck on October 24 with the real onset of the Great Crash, which in time destroyed more than $30 billion in assets of New York stock exchange securities, nearly 10 times greater than the annual budget of the federal government.

Rounding out the year, on November 7, 1929, in New York City the Museum of Modern Art opened. On the 29th of the same month, Admiral Richard Byrd and three others became the first to fly over the South Pole, adding to his North Pole overflight accomplishment of 1926.

On January 13, 1930, the first Mickey Mouse comic strip was published. On March 6, the first frozen foods packaged by Clarence Birdseye went on sale in Springfield, Massachusetts. The Minnesota Mining and Manufacturing Company put Scotch tape on the market this year.

On March 3, 1931, "The Star-Spangled Banner" was adopted as the national anthem of the United States. On March 17, Nevada legalized gambling. This was already taking place under local and regional options in many places in America, but now anyone was invited to come to the Silver State to set up business. On May 1, in New York City, the world's tallest building—the Empire State building—was officially opened.

On January 12, 1932, Hattie Caraway became the first woman to be elected to the United States Senate. On March 1, infant Charles Lindbergh Jr. was kidnapped from the family home near Hopewell, New Jersey. A ransom was paid in bills whose serial numbers were recorded, with the list being distributed nationally. The baby was later found dead. In a controversial trial, ex-convict Bruno Hauptmann was found to be guilty and was executed on April 3, 1936. On March 25, *Tarzan the Ape Man* opened with Johnny Weissmuller, Olympic gold medal swimming champion, in the title role; this was the first of 12 Tarzan films in which he would star.

On July 8 the Dow Jones Industrial average touched its lowest point of the Depression, at 41.22. On July 28, President Hoover ordered the army to evict the so-called Bonus Army of World War I veterans who had gathered in Washington to claim a promised extra payment for their service in the conflict. Near year's end on December 27, Radio City Music Hall opened in Rockefeller Center in New York City. Among the attractions were the Rockettes dancing girls and the largest Wurlitzer theater pipe organ ever made.

Nazi leader Adolf Hitler was appointed chancellor of Germany by president Paul von Hindenburg on January 20, 1932. On the same day, *The Lone Ranger* made its debut on American radio. Prohibition was repealed in 1933, allowing American citizens to once again purchase and consume alcohol if they wished to. Repeal came about, in part, to stimulate the economy and make use of the great stores of grain sitting idle in silos all over the country, and to give farmers a source of income again.

NOTABLE SAYINGS

"Older men declare war. But it is youth who must fight and die."

"Blessed are the young, for they will inherit the national debt."

"Absolute freedom of the press to discuss public questions is a foundation stone of American liberty."

"Peace is not made at the counsel table or by treaties, but in the hearts of men."

32nd President (1933–1945)

FRANKLIN DELANO ROOSEVELT

January 30, 1882–April 12, 1945

Political party: Democratic

Vice president: John Nance Garner, 1933 to 1941; Henry A. Wallace, 1941 to 1945; Harry S. Truman, 1945

First Lady and family: Married a fifth cousin, Eleanor Roosevelt, on March 17, 1905, despite his mother's vehement objections. Eleanor Roosevelt became one of the most prominent and accomplished first ladies in American history, although the relationship with her husband was difficult at best, and in later years devoid of romance. He developed other liaisons. The couple had five children: Anna Eleanor Roosevelt (1906–1975); James Roosevelt (1907–1991); Elliott Roosevelt (1910–1990); Franklin Delano Roosevelt Jr. (1914–1988); and John Aspinwall Roosevelt (1916–1981).

Especially remembered for: Inaugural address comment "The only thing we have to fear is fear itself." Establishment of federal agencies during the Depression, such as TVA, CCC, and SEC, collectively called "alphabet soup." "Fireside chat" radio broadcasts to the public. Trying to pack the Supreme Court with his favorites. Lifting the country from the Depression. Quiet suffering with poliomyelitis. Brilliant conduct of World War II with domestic and foreign policies. Planning to establish the United Nations. A candidate for the most accomplished president, although not without many detractors. Only president for more than two terms. Nickname: "FDR." Roosevelt is frequently rated as one of the top three presidents, the other two being Washington and Lincoln.

The Early Life of Franklin D. Roosevelt

Franklin Delano Roosevelt was born in Hyde Park, New York, son of James and Sara Delano Roosevelt, members of a prominent family. He was a fifth cousin to Theodore Roosevelt. Franklin graduated from Harvard in 1903, and then went to Columbia law school, where he flunked several courses and was so bored he dropped out in 1907. Despite this, he learned enough to pass the bar exam while a student, and soon he was affiliated with a prominent law firm, Carter, Ledyard & Milburn, in New York City.

Like his cousin Theodore, he entered politics. Unlike Theodore, he became a Democrat. New York politicians admired his handsome appearance, intelligence, and fine manner, and persuaded him to run for the State Legislature. His bid was successful, and he served from 1911 to 1913, followed by a position as assistant secretary of the navy from

Opposite: Franklin Delano Roosevelt in December 1933, during his first year as president. The nation's collective spirit was revitalized by FDR's determined optimism and activism.

1913 to 1920. In 1920 he was on the national ticket as vice president, but the Democrats lost to Warren G. Harding.

In August 1921 a worse setback occurred. While swimming in cold water near Campobello Island, New Brunswick, where he had a summer home, he became chilled and sustained cramps. When he tried to stand, his legs would not support him. After some confusion, he was diagnosed with poliomyelitis and was confined to a wheelchair. Undaunted, he set about a regimen of exercise and recovery, including bathing at Warm Springs, a Georgia spa. At first he could pull himself along the floor with his hands and get up with help. Then he was able to stand with braces, and walk, after a fashion, using a cane. In 1924 he made a comeback appearance at the Democratic national convention to endorse Albert E. Smith as the presidential candidate.

After this, Roosevelt could get about, but still required crutches. With great energy he resumed his political ambitions. In 1928 he was elected governor of New York, and in 1932 he was the Democratic choice to oppose incumbent Hoover in the presidential election. He was always careful to avoid being photographed in a wheelchair, and by 1932 most people did not know of his disability. His was an era, quite different from our own, when personal details of a president's health, family activities, and the like were not sought by the press if notice was given that such attention was not wanted.

In the November contest Roosevelt won in a landslide with 57% of the popular vote and carried all but six states. Hoover offered to meet with him to share ideas on how to arrest the downward spiral of the economy, but Roosevelt refused, stating that this would just tie his hands. He set about lining up accomplished men for his Cabinet and held meetings individually with them long before he was inaugurated.

Above: Two FDR portrait pins urge voters to "vote straight Democrat." Roosevelt is the only American president to have been elected to more than two terms.

Roosevelt as President

Roosevelt was sworn into office on March 4, 1933, one day after the Mount Rushmore National Monument was dedicated (featuring presidents Washington, Jefferson, Lincoln, and Theodore Roosevelt). With a great deal of planning, on March 6 he announced that all banks would be closed in a "Bank Holiday" so they could be audited regarding their solvency. Those found to be in sound condition were allowed to reopen soon afterward, while banks in questionable condition were closed or forced to merge. On March 12 he gave his first radio address, inaugurating a series of popular "fireside chats." A few days later on March 15 the Dow Jones Industrial average went from 53.84 to 62.10, or a gain of 15.34%, the highest one-day percentage gain before or since.

With overwhelming support from the public, Roosevelt immediately set about making vast reforms in other areas as well, including public works and relief, aided by his well-informed Cabinet members. His campaign song, "Happy Days are Here Again," became a favorite on the airwaves. Roosevelt's first 100 days in office saw unprecedented changes in his "New Deal," as, metaphorically, a poor hand of cards was thrown away and replaced with one that might include some royal cards and aces. For the first time in several years of national economic depression, citizens had hope. In the meantime, Republicans accused him of anarchy, unconstitutional actions, and more.

The nation went off the gold standard in early 1934, taxes were increased, the national budget ran up a huge deficit, and concessions were made to labor interests. Much of this angered businessmen, many of whom said that Roosevelt's New Deal was filled with jokers, was illegal and improper, and needed to be halted.

Year by year, the opposition notwithstanding, many of Roosevelt's programs worked, although not without encountering hardships, such as the Dust Bowl in the Midwest in the mid-1930s. Roosevelt was reelected in 1936, by which time the economy had improved dramatically. This was not to last, and in 1937 a recession set in. January 20 was now the official inauguration date, replacing the traditional March 4. This reduced the length of time for an ineffective incumbent president to serve who might have lost the November election. On February 5, 1937, President Roosevelt, taking issue with the Supreme Court's resistance to his innovative—radical, many said—government plans to help combat the Depression, proposed increasing the number of people on the Supreme Court. The proposed "packing" of the Supreme Court caused outrage, and nothing was done. On July 22, 1937, the United States Senate voted down Roosevelt's plan.

When World War II commenced in Europe in 1939, Roosevelt worked with British leaders to supply munitions and other goods. This ended the recession, and happy days were truly here again in the economy. In 1940 he sought reelection for an unprecedented third term and won. After America entered the war in Europe in December 1941, Roosevelt worked with the military on strategy, cooperated with allies, and by spring 1945—by then just entering his fourth term of office—had come close to victory. (This saga is related under "The American Scene.")

On November 7, 1944, the president was elected to an unprecedented fourth term, beating challenger Thomas E. Dewey, a former mayor of New York City. Dewey would reappear in the 1948 election contest.

Right: First Lady Eleanor Roosevelt was one of the most distinguished women of the 20th century. A popular speaker and a passionate advocate for human and civil rights, she was also a delegate to the United Nations General Assembly and the first chairman of the UN Commission on Human Rights. President Truman, who succeeded her husband in the White House, called her "First Lady of the World."

FREEDOM FROM WANT · FREEDOM FROM FEAR ·
FREEDOM OF WORSHIP · FREEDOM OF SPEECH ·
FRANKLIN DELANO ROOSEVELT

On April 12, 1945, Franklin Roosevelt died unexpectedly of a cerebral hemorrhage at Warm Springs, Georgia. He was succeeded by his new vice president, Harry S. Truman, who had taken office just five weeks earlier and had not yet been briefed on many important matters, including the development of the atomic bomb.

THE AMERICAN SCENE

In distant Germany, Adolf Hitler and his Nazi party gained an iron-fisted control over the country's politics and economy. Although at first the Nazi actions received little attention in America, by the end of the decade they became one of the great challenges facing President Roosevelt and our nation.

America had been on the gold standard officially since 1900 and in practice since the first U.S. gold coins were minted in 1795. On April 5, 1933, Roosevelt declared a national emergency and issued Executive Order 6102, forbidding Americans to own bullion gold or coins, except for certain numismatic purposes. The price of gold, earlier $20.67 per ounce, was later raised to $35, in effect devaluing the dollar.

Despite enthusiasm for the New Deal, by 1934 most conditions in the United States had not improved greatly, and social conditions were unsettled. Vast dust storms swept through Oklahoma, Kansas, Texas, and other Midwestern states, stripping tens of millions of acres of valuable topsoil and eventually leading to several hundred thousand farmers' leaving the Dust Bowl. Many moved west, primarily to California. For the Ford Motor Company, however, things were beginning to look up, and Henry Ford restored the $5 per day minimum wage to 47,000 of his 70,000 workers.

On May 6, 1937, the *Hindenburg* dirigible (with Nazi emblems) exploded when it attempted to land in Lakehurst, New Jersey. Of the 36 passengers and 61 crew members aboard, 11 passengers and 22 crew members were killed, plus a member of the ground crew. This ended an era of dirigible transportation worldwide. On July 2, Amelia Earhart and her navigator Fred Noonan took off for New Guinea as part of her attempt to be the first woman to fly around the world. Their plane disappeared, creating a mystery that has been contemplated ever since.

On January 3, 1938, the March of Dimes was inaugurated by President Roosevelt. Funds were to be used to find a cure for polio.

Conditions in Europe were worsening as the Nazis expanded their influence and increased persecution of Jews and certain other minorities. On September 30, 1938, British Prime Minister Neville went to Germany, met with Hitler, and returned to assure British citizens that all was well and that there would continue to be peace in the foreseeable future.

On September 1, 1939, the Nazis invaded Poland. Two days later the United Kingdom, France, New Zealand, and Australia declared war on Germany. World War II had begun. However, on the same day the United States declared that it was neutral in the war matter.

In 1940, World War II continued to spread throughout Europe. Nazis occupied France, Belgium, and Holland, adding to the territory already conquered. Neville Chamberlain, who made tragic misjudgments of the Nazis, was replaced as prime minister by Winston Churchill in May. Churchill addressed the House of Commons in relation to the Royal Air Force, whose pilots in Spitfire planes had downed many German bombers, saying, "Never in the field of human conflict was so much owed by so many to so few." The worst was yet to come, for on September 7, Nazi planes began to drop bombs on London; the air strike lasted for 57 consecutive nights.

Although President Roosevelt and Congress continued their neutrality (but not with any official arrangements with the Nazis or the increasing threat of the Japanese), much sentiment was with

Opposite: This bronze plaque honoring Roosevelt was unveiled in 1945. Sculpted by African American artist Selma Burke, the likeness inspired John R. Sinnock's portrait of FDR for the U.S. ten-cent coin.

the "Allies," the oppressed and attacked nations, most notably Britain. On August 1, the president had a secret meeting in Newfoundland with Winston Churchill to formulate the Atlantic Charter. Matters were going from bad to worse. On October 17, the USS *Kearny* destroyer was torpedoed by a Nazi U-boat, killing 11 men, the first direct American military casualties in the war. This was followed on October 31 by the sinking of the destroyer USS *Reuben James* near Iceland with more than 100 sailors killed.

The morning of December 7, 1941, brought a surprise attack by Japanese aircraft against the United States naval installation at Pearl Harbor, Hawaii. Many vessels were damaged or completely destroyed, and thousands of people were killed. The next day the United States, Great Britain, China, and the Netherlands, among others, declared war on the Japanese Empire, Germany, and their allies.

Roosevelt's beloved Scottish terrier, Fala, was a familiar face to the American public, accompanying his master to many events and becoming part of the president's public image. Fala is the only presidential pet to be featured in a presidential memorial.

President Roosevelt spoke to the nation—and the world—when he gave a radio-broadcast address to Congress that afternoon, calling the 7th of December a day that would live in infamy.

Americans volunteered with enthusiasm to serve in the military, while organizations and businesses eagerly scrambled to meet the challenge on the home front. The first U.S. troops arrived in Europe on January 26, 1942, and on February 1 the command staff of the Eighth Air Force reached England.

In a controversial move, President Roosevelt on February 19 signed an executive order setting up "exclusionary zones" where people of "Foreign Enemy Ancestry" were forbidden from entering (following an earlier order of February 2 that required registration of Japanese Americans). This eventually led to the internment (imprisonment) of over 120,000 people, mostly Japanese Americans, but some German and Italian Americans as well.

April 18, 1942, brought the U.S. bombing of Japan by American B-25 twin-engine Mitchell bombers launched from an aircraft carrier. The Battle of the Coral Sea in May was the first time in naval history

that two fleets engaged each other at a distance, with the ships of one side not visible to ships of the other. It was an Allied victory, but at heavy cost. On June 7 the Japanese invaded the Aleutian Islands in Alaska, capturing two of them—their first and only victory on American soil. The Battle of Guadalcanal began in the South Pacific in August and effectively ended in November, with extensive casualties on both sides, but with the United States Navy ending up in command.

On August 17, 1942, came the first raid by heavy bombers of the United States Air Force against occupied France. Eventually, B-17 Flying Fortress and B-24 Liberator bombers would go aloft in formations of several hundred or more in sorties over Nazi territory, at a great loss of aircraft and pilots. A "tour of duty" was 25 such runs, but thousands of airmen did not live long enough to complete it.

The year 1943 was pivotal in Europe, and the tide began to turn as the Nazis were defeated in several areas. In the meantime, the Pentagon, the world's largest office building, was dedicated. The Mall between the White House and the Lincoln Memorial was filled with temporary wooden buildings housing personnel. British bombers devastated Hamburg for eight days and seven nights, starting on July 24, with a firestorm that killed more than 42,000 civilians. One by one, the centers of German cities were being reduced to rubble. Along the way, allied military actions against the Fascist government of Italy, led by Benito Mussolini, reduced that German ally to helplessness, culminating in Italy's surrender announced by General Dwight D. Eisenhower on September 8.

On November 28, 1943, President Roosevelt met with Joseph Stalin and Winston Churchill in the Tehran Conference to discuss strategy for a June 1944 invasion of Europe.

In 1944, victory for the Allies was in the offing. Early in the year American troops occupied several islands in the South Pacific. Air strikes against Germany continued, with devastating effect. On D-Day, June 6, vessels leaving England landed 155,000 Allied troops on the beaches in Normandy in France. On August 24, Paris was liberated from Nazi occupation. Allied troops advanced across the continent. On October 21, 1944, Aachen became the first German city to be captured by American troops.

On February 3, 1945, the Battle of Manila began, leading to the capture of Manila from the Japanese by U.S. forces. Germany and Japan were falling rapidly, but fighting remained intense in many areas and casualties mounted. From February 4 to 11, Roosevelt, Churchill, and Stalin held the Yalta Conference to decide how to rehabilitate the countries under Nazi occupation once the war ended.

Events proceeded quickly. On February 19, about 30,000 Marines landed to do battle on a remote Japanese stronghold in the Pacific, the island of Iwo Jima. On February 23, a photographer captured the moment when the U.S. flag was raised at the summit of Mount Suribachi. On March 9 and 10, American B-29 bombers, used only in the Pacific Theater, attacked Japan with fire bombs. On April 1, troops landed on Okinawa, south of Tokyo, and began battle.

On March 18, 1945, Berlin felt a rain of destruction from 1,250 Allied B-17, B-24, and other bombers. In desperation, the next day Hitler ordered that all industries, military installations, machine shops, transportation facilities, and communication facilities in Germany be destroyed. His generals disobeyed the order. Hitler's days were numbered.

NOTABLE SAYINGS

"We have nothing to fear but fear itself."

"A good leader can't get too far ahead of his followers."

"Happiness lies in the joy of achievement and the thrill of creative effort."

33rd President (1945–1953)

HARRY S. TRUMAN

May 8, 1884–December 26, 1972

Political party: Democratic

Vice president: None 1945 to 1949; Alben Barkley, 1949 to 1953

First Lady and family: Married Elizabeth "Bess" Virginia Wallace on June 28, 1919. The couple had one child, Mary Margaret Truman (born in 1924).

Especially remembered for: His orders to drop atomic bombs on the Japanese cities of Hiroshima and Nagasaki, bringing a quick end to World War II and possibly saving the millions of lives a land invasion might have cost. The "Cold War" with the Soviet Union. The start of the Korean War. His saying "The buck stops here," reflecting his courage to make decisions. Nickname: "Give 'Em Hell Harry"

The Early Life of Harry S. Truman

Harry S. Truman was born in Lamar, Missouri, son of John Anderson and Martha Ellen Truman, who gave him for his middle name the initial S. His parents were well-to-do farmers. Truman spent his youth in Independence, Missouri, where he enjoyed playing the piano (and once contemplated it as a career) and reading, especially history books. His family suffered financial setbacks, and he was unable to go to college. He lived at home until he was in his thirties, employed at various clerking and other jobs.

At age 33 Truman joined the army and went overseas to fight in the Great War. As captain of Battery D, 129th Field Artillery, he distinguished himself in combat and was nearly killed several times. Upon returning home he and a partner opened a haberdashery in Kansas City, Missouri, but it soon failed. Admired as a war hero, Truman attracted the attention of Mike Prendergast, a nephew of Thomas Prendergast, who controlled the regional Democratic political machine. Truman was picked as a likely candidate and successfully put up for election as judge of the Eastern District of Jackson County—a desk job, not on the judicial bench. In 1934, when three possibilities chosen by the Prendergast machine to run for the United States Senate declined, Truman was selected by default, although to the consternation of certain party insiders he was viewed as incorruptible and not subject to outside influence.

Truman went to the Senate, where he performed well but without distinction. In 1940 he sought reelection. By that time Thomas Prendergast was in prison for tax evasion, and the political machine was in shambles. Truman was encouraged to drop out, even by President Roosevelt. He persisted,

Opposite: The official White house portrait of President Harry Truman, painted by Greta Kempton.

Left: A 1934 poster urging voters to choose Truman as the Democratic Party candidate for senator. As senator, Truman decried corporate greed and warned of the hazards of national interests' being influenced too much by stock-market speculators and other wealthy special interests. Below: Truman's official presidential inaugural medal from 1949. It was designed by C. Paul Jennewein.

won the election, and continued in his post. He was appalled at inefficiency in the military, as were certain other senators, who named him to head what became known as the Truman Committee, to investigate waste. When America entered World War II the committee became famous for reforms that led to increased production and savings. For the 1944 election, Truman was Roosevelt's choice as running mate. For whatever reason, the president did not fill Truman in on many war strategies.

Truman in the White House

Upon Roosevelt's death on April 12, 1945, Vice President Truman became president. The war was winding down, with an invasion of Japan imminent. Truman was briefed on military plans, of which he had been given little knowledge earlier, not even of the development of the atomic bomb. He directed that the new weapon be dropped on two Japanese cities to hasten the end of the war. In August the atomic age began. It was said that the destruction of Hiroshima and Nagasaki ultimately saved about two million lives—an estimate of those that would have been lost if the war had continued with a land invasion.

America did emerge victorious (see "The American Scene" below). Truman and his administration faced vast challenges as soldiers returned from war, factories converted to normal peacetime production, and life returned to normal. It was not easy. Shortages of consumer goods were widespread. New automobiles were not available, and when they finally entered the market, black market prices prevailed. Strikes broke out in many industries, resulting in crippling stoppages. Corruption was discovered in Truman's cabinet and elsewhere in his administration.

The plans laid by Roosevelt, Churchill, and Stalin at the 1944 Yalta Conference went awry when Joseph Stalin decided to keep former Nazi countries in servitude and force them into obedience to the Union of Soviet Socialist Republics (USSR) instead of allowing them to rebuild their own governments and economies. An "Iron Curtain" (a term coined by Churchill) descended across part of Europe. The USSR became an enemy to America, and both sides threatened each other. The so-called Cold War began in 1947 and would last into the late 1980s.

On July 18, 1947, Truman signed the Presidential Succession Act, which placed the succession as

vice president, president *pro tempore* of the United States Senate, and the speaker of the House of Representatives.

On April 3, 1948, the president signed the Marshall Plan, authorizing $5 billion in aid for 16 countries—a great boon to towns and cities destroyed during the Nazi regime and to the citizens remaining there. On July 25 he affixed his signature to Executive Order 9981, ending racial segregation in the armed forces.

In 1948 Truman sought reelection. By that time, Republicans were in control of Congress and most of the old Roosevelt appointees and those crucial to related programs had dispersed. Truman's hard line against the emerging strength of Communism in the USSR was resisted by many who felt that Russia would ultimately contribute to world peace. Many Democrats deserted the president, and with the Republicans nominating the handsome and popular Thomas E. Dewey, governor of New York, Truman seemed to be a certain loser. He had no particular talent, it was said. He did not give eloquent speeches. Besides, many felt, the Democrats had won every election since 1932, and it was time for a change.

Just about every political columnist and radio commentator predicted that his challenger would win in a landslide. Public opinion polls verified this. In fact, the outcome was so certain that it was said Truman needn't bother to run. The *Chicago Daily Tribune* prepared its post-election edition with the front-page headline "DEWEY DEFEATS TRUMAN." What else was there to say?

Quite a bit, it turned out. To the surprise of all of the experts, Truman carried a majority of the popular vote, 24,179,347, to Dewey's 21,991,292, and took the electoral votes by a landslide, 303 to 189.

Left: An assortment of campaign and keepsake pins featuring Truman's likeness. Below: President Truman at work. After winning the 1948 election, the president and First Lady had to move out of the White House, whose condition had deteriorated to the point that Truman's own bedroom was considered unsafe. The extensive renovations of the venerable building finally ended in March 1952.

His second term was difficult, and he vetoed 250 bills, of which 12 were overridden by Congress. He approved the Berlin Airlift in 1948 and 1949, which brought supplies to that free city, now encircled by Communist forces. A man of strong principles and determination, he led the nation through difficult and divisive times, including the "police action" in 1950 that started the controversial Korean War. In 1951, President Truman relieved General Douglas MacArthur of command. In the Korean conflict MacArthur was defying the directions of Truman, the commander in chief. This caused a great sensation: the Senate held hearings, and many citizens who disliked the president rallied to MacArthur's side. In time the matter faded away.

In 1953 Truman returned to Independence, Missouri, where he enjoyed his retirement. For many years political observers and historians condemned him and his presidency. After his death, many reevaluated his career, and today he is remembered as a president of unusual strength, even of greatness.

THE AMERICAN SCENE

After President Franklin D. Roosevelt's death on April 12, 1945, it fell to President Truman as commander in chief to make military decisions. He immersed himself in briefings by the military, heads of Senate committees, and other strategists. In the meantime, the Nazi regime was rapidly falling, many German cities had been laid waste by Allied bombers, and many countries once occupied by Germany were free. However, most were disorganized and in chaos, and their inhabitants were short of food and other essentials.

On April 30, Adolf Hitler and his wife of one day, Eva Braun (prior to this his longtime mistress), committed suicide as the Red Army (of the USSR) approached Berlin. The German radio announced that Hitler had died in battle, "fighting up to his last breath against Bolshevism."

On May 3, rocket scientist Wernher von Braun and 120 members of his team surrendered (later, on the 16th of November, 88 of them would be "adopted" and go to the United States to help with America's rocket program, based on the V-2 that had wreaked havoc on Antwerp and London).

On May 7, 1945, Germany signed an unconditional surrender. On May 8, 1945, Victory in Europe (V-E) Day was celebrated with demonstrations, dances, and more. In some towns a conga line of dancers and marchers paraded up and down the streets for hours.

The first general-purpose electronic computer, known as the Electronic Numerical Integrator and Computer (ENIAC), was announced as complete on February 15, 1946. The machine occupied 1,800 square feet of floor space. The utility of such complex and cumbersome devices was debated, but it was thought that surely computers would someday find use with the government and the largest industries.

On July 1 of that year, Germany was divided between the Allied occupation with Russian, French, and American zones. The Russian section eventually became known as East Germany and fell under draconic Communist rule from the USSR. In New Mexico on July 16 the "Trinity Test" of an atomic device was conducted with success, followed on August 6 by the B-29 *Enola Gay* dropping an atomic bomb on Hiroshima and on August 9 by another by the B-29 *Bockscar* on Nagasaki. Faced with annihilation, on August 14 Emperor Hirohito accepted the American terms of surrender. August 15 was proclaimed Victory in Japan (V-J) Day. The greatest war in history, costing an estimated 50 million or more lives (including those lost to Nazi oppression), was over.

On July 1, 1946, an atomic bomb was exploded at Bikini Atoll in the South Pacific, the first of many atomic tests to be conducted by the United States and, later, by other countries, until they tapered off in the late 20th century when the effects of radioactive

Opposite: An undated portrait of Truman. At the time he left office, there was no federal retirement package for presidents, and his only income was his old army pension of $112.56 per month. He wrote his memoirs, sold family property, and in 1958 finally was granted a pension through the new Former Presidents Act.

fallout were finally deemed too dangerous for continuation.

In the national elections of November 5, the Senate and the House both gained Republican majorities, making it difficult for President Truman to facilitate passage that his Democratic Party deemed desirable.

On February 3, 1947, Percival Pratts became the first African American news correspondent to be allowed in the gallery of the United States House of Representatives and the Senate. In the same month, Edwin Land demonstrated his first Polaroid Land Camera, launching instant photography.

In 1947 the Cold War began between United States and the Soviet Union, its former ally. This became the overwhelming international political predicament for many years afterward, as both countries armed themselves, including with atomic weapons, against a possible attack by the other. In late spring and early summer, unidentified flying objects (UFOs) or "flying saucers" made the news, including an extraterrestrial spacecraft that was said to have crashed near Roswell, New Mexico.

On October 14, 1947, Air Force test pilot Captain Chuck Yeager broke the sound barrier, flying a Bell X-1 Rocket plane faster than the speed of sound. On November 29, the United Nations General Assembly voted to partition Palestine between the Arab and Jewish regions, resulting in the creation of the State of Israel, a refuge for many survivors from Nazi persecution.

The Berlin Blockade started in 1948 when East Germany, under the control of the USSR, stopped unauthorized vehicles from bringing supplies to Berlin, part of which was occupied by remaining Allied troops who were helping its citizens to rebuild the economy. The Berlin Airlift was the result, with food and other supplies being flown in to the city airport. This was ended in May 1948.

On August 25, 1948, the House Un-American Activities Committee held its first ever televised congressional hearing, which featured a confrontation between Whitaker Chambers and Alger Hiss. This hearing set the stage for an investigation to identify Americans who might have belonged to the Communist Party or have Communist or subversive inclinations. This search went into high gear in the early 1950s. Led by Senator Joseph McCarthy, this rapidly spiraled out of control, as many prominent

Below: An anti-war poster depicts President Truman as he appeared during his active service in World War I, reminding the public that no one who had been involved in that horrific struggle was eager to go to war again.

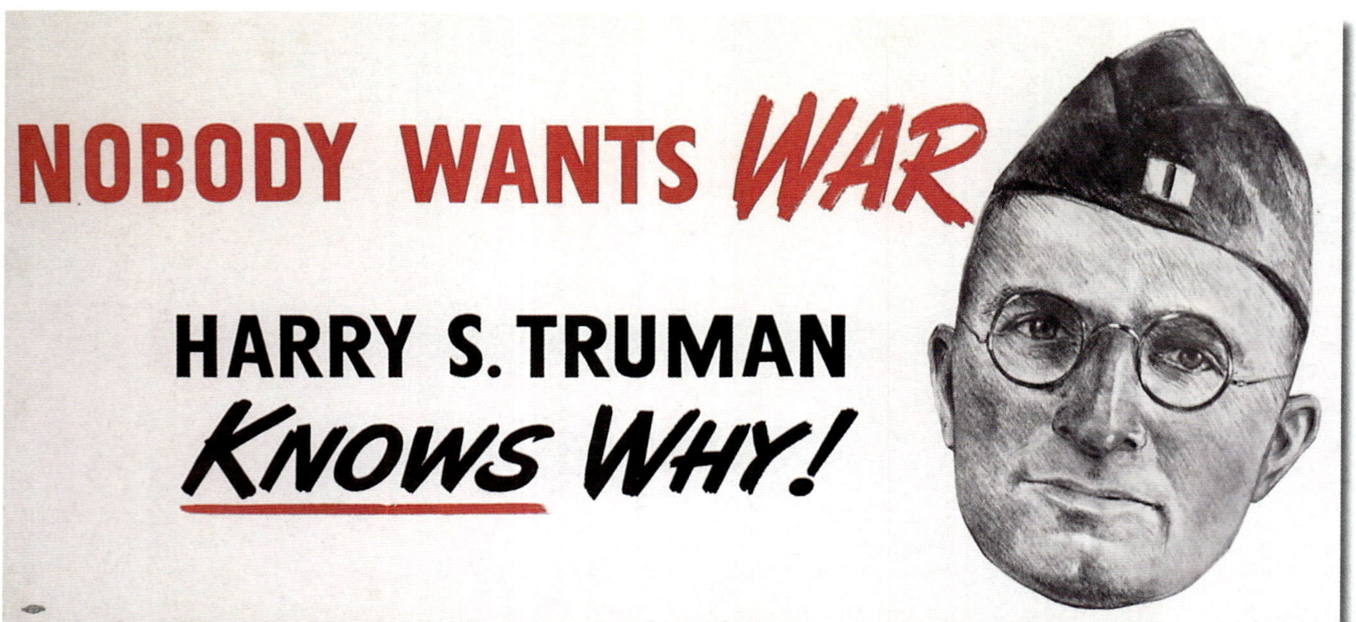

citizens faced baseless accusations, meanwhile surrounded by unending publicity. Citizens with Communist leanings were called "pinkos," meaning they were not fully red (red being the USSR's color). Later, on December 2, 1954, the Senate voted 67 to 22 to condemn McCarthy for "conduct that tends to bring the Senate into dishonor and disrepute."

In 1949, the first year of Truman's second term, the North Atlantic Treaty Organization (NATO) was established as a union of countries to protect themselves against the USSR as the Cold War continued to escalate. The world was hardly at peace, however, as in 1949 Chinese Communist troops overran various areas of Palestine.

On April 7, 1949, Rodgers and Hammerstein's musical drama *South Pacific* opened on Broadway, starring Mary Martin and Ezio Pinza. This was the era of Broadway musicals, which created a sensation in the entertainment world for the next several decades. On July 17 the De Havilland Comet, the world's first commercial jetliner, made its inaugural flight. The USSR tested its first atomic bomb on August 29, shifting the Cold War into higher gear.

In an event that went unnoticed at the time, on February 8, 1950, the first charge was made to a Diner's Club card, launching an era of "plastic" payments that by the end of the century would replace cash and checks for many transactions.

On June 25, 1950, North Korean soldiers invaded South Korea, leading American soldiers into a "police action"—what was never declared a war, but really was one. It lasted well into 1953, with thousands of American troops in service, many of whom paid the ultimate sacrifice. The war ended in a stalemate—the first of a number of American interventions in overseas battle theaters that cost a lot of money and lives, were usually controversial, and ended with inconclusive results. Unlike World War II, these actions often spawned great domestic dissension, especially among young people who were drafted into service or threatened with such a prospect.

On November 10, 1951, direct dialing telephone calls from coast to coast began. In time, this would become universal. Earlier, patrons had to dial 0 and ask for a long-distance operator to make connections. The Cold War expanded. In February 1952 the United Kingdom announced that it had an atomic bomb. In time, many other countries scrambled to develop such devices. In 1952 the United States went one step further, announcing an even more powerful hydrogen bomb, which in 1953 was matched by the USSR.

NOTABLE SAYINGS

"A statesman is a politician who has been dead 10 or 15 years."

"America was not built on fear. America was built on courage, imagination, and unbeatable determination to do the job at hand."

"If you want a friend in Washington, get a dog."

"The buck stops here."

"You need not fear the expression of ideas—we do need to fear their suppression."

"You cannot stop the spread of an idea by passing a law against it."

"A pessimist is one who makes difficulties of his opportunities and an optimist is one who makes opportunities of his difficulties."

"I never did give anybody hell. I just told the truth and they thought it was hell."

" It is amazing what you can accomplish if you do not care who gets the credit."

34th President (1953–1961)

DWIGHT D. EISENHOWER

October 14, 1890–March 28, 1969

Political party: Republican

Vice president: Richard M. Nixon, 1953 to 1961

First Lady and family: Married Mary "Mamie" Geneva Doud on July 1, 1916. The couple had two children: Doud Dwight Eisenhower (1917–1921) and John Sheldon Doud Eisenhower (1923–).

Especially remembered for: The slogan "I like Ike." Truce in Korea. The Interstate Highway system. Mandated desegregation of public schools (including by sending armed forces to Little Rock, Arkansas, in 1957) and the armed forces. Outgoing personality. Enjoyment of golf. Good economic times.

The Early Life of Dwight D. Eisenhower

Dwight David Eisenhower was born in Denison, Texas, son of David Jacob and Ida Elizabeth Stover Eisenhower. He spent his childhood in Abilene, Kansas, which he considered to be his hometown. With an outgoing character and high school achievements in sports he was a natural candidate to go to West Point, from which he graduated in 1915.

Eisenhower began his army career as a second lieutenant in Texas. In succeeding years he filled his assignments well, serving under generals John J. Pershing, Douglas MacArthur, and Walter Krueger. During World War II he was placed in command of the Allied forces in Europe, and he planned strategies in the North Africa campaign and elsewhere. As supreme commander he took charge of the landing of Allied troops in France on D Day 1944. After the war, he returned home as America's greatest military hero.

The general was named president of Columbia University in New York City, and then took a leave of absence in 1951 to command the North America Treaty Alliance (NATO) forces being formed in Europe to resist the spread of Communism and the military reach of the Soviet Union. The Cold War, with its threats and espionage, continued—as did the Korean War, backed by the Communists.

The Eisenhower Presidency

In 1952 both the Democrats and the Republicans sought Eisenhower as a presidential candidate, although "Ike," as he was called, had no elective political experience. He signed on the Republican ticket, campaigning with the "I like Ike" slogan against Democrat Adlai E. Stevenson, and won handily. The Electoral College count was 442 to 89.

Early in his administration his staff participated in negotiations with China to end the Korean conflict

Opposite: The official White House portrait of President Dwight Eisenhower. The artist was J. Anthony Wills of Houston, Texas.

(never officially declared a war), and a truce was perfected on July 27, 1953. North Korea under Communist rule and democratic South Korea were separated by a demilitarized zone. Although warfare ended, for years later, even into the 21st century, the two divisions of Korea remained enemies.

Joseph Stalin, longtime dictator of the Soviet Union, died in 1953, adding further uncertainty to the already tense relations between the United States and that country. On both sides there was much fear of an atomic attack, and during the next 20 years, public and private bomb shelters were constructed on our side of the Atlantic. In the meantime, talks were held with Soviet diplomats, and on occasion tensions were eased, such as at a meeting of government leaders in Geneva in 1955. In the meantime Eisenhower endorsed multiple Central Intelligence Agency (CIA) covert actions, including the removal of certain foreign leaders and even assassinations. This

Top: A banner from the presidential race of 1952, in which Eisenhower's running mate was future president Richard Nixon. Left: A badge for a Wisconsinite to wear to Ike's inauguration in 1953.

led to the overthrow of the leaders of Iran, Guatemala, and possibly the Belgian Congo. The question of whether it is the business of the United States to interfere in other governments not friendly to American interests has been controversial ever since.

On February 10, 1954, after authorizing $385 million more than the $400 million already budgeted for military aid to Vietnam, President Eisenhower warned against American intervention in that country. This advice was not heeded, sowing the seeds for massive anti-war demonstrations in America a decade later.

With an eye on the budget, the president advocated a policy of reducing expenditures on ever more powerful atomic weapons and checking the funding for certain other defense operations that were felt to be getting out of control. Some thought this unusual for a military hero to do. He started the National Aeronautics and Space Administration (NASA), thus beginning the space program.

In November 1955 Eisenhower had a heart attack. He was hospitalized for seven weeks, and then discharged with a good prognosis. In 1956 he won reelection against his old challenger Stevenson (who shared the Democratic ticket with Estes Kefauver), this time by 457 Electoral College votes to 73. In the same year he signed the Federal Highway Act, which authorized the Interstate Highway System, today remembered as a highlight of his administration. In time the nation was linked by limited-access high-speed highways. A provision in the legislation was that in each five-mile stretch there had to be at least one mile of straight road, in case of emergency aircraft landings. The Cold War still dominated much thinking.

Turmoil in the Mideast caused many problems for Eisenhower. The Suez Canal crisis in 1956 closed that important waterway and involved an invasion of Egypt by combined Israeli, British, and French forces. At the United Nations, Eisenhower criticized these three nations, all strong allies of the United States, and forced them to withdraw, after which Gamal Abdel Nasser took command in Egypt and sought to dominate the Arab world while working against American interests. In a later memoir Eisenhower said this was the greatest foreign policy error of his administration.

Segregation continued to be endemic in the South. In 1957 nine African American students sought to enroll in the Little Rock (Arkansas) High School, but in contravention to federal law they were driven away by state authorities. Eisenhower sent federal troops to escort them into the building, and signed into law the Civil Rights acts of 1957 and 1960.

Above: This pin would have been worn by a member of the O'K Ike Club of Sunflower Ordnance Works, located in northwest Johnson County, Kansas. Below: Eisenhower's simple but famous campaign slogan, "I Like Ike," was found on many pins like this one.

By 1960 the Cold War included spy missions by American pilots flying U-2 planes high over Soviet territory. On May 1, the U-2 aircraft flown by Francis Gary Powers was shot down, and the pilot was taken prisoner. At first the government denied this, and one of the greatest diplomatic crises of the Eisenhower administration erupted. Addressing the assembly of the United Nations on May 16, Soviet premier Nikita Khrushchev demanded an apology from Eisenhower about the U-2 flights, which wasn't given, and therefore a summit meeting discussing peace and disarmament collapsed. Things settled down, and years later Powers was exchanged for a Soviet prisoner held by the United States.

In 1960 vice president Richard M. Nixon was nominated as the Republican candidate for president. It seems that Nixon and Eisenhower were not friends, and the latter suggested that Nixon "paddle his own canoe." (Later, a Nixon daughter married an Eisenhower son.) Nixon lost.

Eisenhower continued to be a popular figure until he left office in January 1961. He and his wife Mamie retired to a farm they had acquired in Gettysburg, Pennsylvania. Eisenhower died in March 1969 at Walter Reed Hospital in Washington, D.C., after his seventh heart attack.

THE AMERICAN SCENE

On May 29, 1953, Sir Edmond Hillary and Tenzing Norgay became the first men to reach the summit of Mount Everest. To Americans and others worldwide this was the last great feat of exploration. That summer the first Chevrolet Corvette was built in Flint, Michigan. The decade saw much emphasis on automobiles, emphasizing power and distinctive designs. Tail fins began sprouting in the early 1950s, and by 1959 they may have reached a zenith with the Cadillac, the rear of which looked like a jukebox with its huge fins and red lights. The "big three" auto makers were General Motors, Ford, and Chrysler. Seeking to expand its market, Ford introduced and heavily promoted the Edsel line, which proved to be a poster example of new-product failure.

In 1953 the UNIVAC 1103 became the first computer to use random access memory. Development would continue, and by the late 1950s many universities and businesses had large mainframe computers that filled a room and needed special cooling equipment. Particularly popular were IBM computers that spewed rectangular cardboard punch cards that could be mechanically sorted.

In 1954 the Boeing 707 jetliner was successfully flown, and a few years later would enter regular service. In this year the words "under God" were added to the Pledge of Allegiance. The first transistor radio was announced by Texas Instruments. On November 23, 1954, the Dow Jones Industrial average closed at 382.74, the first time that it had exceeded its 1929 peak.

In April 1955, the singing group Bill Haley and the Comets recorded "Rock Around the Clock," the first widely popular rock and roll tune. The music industry changed almost overnight: dozens of new singing groups were formed, and rock and roll became a sensation that lasted into the early 1960s.

Opposite: President Eisenhower in 1959. Below: Ike with his wife, Mamie. The vivacious First Lady had an inner-ear disorder that made her unsteady on her feet, leading to unjust rumors that she had a drinking problem.

Memorable changes and advances continued. In 1955 the board game Scrabble made its debut, and on CBS TV *The $64,000 Question* became a hit, spawning many copycat game shows, some of which lasted up to the present day. The original show became embroiled in a scandal when it was revealed that contestants who were photogenic were given the answers in advance. In Anaheim, California, Disneyland threw open its gates, launching a new era of "theme parks." In August, Hurricane Diana raked the Northeast, killing more than 200 people and causing over a billion dollars in damage. The first edition of *The Guinness Book of World Records* was published in London and quickly became popular in America.

On February 22, 1956, a rock and roll singer named Elvis Presley entered music charts for the first time with "Heartbreak Hotel." Soon he would become the most popular singer America had ever known. That summer, the Ringling Bros. and Barnum & Bailey Circus had its last tent show, after which it appeared only in auditoriums.

The landmark event of the next year, 1957, was the USSR's launching of Sputnik I, the first artificial satellite to orbit the earth. This created virtual panic in government and technology circles. America, accustomed to being first in many innovations, had nothing equivalent. By early the next year the United States had placed Explorer I into orbit. The economy entered a recession, and in Detroit the unemployment figure touched 20%, a level it had not reached since the Depression. Meanwhile, Toyota, a Japanese automobile outfit, began exporting vehicles to America.

Cuba had long been a friend of America, including under the 1950s administration of dictator Fulgencio Batista. In January 1959 he fled from Havana in the face of advancing troops led by Fidel Castro. Within a week the United States recognized the new Castro government. It was thought that friendship between the two countries would become even stronger. This did not happen. Rather, Castro embraced the Communist policies of the USSR, and late in the Eisenhower administration the Bay of Pigs invasion was planned—to send forces to overthrow Castro.

In 1959 the Barbie doll was introduced, and the first Daytona 500 car race was held. Hawaii was admitted as the 49th state (to be followed by Alaska as the 50th in 1960). In the Congo, the first known human to contract Acquired Immune Deficiency Syndrome (AIDS) died. In Vietnam, where American forces had been helping insurgents for several years, the first large unit action took place and two American companies were ambushed.

The year 1960 saw Joanne Woodward get the first star in the Hollywood Walk of Fame. The Vietnam situation would not go away, and on March 6 it was announced that 3,500 American soldiers would be sent there. No clear explanation of the military objectives or benefit to the United States was forthcoming. In May the first laser beam was projected. Elvis Presley dominated the American musical scene, while in Hamburg, Germany, the Beatles, from Liverpool, England, were attracting notice at the Indra Club. On October 12, Soviet premier Nikita Khrushchev took off his shoe and pounded it on the table during a meeting of the United Nations to protest an open discussion of the Soviet Union's policies toward Eastern Europe.

NOTABLE SAYINGS

"We are going to have peace, even if we have to fight for it."

"America is best described by one word: freedom."

"There is nothing wrong with America that the faith, love of freedom, intelligence and energy of the citizens cannot cure."

"I've never seen a pessimistic general win a battle."

The Early Life of John F. Kennedy

Jack Kennedy, as he was called, was born in Brookline, Massachusetts, son of Joseph Patrick and Rose Elizabeth Fitzgerald Kennedy. His father was a self-made wealthy man, prominent in business and politics. While at Harvard Jack wrote a book, *While England Slept,* which attracted notice. Upon graduating in 1940 he joined the U.S. Navy. In 1943 he was in command of PT-109, a boat sunk by the Japanese in the Solomon Islands. With serious injuries he led survivors through the night in unknown waters to safety.

After the war he served in the House of Representatives from 1947 to 1953, followed by election to the United States Senate. With a warm personality and ready smile, Kennedy was a popular figure. While recuperating from an operation on his back in 1955, he authored *Profiles in Courage,* which won a Pulitzer Prize.

The Pivotal 1960 Election

In 1959 Senator Kennedy decided to seek the Democratic nomination for president. A revision to the Constitution had limited the office to no more than two terms, and thus Eisenhower was not a rival. On January 2, 1960, he began his campaign, challenged by senators Hubert H. Humphrey of Minnesota and Wayne Morse of Oregon. He stumped around the country and won several primaries. As the nominating convention approached his most serious competitor was Senator Lyndon Baines Johnson, who had served in Washington for many years and had built a very strong base of power.

On July 13 Kennedy was chosen as the Democratic candidate. As a matter of strategy he took Johnson as his vice president, believing this would bring many votes from the South. There was no particular warmth between the two men. In a later reminiscence, Kennedy's widow Jackie quoted her husband as saying, "God help us if Johnson should ever become president."

35th President (1961–1963)

JOHN FITZGERALD KENNEDY

May 29, 1917–November 22, 1963

Political party: Democratic

Vice president: Lyndon B. Johnson, 1961 to 1963

First Lady and family: Married Jacqueline ("Jackie") Lee Bouvier on September 12, 1953. She was one of the most popular first ladies in American history, and until her death the media eagerly followed her activities. The couple had three children: Caroline Bouvier Kennedy (1957–); John Fitzgerald Kennedy Jr. (1960–1999); and Patrick Bouvier Kennedy (1963).

Especially remembered for: His saying (borrowed from Churchill) in his inaugural address, "Ask not what your country can do for you—ask what you can do for your country." First Roman Catholic president. The Peace Corps. Failed invasion of the Bay of Pigs. The Cuban missile crisis. Family atmosphere in the White House, popular with news media and public alike—an aura called "Camelot," after the mythical kingdom, by some admirers. Womanizing, although this did not seem to affect his presidential performance. Although his administration was unfortunately brief, he came to be remembered as one of the all-time favorite American presidents. Nicknames: "JFK" and "Jack."

Criticisms arose, including the suggestion that Kennedy, a Catholic, had his first allegiance to the Pope. Famously, he countered, "I am not the Catholic candidate for president, I am the Democratic Party candidate for president who also happens to be a Catholic. I do not speak for my church on public matters, and the church does not speak for me."

In the meantime, in Chicago, on July 25 to 28, the Republican National Convention nominated vice president Richard Nixon as its candidate for president and Henry Cabot Lodge Jr. as his running mate. President Eisenhower endorsed Nixon but did not enthusiastically campaign for him. Perhaps tired after a lifetime of public service, he concentrated on planning his impending retirement and settling pending administration matters.

The nature of American political campaigns changed on September 26. For the first time ever, the opposing candidates were set to debate each other before television cameras, with the unscripted encounter to be broadcast nationwide. At the outset observers anticipated a draw. Both men were accomplished speakers and both were well-known public figures. The reality was different. Nixon, who appeared to be not completely shaven (probably due to his refusal to wear makeup), seemed to be uncomfortable and a bit disorganized, while Kennedy appeared at ease and polished. Afterward, nearly everyone agreed that Nixon finished a distant second. The tenor of the campaign changed instantly. A tradition was established, and televised debates became a staple in future elections. In November, Kennedy, at age 43, edged Nixon by a tiny margin of the popular vote (0.2%) to become the youngest president ever. In the Electoral College he drew 303 votes to Nixon's 219 (with 269 needed to win).

Opposite: President Kennedy was photographed by Cecil Stoughton in the Oval Office on July 11, 1963. Above right: A bold campaign pin for Kennedy echoes a popular sentiment of the day.

President Kennedy in the White House

In a memorable ceremony at noon on January 20, 1961, John Fitzgerald Kennedy was sworn in as president. In his address he took a line (without credit) from Churchill: "Ask not what your country can do for you, ask what you can do for your country." He called upon Americans and nations of the world to fight "the common enemies of man: tyranny, poverty, disease, and war itself."

With his wife Jackie and their two young children, he moved into the White House. Kennedy's personal warmth and the charm of Jackie made the family a favorite with the media and public alike. Unlike the atmosphere of many previous administrations, the White House became a family place, complete with photographs of young Caroline and John (nicknamed "John John").

Kennedy named his brother Robert to be attorney general, generating much criticism because of his lack of experience for such a post. In 1961 his administration worked with a group of armed Cuban exiles to launch the Bay of Pigs invasion,

an attempt to overthrow dictator Fidel Castro. The operation, the groundwork for which had been laid by the Eisenhower administration, failed miserably and caused great embarrassment. On November 18, 1961, newspapers announced that the United States was sending "military advisors" to South Vietnam. On December 1 the Vietnam conflict officially began when the first American helicopters arrived in Saigon with 400 U.S. personnel.

Kennedy's formation of the Peace Corps was received as a brilliant move in humanitarianism and foreign relations, a great step. However, in July 1961, he urged all Americans to build fallout shelters. This program had been underway for some time, but now gained momentum. Many felt that with the race in space being led by the Russians, and with the proliferation of atomic weapons, a nuclear war between the United States and the Soviet Union was inevitable. Many homes and businesses prepared shelters, stocked with food.

In 1962 the Soviet Union shipped ballistic missiles to Cuba, intending to erect launching sites aimed at the United States—the ultimate escalation of the Cold War. Kennedy, uncertain if the outcome would be a nuclear confrontation, demanded that the ships turn around. The world waited with bated breath, but the Soviet Union leaders conceded, and the weapons were returned. This "brinkmanship" was highly acclaimed. Meanwhile, the tensions between the USSR and America continued, and a high wall was erected around the free city of Berlin by the Communist government of East Germany, which held the surrounding land.

President Kennedy helped the space program develop, fostered entertainment and the arts, worked with the civil rights movement, and did many other things that earned him wide admiration.

On November 22, 1963, while riding in a Lincoln convertible in a motorcade in Dallas, President

Left: The president and his elegant First Lady in the Yellow Oval Room of the White House, in March 1963. Opposite: The Kennedy family in 1961 at Hammersmith Farm in Newport.

Kennedy was fired upon by Lee Harvey Oswald. He died soon afterward. Lyndon B. Johnson, his vice president, took the oath of office aboard the presidential plane, Air Force One. The nation went into mourning. Conspiracy theories arose. Did Cuba mastermind the assassination? Did Johnson have something to do with it? What about the USSR? The Warren Committee was formed to investigate and concluded that Oswald had acted alone.

Left: This 1958 portrait Christmas card was sent during Kennedy's tenure as a senator. He and Jacqueline are shown with their baby daughter, Caroline.

Widow Jackie remained in the public eye for years afterward (including in a widely commented-upon marriage to Greek tycoon Aristotle S. Onassis) and was a favorite cover subject for popular magazines.

THE AMERICAN SCENE

The so-called space race proceeded at full speed during the Kennedy administration. On April 12, 1961, Yuri Gagarin, aboard the USSR satellite Vostok I, became the first human to orbit the earth, while America could claim only small satellites. The Century 21 Exposition opened in Seattle a few days later on April 21, the first world's fair on American soil since 1939. The iconic Space Needle featured a rotating restaurant at the top.

Events of 1962 included the opening of the first Wal-Mart store in Rogers, Arkansas, the brainchild of Samuel Walton. At the time, retailing was dominated by Sears, followed at a distance by Montgomery Ward. Rachel Carson's book *Silent Spring* was published, giving impetus to the environmentalist movement. The volume told of a spring without any birds, chirping insects, or wildlife, all victims of pollution.

Despite federal laws and occasional intervention by the military, segregation continued to be the rule in many parts of the South. On January 14, 1963, George C. Wallace became governor of Alabama and in his inaugural speech said, "segregation now, segregation tomorrow, and segregation forever." The audience cheered. On April 3 the Southern Christian Leadership Conference (SCLC) began a campaign in Birmingham against racial segregation starting with a sit-in. On the 12th of the month Martin Luther King Jr., Ralph Abernathy, Fred Shuttlesworth, and others were arrested in Birmingham for "parading without a permit." King became a popular hero. On August 28 he gave his "I Have a Dream" speech on the steps of the Lincoln Memorial to an audience of at least 250,000 people during the March on Washington for Jobs and Freedom.

Elsewhere on the American scene, in November 1963 the first push-button telephone was offered to AT&T customers. The company had a stranglehold on that form of communication and would not allow private devices such as recorders to be attached. The AT&T monopoly would later be broken up in anti-trust procedures.

NOTABLE SAYINGS

"Forgive your enemies, but never forget their names."

"If we cannot end now our differences at least we can help make the world safe for diversity."

"The American, by nature, is optimistic. He is experimental, an inventor and a builder who builds best when called upon to build greatly."

The Life of Lyndon B. Johnson

Lyndon Baines Johnson was born near Stonewall, Texas, not far from Johnson City (which his family had helped settle), son of Sam Ealy Johnson Jr. and Rebekah Baines Johnson. He worked hard as a teenager and earned his way through the Southwest Texas State Teachers College (now the Texas State University at San Marcos), graduating in 1930. He became a teacher at a Houston high school. As a volunteer in a regional campaign for a congressman, Johnson developed a taste for politics. From 1931 to 1937 he was a congressional secretary, after which he served his own terms in the House of Representatives from 1937 to 1949, during which he made an unsuccessful Senate bid. In World War II he served as an officer in the Navy.

Entering the Senate race in 1948, he won by a questioned and highly controversial margin of just 87 votes. For the rest of his life he would be perceived by some as a manipulator, a "political animal" with great skill. Along the way Johnson became a very wealthy man. He served as a senator until 1961, when he went to Washington as vice president to John F. Kennedy, although he had been his chief rival for the Democratic nomination.

After Kennedy's assassination on November 22, 1963, Johnson became president. He sought to further his predecessor's programs and also to launch a program called the Great Society—so that "man's life matches the marvels of man's labor." On January 8, 1964, in his first State of the Union address, Johnson declared the "War on Poverty." On July 2, he signed the Civil Rights Act of 1964 into law, abolishing racial segregation in the United States. In recent years, there had been many incidents, particularly in the South, where black students had been denied admission into certain schools, patrons to restaurants, guests to hotels, and the like. Within walking distance of the White House, many Washington restaurants turned African Americans away.

Running for reelection against Republican Barry Goldwater in 1964, Johnson won with the

36th President (1963–1969)

LYNDON B. JOHNSON

August 27, 1908–January 22, 1973

Political party: Democratic

Vice president: Hubert H. Humphrey, 1965 to 1969

First Lady and family: Married Claudia ("Lady Bird") Alta Taylor on November 17, 1934. The couple had two children: Lynda Bird Johnson (1944–) and Luci Baines Johnson (1947–).

Especially remembered for: A mixed legacy with pluses for the Great Society, Medicare, and other programs, and minuses for the conduct of the Vietnam War and domestic racial unrest. Nickname: "LBJ."

ARNOLD NE

Opposite: President Lyndon Johnson photographed in the White House. Above: Johnson first ran for the Senate in 1941, when he lost by only 1,311 votes. In 1948, he won a Senate seat by a margin that earned him the nickname "Landslide Lyndon".

greatest popular margin up to that time, more than 15 million votes. In office he had many accomplishments, including the Medicare amendment to the Social Security Act, and encouraging the space race, started under Kennedy, which put the first men on the moon soon after he left office.

Although segregation in the South was now officially outlawed, in practice it endured in many places. On March 25, 1965, Martin Luther King Jr. and 25,000 civil rights activists ended their four day march from Selma, Alabama to the State Capitol in Montgomery.

The administration also had its troubles, including the Vietnam War, which spawned riots among draft-age men and protests by the public. Military policy seemed to lack direction, and there was no winning strategy evident. The nation became sharply divided on this question. In another area of tension, African Americans rioted in Los Angeles and elsewhere, in protest of the country's lack of racial justice and equal opportunities, among other concerns.

In 1968 Johnson did not seek reelection but retired to his ranch in Johnson City, Texas. The war continued in progress, and racial tensions remained high, becoming the problems of the next administration. Lyndon Johnson died of a heart attack on his ranch in January 1973.

Above: President Johnson decorating an American soldier in Cam Ranh Bay, Vietnam, in October 1966.

THE AMERICAN SCENE

Toward the end of 1963, Beatlemania became a great fad in the United States. British music stars flared into prominence in America and would be popular for a long time. On April 4, 1964, the Beatles held the top five positions in the Billboard Top 40. The songs were "Can't Buy Me Love," "Twist and Shout," "She Loves You," "I Want to Hold Your Hand," and "Please, Please Me."

In Detroit in 1964 the first Ford Mustang came off the assembly line. In the line of luxury automobiles, Cadillac was solidly number one in fame and desirability, with Lincoln a distant second and the Chrysler Imperial an also-ran. Imports, particularly various Volkswagen models, were attracting a lot of attention through innovative advertising. The New York World's Fair opened the same year but was not an "official" world's fair as it took place within 10 years of the Seattle event. Nonetheless, some foreign countries set up exhibits.

The Vietnam War, with loosely defined objectives and strategies that few Americans could understand, caused great unrest and dissension. Young men in the prime of life were being drafted to risk their lives in a distant conflict that seemed to be meaningless. On May 2, 1964, hundreds of students marched through Times Square in New York City and hundreds more in San Francisco in the first major student demonstration against the war. Other, smaller demonstrations occurred in Boston, Seattle, and Madison, Wisconsin. On May 12 a dozen young men in New York City publicly burned their draft cards, in the first of many such demonstrations. Still, President Johnson remained relatively popular, and on November 3, 1964, he trounced Republican challenger Barry Goldwater with more than 60% of the vote.

On March 8, 1965, 3,500 U.S. Marines arrived in South Vietnam, the first large contingent of openly acknowledged combat troops. Thousands of other servicemen sent earlier were mainly "advisors" and the like. On May 15, 1966, there was a massive anti-war demonstration in Washington, D.C., with protestors picketing the White House then rallying at the Washington Monument. On July 28, Johnson announced the plan to increase the number of troops in South Vietnam from 75,000 to 125,000 and to more than double the number of men drafted every month, from 17,000 to 35,000. On November 27, tens of thousands of Vietnam War protestors picketed the White House and then marched to the Washington Monument. Johnson said that if the new draft measures did not succeed, the number of American troops in Vietnam would have to be increased from 125,000 to 400,000 within the next year. Students calling themselves cannon fodder continued protests across America.

Below: The president and Lady Bird in 1968. Lady Bird actively worked for the conservation of natural resources and was awarded both the Presidential Medal of Freedom (1977) and the Congressional Gold Medal (1988).

The price of silver bullion had been rising on world markets. In 1964 it was realized that if the United States were to continue to produce silver coins beyond this time, they would cost more than face value to mint. Accordingly, beginning in 1965, a new copper-nickel alloy was used. Silver coinage became history, except for special pieces made to be sold at a premium to collectors.

President Johnson had a secret meeting with leaders on November 2, 1967, and requested them to suggest ways to unite the American people in support of the Vietnam War by giving out more optimistic reports. In 1968 things went from very bad to even worse. The My Lai Massacre on March 16, 1968, which was not revealed until the following year, consisted of American soldiers killing helpless men, women, and children with machine guns in a peaceful Vietnam village. Matters were spiraling wildly out of control. The military would not give up, however.

On April 4, 1968, Martin Luther King Jr. was shot and killed in Memphis, Tennessee, causing riots in major American cities. On June 8, James Earl Ray was arrested for the foul deed.

NOTABLE SAYINGS

"A president's hardest task is not to do what is right, but to know what is right."

"You ain't learnin' nothin' when you're talkin'."

"If government is to serve any purpose it is to do for others what they are unable to do for themselves."

37th President (1969–1974)

RICHARD M. NIXON

January 9, 1913–April 22, 1994

Political party: Republican

Vice president: Spiro Agnew, 1969 to 1973; none for part of 1973; Gerald Ford, 1973 to 1974

First Lady and family: Married Patricia Ryan on June 21, 1940. The couple had two children: Patricia Nixon (1946–) and Julie Nixon (1948–).

Especially remembered for: Opening trade with China. Resignation of dishonest, discredited vice president Agnew. The Watergate cover-up and scandal; the indictments of more than a dozen Cabinet members and key officials. Unprecedented resignation in shame from the presidency. Nickname given by detractors: "Tricky Dick."

The Life of Richard M. Nixon

Richard Milhous Nixon was born in Yorba Linda, California, son of Francis Anthony and Hannah Milhous Nixon. He was a gifted student at Whittier College, from which he graduated in 1934; he graduated from Duke University Law School in 1937. He went into law practice in Whittier as a partner in the firm of Bewley, Knoop & Nixon. During World War II he served in the Navy as a lieutenant commander in the Pacific and as an attorney for the United States Office of Emergency Management.

After the war Nixon campaigned for and won a seat in the House of Representatives. In a smear campaign (perhaps a harbinger of things to come?) against incumbent Jerry Voorhis, he stated that Voorhis was influenced by Communists, and made other accusations, mostly distorted or false. Nixon held his seat in the House until 1951. In 1950 he ran for the Senate against Helen Gahagan Douglas, in another smear campaign that unfairly branded her as a Communist sympathizer. In disgust, a California paper, the *Independent Review,* printed Nixon's picture with the caption "Tricky Dick," a nickname that stuck with him for the rest of his life.

At the Republican nominating convention, after besmirching other contenders (including California governor Earl Warren and Robert Taft), Nixon was named as running mate to Dwight Eisenhower. From 1953 to 1961 he served as vice president. Entering the 1960 presidential campaign against John F. Kennedy, Nixon was unable to get a warm recommendation from Eisenhower, who in view of the candidate's somewhat tarnished reputation told him he would have to go it alone. In November, Nixon came in second, after which he ran for the California governorship in 1962 and lost, and complained about his treatment by the press ("You won't have Nixon to kick around anymore, because,

Opposite: President Richard Nixon in the White House, July 8, 1971. Nixon had served as vice president from 1953 to 1961.

PHOTO BY FABIAN BACHRACH
Richard M. Nixon
To Fred Eckert
with every good wish for the years ahead
from Richard Nixon
LITHO. IN U.S.A. BY LA SALLE LITHO CORP. N.Y.C., N.Y.

Opposite: Nixon in a 1960 campaign photograph. Right: Also from the 1960 campaign is this portrait pin. Nixon lost the 1960 presidential race narrowly to John F. Kennedy.

gentlemen, this is my last press conference"), and in general was a sore loser.

Nixon went back into private life and landed a $200,000-per-year job with a Wall Street law firm. In 1968 he returned to politics and, based on his record as a strong campaigner, became the Republican nominee for president. In his campaign he earned votes by claiming the Vietnam War was a mistake, many soldiers had been sacrificed, and time had come for a change. "I pledge to you: We will have an honorable end to this war in Vietnam." His opponent was Democrat Hubert H. Humphrey, who was saddled with the perceived onus of the unpopular Johnson administration, in which he had been vice president, and its conduct of the despised war. Nixon and his running mate, Spiro T. Agnew, gathered only 43.4% of the popular votes, in a three-way contest in which a renegade candidate, Alabama's virulently racist George Wallace of the American Independent Party, took 13.5%.

After taking office in January 1969, Nixon and his staff, with secretary of state Henry Kissinger playing an especially prominent role, worked hard

Below: A promotional flag from his unsuccessful 1960 campaign features Nixon's portrait and urges "World Leadership thru Nixon."

on foreign affairs, including a gradual withdrawal of troops from Vietnam. In 1972 he was the first sitting president in history to visit China, a country that had been isolated from America since the Communist regime took over after World War II. In the same year Nixon was reelected by a large margin in a contest in which the campaign of his opponent, Senator George McGovern of South Dakota, was characterized by disorganization and infighting in the Democratic Party.

In 1969 the Vietnam War finally took a turning point for the better. Nixon met with the president of that country on June 8 and announced that 25,000 American troops would be withdrawn by September. Despite this, criticism of Nixon mounted. In November the president addressed the nation and asked citizens to join the "silent majority" of millions of Americans who supported him and his policy. Meanwhile, Vice President Agnew weighed in and said that critics were an "effete corps of impudent snobs" and "nattering nabobs of negativism." The press had a grand time with these statements, and "silent majority" became an idiom. On November 15 in Washington, D.C., an estimated 250,000 to 500,000 people gathered to protest the ongoing war.

On January 27, 1973, a cease-fire in Vietnam ended the direct involvement of the U.S. ground troops in the military action there, a high accomplishment. The North Vietnamese would take Saigon on April 30, 1975.

Enmeshed in the taking of bribes and other scandals unrelated to the White House, Vice President

Below: Presidential candidate Nixon makes his famous "V for victory" gesture while campaigning in Philadelphia in 1968. This time Nixon would win the election.

Agnew was forced to resign in 1973. Nixon nominated House minority leader Gerald R. Ford to be Agnew's successor, and this was confirmed by Congress. Almost immediately the Watergate scandal erupted, created when operatives of Nixon's 1972 campaign, members of the Committee to Re-Elect the President (CREEP), broke into the offices of the Democratic National Committee in the Watergate office complex in Washington. When this was revealed by *Washington Post* columnists Bob Woodward and Carl Bernstein, Nixon denied any personal knowledge. The matter escalated, and it was revealed that Nixon had secretly recorded most of the conversations he had held with his strategists and other visitors to the White House.

The matter reached the explosive state, many of his closest appointees were indicted for lying under oath, and, eventually, the playing of the secret tapes revealed that Nixon himself had tried to engineer a cover-up and had repeatedly lied to investigators. On August 8, 1974, with the nation watching on television, he stated he would resign the following day so that the nation could begin the "process of healing." Gerald R. Ford was sworn in as his successor.

In his retirement, Nixon was consulted on international affairs by presidents of both parties, and he gradually took on the mantle of a Republican elder statesman. Watergate remained a millstone around his neck, but he was unrepentant, and supporters praised domestic-policy successes seen in his terms (such as establishment of the Environmental Protection Agency, the Drug Enforcement Administration, and the Office of Minority Business Enterprise); his skillful foreign policy, especially in regard to China and the Soviet Union; and the influence and political longevity of many Nixon administration employees and Cabinet members. Nixon wrote his memoirs and several books on politics and foreign affairs, and traveled. On April 18, 1994, he suffered a severe stroke; later he slipped into a coma, and he passed away on April 22. He was buried beside his wife in Yorba Linda, California.

THE AMERICAN SCENE

In 1969, a St. Louis a teenage boy died from a baffling disease that was later determined to be the first fatal case of AIDS in America. On July 16, *Apollo 11,* captained by Neil Armstrong, lifted off for its journey to make the first landing on the moon. July 20, 1969, the lunar module the *Eagle* landed on the lunar surface, returning on July 24. The Woodstock Festival was held on an upstate New York farm in August and drew thousands of mostly younger people, including Vietnam War protesters, to enjoy several days of music by prominent artists. Word of the success of the event spread, and it became famous. In November the ARPANET computer link was established, predecessor to the Internet. Awareness of computers was growing by leaps and bounds, and in contrast to the monolithic devices of earlier times, many relatively small models were on the market, with the business led by IBM.

Among events of 1970, the Concorde supersonic transport (SST) made its first flight. In time, these airplanes would fly in and out of Kennedy and Dulles airports in the United States, connecting to London and Paris. The Public Health Cigarette Smoking Act became law, prohibiting cigarette advertising on television. The legal voting age was lowered from 21 to 18.

Going into the year 1971, gold was rising in value on the international market, causing investor demand, although American citizens still could not legally hold it—the result of regulations imposed by the government in 1933. In an attempt to stop inflation, President Nixon imposed a 90-day freeze on wages and prices on August 15. As an indication of national priorities, a study found that the average American taxpayer gave the U.S. government $7 for medical research (part of $315 for health-related activities), $30 for space exploration, and $30 for highway construction, but $400 for defense and $125 for the Vietnam War. American research was halted on our version of an SST, leaving the field open to Russia with its TU-104 and to Britain and

Above: On December 21, 1970, rock-and-roll legend Elvis Presley requested, and was granted, a meeting with President Nixon at the White House.

France with their Concorde. As it turned out, only the Concorde ever saw commercial use.

On January 5, 1972, President Nixon signed a $5.5 billion bill for a program to develop a reusable space shuttle. On March 22, the National Commission on Marijuana and Drug Abuse urged that criminal penalties be ended for the possession and use of marijuana. This was not done, and in ensuing years millions of Americans were prosecuted for using the substance, and prisons became crowded. In time, five times as many Americans were behind bars, in terms of percentage, than any other civilized country. *The Economist* mused that either huge numbers of citizens were criminals or else there was something wrong with the laws. On November 14, the Dow-Jones Industrial Average of blue-chip stock prices closed above 1,000 for the first time in history, reaching 1,003.16.

In April 1973 a committee of U.S. manufacturers and grocers recommended the adoption of a Universal Product Code (UPC), which became known as the bar code, designed to permit electronic scanning of labels to create invoices and to monitor inventories. In time the "ka-ching" of the cash register would be history. At Wounded Knee, South Dakota, members of the American Indian Movement (AIM) seized the town and barricaded themselves within to protest the mistreatment of Native Americans. The town was later stormed by police and the National Guard, but not before AIM and its leader Russell Means had gotten their message to the world. In the lighter side of the news, Willie Mays, the "Say Hey Kid," retired from professional baseball after spending his entire career with the New York (later San Francisco) Giants. His illustrious career included several Most Valuable Player awards; his 660 career home runs place him third on the all-time list, behind the legendary Babe Ruth (714) and Hank Aaron (744).

The oil crisis began in earnest, with prices skyrocketing and long lines forming at service stations, prompting rationing and purchase limits. Uncontrolled inflation was a national problem, and the value of gold bullion rose sharply on international markets.

In 1974, national focus was on the Watergate scandal, plus inflation, rising unemployment, and continuing gas shortages. These were not happy times.

NOTABLE SAYINGS

"I was not lying. I said things that later on seemed to be untrue."

"I am not a crook."

"I like the job I have, but if I had to live my life over again I would like to have ended up a sports writer."

"Always give your best, never get discouraged, never be petty; always remember, others may hate you. Those who hate you don't win unless you hate them. And then you destroy yourself."

The Life of Gerald Ford

Gerald R. "Jerry" Ford was born in Omaha, Nebraska, son of Leslie Lynch and Dorothy Ayer Gardner King Ford. He spent his youth in Grand Rapids, Michigan. Attending the University of Michigan, he was a star football player and graduated in 1935. He took his advanced degree in law from Yale, graduating in 1941. Meanwhile, he helped coach the football team. During World War II he was a lieutenant commander in the navy. After the conflict ended, he went back to Grand Rapids, where he practiced law.

Entering politics, Ford served in the House of Representatives from 1949 to 1973; from 1965 onward he was minority leader. In 1973 he was appointed as vice president to replace the disgraced Spiro T. Agnew, and then in 1974 he became president when Richard M. Nixon resigned. Thus, under the 25th amendment of the U.S. Constitution, he became the first president of the United States who had not been elected to either the presidency or vice presidency.

At his swearing in on August 9, 1974, President Ford inherited the Watergate imbroglio, which had tarnished the entire Republican Party. Nixon remained in disgrace, as did many of his appointees and staff. There were calls for Nixon to go to trial so that all elements of the cover-up would be revealed and the full extent of the scandal known. Ford, stating that this would be a media circus for months and a great disruption to national progress, elected to grant Nixon a full pardon. This was probably the death knell for Ford's political future, as it meant that Nixon, who was viewed as criminal and reprehensible, never had to be held accountable for his actions. Public faith in the executive office hit an all-time low.

The new president was faced with many challenges in addition to restoring the integrity of the White House. Inflation was on a runaway course; energy supplies were in crisis, resulting in long lines at gasoline pumps; and the economy was sagging.

38th President (1974–1977)

GERALD FORD

July 14, 1913–December 26, 2006

Political party: Republican

Vice president: None at the beginning; Nelson Rockefeller, 1974 to 1977

First Lady and family: Married Elizabeth ("Betty") Bloomer Warren on October 15, 1948. The couple had four children: Michael Gerald Ford (1950–); John Gardner Ford (1952–); Steven Meigs Ford (1956–); and Susan Elizabeth Ford (1957–).

Especially remembered for: First (only) president to succeed a president who had resigned. Only president not elected to either the vice presidency or the presidency. Widely criticized pardon of Richard Nixon (which probably cost him his election bid in 1976). Widely recognized as a fair, kind, and gentle man of good principles and intent.

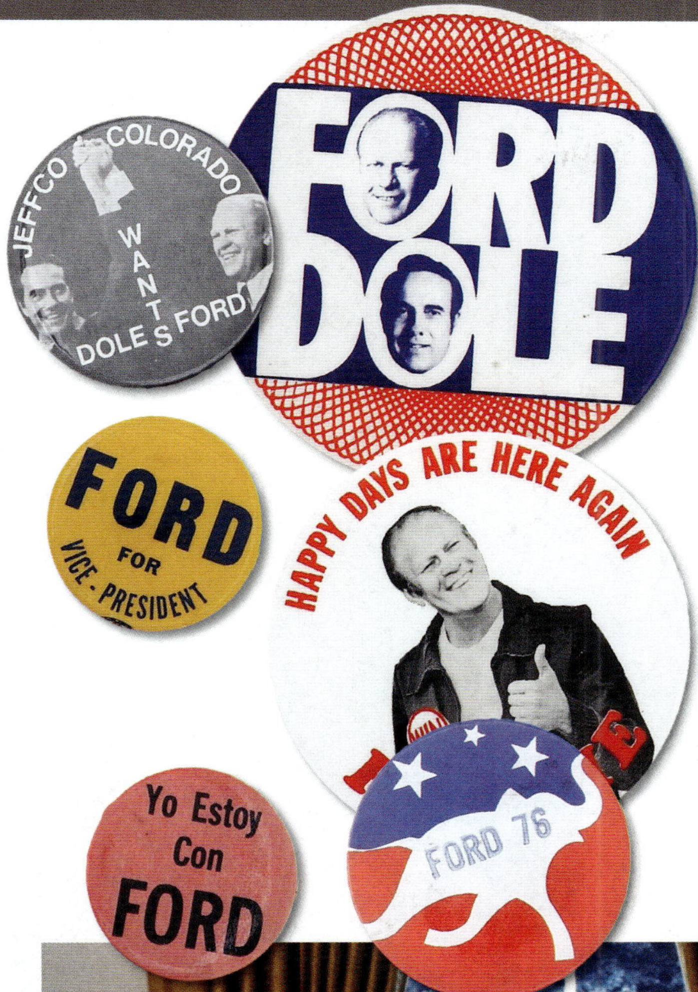

Ford encouraged businesses to solve these problems without government mandates or intervention.

On the world scene, the governments of South Vietnam and Cambodia collapsed, creating a new set of problems, while in Israel the situation between the Israelis and Palestinians, a hot spot since the country was formed in 1948, required constant diplomacy, as did the relationship between Israel and Egypt, which threatened to break out into war. With the Soviet Union, Ford negotiated limitations on the development and stockpiling of nuclear weapons.

Although Gerald Ford tried hard to do what he thought was right, domestic problems in particular were overwhelming, and the hostile Congress, under Democratic control, was constantly critical. In 1976 he ran for election, but he was narrowly defeated by

Opposite: President Gerald Ford in his official presidential photograph, taken August 27, 1974. Left: Among this assortment of campaign pins is one depicting Ford as Fonzie from *Happy Days.* Below: The president speaks to the crew of the *Apollo Soyuz* Test Project space mission while watching them on TV.

the Democratic candidate, Jimmy Carter. The popular vote was 39,148,940 for Ford and 40,828,929 for Carter, and the Electoral College voted 297 to 241. In his inaugural address, Carter expressed the country's gratitude: "For myself and for our nation, I want to thank my predecessor for all he has done to heal our land."

Ford stayed active in retirement, especially in historical, educational, charitable, and political activities. He died on December 26, 2006, at his home in Rancho Mirage, California.

Below: The president and First Lady hold hands during a limousine ride in 1974. Betty Ford became known for her candor on controversial subjects and raised awareness of alcoholism when she disclosed her own struggle with addiction. She went on to found the Betty Ford Center for substance abuse and addiction, and was awarded both the Presidential Medal of Freedom (in 1991) and the Congressional Gold Medal (in 1998, an honor shared with her husband). Right: Ford's autobiography was published in 1979.

THE AMERICAN SCENE

In 1974, revelations that the Federal Bureau of Investigation had carried on operations against civil rights groups in the United States, and that the Central Intelligence Agency had attempted to overthrow foreign governments, did nothing to enhance the government's reputation. Meanwhile, secretary of state Henry Kissinger did much for American foreign policy and helped bring an element of stability to the Middle East. Meanwhile, in the sports world, the irrepressible Muhammad Ali won the world heavyweight boxing title for the second time.

A 10.3% inflation rate contributed to a 20% slump in automobile sales, while housing starts dropped 40% and unemployment hit 7.2% by December 1974. On October 8, President Ford announced a program called Whip Inflation Now (WIN) to help stem rising oil prices. The "energy crisis" gripped the country and would dominate much of America's economy and international politics over the next 15 years.

In 1975 the Watergate investigations continued, and Nixon insiders John N. Mitchell, H.R. Haldeman, and John D. Ehrlichman were found guilty of aiding in the cover-up and were sentenced to jail. The cost of a first class stamp went from 10 cents to 13 cents. On television, *Saturday Night Live* premiered with comedian George Carlin as host. In Japan, two competing videocassette recorder (VCR) systems were developed by Sony (Betamax format) and Matsushita (VHS format), with VHS eventually dominating the marketplace. Computers became a challenge for craftsmen and the Altair kit, for one, allowed them to build and program their own personal devices. By this time, computers were in common use in business.

On February 17, 1976, President Ford created a board to oversee foreign and United States intelligence operations overseas, and the next day he placed limits on surveillance of U.S. citizens by government agencies. His administration accomplished many good things, but being Republican it continued to suffer from the backlash of Watergate and lingering anger from the Nixon pardon. In the same year it was revealed that Lockheed Aircraft Corporation illegally paid tremendous bribes and payoffs to agents to secure aircraft sales overseas. Conrail, set up by the government, took over the operation of six railroads in the Northeast. On April 21, 1976, the last Cadillac convertible left the assembly line, the last open-top vehicle to be made in quantity in America until the concept was revived in the 1980s. Barbara Walters signed a five-year contract for $5 million with NBC on April 22, becoming the first anchorwoman on a major network news program.

Sylvester Stallone's low-budget movie *Rocky* was released and quickly became one of the most popular films in history. The novel *Roots* by Alex Haley made the *New York Times* bestseller list and met with wide acclaim as a view of the African ancestry of black Americans. Later, a dramatization of *Roots* broke television viewership records.

The 1976 Bicentennial of American independence was to have been a grand event, and years earlier it had been hoped that a world's fair would be held in Philadelphia, where in 1876 the Centennial Exhibition had taken place. This did not come to pass. When the Bicentennial arrived, many local historical societies published booklets, new coin designs were issued, and celebrations took place, but there was hardly any nationwide excitement. America was still preoccupied with inflation, unemployment, and other problems.

NOTABLE SAYINGS

"Things are more like they are now than they ever have been."

"Truth is the glue that holds governments together. Compromise is the oil that makes governments go."

"A government big enough to give you everything you want is a government big enough to take from you everything you have."

39th President (1977–1981)

JAMES EARL CARTER JR.

Born October 1, 1924

Political party: Democratic

Vice president: Walter Mondale, 1977 to 1981

First Lady and family: Married Rosalynn Smith on July 7, 1946. The Carters had four children: John William "Jack" Carter (1947–); James Earl "Chip" Carter III (1950–); Donnel Jeffrey "Jeff" Carter (1952–); and Amy Lynn Carter (1967–).

Especially remembered for: Being a humanitarian with the interests of everyday citizens at heart. Struggling with overwhelming energy and economic problems. Distinguished service following his presidency. Recipient of the Nobel Peace Prize in 2000.

The Life of Jimmy Carter

James Earl Carter Jr.—"Jimmy," as he likes to be called—was born in Plains, Georgia, son of James Earl and Lillian Gordy Carter. His family was important in peanut farming and lived comfortably. As a youth he worked on the family farm, followed the Baptist religion closely, and enjoyed observing the political scene.

During World War II Carter attended the United States Naval Academy in Annapolis, from which he graduated in 1946. He served seven years as a naval officer, after which he went back to the family business in Plains. He entered state politics in 1962 and was elected as a senator, serving from 1963 to 1966. In 1970 he was elected governor of Georgia, and remained in the post until 1975. In politics he was always an independent thinker, outspoken on the subjects of racial equality, government efficiency, and conservation—the opposite of many politicians who measured what their responses should be, in terms of getting votes.

Relatively unknown on the national scene, Carter announced in December 1974 that he would seek the Democratic nomination for president. For the next year and a half he campaigned tirelessly, in time gaining the support of party leaders. On the first ballot of the convention he was chosen. His campaign against incumbent Gerald Ford was vigorous and involved three televised debates. In November 1976 Carter was the winner by a narrow margin.

At the White House, the new president inherited problems of energy consumption and economic inflation. Under his watch, interest rates spiraled wildly out of control (at one time exceeding 20% per year), and much of the nation's banking system was in disarray. In the meantime the energy crisis and gasoline shortage worsened, with both the president and Congress appearing to be helpless.

Opposite: President Carter was photographed in the White House on January 31, 1977, by Karl Schumacher. The president's broad grin was one of his most recognizable—and most widely caricatured—features.

An assortment of pins from Carter's presidential campaign. When the former Georgia governor entered the Democratic primaries in 1976, he was almost unknown compared to the other candidates. After the scandal of Watergate, however, Carter's position as a Washington outsider worked to his advantage.

Carter was a true humanitarian and sought to make the government "compassionate" and responsive to the needs of the people. He added the Department of Education to the list of Cabinet offices. Minority applicants were added to the government payroll in unprecedented numbers. Nationwide employment increased, and the federal budget was held in check. Effective discussions were held with the Soviet Union, and diplomatic relations were restored with China after a lapse of many years. He relinquished control of the Panama Canal to the country wherein it was situated—a move highly criticized in view of the importance of the international waterway.

Problems arose when the Soviets invaded Afghanistan, precipitating a war with no certain end. The shah of Iran was deposed, many Iranian businesspeople and their families fled that land, and the government was taken over by a religious ayatollah who was hostile to American interests. At the U.S. embassy in Tehran the Iranians held 52 Americans hostage. In the last year of Carter's administration, news coverage was dominated by the hostage crisis and runaway inflation.

The Carter administration continued to experience a great deal of difficulty into 1980 despite the president's well-meaning and honest intentions. The hostages were still being held at the U.S. embassy, casting a cloud over the international scene. Soviet occupation of Afghanistan was agonizing, and relations between the United States and the USSR became very cold. To many observers Jimmy Carter seemed to occupy an office larger than he was capable of managing, and he seemed unable to cope with its many problems. Carter canceled a grain order to Russia in protest of the Afghanistan situation, withdrew sales of high technology equipment, and declared that the United States would boycott the 1980 Olympic Games in Russia. On January 23, 1980, Carter stated that force would be used if necessary to keep supply routes open to the Persian Gulf. In February an FBI sting operation called

ABSCAM incriminated 31 public officials, including one senator and six representatives.

In a humanitarian move, Carter signed the Refugee Act of 1980 on March 17, broadening the term "refugee" to include people from any part of the world, and increasing the maximum admitted annually to 320,000 from 290,000. On April 7, diplomatic relations with Iran were suspended. On April 24 a rescue mission to free the hostages failed, and eight were killed in a plane crash associated with the mission. President Carter deregulated certain trucking rates on July 1 and certain railroad rates on October 14. He sought reelection in 1980. The country wanted a change, however, and Carter's challenger, Ronald Reagan, took the contest in a landslide.

In retirement Jimmy Carter went back to Georgia, where he wrote books, became a willing interviewee for the media, and distinguished himself as a humanitarian, including taking tools and working with Habitat for Humanity to construct houses. In 2000 he was awarded the Nobel Peace Prize. While he may not have distinguished himself greatly in the White House, it is a popular saying that "Jimmy Carter is the best *ex*-president we have ever had."

The president and his First Lady, Rosalynn Carter, at the inaugural ball, January 20, 1977. A leading advocate for mental health causes, Mrs. Carter is also president of the board of directors for the Rosalynn Carter Institute for Caregiving.

THE AMERICAN SCENE

As one of his first official acts after his inauguration in January 1977, President Carter pardoned most of the draft resisters to the Vietnam War, which earned him many accolades. The stock market was in a slump, and the Dow-Jones Industrial Average declined more than 165 points during the year. The unemployment rate was 7%, a figure considered to be unsatisfactory. Coffee prices rose to $5 per pound retail, causing an increase in tea consumption. On March 9 the Food and Drug Administration suggested that saccharine might cause cancer and proposed a ban that was postponed for 18 months pending new tests. On July 28, the 799-mile Trans-Alaska oil pipeline connected Prudhoe Bay to the port of Valdez, a welcome help for the energy crisis.

Two films were hits at the box office in 1977—*Star Wars* and *Close Encounters of the Third Kind.* Former secretary of state Henry Kissinger sold his memoirs for $2 million, matching the figure guaranteed in a contract signed on September 29, 1976, by Richard Nixon for his memoirs. On March 9, former president Gerald R. Ford and his wife Betty were reported to have signed contracts for their memoirs for about $1 million each. Attendance at professional sports burgeoned, with an increase of 24% in baseball attendance over the preceding year. The "King of Rock and Roll," Elvis Presley, died in his palatial Graceland estate in Memphis; and two of the greatest funnymen of all time passed away, Charlie Chaplin and Groucho Marx.

By 1978 the computer age in combination with government and other programs was turning the practice of medicine into a sea of paperwork and red tape. Costs for health care escalated rapidly, and the Carter administration blamed organized medicine, which did nothing to advance medical progress. Welfare programs were very inefficient as well. Later, popular radio commentator Paul Harvey calculated that it cost layers of government agencies $21,000 to deliver $8,000 of aid, and money would

Above left, below, and opposite: Carter is a prolific author, having written 21 books since leaving the Oval Office. They cover a wide range of topics, including politics, autobiography, religion, human rights, and aging, and even include a children's book illustrated by his daughter, Amy.

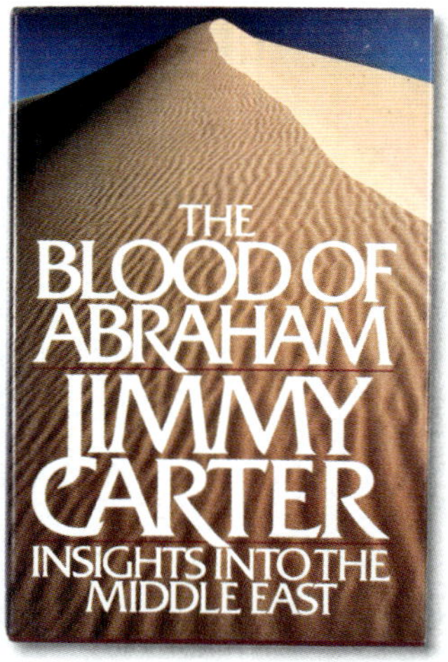

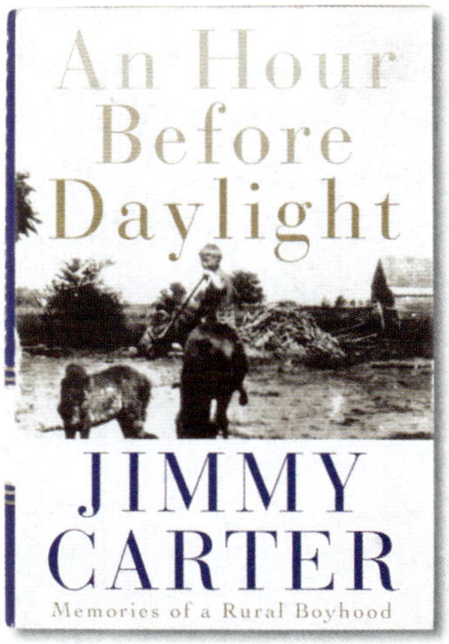

be saved if the government simply mailed each recipient $10,000 in cash!

New York City, facing bankruptcy, received a federal loan guarantee of $1.65 billion for its bonds. On December 15, Cleveland, Ohio, could not pay $15.5 million in short-term notes, becoming the first of several cities to default in modern times; nothing like this had happened since the 1930s. Inflation rose to 8%, but productivity increased only 0.4%. The annual U.S. trade deficit increased and continued to be a problem. General Motors led the roster of U.S. corporations in 1978 with sales of more than $63 billion.

In 1979, the energy crisis worsened in view of the political situation in Iran. On July 15, President Carter announced an energy conservation program that would limit oil imports and reduce domestic use. Congress passed a bill authorizing $1.5 billion to bail out the Chrysler Corporation from its economic woes, following a presentation by its president, Lee Iacocca, who became an American folk hero as he subsequently turned the fortunes of the company around. Suggestions were made that he could run the country and should throw his hat in the ring for president.

Problems continued in the economy, with the biggest increase in the consumer price index in 33 years—13.3%, known as "double digit inflation." The stock market remained relatively stable, with the Dow-Jones Industrial Average standing at 838.4 at the end of the year, an increase of 4.2% over the preceding 12 months, although a record 8.2 billion shares were traded.

In October the Federal Reserve raised the discount rate to 12% in an effort to control the money supply, causing stock and bond prices to drop. Many banks raised the prime rate to 14.5%. Fear of holding money increased, and people rushed to acquire tangible assets including gold and silver, which rose to record prices. The Hunt brothers, Texas billionaires, endeavored to corner the world market on silver bullion.

Inflation continued rampant in 1980 and by the end of the year had risen to 12.4%, the second year of double-digit inflation, causing annuities and pensions to lose their value and increasing concern over the soundness of the American dollar. Unemployment reached 7.1%, automobile sales were at their lowest in 19 years, and the Ford Motor Company reported losses of $575 million, the largest ever sustained by an American corporation. The country's largest corporation, Exxon, attained $79.1 billion in sales; General Motors was the second largest.

The Mount St. Helens volcano in Washington State erupted on May 18, flattening timber for miles around. The volcano, inactive since 1857, filled the air in the northwestern United States with clouds of microscopic dust. The November 21 episode of *Dallas*, a popular television soap opera, drew more viewers than any other single television program in U.S. history when it revealed "who shot J.R."

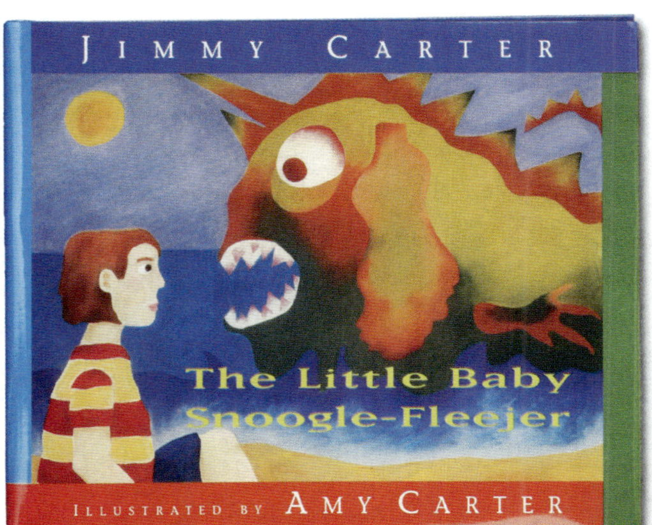

NOTABLE SAYINGS

"The best way to enhance freedom in other lands is to demonstrate that here our democratic system is worthy of emulation."

"We must adjust the changing times and still hold to unchanging principles."

40th President (1981–1989)

RONALD WILSON REAGAN

February 6, 1911–June 5, 2004

Political party: Republican

Vice president: George Bush, 1981 to 1989

First Lady and family: Married well-known film actress Jane Wyman on June 25, 1940 (divorced in 1948). His second wife was Nancy Davis (1923–), whom he married on March 4, 1952. Reagan had four children, two from his first marriage: Maureen Elizabeth Reagan (1941–2001) and Michael Edward Reagan (adopted; 1945–); and two from his second marriage: Patricia Ann Reagan (1952–) and Ronald Prescott Reagan (1958–).

Especially remembered for: His career as a movie star. His understanding of human nature, communication, and how to motivate his associates. Restoring the national economy to normal interest and inflation rates. The Iran Contra scandal engineered by subordinates. Persuading Soviet leader Mikhail Gorbachev to tear down the Berlin Wall, which happened under the next administration, leading to the dissolution of the Communist bloc and freedom for many countries; one of the greatest diplomatic accomplishments in American history. A popular and charismatic president.

The Life of Ronald Reagan

Ronald Reagan was born in Tampico, Illinois, son of John Edward and Nelle Wilson Reagan. His father was a traveling salesman whose earnings were erratic at best. Young Reagan worked hard, attended high school in nearby Dixon, and became a popular figure. As a local lifeguard, over a period of time he rescued dozens of people. He attended Eureka College, where he studied economics and other subjects, acted in plays, and was on the football team. He graduated in 1932.

Soon, Reagan became a radio sports announcer in Davenport, Iowa, often giving what seemed to be on-the-spot coverage, although he improvised the plays and the crowd excitement from reading raw scores telegraphed from Chicago or another location. In 1937 he took a screen test and landed a contract in Hollywood, launching a career in which he played in 53 films, some of them box-office hits. Elected president of the Screen Actors Guild, he championed the rights of entertainment personalities in the era of witch-hunting by Senator Joseph McCarthy for suspected Communists.

Speaking frankly and with a compelling charm, Reagan campaigned for and won the post of governor of California by a wide margin in 1966, and was reelected in 1975. In 1980 he was the Republican nominee for president, opposing incumbent Jimmy Carter. Reagan posted an overwhelming victory. On the day of his inauguration in January 1981, the government of Iran released its 52 American hostages, eliciting a roar of applause from the audience seated on the lawn beneath the podium on the back side of the White House.

In an attempt to improve economic conditions, on February 18, President Reagan recommended a cut of $41 billion in the federal budget drafted by Carter, and also proposed income tax decreases. These actions were derided as "Reaganomics" by

Opposite: President Reagan in 1981. The president's face was already familiar to the American public from the numerous Hollywood films he had appeared in.

his opponents, but with much effort and some setbacks, the economy was eventually turned around and double-digit inflation faded into history—but not without a lot of controversy. On his 69th day in office Reagan was shot by the deranged John Hinckley, a would-be assassin. Interviewed in the hospital afterward, on the way to what proved to be a full recovery, Reagan lightly joked about the matter. His public ratings soared.

On August 3, 1981, nearly 13,000 air traffic controllers went on strike nationwide. Reagan announced that unless they returned to work on August 5 they would be fired. Those who did not return to work were eventually replaced; America's labor unions had lost power and would continue to do so.

In the White House, First Lady Nancy Reagan dazzled fashion reporters with lavish expenditures on fancy clothes. Not since the Kennedy administration had there been such an interest in this area.

On August 19, 1981, navy planes shot down two Libyan fighter planes about 60 miles off the coast of Libya after the fighters, claiming sovereignty over the area, opened fire. President Reagan slept through the engagement and learned about it the next morning, quipping that if American planes had been shot down, he would have been awakened to spring into action. Relations with Russia worsened as martial law was imposed in Poland and the solidarity movement there was outlawed.

In 1984 Reagan ran for reelection against Democrat Walter F. Mondale, scoring an all-time high 525 Electoral College votes, with only 13 going to his opponent. Although the economy had stabilized, the unemployment rate was still more than 7%, considered to be an unsatisfactory

Top right: A World War II–era likeness of the young Ronald Reagan. Center right: One of Reagan's most famous film roles was as George "the Gipper" Gipp in *Knute Rockne, All American.* Bottom right: Souvenir pins from Reagan's political campaigns.

figure. Reagan worked on many fronts, including restoring the economy, easing the energy crisis, building national defense (a proposed anti-missile protection system, dubbed "Star Wars" by critics, was eventually rejected by Congress), and income-tax code reform. His effective negotiations with Soviet leader Mikhail Gorbachev led to the tearing down of the Berlin Wall, which happened early in the next administration, and the dissolution of the Communist bloc. With this came independence for Eastern European countries as well as various states within the Soviet Union. In Reagan's negative column was the Iran Contra scandal, a secret plan to supply arms to those opposing the new regime in that country. The matter went to Congress and brought embarrassment to the administration, but no direct connection to Reagan himself was proven.

In 1989 Ronald and Nancy Reagan left Washington and returned to California, where the couple had acquired a home in Bel Air, a Los Angeles suburb. Later, the former president struggled with Alzheimer's disease, with the public kept apprised of its progress. He died peacefully in Bel Air in June 2004.

President Reagan with First Lady Nancy, who like her husband was a former movie actor. She launched the anti-drug campaign whose famous motto was "Just Say No."

THE AMERICAN SCENE

Despite efforts by the new president, the inflation rate in 1981 was 14%, showing double-digit figures for three years in a row. National unemployment was at a 7.4% rate. Car sales plummeted. Reagan lifted price controls on oil, and prices bounded upward. Airlines operated at a record loss. "Reaganomics" had yet to be effective. Car sales plummeted. The space shuttle *Columbia* lifted off for its first mission and for "work" deployed two communications satellites. The shuttles would remain prominent for years afterward, until the program ended in 2011, by which time they were no longer particularly useful in new scientific discoveries.

Maya Yang Lin, a Yale undergraduate student in architecture, won a nationwide competition to design the Vietnam War Memorial. "The Wall," as it came to be known, was subsequently built in Washington, D.C., and the names of all who died in the war were inscribed on its surfaces.

The music album of the year 1982 was *Double Fantasy* by John Lennon (formerly of the Beatles) and his wife, Yoko Ono. The Federal Communications Commission authorized Motorola to commence testing cellular telephones, starting in Chicago.

The second space shuttle, the *Challenger,* was launched in 1983. Popular singer Karen Carpenter died of anorexia, or self-starvation to improve one's appearance, focusing nationwide attention on a syndrome that mostly affected young women. More than 125 million people, a record, tuned in to see the last episode of the television series *MASH*.

On January 1, 1984, AT&T's Bell Telephone System was broken up, launching a dynamic industry in telecommunications. Soon, many different devices to attach to phones were available to the general public. Having a recorder and answering system became so popular that the majority of citizens used them. *The Cosby Show* made its debut and was soon the most popular program on television. In the meantime the use of VCRs expanded, making it possible to record a show at any time and view it later.

Ronald Reagan
AMERICA
REAGAN COUNTRY

By 1985, personal computers (PCs), some of which cost less than a thousand dollars, were very popular, although operating them was tedious, usually involving adding code script. In this era the Apple Macintosh made its appearance, with changes vastly simplifying the process. The Microsoft Corporation, holder of the MS-DOS patents, created Windows. By decade's end the PC was in very wide use and the Internet liked computers worldwide.

The space program suffered a severe setback on January 28, 1986, when the *Challenger* shuttle exploded shortly after takeoff, killing all seven aboard.

The News Corporation, based in England, created the Fox television network, which at first offered 10 hours a day of prime time programming. In time it and the already established CNN (Cable News Network) each had round-the-clock offerings, typically based on current news events. The *Oprah Winfrey Show* first appeared on national television and soon attracted a wide following. The CD-ROM rapidly took the place of magnetic tape and other storage media. The rather obscure *Academic American Encyclopedia* became the first reference work to be available on these discs. The return visit of Halley's Comet, last seen in 1910, was widely anticipated but proved to be a flop and was scarcely visible, unlike the earlier time when it blazed across the night sky and caused a sensation.

In 1987 Colonel Oliver North Jr., who participated in secret negotiations in the Iran-Contra arms deal, told congressmen that it was authorized by higher officials; President Reagan disavowed any specific knowledge but assumed responsibility. The matter remained controversial for a long time. On July 3, 1988, a United States Navy gunner mistook an Iranian airliner for a warplane, so he said, and shot it down in the Persian Gulf, killing 290 people. By this year, the last in the Reagan administration, the economy was back on an even keel and unemployment had been reduced to an acceptable 5.5%. As a harbinger of things to come, NASA scientist James Hansen told Congress that mankind was directly responsible for global warming, giving impetus to a growing interest in helping to prevent it.

As 1988 drew to a close there was a feeling of contentment and well-being across much of America, although many social problems remained to be solved.

Opposite: A 1980 campaign poster declares America to be "Reagan Country," a phrase that became part of the cultural lexicon.

NOTABLE SAYINGS

"The best minds are not in government. If they were, business would hire them away."

"Double—no, triple—our troubles, and we would still be better off than any other people on earth. It is time that we recognize that ours was, in truth, a noble cause."

"If some among you fear taking a stand because you are afraid of reprisals from customers, clients, or even government, recognize that you are just feeding the crocodile hoping that he will eat you last."

"The government's view of the economy could be summed up in a few short phrases: if it moves, tax it. If it keeps moving, regulate it. If it stops moving, subsidize it."

"The most terrifying words in the English language are 'I'm from the government and I'm here to help.'"

"Mr. Gorbachev, tear down the wall."

"We are a nation that has a government—not the other way around. And that makes it special among the other nations of the earth."

41st President (1989–1993)

GEORGE HERBERT WALKER BUSH

Born June 12, 1924

Political party: Republican

Vice president: Dan Quayle, 1989 to 1993

First Lady and family: Married Barbara Pierce on January 6, 1945. The couple had six children: George Walker Bush (1946–), who would be elected president in 2000; Robin Bush (1949–1953); John Ellis ("Jeb") Bush (1953–); Neil Bush (1955–); Marvin Bush (1956–); and Dorothy Bush (1959–).

Especially remembered for: The demolition of the Berlin Wall and the dissolution of the Communist bloc, after which many countries became free and independent. Operation Desert Storm (the invasion of Iraq after that country occupied Kuwait).

The Life of George H.W. Bush

George Herbert Walker Bush was born in Milton, Massachusetts, son of Prescott Sheldon Bush and Dorothy Walker Bush. A young man with talent, he enrolled in Phillips Academy in Andover in the same state, where he was among the student leaders. Enlisting in the navy, he was the youngest pilot up to that time in that service to receive his wings. During World War II Bush flew 58 combat missions and was shot down in action by an anti-aircraft battery, to be rescued at sea by a submarine. He was awarded the Distinguished Flying Cross.

After the war Bush attended Yale University, where he was a Phi Beta Kappa scholar and captain of the baseball team. After graduating in 1948 he went to western Texas, where he began a career in the oil industry. Entering politics with the election of 1966, he served in the House of Representatives from 1967 to 1971, following this with service as ambassador to the United Nations for two years. Two bids to become a U.S. senator were unsuccessful. In 1976 and 1977 he directed the Central Intelligence Agency. In 1980 he aspired to be Republican candidate for president, but lost. Selected by Ronald Reagan to be vice president on the ticket, he served with distinction in that office from 1981 to 1989.

He tossed his hat in the ring for the 1998 presidential election and campaigned extensively, but in the bellwether Iowa caucus came in third, behind Bob Dole and Christian televangelist Pat Robertson. With renewed energy, he went to New Hampshire, held many meetings, ran extensive advertising, and was the winner of that state's primary election, the first in the nation. Other successes followed. At the summer convention the Republican Party selected him as its candidate in the forthcoming presidential

Opposite: President George H.W. Bush, sometimes known as "Bush 41," "Bush the Elder," or "George Bush Sr." to distinguish him from his presidential son. The 41st president, he began his term immediately after completing a second term as vice president.

election. At the nominating event he uttered a phrase that would become famous: "Read my lips. No new taxes."

For a running mate he picked J. Danforth "Dan" Quayle, a relatively unknown senator from Indiana. Reagan, with his outgoing personality and skill as a public speaker, was a hard act to follow, and some detractors suggested that Bush was not a worthy successor. His Democratic opponent was governor Michael Dukakis of Massachusetts, who chose Texas Senator Lloyd Bentsen as his vice presidential candidate. Many polls favored Dukakis, but the voters picked Bush by 54.4%. In the Electoral College he took 426 votes to his opponent's 111.

Upon entering the White House he inherited Reagan's policies and momentum, which he handled with extensive knowledge and experience. The Cold War came to an end and the Communist empire dissolved, one of the greatest advances on the diplomatic scene in world history. He also inherited a huge budget deficit. Faced with the alternatives of cutting the budget or raising taxes, Bush proposed cuts and also increased taxes to reduce the deficit by $500 billion over five years. On the tax matter many of his Republican supporters felt betrayed.

President Bush sent troops to Panama to oust the corrupt general Manuel Noriega from power. When Saddam Hussein, president of Iraq, invaded and occupied Kuwait, Bush, with the endorsement of Congress, sent 425,000 American troops, aided by 118,000 from other nations, to liberate that country. This was handily accomplished in a quick operation known as Operation Desert Storm. The Iraqis retreated north back into their own country. At one time the president registered an incredible 89% approval rating.

Below: Chief Justice William Rehnquist administers the oath of office to the new president during inauguration ceremonies on January 20, 1989. Barbara Bush, at right, looks on.

In his administration the Americans with Disabilities Act (ADA) was signed, providing easy access to public buildings by people who could not climb steps and putting in place other features to improve accessibility. The Clean Air Act led the way to reduce toxic emissions by automobiles, factories, and other fuel-burning sources.

By the time that Bush sought reelection in 1992, the American economy was faltering, the federal budget registered a deficit that many found untenable, and racial problems continued in several cities. Although there was little controversy surrounding the president or the actions of his administration, there was enough dissatisfaction to effect a change. Democratic challenger William "Bill" Clinton took the November contest by a large margin.

Above left: President Bush and Vice President Quayle in their official portrait, June 1989. Above right: A keepsake pin marked the start of Bush's presidential campaign in 1987.

The president left Washington and went into retirement, spending time in Texas and at his long-time summer home in Kennebunkport, Maine, as well as pursuing private interests, investments, and charitable work. In 2002 one of his sons, George W. Bush, was elected president.

THE AMERICAN SCENE

A notable event early in 1989 was the rupture of the tanker *Exxon Valdez,* which spilled 11 million gallons of crude oil into Prince William Sound in Alaska, a major ecological disaster, the effects of which echoed for many years afterward. On August 9 army general Colin R. Powell was tapped by the president to become chairman of the Joint Chiefs of Staff. Powell proved to be very popular in the position and in later years was even mentioned as a possible candidate for president. In Europe, Salman Rushdie's novel *The Satanic Verses* was said to be an insult to the Islamic religion, and militants offered a bounty to anyone who would kill the author (this didn't happen). For the first time. Islamic extremists became important in the news.

In recent years, explorations of the outer planets resulted in many fascinating discoveries, especially odd facts about the moons of Jupiter and Neptune.

In 1990 the United States Supreme Court overturned a law banning the burning of the American flag. By this time patriotism had taken many twists and turns, and many citizens said that mention of God should be forbidden in official statements, never mind that the national motto is "In God We Trust," and "one nation under God" is part of the Pledge of Allegiance. Increasingly in the age of recorded television speeches and the Internet, statements of politicians on all levels from regional to international were dissected, taken out of context, and distorted. This was hardly new, but now it became easier to do. The 1990 Grammys honored Bette Midler's "Wind Beneath My Wings" as Record of the Year; *Seinfeld* was launched on

television and soon became popular, as did *The Simpsons;* and in movie theaters *Dances with Wolves* earned accolades.

In 1991 President Bush nominated Judge Clarence Thomas for the Supreme Court, but confirmation, which finally occurred, was complicated when Professor Anita Hill accused him of sexual harassment. AIDS had developed into a worldwide problem, and many medical researchers were at work on medicine to reduce or delay its effects, although no cure was in sight. During the Bush administration Dan Quayle became the butt of many jokes, especially after he told a grade-school class that the correct spelling for a certain vegetable was "potatoe."

In 1992 the last U.S. military forces left the Philippine Islands, which America had occupied after the War of 1898 and where they had later kept an armed presence (except during World War II). In Los Angeles, an African American man named Rodney King was brutally beaten by police officers, who were taken to court but acquitted. Violence erupted in the city upon word of the verdict.

For the first time, sales of CDs eclipsed cassette tapes in sales of recorded music. An era ended when emcee Johnny Carson retired from hosting the NBC *Tonight Show* after 20 years.

Above left: In 1990 the president and British prime minister Margaret Thatcher addressed the Aspen Institute Symposium in Colorado. Above right: The former president aboard the aircraft carrier named for him, the USS *George H.W. Bush,* in 2010.

NOTABLE SAYINGS

"If anyone tells you that America's best days are behind her, they are looking the wrong way."

"The United States is the best and fairest and most decent nation on the earth."

"You bet I cut the taxes at the top. That encourages entrepreneurship. What we Republicans should stand for is growth in the economy."

"I know that human beings and fish can coexist peacefully."

"Being a dictator would be a heck of a lot easier; there is no question about it."

The Life of William Clinton

Bill" Clinton, as he liked to be called, was born in Hope, Arkansas, son of William Jefferson Blythe III and Virginia Divine Cassidy Blythe Clinton Kelley. Three months before his birth, his father was killed in a traffic accident. When Bill was four years old his mother wed Roger Clinton of Hot Springs, Arkansas, and Bill later took the new family name.

A brilliant student and with a winning personality, Clinton made friends wherever he went. He played the saxophone and for a time considered becoming a professional musician. During a visit to the Rose Garden at the White House when he was in high school he met John F. Kennedy, after which he decided to devote his life to public service. At Georgetown University he earned a Bachelor of Science degree in foreign service. In 1968 he won a Rhodes scholarship to University College, Oxford, in England. He also studied at Yale and graduated with a law degree in 1973.

In 1974 Clinton ran for Congress as the representative from the 3rd District of Arkansas, but lost. In 1976 he was elected attorney general of the state, and in 1978 he was voted in as governor. A bid for a second term failed, but four years later he was again a winner. He remained governor from 1982 until his run for the presidency.

In 1992 he sought the Democratic nomination and campaigned vigorously, but in the first contest, the Iowa caucus, he finished third, far behind the winner, Iowa senator Tom Harkin, who had the home court advantage, so to speak. He then pursued New Hampshire voters in hopes of winning that state's primary, the first election in the nation, but rumors of an extramarital affair with Gennifer Flowers dampened the enthusiasm of many voters, despite his going on CBS *60 Minutes,* accompanied by his wife Hillary, to refute the charges. The winner was Paul Tsongas (a former senator from the adjacent state of Massachusetts), but only by a narrow margin. Undaunted, Clinton went on to win primaries in Texas, Florida, and several other states.

42nd President (1993–2001)

WILLIAM JEFFERSON CLINTON

Born August 19, 1946

Political party: Democratic

Vice president: Al Gore, 1993 to 2001

First Lady and family: Married Hillary Rodham on October 11, 1975. They had one daughter, Chelsea Victoria Clinton, born in 1980. Hillary was a very active and well-liked First Lady. Later she became a U.S. senator from New York and then secretary of state in the Barack Obama administration beginning in 2009.

Especially remembered for: Best academic credentials of any president. Presidency marked by excellent economic conditions and relatively peaceful world conditions. Enjoyment of the office of president, with enthusiasm in most of his efforts. Headline-grabbing affair with a White House intern, which resulted in impeachment proceedings in Congress. In retirement accomplished much in charitable and other causes.

At the nominating convention that summer he secured the party's nod, with the only other serious contender being Jerry Brown, a former governor of California. In November Clinton and his running mate, Al Gore, competed against incumbent George H.W. Bush and third-party contender Ross Perot, and was the winner by a significant margin.

For the first time in 12 years the presidency and Congress were controlled by the same party, which facilitated the passage of legislation. To most observers, this advantage was not abused, and many advances were made. In 1996 Clinton sought reelection against Robert Dole on the Republican ticket and Ross Perot again as a third-party candidate. Clinton won in another landslide.

Clinton's administration was perhaps a modern counterpart to President James Monroe's "Era of Good Feelings" of the early 19th century. The economy was robust, as was employment (the highest in modern times), the crime rate dropped, advances were made in civil rights, progress in conservation and ecology took place, and a budget *surplus* was achieved. On his foreign trips Clinton was welcomed by crowds. On the negative side, his far-ranging program of health-care reform did not become a reality, and an affair with a female intern in the White House led to impeachment proceedings (which came to nothing). Clinton apologized to the nation for his indiscretion and continued to enjoy high public-approval ratings.

Opposite: The official White House photo portrait for President Clinton's first term was taken in January 1993. Below: On January 20, 1997, President Clinton was inaugurated for a second term. Here he and First Lady Hillary wave to the crowds gathered to watch the inaugural parade.

Above: Clinton's autobiography *My Life* was published in 2004. The former president received what was then the highest advance on royalties ever given an author, estimated at $12 million. Below right: Two campaign pins show support for Clinton at the Democratic National Convention of 1992.

In retirement, Clinton and wife Hillary acquired a home in Chappaqua, New York. The ex-president wrote his memoirs, arranged profitable speaking engagements, participated in humanitarian groups—including his own William J. Clinton Foundation—and enjoyed the friendship of a large following. When Hillary embarked on a political career of her own, Clinton helped her campaign for senator and, later, for the presidential candidacy. Although Hillary lost the 2008 Democratic presidential nomination to Barack Obama, she was named Obama's secretary of state in 2009.

THE AMERICAN SCENE

Early in the Clinton administration, the compound of the Branch Davidian religious cult in Waco, Texas, consisting of leader David Koresh and about 140 followers, became the focus of international attention. On February 28, 1993, agents of the Bureau of Alcohol, Tobacco, and Firearms endeavored to execute a search warrant and were met with gunfire in a battle that lasted nearly two hours, in which four federal agents and five cult members died. The FBI initiated a siege of the compound, and on April 19 attempted another entry. A fire broke out, the facility was destroyed, and 76 people died, including leader David Koresh.

Up to this year homosexuals were prohibited from serving in the military. Clinton agreed to a compromise that became widely known as "don't ask, don't tell." The gay rights movement had been gaining force, and in coming years there would be great advances.

Despite much opposition that it would cost countless jobs, Congress in November passed the North American Free Trade Agreement to allow unimpeded business exchanges with Canada and

Mexico. The latter country in particular had offered labor much cheaper than in the United States.

On July 12, 1994, Nicole Brown Simpson, wife of football star O.J. Simpson, was found dead outside of her condominium, where she had lived since being separated from her husband. Her friend Ronald Goldman had been killed as well. The matter went to court in 1995 and was televised, with some calling it the "trial of the century." Day after day viewers heard testimony for and against O.J., who did not say a word. The jury acquitted him for failure to prove guilt beyond a reasonable doubt.

Republican congressman Newt Gingrich was named speaker of the House in 1994, after which he became well known in national politics, later making runs as a presidential candidate. Steven Spielberg's film *Schindler's List* won the Academy Award for Best Picture, an honor that had not gone to his famous earlier success *Star Wars.* Chain bookstores such as Barnes & Noble, Borders, Books-A-Million, and several others had seen great increases in popularity in recent years, offering coffee, sometimes music, and a relaxing atmosphere among shelves of books and racks of recordings. In 1994 for the first time chain-store sales surpassed those of independent book stores.

On April 19, 1995, two paramilitary renegade men, later identified as Timothy McVeigh and Terry Nichols, filled a rented Ryder truck with explosives and detonated it in front of Oklahoma City's Alfred P. Murrah Federal Building, killing 168 people, including 19 children under the age of six, a horrific incident that emphasized the need to protect government and other facilities against bombings. Earlier an unrelated bombing had occurred in a garage under the World Trade Center in New York City. Soon barriers were erected in front of many buildings and the parking of vehicles in front of many facilities was banned. In October the Million Man March saw several hundred thousand African Americans and others in Washington to protest inequalities. *Forrest Gump* was the Academy's selection for Best Picture. In the United Kingdom two doctors created the world's first cloned sheep from embryo cells, initiating worldwide discussion of the practice and how far it should be extended with humans.

A pin from the president's inaugural gala of 1993 boasts what would become a famous image: the president playing the saxophone. Another pin honors First Lady Hillary Rodham Clinton, who would go on to have a distinguished political career of her own.

For nearly 20 years a secretive individual had been mailing bombs to unsuspecting recipients, including at universities, giving him the press nickname of Unabomber. On April 3, 1996, "Ted" Kaczynski, a Montana hermit with a Harvard degree, was arrested and charged after his brother identified him from a published manifesto.

On a 1999 visit to Peterson Air Force Base in Colorado, President Clinton receives a coin from 84th Airlift Flight Commander Major Sandy J. Krigel and his wife.

On July 17 Trans World Airlines Flight 800, bound from New York to Paris, exploded over Long Island Sound, killing all 230 aboard. The cause was officially stated to be an explosion in a fuel tank, but was thought by some others to have been a test firing of a military missile that went astray.

The economy was running smoothly in 1997, with the unemployment rate at a low 4.9%. Comet Hale-Bopp was a fixture in the night sky in March, the first bright comet in many years. On Mars an unmanned NASA "rover" began exploring the surface and radioing back its findings.

On the big screen, *Titanic,* directed by James Cameron, took in more than $580 million in the United States, the highest gross ever. Construction of the International Space Station began with the delivery of two sections of it by the shuttle *Discovery.*

In early 1999 the Senate took up the impeachment question, acquitted President Clinton, and rejected the House's censure. On July 16 a plane piloted by John F. Kennedy Jr., and with his wife and sister-in-law aboard, disappeared at sea while on the way to the island resort of Martha's Vineyard. *The Blair Witch Project,* a film that cost a mere $30,000 to produce, became a cult classic on the screen and grossed more than $125 million, providing an inspiration to amateur filmmakers worldwide. In the meantime, personal computers were in use by many Americas, and web sites on the Internet were proliferating.

Internet company America Online (AOL) agreed to buy publishing and media giant Time Warner for $164 billion in January 2000. Excitement prevailed. The Internet beckoned as the potential source of immense profits. The stock market was afire, fueled by initial public offerings of companies projecting profits from Internet sales of everything from groceries to cat food. Prices of some securities rose steadily, and many brokers, happy to encourage trading, offered desk space in their offices to amateur investors. On February 25, there was a break, and many securities on NASDAQ, the primary exchange for Internet stocks, dropped. A crash soon followed, and the index of NASDAQ stocks (which mostly consisted of non-Internet-based companies) plunged to less than half of its high. Many Internet businesses were liquidated, and in time the AOL acquisition proved to be a dismal failure.

Popular writer Stephen King published a novella, *Riding the Bullet,* which was released only as an electronic book (e-book) for downloading to computers. More than 500,000 downloads were sold in the first three days. No printed version was issued. This called attention to a coming wave of e-publications, which a decade later would be an important part of the trade.

NOTABLE SAYINGS

"There is nothing wrong in America that can't be fixed with what is right in America."

The Life of George W. Bush

George Walker Bush was born in New Haven, Connecticut, son of George Herbert Walker Bush and Barbara Pierce Bush. He spent his youth in Midland and Houston, Texas, where his father was a highly prosperous oilman. In 1968 Bush graduated from Yale with a degree in history, and then joined the Texas Air National Guard, where he went into training and became a fighter pilot, flying an F-102. Afterward he went to Harvard, earning an MBA in 1975.

Bush returned to Texas, where he went into the oil business in Midland with the encouragement and assistance of his father. In 1989 he was part of a group of investors who purchased the Texas Rangers baseball franchise. However, he was not particularly successful in the business world. He soon turned to politics. In 1994 Bush ran for and was elected governor of Texas, and in 1998 he was reelected, becoming the first governor in state history to earn two consecutive terms. While serving in that post he was a popular figure viewed as a nice guy, the kind of neighbor anyone would like to have next door.

In June 1999, while serving as governor of Texas, Bush announced his bid for the Republication nomination for the presidential contest of 2000. He became part of a large field of Republican hopefuls, including Lamar Alexander, Gary Bauer, Pat Buchanan, Elizabeth Dole (wife of earlier presidential candidate Bob Dole), Steve Forbes, Orrin Hatch, John Kasich, John McCain (who would be heard from again in 2008), former vice president Dan Quayle, and Robert C. Smith. Eventually, the Republican contest effectively narrowed to Bush versus McCain. Bush won the Iowa caucus hands down and was predicted to sweep the New Hampshire primaries. This did not happen, however, and he received 19% fewer votes than his competitor.

Dismissing New Hampshire as a "bump in the road" he carried to other states his messages—cutting taxes, assisting minorities, improving education, and strengthening the military—plus, as expected,

43rd President (2001–2008)

GEORGE W. BUSH

Born July 6, 1946

Political party: Republican

Vice president: Dick Cheney, 2001 to 2008

First Lady and family: Married Laura Welch on November 5, 1977. The couple had twin girls: Barbara Pierce Bush (1981–) and Jenna Welch Bush (1981–).

Especially remembered for: Robust economy. War on terrorism precipitated by the attacks of September 11, 2001. Controversial Iraq war. Nickname: "W," sometimes spelled out as "Dubya."

criticizing his Democratic opponent, Vice President Al Gore. At the nominating convention in July he secured first place on the ticket and selected Texas businessman and former White House chief of staff, representative to Congress, and secretary of defense Dick Cheney. In November Bush edged Gore by a narrow margin, with the outcome resting on the pivotal state of Florida. A recount was ordered, then a second recount, after which the Florida Supreme Court ordered a third recount. The public was told of seemingly unusual situations, such as punched machine tickets with little tabs still hanging, called "chads." The matter went to the Supreme Court, which ruled that a recount showing Bush the winner by 537 votes was correct. Nationwide, Bush received 543,895 fewer popular votes than did Gore. The Electoral College decided the question, with 271 for Bush and 266 for his opponent—the narrowest election in many years.

George W. Bush was sworn in as president on January 20, 2001, and started his administration by supporting a tax-relief bill that resulted in more money in the paychecks of average workers, and by reform efforts in education, notably the No Child Left Behind Act of 2001. Medicare benefits were expanded to provide increased benefits and prescription drugs.

On September 11, 2001, terrorists hijacked four commercial aircraft. Two were crashed into the World Trade Center in New York City, destroying both of the twin towers and costing nearly 3,000 American lives. Another was crashed into the Pentagon, causing extensive damage and loss of lives. Aboard the fourth, passengers overcame the hijackers, and the plane crashed into a field in Shanksville, Pennsylvania, killing all aboard. President Bush declared war on terrorists, particularly those affiliated with an extremist group known as al-Qaeda. The United States launched Operation Enduring Freedom to destroy the al-Qaeda network harbored by Afghanistan's Taliban regime. Back home, vast changes were made in domestic security procedures in the hope of preventing future tragedies. This overwhelmed all other planned agendas and defined the rest of the Bush administration. Everything else was secondary.

Believing that Iraqi leader Saddam Hussein possessed "weapons of mass destruction" and would not hesitate to use them, Bush ordered an invasion of Iraq. Hussein's military forces were neutralized,

Opposite: In this White House photo portrait, President Bush's resemblance to his father, the former president, is evident. Above right: An assortment of campaign and keepsake pins from Bush's career. Below right: Artist George Rodrigue customized his iconic blue dog for a canine variation on the presidential seal.

the dictator went into hiding (and was later hunted down, tried, and executed), and hopes were high that Iraq would become a free land with elected officials. At the outset all seemed to go well, and soon President Bush was photographed aboard an aircraft carrier with a huge "Mission Accomplished" sign in the background. In 2004 he sought reelection against Senator John Kerry, and won the first majority of the popular vote since his father's election in 1988.

The Iraq war was not over, and the worst was yet to come. Continued American presence drew condemnation and wide criticism, which also embraced the United Nations and which came from some of America's closest allies, and this criticism accelerated when no weapons of mass destruction were found. International indignation was caused when photographs appeared of American guards at the Abu Ghraib detention camp making Iraqi prisoners undress and otherwise intimidating them. A Pentagon inquiry found irregularities not only at the prison but at "all levels" in the conduct of the attack and capture of Iraq. Anti-American sentiment increased abroad, especially in Arab countries. America itself became polarized, and the approval ratings of the president fell precipitately. Through the criticism President Bush remained firm in his convictions and supportive of his advisors.

In time, many domestic improvements were indeed made in such fields as health care, education, and the treatment of immigrants, among other areas. Bush campaigned hard to allow Social Security funds to be invested in the private sector, such as stocks and mutual funds. In hindsight it was fortunate that this did not happen, for many retirement nest eggs depreciated in value once the economy took a downward turn in 2007. In the

Below: In a 2002 visit to Naval Station Mayport in Jacksonville, Florida, the president thanks sailors for their sacrifices and efforts in the name of freedom. "The United States Navy carries the might and the mission of America to the farthest parts of the world," he declared.

meantime, vice president Dick Cheney was perceived as directing many White House policies and decisions, although this was denied by Bush, who called himself "the decider." In his last year in office, 2008, President Bush tried to deal with the longest economic recession since World War II. His approval ratings dropped. By December 31, 2008, 1.9 million American jobs had been lost, the most in many years. When he left office in January 2009 the economy was a challenge for his successor, Barack Obama.

THE AMERICAN SCENE

In early 2001 the budget surplus that had been posted by the Clinton administration dwindled rapidly, with prospects for future surplus dimmed by a tax cut, the most substantial in 20 years, that became law on June 7. In view of later events, this proved to be unwise. In August the Congressional Budget Office stated that the rapid change from surplus to deficit was indeed due to the tax cuts and also to the difficult economic conditions. Everything changed on September 11 following terrorist attacks and destruction of the World Trade Center, damage to the Pentagon, and nearly 3,000 deaths. Security was tightened everywhere, airplane passengers became subject to screening and even body searches, new rules were enacted, and the nation took on a warlike footing against terrorism.

In publishing, the Harry Potter series of novels by J.K. Rowling were a sensation, and the first novel's film adaptation, *Harry Potter and the Sorcerer's Stone,* scored a home run at the box office. *John Adams* was written by historian John McCullough, whose well-researched books influenced his contemporaries (e.g., changing the perception of Harry Truman from a mediocre to an accomplished president).

Below: The president attends the opening ceremonies at the 105th Army vs. Navy game in December 2004. The Navy went on to beat the Army 42–13.

On the business front, executives of such well-known firms as Arthur Anderson, Tyco, Qwest, Global Crossing, and Adelphia were investigated in 2002 for fraud and false accounting by federal authorities, and some went to jail.

In October a mysterious sniper killed 10 people and wounded others in the Washington, D.C., area. The miscreant sniper and his follower were caught and convicted. Scientists constructed two complete maps of the genomes of a mouse and a human, revealing many similarities. Genetic research, an important branch of medicine, saw many advances. The reality television show *American Idol* was launched and quickly became popular.

On February 1, 2003, the space shuttle *Columbia* tore apart during its descent to earth across the Southwest, killing the seven astronauts aboard.

The economy worsened, and the Congressional Budget Office predicted a deficit of $480 billion by 2004, ballooning to $5.8 trillion by 2013. No meaningful action was taken to prevent this, such as cutting federal expenditures and raising taxes.

The iPod, a best-selling product by Apple Computer, allowed the user to carry dozens to thousands of songs, which could be downloaded from the Internet for 99 cents each. Overnight, portable CD players such as the Sony Discman became obsolete, and no longer did fans need to buy a tape or compact disc to enjoy their favorite music. The illegal downloading of songs and films became endemic, prompting the Recording Industry Association of America to prosecute with lawsuits those who illegally downloaded large numbers of titles, including, in one much-publicized case, a 12-year-old girl.

In 2004 Massachusetts became the first state to allow same-sex marriage. Tax cuts set to expire in 2005 were extended. In an almost comic situation, popular television personality and author Martha Stewart was sentenced to five months in prison and fined $30,000 on charges of insider trading. Meanwhile, unknown to the general public and not watched closely by regulators, billions of dollars of mortgage loans, investment packages, and other securities, often prepared with little investigation of their true worth, were sold by banks and brokers to retirement funds, state treasuries, and private individuals. A few years later when these malfeasances were uncovered, including inappropriate behavior by officers of the Fannie Mae and Freddie Mac agencies, little was done at all to prosecute the perpetrators, although in some instances fines were levied. In August the Internet search site Google went public, making its founders, Sergey Brin and Larry Page, billionaires. Existing billionaires such as Bill Gates (Microsoft) and Warren Buffett (Berkshire-Hathaway) were popular figures for interviews, and when *Forbes* magazine published its list of the 400 richest people the issue was always a sellout.

In early 2005 President Bush, beginning his second term, emphasized his plan to privatize Social Security, campaigning across America, but with little support in Congress. As the sales of iPods increased, so did downloads of music. Selections of CDs at stores became smaller as the market for them dwindled. On the television screen, *Desperate Housewives, Lost, American Idol,* and *Gray's Anatomy* were among the favorites. Round-the-clock news coverage by Fox and CNN disclosed the latest events worldwide as soon as they happened, with MSNBC joining the news coverage. Larry King, a popular interviewer on CNN, reached a wide audience. Newspaper subscriptions declined, as by the time happenings were related in print, they had been treated to the point of exhaustion on television and the Internet.

In late summer of 2005 Hurricane Katrina raked the Gulf Coast, laying waste low-lying coastal towns and buildings and submerging much of New Orleans. More than 1,800 people lost their lives. A later investigation revealed gross mismanagement by the Federal Emergency Management Agency (FEMA) and poor design and construction of levees by the U.S. Army Corps of Engineers.

By 2006 the American oversight of conquered Iraq became a first-class headache: crime increased,

soldiers were killed, citizens remained restive, and it became clear that attempts to install a peaceful democratic government would fall far short of success. In the meantime, anti-American sentiment increased in other Arab countries that resented the interference and influence of the United States in that area of the world. Matters worsened in early 2007 when President Bush ordered a temporary "surge" of 30,000 more American troops to Iraq to quell unrest. The actions of Blackwater, a private security company founded in that year and hired by the United States, were called into question when it was found by the House Committee on Oversight that more than 200 people had been shot by their employees. The use of mercenaries continued, but Blackwater, in an attempt to avoid more bad publicity, changed its name to Xe Services.

In early 2008 the stock market plunged as a result of continuing news of the mortgage crisis brought about by banks and other financial institutions that granted generous mortgages on residential and other properties that were sometimes falsely valued or not appraised at all. The economy began what would be a year of recession, with unemployment rising. Some of the nation's largest banks were faced

Above: In a 2003 visit to Naval Station Pearl Harbor in Hawaii, President Bush and First Lady Laura Bush converse with military personnel. The president also met with survivors of the Pearl Harbor attack in 1941.

with nonperforming mortgages and insufficient capital. A crisis was in the making. Matters were not helped by the fact that the majority of consumer goods sold in the United States were made in China and other countries on the other side of the world. In October the president signed a revised version of the Emergency Economic Stabilization Act to allow the Treasury to earmark $700 million for banks that were "too big to fail." In the meantime, there was little interest in helping small businesses and individuals that were in financial trouble. Wall Street was the focus, and Main Street was ignored.

In February 2008, the president visited tornado-stricken areas in the southern states. Here he consults with Federal Emergency Management Agency (FEMA) administrator David Paulison.

NOTABLE SAYINGS

"If you don't feel strongly you are not going to achieve."

"We will bring the terrorists to justice, and we will bring justice to the terrorists. Either way justice will be done."

The Life of Barack Obama

Barack Obama was born in 1961 in Honolulu, Hawaii, son of Barack Obama Sr., of Kenya, and Stanley Ann Dunham, of Kansas. His parents divorced in 1964. His mother later married a student from Indonesia, and Barack Jr. grew up in Indonesia and Hawaii. After high school he went on to graduate from Columbia University and Harvard Law School. (The story of his childhood, adulthood, and early political career are discussed in greater detail in part 1 of this book.)

Obama was elected to the Illinois State Senate in 1996 and reelected in 1998. In 2004, four years after a coming up short in the Democratic primary for the House of Representatives, he made a bid for the U.S. Senate, winning handily.

In February 2007, Senator Obama announced his bid for the Democratic nomination as president. His campaign platform included ending the occupation of Iraq, increasing domestic energy production, and expanding health care to cover all citizens. In August he was nominated by his party and chose Delaware senator Joe Biden as his running mate. Together they faced and defeated Republican senator John McCain and his running mate, Sarah Palin, governor of Alaska. On January 20, 2009, he was inaugurated as president, and later that same year was awarded the Nobel Peace Prize.

Obama's main accomplishments in his first term consisted of a $787 billion stimulus bill, aimed at preventing a second Great Depression; repealing the "Don't Ask, Don't Tell" policy regarding gays in the military; and the sweeping healthcare-system overhaul that came to be known as "Obamacare." He also appointed two women to the Supreme Court, Sonia Sotomayor and Elena Kagan. He ended the war in Iraq, began the process for withdrawal from Afghanistan, and restored broken relationships with several allies. On May 1, 2011, Obama ordered a raid by Navy SEALs on Osama bin Laden's compound in Pakistan—a successful operation in which the terrorist leader was killed.

44th President (2009–2016)

BARACK OBAMA

Born August 4, 1961

Political party: Democratic

Vice president: Joe Biden (1999–2016)

First Lady and family: Married Michelle Robinson on October 3, 1992. The couple had two daughters: Malia Ann (1998–) and Natasha ("Sasha") (2001–).

Especially remembered for: First African-American to be elected president. Dealing with difficult economic conditions and worldwide unrest.

On November 6, 2012, Barack Obama was reelected, defeating former Massachusetts governor Mitt Romney.

THE AMERICAN SCENE

During Barack Obama's presidency the war against terrorism committed by Islamic radicals called *jihadists* continued. In recent years several attempts at destroying civilian targets, aircraft, and buildings had been thwarted by government agents. Overseas, American soldiers continued their guard in occupied Iraq and in military actions in Afghanistan, in areas in which many if not most citizens disliked the interference, and where there was much government corruption. Increasing calls were made to bring American troops back home and let the Arab countries sort out their own differences. In the meantime Israel, which America has strongly supported since the late 1940s, was increasingly threatened by its neighbors while internally dealing with the plight of Palestinians who were treated as second-class citizens. It seemed to be a lose-lose situation for all involved.

On January 12, 2010, a magnitude 7.0 earthquake devastated much of Port-au-Prince, Haiti. Thousands of people were killed and injured. Aid from private and public interests in the United States and abroad was immediate. On April 14 an eruption of the Eyjafjallajokull volcano in Iceland closed down much European air traffic for several days, including flights to and from the United States. One disaster followed another, and on April 20 a huge explosion demolished a British Petroleum oil rig in the Gulf of Mexico off the coast of Louisiana and leaked tens of thousands of gallons of crude oil per hour. Finally, 96 days later, the well was capped. The ecological damage to coastal beaches and wildlife was immense, and legal actions continued long afterward.

Into 2011 it was more of the same: American troops fighting in Afghanistan, punctuated by a secret raid by Navy Seals into Pakistan where al-Qaeda leader Osama bin Laden, who had masterminded the 9/11 terrorist attacks on America, was cornered and killed.

The American economy showed few signs of getting better.

On the home front, e-book readers became very popular, led by Amazon's Kindle and the Barnes and Noble Nook. Apple's iPad launched a craze for tablet computers. Cell phones were in use everywhere, and land lines were abandoned by many Americans.

Opposite: President Barack Obama's official photographic portrait from January 2009.

NOTABLE SAYINGS

"Change will not come if we wait for some other person or if we wait for some other time. We are the ones we've been waiting for. We are the change that we seek."

"We lose ourselves when we compromise the very ideals that we fight to defend. And we honor those ideals by upholding them not when it's easy, but when it is hard."

"If you are walking down the right path and are willing to keep walking, eventually you will make progress."

Appendix

A SELECTION OF NOTABLE FIRST LADIES

One of the most challenging public positions in the United States is that of the first lady. The Constitution gives no definition of her powers or duties. The role is constantly evolving to meet the goals of the current administration, serve the needs of the nation, and match the personality of the woman filling the post.

The most obvious (and originally, the most important) function the first lady performs is a social one: as the official hostess for the White House, she oversees diplomatic parties and society events. As part of those responsibilities, she also supervises the household—serving, for all intents and purposes, as both homemaker and museum curator. When Martha Washington became the first lady in 1789, her duties were like those of any other upper-class woman of the time. Instead of hosting small parties among the local gentry, though, she was entertaining the men of rank who represented the United States to the rest of the world.

As the roles of women in America have changed, the roles of the first lady have expanded as well. Social responsibilities are no longer the main focus of her position. Because she is one of the few people totally loyal to the president, she can be his partner in the job. Modern first ladies have taken roles that are more actively political—campaigning, advising, and speechwriting for their husbands; helping draw support for administration policies; and at times acting as diplomats and intermediaries between the president and foreign governments.

In addition to her political and social duties, the first lady traditionally has a platform (or several of them)—specific charities and social issues that she wants to champion during her time in office. These have included movements as varied as environmental protection, animal rights, childhood and adult literacy, and health care. As an international celebrity, she can use her title to influence policies

First Lady Michelle Obama joins the president and Staff Sgt. Salvatore Giunta (center) as they enter the East Room of the White House to begin the Medal of Honor ceremony on November 16, 2010. Giunta, of Hiawatha, Iowa, is the first living veteran of the wars in Iraq and Afghanistan to receive the award.

relating to her cause. This advocacy usually continues long after her position in the White House has passed to the next administration.

Though the first lady is not an elected official, as a public figure she is under intense pressure and scrutiny throughout her time in Washington. Americans have always been fascinated by the first family, whose behaviors reflect on the president and his ability to lead the nation. The presidential inauguration marks the end of the first lady's private life. The public wants to see her properly prioritize her time for her family and her expected duties—though the definition of "properly" is, of course, left to each person's reckoning. Expectations are high and are easy to disappoint.

The president's wife has always been required to balance an array of roles for the American people and her family. Throughout such challenges, these women have provided great service to the country. Their position is not necessarily one to be desired—but handled well by the right woman, it is one worth admiring.

The following are some of the remarkable ladies who have held this most challenging and important role over the years.

Michelle Obama

"Mom-in-Chief"

"I come here as a mom," Michelle Obama said to the screaming thousands gathered in Denver the night in August 2008 when her husband was nominated to run for president, "whose girls are the heart of my heart and the center of my world. They're the first things I think about when I wake up in the morning and the last thing I think about before I go to bed at night.

"Their future, and all our children's future, is my stake in this election."

Long before the 2008 Democratic National Convention, Barack Obama's campaign had made the strategic decision to ease off Michelle's impressive professional achievements and focus media attention on her credentials as mother to the couple's two daughters, Malia and Sasha.

The move was anything but a political ploy. For all her career success, Michelle Obama is every bit the dedicated mother and caregiver she appeared to be on that Denver stage, and the evidence stretches back years before her husband announced his bid for the presidency.

By the time Malia was born in 1998, her mother had left a dream job (as executive director of the volunteer organization Public Allies) and taken another, closer to home, in preparation for the couple's first child. Barack had been elected to the Illinois state senate and was practicing law and teaching at the University of Chicago. Michelle adjusted her career path to accommodate their new family, which by 2001 included a second daughter, Natasha ("Sasha").

"In her own mind, two visions of herself were at war with each other," Barack wrote of his wife in *The Audacity of Hope*. "The desire to be the woman her mother had been, solid, dependable, making a home and always there for her kids, and the desire to excel in her profession, to make her mark on the world and realize all those plans she'd had on the very first day that we met."

As the trajectory of her husband's political career became meteoric, Michelle gradually accepted that the Obamas' best opportunity to make their mark would be with Barack serving as president of the United States. After he launched his campaign in early 2007, Michelle reduced her hours as a vice president at the University of Chicago Hospitals. During the campaign's home stretch in 2008, she remained close to their children, spending about two-thirds of the final months in Chicago.

In fact, with Barack no longer forced to shuttle between Washington and Chicago (and no longer on the campaign trail), the Obamas looked forward, as they moved into the White House, to watching their family life return to "normal."

"We get to be together under the one roof, having dinners together," she told *60 Minutes* in January 2009. "I envision the kids coming home from school and being able to run across the way to the Oval Office and see their dad before they start their homework."

Indeed, homework—and chores—were very much part of the plan as the Obamas arranged their transition. During a post-election visit to the White House, Michelle specifically instructed staff that they were *not* to make Malia's and Sasha's beds, nor were they to clean the girls' rooms. "They have to learn these things," their mother told Barbara Walters in an interview for ABC.

Michelle also solicited advice for presidential child-rearing from former first lady Rosalynn Carter and also from her husband's secretary of state, Hillary Clinton (whose lead the Obamas already followed by enrolling their daughters in Sidwell Friends School, which Chelsea Clinton attended).

Whatever Michelle Obama has done, whatever choices she's made, to raise her two daughters in the midst of her husband's political campaigns—it's working. Everyone who knows the family or has been around them says Malia and Sasha have emerged from the first four years of their father's presidency as delightful children, respectful, kind, and well behaved. That trend is likely to continue during the next four years.

Volunteer

For much of Michelle Obama's adult life, she has been in the unusual position of being paid to coordinate volunteer efforts and community service. But before she reached that point, as a law student at Harvard, Michelle spent long, unpaid hours in the student-run Legal Aid Bureau, which provided legal assistance to low-income clients. On top of her grueling law-school schedule, she often worked 20 hours a week handling landlord-tenant disputes and other cases.

When she graduated from Harvard, Michelle (then Robinson) was offered a position with a "silk-stocking" law firm in Chicago. She was worried that she wouldn't be doing much to help others, but, as she later put it, she couldn't pass up the chance to earn more than her parents had ever earned in their lives. She worked in the area of entertainment law—relatively interesting and glamorous work for a second-year associate. At one point, the firm was hired to handle legal issues for Barney (the familiar purple dinosaur); because everyone knew of Michelle's commitment to community service, the public-television link made her a logical candidate.

Yet Michelle didn't feel like her work was making a difference. She left the law firm to work for the mayor's office, where she helped develop programs for low-income children, dealing with infant mortality, mobile immunization units, and similar issues.

After a "Let's Move! London" event, the First Lady gets a monster hug from the children of former Olympic swimmer Summer Sanders.

She soon realized how slowly change takes place in government. After 18 months she left the mayor's office and helped found the Chicago chapter of Public Allies, an organization that trains young people from diverse backgrounds—from college students to welfare mothers—to work together on community-service projects. After three years, she took a position at the University of Chicago, where she worked to put students together with service opportunities in the community; she later moved on to the University of Chicago Hospitals, where she once again demonstrated her special talent for matching volunteers with opportunities, in the hospital system and the community.

In 2009, Michelle Obama undertook the biggest volunteer position of her life: first lady of the United States. Like all first ladies, she appears at benefit galas and makes the rounds of soup kitchens, children's hospitals, and homeless shelters. Her signature causes, however, have been the welfare of military and working families, and the reversal of the national trend toward obesity in children. She continually promotes fitness and healthy eating, and in February 2010 she launched a program she calls "Let's Move!"

Perhaps best of all, she is in a position to encourage and motivate others to volunteer their time, as well. "We need every American to serve their community, including our young people," Michelle has said: kids can volunteer in a homeless shelter, visit an elderly person, or write letters to soldiers.

Perhaps the first lady's greatest achievement as a volunteer will be recruiting a new generation to whom giving is as natural as it is to her.

Sorting toys for the Toys for Tots charity.

Heading up the third annual White House kitchen garden fall harvest—an essential part of her Let's Move! initiative.

Fashion Icon

As first lady, Michelle Obama is in the position of being the most-watched fashion leader in the country. The verdict among fashion fans has been swift and emphatic: not since Jacqueline Kennedy graced the White House has the wife of a U.S. president brought such a flair for fashion to her position. The new first lady has already established herself as a woman with a unique sense of style. Instead of playing it safe with conservative suits and established designers, Michelle has brought a breath of fresh air to Washington with bold choices, up-and-coming designers, and a mixture of couture and off-the-rack pieces. Whether going casual in J. Crew or blazing a new trend in runway fashions, Michelle Obama is making her mark on the fashion world.

In an era when most women in the public eye have a personal stylist to decide what they will wear, Michelle stands out by making her own fashion choices. Her style reflects her individuality and confidence. "There's nothing imposed on her that isn't generated by who she is," says Amy Fine Collins, a special correspondent at *Vanity Fair.* "She has a very definite sense of herself." Michelle often personalizes an ensemble by adding a sweater, sparking it with unexpected jewelry, or even altering design details. She is not afraid to be bold, and that has made waves among some of the more traditional fashion commentators. On election night in 2008, her stunning red-and-black ensemble from Narciso Rodriguez caused a sensation: some found the dress too daring, while others lauded the individuality that it heralded. According to Julie Gilhart, fashion

With Caroline Kennedy Schlossberg in the Green Room of the White House.

director of Barney's New York, "It said, 'Be who you are—don't let someone else tell you how to be.'"

Although part of the first lady's signature style is her ability to surprise with the unexpected, some defining characteristics of her distinctive look have emerged: streamlined silhouettes, waist-cinching belts, and a bold brooch or bead necklace to draw the eye. Michelle Obama's style also has a down-to-earth quality that allows the average American woman to relate to her: by mixing couture pieces with lower-priced off-the-rack items, she has proven that dressing stylishly doesn't have to mean breaking the bank. In the words of *Los Angeles Times* fashion critic Booth Moore, "She reflects the American-led democratization of fashion." The first lady is even credited with reinvigorating the fashion industry in America and providing a one-woman economic stimulus package, as new customers flock to the retailers and designers she frequents. Her fashion choices have set off shopping frenzies, as when women rushed to purchase the black-and-white print dress she wore on television's *The View*.

The *Washington Post* dubbed Michelle "the leader of the fashionable world"—and she even made the cover of the March 2009 issue of fashion magazine *Vogue*. This is only the second time an American first lady has taken the place of a model on the cover (the other was Hillary Clinton in 1998).

Whatever lies ahead in the next four years for the dynamic first lady, there is no doubt that America will continue taking its fashion cues from her.

A walk on the beach in Panama City, Florida.

Martha Washington

Born in 1731 to John and Frances Dandridge, Martha grew up on a plantation near Williamsburg, Virginia. As a girl, her education was focused on domestic and social skills, honed in Tidewater Virginia society. At the age of 18, she married her first husband, Daniel Parke Custis. Two of their four children died in infancy, and Daniel himself died in 1757, leaving Martha a large inheritance. By the age of 26, she had considerable business sense and social power, which may have helped to attract the attention of George Washington, then a young colonel in the Virginia militia.

In 1759, Martha married George at her estate, known as the White House, on the Pamunkey River, northwest of Williamsburg. After a short honeymoon there, they moved to George's home at Mount Vernon. They had no children together, but they raised Martha's surviving children, Martha and John. Sadly, young Martha died at the age of 17 of an epileptic seizure, and John, who had served as an aide to George during the siege of Yorktown, died of fever shortly after the siege ended, in late 1781. After John's death, the Washingtons raised the younger two of John's children and provided personal and financial support to other family members.

While she preferred a quiet life at home, she accompanied George when he served as commander-in-chief of the Continental Army. She spent the winter at Valley Forge and helped maintain morale among the troops. She supported a formal effort to enlist women to volunteer for the Continental Army. Revolutionary veterans honored her with the title "Lady Washington."

Although she valued privacy and was disturbed by press coverage of her shopping trips and family outings, Martha rose to the challenge of supporting her husband's career in public life with tact and discretion. While the Washingtons entertained in a formal style to convey equal status with the governments of Europe, Martha was known as a gracious hostess who made guests feel welcome. She later confided to a niece that she felt constrained by her role as first lady. George's secretary created rigid protocol rules based on his experience in Europe—for example, they were forbidden from accepting invitations to dine in private homes.

The Washingtons retired from public life in 1797, returning to Mount Vernon, where they continued to entertain guests constantly. After George died in 1799, Martha burned their letters to ensure privacy. She freed many of the family's slaves in 1801. The nation's *first* first lady died of fever in 1802, and lies buried next to her husband at Mount Vernon.

Abigail Adams

Born in 1744 at Weymouth, Massachusetts, to William Smith and Elizabeth Quincy Smith, Abigail was descended from the prestigious Quincy family. Her father was a Congregational minister who emphasized the importance of reason and morality. Though she was not formally educated, Abigail was an avid reader of history and studied both English and French literature. She shared her love of reading with John Adams, a young lawyer and Harvard graduate, who was impressed by her intellect. They married in 1764 and moved to a small cottage and farm that John had inherited from his father in what would later become Quincy, Massachusetts.

Abigail bore three sons and two daughters as her husband's law practice grew. One of her sons, John Quincy Adams, would later become the sixth president of the United States.

Abigail took an active role in politics. She advocated for married women's property rights and more opportunities for women in education. They sometimes disagreed on women's rights issues; in a March 31, 1776, letter to her husband, Abigail Adams wrote, "I long to hear that you have declared an independency. And, by the way, in the new code of laws which I suppose it will be necessary for you to make, I desire you would remember the ladies and be more generous and favorable to them than your ancestors. Do not put such unlimited power into the hands of the husbands. Remember, all men would be tyrants if they could. If particular care and attention is not paid to the ladies, we are determined to foment a rebellion, and will not hold ourselves bound by any laws in which we have no voice or representation." Despite their sometime disagreement on the subject, John often asked Abigail for advice in political matters. They both believed that slavery was evil and a threat to American democracy.

Abigail joined John at his diplomatic post in Paris in 1784. When he became the first U.S. minister to Great Britain after 1785, she supported him with dignity and tact. In 1789, just a year after they returned to Massachusetts, John Adams was elected first vice president of the United States.

During her husband's two terms as vice president, Abigail drew on her experience in foreign society while entertaining, and became a good friend to Martha Washington. After 1791, however, poor health forced her to spend much of her time at home in Quincy.

In 1797, John Adams was elected president. In 1800, Abigail became the first of the first ladies to preside over the president's house, later known as the White House. Washington, D.C., was then a primitive wilderness, with the president's house not yet completed. However, determined to perpetuate the style of entertaining initiated by the Washingtons, Abigail continued to host formal dinners and receptions.

The Adamses retired from public life in 1801 and enjoyed 17 years together at home in Quincy. Abigail died of typhoid fever in 1818, seven years before her son became president. She is buried beside her husband at United First Parish Church.

Mary Todd Lincoln

Born in 1818 to Eliza Parker and Robert Smith Todd (a wealthy merchant, lawyer, and politician), Mary received an unusually extensive private education and led an active social life among the aristocracy of Lexington, Kentucky. Exposed to such politicians as her father's close friend Henry Clay, she developed intense interest in political issues, ultimately supporting the abolition of slavery.

At the age of 20, Mary moved to Springfield, Illinois, to live with her sister. This is where she met Abraham Lincoln. Though quite different in their backgrounds and their personalities, the two endured a tumultuous three-year courtship (and a broken engagement) and finally married in 1842. Mary's love for Abraham and her trust in his abilities carried her though their early years of hardship in Springfield. Limited funds and social opportunities while caring for their sons may have influenced her unusual decision to board with him in Washington for a winter during his term in Congress from 1847 to 1849.

Mary actively promoted Abraham's political career, handwriting solicitations to Whig leaders for a political appointment. She advised him to reject the offer of the governorship of Oregon Territory, which would remove him from national politics. Attending state legislature sessions, she recorded the partisan allegiance of each member. In correspondence, she conveyed her husband's views on slavery to influential friends in Kentucky. Mary realized her high social ambitions when Abraham was elected president in 1860.

As first lady, Mary Todd Lincoln faced extraordinary challenges during the Civil War. In spite of her refined social skills, she was viewed by Washington's elite as a Westerner unsuited to society's leadership. When she redecorated the White House in an effort to promote an image of stability that would command respect for both the president and the Union, the press portrayed her as selfish and indulgent. A gracious hostess, she was nonetheless accused of unpatriotic extravagance when she entertained, and of shirking her social duties when she limited her entertaining after the death of her son Willie in 1862.

In spite of such obstacles and criticism, Mary made significant contributions to the war effort. She volunteered as a nurse in Union hospitals, provided intelligence and advice about military personnel, recommended minor military appointments, and accompanied Abraham on tours of Union Army camps. She used entertaining to lift morale. By raising funds through the Sanitary Commission fairs and the Contraband Relief Association, she publicly encouraged the Union Army and supported freedom for slaves.

Mary was devastated by her husband's assassination in 1865. Her son Robert later had her committed to an asylum, but one of the nation's first female lawyers, Myra Bradwell, appealed her case, enabling release to her sister's care. Mary died in 1882 at her sister's home in Springfield. She is buried at the Lincoln Tomb.

Anna Eleanor Roosevelt

Born in New York City on October 11, 1884, Anna Eleanor Roosevelt was the daughter of Elliott Roosevelt, the younger brother of (later) U.S. president Theodore Roosevelt. Both of Eleanor's parents died while she was still a young girl. She was sent to live with her grandmother, but Eleanor did not begin to blossom until her mid-teens, when she went to a finishing school in London. It was there that she first began to exhibit her independence and high intelligence.

Eleanor Roosevelt was 20 years old when she married Franklin Delano Roosevelt, a distant cousin she had known practically her entire life. At age 23, Franklin was handsome, fun-loving, and confident. They seemed to be an odd match, but he understood her inner strength and her compassionate nature. They lived in New York City and Hyde Park and had six children together; the last, a son, John Aspinwall Roosevelt, was born in 1916 in Washington, D.C. The family had moved there after Franklin was appointed by President Woodrow Wilson to be under-secretary of the Navy.

In 1921, Franklin Roosevelt contracted polio. The disease did not deter his political ambitions, and his wife's responsibilities grew exponentially as a result. She traveled and spoke on his behalf, while also teaching and writing on her own. Eleanor Roosevelt would campaign for her husband in his successful bid to become New York's governor. After Franklin won the first of his four terms as president of the United States, Eleanor began to reinvent the role of first lady. She had little interest in overseeing the domestic duties of the White House, and instead traveled the world and spoke vigorously and compassionately on the behalf of black and impoverished Americans.

Even after the start of World War II, Eleanor Roosevelt continued to travel the globe. She visited soldiers, toured army hospitals, and, upon her return to the White House, advised her husband on all matters she considered vital. The war years were difficult ones, however. All four of the Roosevelts' sons fought in the conflict, and Franklin's own health continued to decline.

After Franklin Roosevelt died in 1945, Eleanor continued to find energy for worthy causes. She focused intensely on human rights, and particularly the needs of women and minorities. Eleanor Roosevelt passed away on November 7, 1962, and was buried in Hyde Park, New York.

With the visiting Queen Elizabeth, at left

Jacqueline Lee Bouvier Kennedy

Jacqueline Lee Bouvier was born on July 28, 1929, in Southampton, New York, to John "Jack" Bouvier III and Janet Norton Bouvier. Her father was a successful New York Stock Exchange broker, and Jacqueline was educated at the finest schools. She finished high school at Miss Porter's School in Farmington, Connecticut, and continued her higher education at Vassar College and, through Smith College, the University of Grenoble and the Sorbonne in Paris, ultimately graduating with a bachelor of arts in French literature from George Washington University, in 1951. As a young woman, Jacqueline, while stylish and beautiful, also excelled in the literary arts. She won an essay contest sponsored by *Vogue* magazine, then turned to journalism, working as a photographer and a reporter for the *Washington Times-Herald*. One of her early interviews was with Massachusetts senator John Fitzgerald Kennedy, who became her first husband.

Jacqueline Bouvier married John Kennedy on September 12, 1953, in Brookline, Massachusetts. At the time, she still had aspirations of being a novelist, but her duties as Kennedy's wife rearranged her life's work. Her writing involved answering mail from his constituents; she also contributed to the editing of John's astounding autobiography, the Pulitzer Prize–winning *Profiles in Courage*. She and John had three children: Caroline Bouvier Kennedy, born in 1957; John F. Kennedy Jr., born in 1960, just a few weeks after John Sr. was elected to the presidency; and Patrick Bouvier Kennedy, who was born prematurely in 1963 and died at two days old.

As first lady, Jacqueline Kennedy maintained her intense interest in the arts. She met with French minister of culture André Malraux in 1961; Malraux was so taken with her that he loaned to the United States the famous *Mona Lisa* painting from the Louvre Museum. "Jackie," as she was known, brought a fresh new sense of style, fashion, and elegance to the role of first lady. Her clothing—sometimes based on her own sketches—made international headlines. She appeared on hundreds of magazine covers, and was the first presidential spouse to have her own press secretary. Her well-publicized interests brought national attention to culture, fashion, and the arts.

Jacqueline Kennedy traveled extensively in her role as first lady and met with the leaders of many nations. After her husband was assassinated in Dallas in November 1963, she wrote to Soviet leader Nikita Khruschev, encouraging him to honor his commitment on the Nuclear Test Ban Treaty.

After leaving the White House, Jacqueline Kennedy reared her two children in New York. She played a significant role in the creation of the John F. Kennedy Library. She also would remarry, to Greek businessman Aristotle Onassis, in 1968, and subsequently she spent a majority of her time in Athens, Greece, as well as in Paris. Following the death of Aristotle Onassis, she moved back to New York City, and worked as an editor for Viking Press and Doubleday. Jacqueline Lee Bouvier Kennedy Onassis died in New York City on May 19, 1994, and was laid to rest next to John F. Kennedy at Arlington National Cemetery in Arlington, Virginia.

Nancy Reagan

Anne Frances "Nancy" Robbins was born on July 6, 1921, in New York City. Her parents divorced shortly after her birth. When she was eight, her mother, a stage actress, married a prominent neurosurgeon, Loyal Davis, whom Nancy always thought of as her father. She attended Smith College, where she graduated in 1943 with a degree in drama. With the help of her mother's theater connections, she pursued a career as an actress, appearing in various television shows and a dozen films (including *Hellcats of the Navy*, with her husband, Ronald Reagan).

Being an actress, though, had never been Nancy's main goal—MGM's promotional materials said that her "greatest ambition was to have a successful, happy marriage." Nancy met Ronald in 1949, when he was the president of the Screen Actors Guild. They began dating then and married in 1952. They had two children of their own—Patricia Ann Reagan (professionally known as Patti Davis) in 1952 and Ronald Prescott Reagan in 1958—in addition to Ronald's two children from a previous marriage. Nancy retired from acting shortly after their marriage to devote herself to her family.

Nancy played a prominent role in her husband's political campaigns and presidency, managing staffers and organizing schedules. His confidence was boosted when she went to his rallies and meetings. Following John Hinckley's attempt on President Reagan's life in 1981, Nancy took on the role of her husband's "protector," strictly controlling access to the president and arranging his schedule.

While Ronald was governor of California, and continuing through his time as president, Nancy was very active in charitable ventures, visiting veterans, the elderly, and the handicapped. As first lady, her focus turned to the fight against substance abuse among young people. She launched the "Just Say No" drug awareness campaign in 1982, and that remained her primary project during her time as first lady. Toward the end of her husband's presidency a mammogram revealed a malignant tumor in her left breast. Her resulting surgery brought attention to breast cancer and encouraged women across the country to get mammograms.

Following her time in the White House, Nancy continued to campaign against drug abuse until Ronald was diagnosed with Alzheimer's disease in 1994. From that point on, the Reagans retired from public life. She dedicated herself to caring for her husband and supporting the National Alzheimer's Association, including through the Ronald & Nancy Reagan Research Institute, which they helped create and fund as an affiliate of the NAA. In 2002 Nancy was awarded the Presidential Medal of Freedom, the nation's highest civilian honor, and she and her husband were jointly awarded the Congressional Gold Medal. Since Ronald's death in 2004, she has remained active in politics, supporting stem-cell research and in 2007 hosting a Republican presidential debate.

Hillary Diane Rodham Clinton

Hillary Diane Rodham was born to Hugh Ellsworth Rodham and Dorothy Emma Howell Rodham in Chicago on October 26, 1947. Her father, originally from Scranton, Pennsylvania, worked in the textile business, as a supply owner. Hillary, the eldest of three siblings, was educated through high school in Park Ridge, Illinois, then went on to graduate from Wellesley College in Massachusetts. She graduated from Yale Law School with honors. As a teenager, she tried a variety of jobs, including babysitting and working in a cannery, and was active in young-Republican organizations. In 1968 she switched party affiliations. She served as the staff attorney for the Children's Defense Fund in Cambridge, Massachusetts, and in 1972 worked in the Western states for the presidential campaign of George McGovern. During the impeachment hearings of President Richard Nixon in 1974, Hillary worked as an adviser to the Judiciary Committee for the House of Representatives.

Hillary Rodham eventually moved to Fayetteville, Arkansas, and joined the faculty of the University of Arkansas Law School, where her boyfriend and future husband, William "Bill" Jefferson Clinton, was also on staff. They married in Fayetteville on October 11, 1975. They had one child, a daughter, Chelsea Victoria Clinton, born five years later.

In 1978, Bill Clinton was elected to the first of his five terms as Arkansas governor. That same year, Hillary accepted an appointment from President Jimmy Carter to the board of the Legal Services Corporation. She became a full partner at Rose Law Firm in 1979 and worked tirelessly on behalf of multiple organizations dedicated to the welfare of Arkansas children. Her independent nature and high profile became something of a lightning rod for Republican pundits during Bill Clinton's presidential bid in 1992. After he won the election over incumbent George H.W. Bush, Hillary was appointed by her husband to head the President's Task Force on Health Care Reform. Her plan failed to gain significant support; however, she was eventually credited with helping guide the State Children's Health Insurance Program during his second term.

She displayed remarkable resilience while standing by her husband's side after he acknowledged his infidelity with a White House intern. After his second term as president, Hillary Clinton successfully ran for an open seat in the U.S. Senate (representing the state of New York) in 2000. Her victory there marked the first time a former first lady was elected to public office. Though her presidential bid in 2008 was unsuccessful, Hillary Clinton was subsequently appointed by the newly elected president, Barack Obama, to the post of secretary of state for the United States.

Laura Bush

Laura Lane Welch was the only child of Harold Welch, a builder and real-estate developer, and Jenna Louise Hawkins Welch. Born in Midland, Texas, on November 4, 1946, Laura fell in love with reading at a very early age. Her fondness for books and learning led her to pursue a bachelor's degree in education at Southern Methodist University, and she became a grade-school teacher after graduation. She returned to school after several years as a teacher, earning a master's degree in library science from the University of Texas at Austin.

Laura met her future husband, George W. Bush, at a friend's backyard barbecue in 1977. After a three-month courtship, they became engaged, and they were married in November of that year. Almost immediately after their wedding, the two began campaigning for George's congressional candidacy in 1978. George lost that race and returned to the life of a businessman. He was still involved in oil and gas exploration in 1981, when Laura gave birth to twins Barbara and Jenna. The girls were 12 years old by the time George returned to the political arena, declaring his candidacy in 1993 for the governorship of Texas.

Though a supportive political wife, Laura held no formal events during her five years in the governor's mansion. She was extremely active, however, in working for causes she believed in. As the first lady of Texas and then of the nation, Laura was a staunch advocate of women's and children's issues, particularly in education and health. She focused on teacher training and promoted early-childhood education and early-literacy programs. She established the Women's Health and Wellness Initiative and promoted awareness of heart disease—the number-one killer of American women—and breast cancer. Since the September 11 terrorist attacks, she has been a great supporter of the women in Afghanistan, speaking out against the oppression of women and children.

Laura Bush was one of the most popular first ladies, with approval ratings as high as 82 percent. Though the Bushes have returned to private life, Laura says that she will continue to work for women's rights in Afghanistan. Of how her life would change when she left the White House, she said, "I'll miss all the people that are around us all the time. From the ushers and the butlers who are there for every president and have been there four or five administrations, to our own staff, of course, that we love to laugh with and talk with and solve problems with . . . I'll miss the people the most."

About the Authors

Q. David Bowers is the author of more than 50 books, primarily on history, antiques, and collectibles, including his specialty of numismatics (coins, medals, tokens, and paper money), but also in such fields as the California Gold Rush, silent movies, the Thanhouser film studio, nickelodeon theaters, the postcard art of Alphonse Mucha, the voyages of diplomatic envoy Edmund Roberts in the 1830s, a three-volume town history, and more. Among Bowers's recent books are *Collecting Rare Coins for Pleasure and Profit*; *Ronald Reagan: An American Legend;* the *Whitman Encyclopedia of Colonial and Early American Coins*; and *One Thousand Nights at the Movies*.

Bowers's byline has appeared in newspapers, magazines, and the Internet. When *American Heritage* celebrated its 25th anniversary, he was tapped to write the cover feature. He has appeared on ABC, CBS, NBC, Fox, and all other major networks, and has been featured in television documentaries popular with viewers of the Discovery Channel and the History Channel. In recent years he has given annual lectures at Harvard University on the subject of collecting, museum curatorship, and connoisseurship.

Bowers is chairman of Stack's Bowers Galleries of New York and New Hampshire, and serves as numismatic director of Whitman Publishing, LLC. He is a fellow of the Massachusetts Historical Society, the American Antiquarian Society, and the American Numismatic Society, is a trustee of the New Hampshire Historical Society, and serves as a selectman on the town board of Wolfeboro, New Hampshire, "America's Oldest Summer Resort."

Like millions of Americans, author Dave Lifton first learned of Barack Obama during the 2004 Democratic National Convention. He was immediately inspired by Obama's message of common ground over ideological division.

Lifton runs three Web sites the pop-culture blog and podcast *Wings for Wheels;* the soccer-dedicated site Booked for Dissent; and DC to Chicago, which chronicles his adventures in the Windy City. He is a firm believer in the power of new media to establish new voices and tones.

A native of Long Island, Lifton moved to Chicago in November 2008 after 15 years in Washington, D.C. He enjoys traveling, photography, and playing guitar.

Image Credits

Listed in page order. Where two images appear on a single page, the first credit is for the image closer to the top; where three or more images appear on a page, credits are listed clockwise from top left (or leftmost, if applicable).

5: Official White House Photo by Pete Souza. 7: Chip Somodevilla / Getty Images. 8: AP Photo / Obama Presidential Campaign; AP Photo / Obama for America. 9: Obama Presidential Campaign (2008). 11: AP Photo / Obama for America. 12: AP Photo / Ron Edmonds. 13: AP Photo / Paul Sancya; AP Photo/Ted S. Warren; AP Photo / Alex Brandon. 15: AP Photo / Laramie Boomerang, Ben Woloszyn. 17: AP Photo/Charlie Neibergall, File. 18: AP Photo / Alex Brandon; AP Photo / M. Spencer Green. 19: AP Photo / Jae C. Hong. 20: AP Photo / Jeff Roberson. 21: AP Photo / Alex Brandon. 23: AP Photo / Alex Brandon. 24: AP Photo / Alex Brandon. 25: AP Photo / Ted S. Warren. 26: AP Photo / Jeff Chiu. 27: AP Photo / Jeff Chiu. 29: AP Photo / Alex Brandon. 30: AP Photo / Jae C. Hong. 31: AP Photo / Alex Brandon. 32: AP Photo / Charles Rex Arbogast. 33: AP Photo / Alex Brandon. 34: AP Photo / Charles Dharapak. 35: AP Photo / Pablo Martinez Monsivais. 36: AP Photo / Pablo Martinez Monsivais. 37: Official White House photo by Pete Souza. 38: AP Photo / Gerald Herbert. 39: AP Photo / The White House, Joyce N. Boghosian; AP Photo / Obama Transition Office, Callie Shell. 40: AP Photo / Gerald Herbert, File. 41: AP Photo / Pablo Martinez Monsivais. 42: AP Photo / Alex Brandon. 43: AP Photo / Carolyn Kaster. 45: Photo by Owen Byrne. 46: AP Photo / Marco Garcia. 47: AP Photo / Nam Y. Huh. 48–49: Official White House Photo by Annie Liebowitz. 50: AP Photo / Charles Dharapak. 51: AP Photo / Charles Dharapak; AP Photo / Gerald Herbert. 52: AP Photo / Charles Dharapak. 53: AP Photo / Kevin Wolf. 54: AP Photo / Jacquelyn Martin. 55: AP Photo, U.S. Air force Master Sgt. Cecilio Ricardo; AP Photo / Jacquelyn Martin; Photo by Lance Cpl. Bryan G. Carfrey. 56: AP Photo / Ron Edmonds. 57: AP Photo / Ron Edmonds. 58: AP Photo / Carolyn Kaster. 59: AP Photo / Ron Edmonds, File. 60: MSgt Cecilio Ricardo. 61: Dan Renaldo / NBC NewsWire. 64: SMSgt Thomas Meneguin. 65: AgnosticPreachersKid. 66: SSG Jim Greenhill. 67: USCapitol. 68: MC1 Mark O'Donald. 69: SPC Daniel J. Herrera. 70–71: AP Photo / Mark Wilson, Pool. 72: AP Photo / Luis M. Alvarez. 73: AP Photo

/ Matt Rourke. 74: AP Photo / Matt Rourke. 75: AP Photo / Jason DeCrow. 76: AP Photo / Kevin Wolf. 77: AP Photo / Maya Alleruzzo. 78: AP Photo / Luis M. Alvarez. 79: AP Photo / M. Spencer Green. 80–81: Dan Renaldo / NBC NewsWire. 82–83: Dan Renaldo / NBC NewsWire. 85: AP Photo / Department of Defense, Petty Officer 1st Class Michael Heckman. 86: AP Photo / Elise Amendola. 87: AP Photo / Lauren Victoria Burke. 88: AP Photo / Ron Edmonds. 89: AP Photo / Jim Bourg, Pool. 90: AP Photo / David Kohl. 91: AP Photo / John Bazemore. 92–93: Photo by Mass Communication Specialist 1st Class Mark O'Donald, U.S. Navy/Released. 93: Photo by Yeoman 1st Class Donna Lou Morgan, U.S. Navy/Released. 94: AP Photo / Elise Amendola; AP Photo / Susan Walsh; AP Photo / J. Scott Applewhite. 95: AP Photo / Riccardo Gangale. 96–97: AP Photo / Bertrand Combaldieu. 97: AP Photo / Achmad Ibrahim. 98: AP Photo / Charles Dharapak. 99: AP Photo / Saul Loeb, Pool. 100: Official White House photo by Pete Souza. 101: AP Photo / White House, Eric Draper. 102–103: AP Photo / Evan Vucci. 104: AP Photo / Charles Dharapak. 105: AP Photo / Pablo Martinez Monsivais; AP Photo / Manuel Balce Ceneta. 106–107: Photo by SrA Kathrine McDowell. 108: AP Photo / Haraz N. Ghanbari. 109, both: Official White House photo by Pete Souza. 110: AP Photo / Charles Dharapak. 111: UpstateNYer. 112: TSgt Larry Simmons. 113: Tech. Sgt. Andy Dunaway. 114: Official White House photo by Pete Souza. 115: ChadH. 116: Official White House photo by Pete Souza. 117, both: Official White House photo by Pete Souza. 118, all: Official White House photo by Pete Souza. 119, both: Official White House photo by Pete Souza. 120, both: Official White House photo by Pete Souza. 121, all: Official White House photo by Pete Souza. 122: Official White House photo by Pete Souza. 123: Official White House photo by Pete Souza. 124: Steve Petteway, Collection of the Supreme Court of the United States; U.S. Navy photo. 125: Photo by Alex Wong / Getty Images; Photo by Justin Sullivan / Getty Images; Mikael Häggström. 126: Official White House photo by Pete Souza. 127, both: Official White House photo by Pete Souza. 129: AP Photo / Gerald Herbert. 131: AP Photo / Amy Sancetta. 133: AP Photo / Gerald Herbert. 134: Photo by Molly Theobald, AFLCIO. 135: AP Photo / Charles Dharapak. 137: Official White House photo by Pete Souza. 138, all: Official White House photo by Pete Souza. 141, top and middle: Official White House photo by Pete Souza; bottom, Official White House photo by Chuck Kennedy. 142, both: Official White House photo by Pete Souza. 143: Official White House photo by Pete Souza. 145: Official White House photo by Chuck Kennedy. 146: Official White House photo by Pete Souza. 147: Official White House photo by Pete Souza. 149: Official White House photo by Pete Souza. 150–151: Official White House photos by Pete Souza. 152: Cpl Jason Ingersoll; TheMachineStops and UpstateNYer; PH2 Jim Watson. 153: U.S. Department of Defense; U.S. Navy; U.S. Department of Defense. 154: Official White House photo by Pete Souza. 155: SSgt. Stephen Schester; Official White House photo by Pete Souza. 157: Official White House photo by Pete Souza. 158: SPC Monte Swift. 159: SrA Perry Aston. 160: Staff Sgt. Lynette R. Hoke. 161: Cpl. Jordan Johnson. 162: top left, Austen Hufford; all others, Gage Skidmore. 163: Washington Post; Majunznk. 164: AP Photo / Charles Krupa, File. 165: Katherine Cresto. 166: Rex Features via AP Images. 167: AP Photo / Alex Menendez. 168: Official White House Photo by Pete Souza. 169: Alex Wong / Getty Images. 170: AP Photo / Jae C. Hong; Alex Wong / Getty Images; AP Photo / Charles Dharapak. 171: AP Photo / David Goldman; Tom Pennington / Getty Images. 172: Andrew Harrer / Bloomberg via Getty Images. 173: Mario Tama / Getty Images; Win McNamee / Getty Images; Official White House Photo by David Lienemann. 174–175: AP Photo / Alan Diaz. 175: Scott Olson / Getty Images. 176: AP Photo / Mark Lennihan. 177: Official White House Photo by Pete Souza; AP Photo / Steve Helber. 178–179: Official White House Photo by Pete Souza. 179: SAUL LOEB / AFP / Getty Images. 180: AP Photo / Matt Rourke. 181: JEWEL SAMAD / AFP / Getty Images. 182: - / AFP / Getty Images. 183: AP Photo / Carolyn Kaster. 184: AP Photo / Ben Curtis. 185: SAUL LOEB / AFP / Getty Images. 186: AP Photo / Wong Maye-E. 187: Chip Somodevilla / Getty Images. 188: ROBYN BECK / AFP / Getty Images. 189: AP Photo / Kathy Willens. 190: Official White House Photo by Pete Souza. 191: Official White House Photo by Pete Souza. 192: Official White House Photo by Pete Souza. 193, both: Official White House Photo by Pete Souza. 194: Official White House Photo by Pete Souza. 195: Official White House Photo by Pete Souza. 196, both: Official White House Photo by Pete Souza. 197: Official White House Photo by Chuck Kennedy. 198: Official White House Photo by Chuck Kennedy. 199: Official White House Photo by Lawrence Jackson; Official White House Photo by Pete Souza. 201: Official White House Photo by Pete Souza. 203: Official White House Photo by Pete Souza. 204: AP Photo / Markus Schreiber. 205: AP Photo / Charles Dharapak, File. 206: Official White House Photo by Pete Souza. 207: Official White House Photo by Chuck Kennedy; Official White House Photo by Pete Souza. 208: Official White House Photo by Chuck Kennedy. 209: Metrolina photo by Holly Hess. 211: Official White House Photo by Pete Souza. 214–431: Heritage Auction Galleries of Dallas, Texas (the largest auction house founded in America, the world's largest collectibles auctioneer, and the third-largest auction house; www.ha.com) provided many images of historical artifacts and other Americana. Additional image credits are as follows. 218, top (Mount Vernon): photo by Ad Meskens. 225, Adams birthplace: photo by Daderot. 230: photo by Joe Ravi. 356: the George F. Landegger Collection of District of Columbia Photographs in Carol M. Highsmith's America, Library of Congress, Prints and Photographs Division. 420: photo by Staff Sergeant Alex Lloyd, United States Air Force. 424: photo by Photographer's Mate Second Class Chuck Hill. 425: U.S. Navy photo by Mr. Damon J. Moritz. 427: U.S. Navy photo by Photographer's Mate First Class Keith W. DeVinney. 433: D. Myles Cullen, U.S. Army (released). 434: Library of Congress. 435: Official White House Photo by Sonya N. Hebert. 436: U.S. Air Force photo by Staff Sgt. Brittany E. Jones (released); Official White House Photo by Chuck Kennedy. 437: Official White House Photo by Lawrence Jackson. 438: Official White House Photo by Samantha Appleton. 439: Library of Congress. 440: Library of Congress. 441: Library of Congress. 442, both: Library of Congress. 443: Library of Congress. 444: Library of Congress. 446: Official portrait by Krisanne Johnson.